TEACHING FOR MORAL GROWTH

**A GUIDE FOR THE CHRISTIAN COMMUNITY
TEACHERS, PARENTS, AND PASTORS**

BridgePoint,
the academic
imprint of
Victor Books, is
your connection
for the best in
serious reading
that integrates
the passion of
the heart with
the scholarship
of the mind.

TEACHING FOR MORAL GROWTH

A GUIDE FOR THE CHRISTIAN COMMUNITY
TEACHERS, PARENTS, AND PASTORS

BONNIDELL CLOUSE

A
BRIDGEPOINT
BOOK ®

Copyediting: Robert N. Hosack
Cover Design: Joe DeLeon

Library of Congress Cataloging-in-Publication Data

Clouse, Bonnidell.
    Teaching for moral growth: a guide for the Christian community — teachers, parents, and pastors / by Bonnidell Clouse.
        p.   cm.
    Includes bibliographical references.
ISBN: 1-56476-078-2
1. Christian ethics — Study and teaching. 2. Moral development. 3. Youth — Conduct of life. 4. Christianity — Psychology   I. Title.
BJ1251.C66   1993   93-2316
241'.07 — dc20   CIP

BridgePoint is the academic imprint of Victor Books.
© 1993 by Victor Books/SP Publications, Inc. All rights reserved. Printed in the United States of America.

1   2   3   4   5   6   7   8   9   10   Printing/Year   97   96   95   94   93

CONTENTS

To the memory
of my mother and father,
Lela and Ranselaer Barrows

ACKNOWLEDGMENTS

There are a number of people who make a book like this possible. To recognize them all would be impossible. I especially wish to thank Robert Hosack, Academic Resources Editor, Victor Books, for working with me on this project and seeing it to its completion; Perry Downs, Professor of Christian Education, Trinity Evangelical Divinity School, for reading the manuscript, giving valuable input, and suggesting the title *Teaching for Moral Growth;* Kenneth Walker, Chairperson of Educational and School Psychology, Indiana State University, for letting me use his computer for weeks at a time when mine ceased to function; and Nancy Kiger, my graduate assistant, who brightened my days with her cheerful disposition, made many trips to the library, typed tirelessly, and proofread every word of the manuscript.

Special appreciation goes to my husband, Robert, who assured me that writing this book took precedence over many other things I felt needed to be done. It was with his support and encouragement that a difficult task was made easy and a seemingly endless project came to fruition.

INTRODUCTION

On the pages that follow you will find a number of ways that parents, educators, and church leaders can impact the lives of children and adolescents so that moral development is more likely to occur. It will not be a "cookbook" approach, as children are too complicated for that. What works for one child may not work for another; any parent with two or more children can tell you that. However, some methods appear to be more effective than others, and as concerned adults we can use those techniques the research has shown to be apt to produce the desired results.

You will notice that the book has a decidedly Christian emphasis. This does not mean that if you are of a different religious persuasion or tend not to be religious at all that you cannot profit from the ideas given. The techniques presented can be used by anyone. Nor does it mean that a person must be a follower of Christ to appreciate the moral quest. Caring citizens regardless of religious affiliation have always been interested in morality as it relates to personal conduct, strength of character, and social conformity. Some excellent research has been conducted by those who according to their own confession are not followers of Jesus Christ. But it does mean that I as a Christian firmly believe that by looking at the Bible, the written Word of God, as the only unerring guide to faith and morals, and to Jesus Christ, the living Word, as the ultimate example of ethical conduct and mature moral discernment, a dimension has been added that helps us in our quest of finding out what it means to be a truly good person.

C.S. Lewis (1960) developed this thought in *Mere Christianity* when he wrote that morality is concerned with three things: "Firstly, with fair play and harmony between individuals. Secondly, with what might be called tidying up or harmonising the things inside each individual. Thirdly, with the general purpose of human life as a whole: what man was made for" (p. 71). The first has to do with relations between one person and another, the second with what a person is like within the self, and the third with how the person relates to the Power that made him. Lewis noted that most people think of morality as encompassing only the first of these, that of interpersonal relationships. They say that as long as no one else is hurt it does not matter what they do. But the first cannot be separated from the second, nor the second from the third. Fair play and harmony between individuals is not possible unless individuals are right within themselves and unless they understand who they are in relation to the One who created them.

Lewis likened morality to a fleet of ships sailing in formation. First, all ships must be in the proper position. It simply will not do for one ship to go off on its own or to turn into another ship, crippling them both. Second, each ship must be in good operating condition; all parts must be functional. Third, the purpose of the voyage must be known. Why are the ships sailing? What is their destination? Lewis graphically illustrates how the first condition is dependent on the second:

> What is the good of telling the ships how to steer so as to avoid collisions if, in fact, they are such crazy old tubs that they cannot be steered at all? What is the good of drawing up, on paper, rules for social behavior, if we know that, in fact, our greed, cowardice, ill-temper, and self-conceit are going to prevent us from keeping them? . . . Without good men you cannot have a good society. (p. 72)

But how do we get "good men"? This second condition is dependent on the third. Unless people understand the purpose of life, unless they are aware of their destination, they will not know when the parts within them (mind, will, and emotions) are in good working order. This third aspect of morality is considered even less by secular writers than is the second. "It is in dealing with the third that the main differences between Christian and non-Christian morality come out" (Lewis, 1960, p. 73). It is the believer in Christ who better understands the true reason for humanity's existence. It is the Christian who is aware of the destination of the human race. The written Word of God provides a guide for how one is to relate to others, and the living Word provides the power to keep the parts within oneself in good working order.

HOW DOES PSYCHOLOGY FIT INTO THE PICTURE?

Christians in all walks of life enjoy thinking through how their occupations relate to their faith. Christian psychologists are no exception. Within the past twenty years there has been an explosion of materials in both books and journals on the topic of how psychology and Christian theology interrelate. Christian counselors, clinicians, academicians, experimental researchers, pastors, and youth workers have joined the movement. As a professor of psychology in a state university as well as a parent, Sunday School teacher, and minister's wife, I have worked for a number of years in the area of integrating psychology and Christian belief as these disciplines impact an understanding of how moral growth takes place. Call it a labor of love, missionary call, or whatever but it has become a consuming passion. Too many young people, including Christian youth, are desperately in need of some type of moral guidance. Hopefully, the ideas presented in this book will help us to help them.

In the fall of 1989 a massive survey was taken of over 5,000 children and adolescents in grades four through twelve throughout the United States asking them a number of questions including, "How do you decide what is right and wrong?" and "What system of values informs your moral decisions?" The survey was sponsored by the Girls Scouts of America, the Lilly Endowment, and the Mott Foundation with Roberts Coles, Professor of Psychiatry and Medical Humanities at Harvard University, designated as the project director. The results showed a wide diversity in the "moral compass" used by young people today. Only 16 percent adhered to some kind

Within the past twenty years there has been an explosion of materials in both books and journals on the topic of how psychology and Christian theology interrelate.

of religious authority such as Scripture or what the church teaches. Another 20 percent deferred to other authorities such as parents or youth leaders. Twenty-five percent said they would do what they felt was best for everybody, whereas 18 percent said they would do what felt good at the time or made themselves happy. Ten percent used the criterion of whether it would help them improve their situation or get ahead, and the other 11 percent had no rationale to help them decide right from wrong (Coles & Genevie, 1990). When asked about their attitude toward premarital sex, 54 percent of boys and 22 percent of girls in junior and senior high school said they would have sex with someone they loved; 11 percent of boys and 22 percent of girls would "try to hold off" if they could. Sixty-five percent of those in high school said they would cheat on an important exam (Hellmich, 1990).

Many adults are surprised to find that today's youth do not have the values prevalent a generation or two ago. We wonder what went wrong. How could this have been prevented? We are quick to place the blame on any number of possible causes: the influence of peers, secular humanism in the schools, both parents working outside the home, the pervasiveness of MTV, drug abuse, or whatever comes to mind. But placing blame does not change the situation. We need to start with where we can make a difference, that is, we need to start with ourselves. Then we can move on to the social problems that at times seem so overwhelming.

We should ask ourselves if our speech and our actions are in line with our moral principles. What do we talk about? How do we spend our time? Does our speech betray an emphasis on material possessions? Do we help others and encourage our children to do the same? Do we communicate to our children the importance of a cause greater than themselves? Do we take the time to be with the family? None of us upon rising for the day would say, "How can I plan my day so I spend as little time as possible with my kids?" yet the end result seems to be the same. What messages are conveyed on the TV programs we watch? If our children observe us enjoying shows that depict violence and recreational sex, will it not be more difficult to communicate to them that these behaviors are wrong?

Those of us who are teachers in the school or youth ministers in the church will have an effect not only on our own children but on other people's children as well. This is a great responsibility and one to be taken seriously. What kind of example do we provide? How do we help our youth choose the goals and values that will make their lives meaningful to themselves and to others? How do we teach so that moral growth will take place?

PLAN OF THE BOOK

In this volume we will begin by describing some traditional approaches to moral development. This will include the use of storytelling as well as what the Bible says about being a good person. It will also include the character education method so popular in the past and still used by many teachers and parents today.

12

We will then move on in successive chapters to four major psychologies, each giving us some pointers as to how we as adults can help children and teenagers develop into caring and responsible persons. These psychologies and their application will comprise the major portion of the book. Each psychology emphasizes a different expression of morality, begins with a different assumption as to what people are like, and employs a different method for enhancing moral growth. Taken together, they can tell us a great deal. You can use this book, then, to apply psychology to your own situation. Prior expertise in the field is not required; psychological ideas are presented in as clear a way as possible, especially for the reader unfamiliar with the terminology. Words you may not already know are defined and illustrated. *Teaching for Moral Growth* will not read like a novel, but neither is it so difficult that it becomes a Herculean task.

We will then look again at Scripture as a way of evaluating the basic ideas presented by the major psychologies, seeing to what extent the philosophical assumptions of each psychology line up with the teachings in the Bible. Finally, we'll summarize it all in a concluding statement, endeavoring to answer the question: How shall we then teach?

References

Coles, R., & Genevie, L. (1990, March). The moral life of America's schoolchildren. *Teacher Magazine,* pp. 43–49.

Hellmich, N. (1990, February 1). Those adolescent years are a turbulent period. *USA Today,* p. 1.

Lewis, C.S. (1960) *Mere Christianity.* New York: Macmillan.

PART I

TRADITIONAL APPROACHES TO MORAL GROWTH

ONE

The Role of Stories

Storytelling has been around for as long as recorded history and is a major way in which people all over the world communicate to their offspring what behaviors are acceptable and what ones will bring disfavor and possible punishment.

Long before the advent of radios, videos, computers, or even the printed page, there were stories. The stories were told by the wise men to the people, by the old folk to the children, by those who ventured beyond the village to those who remained close to their place of birth. The stories told of how the world was formed, of those who had gone before them, of heroes and villains, of brave people and cowards. The stories were the wisdom of the ages passed from generation to generation.

As the people listened, they learned what was good and evil, what was clever and stupid, what was condoned and offensive, and what would bring honor or disgrace. Stories gave the people roots, telling them where they came from, who they were, and what they might expect in the future. The children loved the stories, for stories took them to far away places and to the times of their forefathers. And the children vowed they would grow up to be good, brave, and wise like those who came before them. They would make their elders proud. And, like millions of children since, they identified with the heroes of the story, imitating their speech and their actions.[1]

THE USE OF STORIES

Stories provide both entertainment and instruction. Whether real or imaginary, stories tell of people whose circumstances differ from our own, people who by eventualities of birth live their lives differently than we live ours. By hearing their stories we experience what they experience, feel what they feel, understand what they understand. We are repulsed by some and vow we will never be like them. We are drawn to others and imagine ourselves to be as daring, attractive, and successful as they. It is by putting ourselves in the place of others that we enlarge our perspective of life. It is by vicariously experiencing what they experience that we learn to appreciate the multifaceted and complex nature of human existence.

> **But more than entertaining, instructing, and making us wonder about our own lives, stories illustrate truths that are difficult to grasp in any other form. This is especially true for children who are not yet ready for abstract thinking.**

Stories stir the imagination. We question what would have happened if some detail of the story had been altered. A chance meeting, an unexpected opportunity, a different decision could have made all the difference. We wonder about the role of a Supreme Being who oversees the sequence of people's stories and to what extent we are following the pattern set for us before birth? Or, could it be that we set our own pattern and bring about the eventualities of our own story? What of the circumstances that lie beyond our control? They surely must play a part as well. Fate, providence, our own wills, daily circumstances — how do they all enter the picture?

But more than entertaining, instructing, and making us wonder about our own lives, stories illustrate truths that are difficult to grasp in any other form. This is especially true for children who are not yet ready for abstract thinking. Maxims, moral principles, and rules are not as well understood when stated directly as when illustrated in story form. Being told to be honest, brave, or obedient is not the same as hearing the real-life experiences of someone who possessed these traits. William Bennett (1991), gives the following examples:

> We want our children to recognize greed, and so they should know King Midas. . . . We want them to know about overreaching ambition, so we should tell them about Lady Macbeth. We want our children to know that hard work pays off, so we should teach them about the Wright brothers at Kitty Hawk and Booker T. Washington's learning to read. . . . We want them to see that one individual's action can make all the difference, so we should tell them about Rosa Parks, and about Jonas Salk's discovery of a vaccine against polio. We want our children to respect the rights of others, and so they should read the Declaration of Independence, the Bill of Rights, the Gettysburg Address, and Martin Luther King, Jr.'s "Letter from Birmingham City Jail." (p. 136)

It matters not to the young child if the characters are human or animal, real or imaginary. Even fairy tales can be used to teach moral lessons (Vandenplas-Holper, 1990). Some of the most popular stories combine real people, animals, cartoon characters, and inanimate objects. In *Aesop's Fables* each story is followed by a moral. "Slow and steady wins the race" we learn from the hare and the tortoise. "Sometimes the weak are able to help the strong" we see as the little mouse gnaws the ropes so the great lion can go free. "It is better to have less and be safe than to have more and be in danger" we realize when the country mouse is almost killed visiting the home of the city mouse. "Pride comes before a fall" we learn as the lamp which compares itself with the sun, moon, and stars is snuffed out by a puff of wind.

"Children find as much pleasure in stories which they know are the product of another's fancy as they do in playthings which by the power of their own imagination they transform into something very different from what they are" (St. John, 1918, p. 17). "The Little Engine That Could" teaches perseverance. "Stone Soup" teaches resourcefulness, and "Peter Rabbit" teaches obedience. Stories make abstractions come alive. They remain etched in our brains and we remember the lessons taught long after other information is forgotten. "A story is a way to say something that can't be said in any other way" (Ryan, 1991, p. 317).

PROBLEMS

The use of stories with the intent of teaching morality was greatly reduced during the third quarter of the twentieth century. It was thought by some educators that children have a natural inclination to develop morally and will do so without outside help. Stories could be read for enjoyment or for acquiring information, but they were not to be used for the purpose of teaching what was right and wrong.

There was also an objection to stories being used to frighten the child into being good. There have always been teachers, parents, and preachers who have used narrative in this way, but the method was considered unacceptable in the fifties, sixties, and seventies and continues to be viewed with suspicion today. Stories that frighten a child into behaving usually distort reality and often involve lying to the child. The punishment given to the culprit in the story is exaggerated or may not exist at all. At best, the consequences of a misdeed come to the character in the story much more swiftly than they would in real life.

Examples I have seen in picture books include the following: a boy took his pet fox to school, hiding it under his shirt because he knew it was against the rules to bring animals to class. His stomach was literally eaten away by the fox but he dared not cry out in pain. A little girl wandered off from her family while on a picnic and was swooped up by a large bird and fed to its babies. A child made fun of a classmate for being black; his punishment was that he became black. (You can imagine what that does for race relationships.) A boy was pictured sitting at the supper table with a steaming bowl of soup before him. In each successive picture the boy was perceptively thinner with the bowl of soup still before him. The last picture showed a newly dug grave with the cold bowl of soup on top.

From these stories the child is to learn obedience, the importance of staying with those who will protect, to respect the feelings of others, and not to waste food. But lying to children to get them to act in these ways creates other problems. In the first place, the storyteller becomes a poor model for children to emulate. "Your eyes turn green when you lie to me" does little to encourage truth telling. Secondly, the consequences do not occur in real life. Pinocchio's nose may get longer when he tells a lie, but children's noses do not. Wandering off alone when you should stay with the family does not mean you will become bird

18

food, and making fun of a dark skinned child will not affect the pigmentation of your own skin. In James Whitcomb Riley's poem "Little Orphant Annie," the goblins got a little boy who didn't say his prayers and a little girl who made fun of her elders. But as important as prayer is and as socially desirable as respecting older people is, goblins do not whisk away children who forget to pray or who are disrespectful of others.

This does not mean, of course, that stories of this nature should not be read to children for they provide entertainment and teach moral lessons. But it does mean that when stories like this are read, the adult should talk with the child about the story, making certain the child knows what is real and what is fantasy. Together, adult and child, can discuss the reason for the story being written while at the same time enjoying its imagery and the unfolding of the plot. After the age of five or six, most children have no difficulty separating what could actually happen with what is in the imagination of the author.

The problem we are more apt to face as we enter the twenty-first century is that many of the stories children are exposed to are unsuitable and may do more harm than good. It would appear that the television now tells the stories children hear. Saturday morning cartoons, afternoon soaps, talk shows that cater to the bizarre, and movies where aggression is met by aggression and explicit sexual situations abound—all are part of the regular fare of the child. Parents are asked to monitor what their children watch, but it would appear that few parents are taking the assignment seriously. Kevin Ryan (1993), of Boston University's Center for the Advancement of Ethics and Character, gives the following suggestions:

- Read stories to or with children and discuss the moral implications of the story.
- Watch television with them, then turn it off and talk about the program, whether good or bad behavior was shown.
- If the children are going to watch "The Simpsons," for example, parents should be there to explain Bart is funny because he's way out of line. Children clearly have to understand why he is out of line.

Ryan adds: "My own belief is that parents have been on an extended vacation from their responsibilities to raise good children" (p. 7D).

Stories Again Used To Teach Morality

Some parents *are* serious about providing good books and videos that teach for moral growth. They *are* aware of the effect stories have on children and *do* talk with them about the moral implications of what is seen or read. They know that even as children do not grow without food and even as they do not become strong without exercise, neither will they become morally educated without guidance and instruction. *Teaching for moral growth* is essential for moral maturity to occur. Today, once again, stories are an accepted form of communication. Once again, stories are in vogue for teaching the child the difference between right and wrong. A perusal of Christian literature will show that there is no scarcity of books for all age levels that teach children what they need to know to be good persons.[2]

NARRATIVE AND SCRIPTURE

Bible stories are a rich source from which to draw. The child can learn obedience from Abraham, bravery from Joshua and Caleb, loyalty from Ruth, friendship from David and Jonathan. The child hears that Joseph showed kindness to his brothers even though they had mistreated him; Job trusted God although he could not understand why terrible things were happening to him; and Daniel kept his faith despite the fact that he was put in the lions' den for doing so. In each story, God intervened and helped the one in need. God is more powerful than Satan. Good will triumph over evil. What God wants from each of us is a willingness to forgive those who would harm us, to trust Him to work things out in the long run, and to continue to worship Him despite our circumstances.

Jesus used stories or parables to teach what He wanted the disciples to know. He told about the farmer who sewed the seed, the shepherd who cared for the flock, the father who welcomed home his delinquent son, and the woman who was so sick the doctors could not help her. In each case, those who listened learned more about themselves, God's character, and what it meant to enter the kingdom of heaven. Storytelling or narrative is a very effective means of communication. "Jesus was a master story-teller. He did not invent the parable; the rabbis used it constantly; but so skilful was his use of this device that in our thought it is associated almost wholly with his name....His stories were marvels of perfection both in form and use. When we study them we do not wonder that the common people heard him gladly. It is not strange that the stories impressed his followers so strongly that many of them found place in the record of his life and teaching" (St. John, 1918).

On occasion, Jesus would use a story to answer a question asked by someone who listened to His words. When Peter asked, "Lord, how many times shall I forgive my brother when he sins against me?" (Matt. 18:21), Jesus told of a king who forgave his servant a debt but then changed his mind when the servant did not forgive the debt of another. If Peter wanted God's forgiveness, he in turn should forgive others. When an expert in the law asked, "Who is my neighbor?" (Luke 10:29), Jesus told the Parable of the Good Samaritan in which neighbor was defined as anyone a person comes in contact with who needs assistance, including someone of a different ethnic, social, or religious group. When some of the disciples asked when the kingdom of God would come, Jesus answered with an account of Lot and the sin-filled lives of those who lived in Sodom. Even as Lot and his neighbors did not know when the promised destruction would come, the disciples would not know when the kingdom of God would appear (Luke 17:20-28).

STORIES THAT ANSWER CHILDREN'S QUESTIONS

It was Joshua who was the leader of the Israelites after Moses died, and he had something to say to parents about using stories to answer children's questions.

> When your descendants ask . . . "What do these stones mean?" tell them, "Israel crossed the Jordan on dry ground." For the Lord your God dried up the Jordan before you until you had crossed over. The Lord your God did to the Jordan just what he had done to the Red Sea when he dried it up before us until we had crossed over. He did this so that all the peoples of the earth might know that the hand of the Lord is powerful and so that you might always fear the Lord your God (Josh. 4:21-24).

The stones had been placed there for just this purpose. The adults knew that children were good at asking questions and that a pile of stones beside the river would make them curious. Then, when the question came, "What do these stones mean?" the parents could tell the story of how God helped their grandparents enter the Promised Land and about all the things they had because He loved them and had chosen them as His special people.

This story must have been a favorite with the younger set and was asked for time and again. The best stories are the ones that come from the experiences of people we know. Young children, especially, are fascinated by the fact that their parents were once their same age, and they enjoy hearing what happened to mom or dad when they were young and living with grandma and grandpa.

STORIES THAT TEACH THE IMPORTANCE OF GOD'S WORD

Through Moses, Jehovah had explained to the Israelites how they and their children were to remember the Lord:

> Love the Lord your God with all your heart and with all your soul and with all your strength. These commandments that I give you today are to be upon your hearts. Impress them on your children. Talk about them when you sit at home and when you walk along the road, when you lie down and when you get up. Tie them as symbols on your hands and bind them on your foreheads. Write them on the doorframes of your houses and on your gates (Deut. 6:5-9).

These were not mere suggestions given to Jewish parents at that time. Rather they were commandments to be enacted. One *must* love the Lord with one's whole being and observe the "decrees and laws." Parents *must* impress upon their children the importance of knowing the law and obeying it in order that they too would serve God. This was to be done as naturally and regularly as getting up in the morning, sitting in one's house, walking from place to place, or lying down at night. And the tangible reminders were to be all around them — on the gates and doorframes and even on their hands and foreheads, showing the commandments' relevancy to everyday life.

Again, parents were instructed to give their personal testimony in the form of a story to their children, recounting God's goodness in the past and reiterating His promises for the future. Educative stories developed through remembering and rehearsing the acts of God.

When your son asks you, "What is the meaning of the stipulations, decrees and laws the Lord has commanded you?" tell him: "We were slaves of Pharaoh in Egypt, but the Lord brought us out of Egypt with a mighty hand . . . brought us out from there to bring us in and give us the land that he promised on oath to our forefathers. The Lord commanded us to obey all these decrees and fear the Lord our God, so that we might always prosper and be kept alive, as is the case today. And if we are careful to obey all this law before the Lord our God, as he has commanded us, that will be our righteousness" (Deut. 6:20-25).

Thus we see in Scripture, and especially in the Old Testament, that stories were used to tell children of God's love and care for them. Stories were told to remind them that some behaviors are good and right in the sight of God and would be followed by blessing, and other behaviors are despised and hated by God and would be followed by punishment. In the New Testament, Jesus spoke in parables to enlighten His listeners as to the nature of God and what His kingdom would be like. He gave a word picture of the last times when God as King would judge all peoples, separating the righteous from the unrighteous, the caring from the uncaring, the "sheep" from the "goats" (Matt. 25:31-46).

After Jesus ascended into heaven, His disciples related to others the stories of what the Lord had said and done, how He appeared to many people after the resurrection, told them to be witnesses of Him, and promised they would receive the power of the Holy Spirit (Acts 1:3-7). The disciples wrote much of it down so these episodes would not be forgotten. "Gospel writings were the response of first-generation Christians who had lost One who had held them together. . . . Through the telling of the stories of Jesus they regained their focus and the church grew" (Nelson, 1990, p. 95).

Narrative, then, is the method God chose to reveal Himself to us, to tell the story of creation and redemptive love. It is the history of the human race, individually and collectively. And because we see our own lives as narrative, we are able to understand what God has revealed to us through His Word. The Scriptures speak to us not only of what we should know, but how we should feel as we look at the total picture of who we are in relation to our Maker and to our fellow human beings. Without stories we would have no concept of self, no roots to the past, no hope of a glorious future.[3]

WHERE WE ARE TODAY

The directions given to Jewish parents many centuries ago are as appropriate today as they were then. But it is harder now, we say. Time is taken up with many responsibilities, places to go, and things to do unheard of during biblical times. If both parents work outside the home, as is quite common, there is even less time to be with one's children.

In many ways, Christian homes are not very different than the homes of unbelievers. We and our children live in a world of television, computers, radios, and movies; a world of scouts, basketball games, music lessons, and school; a world of mountain bikes, mopeds, motorcycles, and cars; a world of clothes, parties, and the constant display of sex in advertising. It is also a world of work and responsibility, of caring for our homes and families. And if we take our jobs seriously, more and more demands are placed upon us, leaving less and less time to consider ways to help our children develop morally. Unless we make a concerted effort to plan our lives so that the pressure of each day does not take precedence over what really matters in the long run, teaching our children what is true and beautiful and good is less apt to occur.

Even the busiest of parents will find some time to talk with their children, to answer their questions, and to read them a story. What we say, how we respond, and what we read will make a difference. And as our children get older, there will be other influences as well. Children cannot be isolated from the outside world, nor would we want them to be. Peers will take on increasing importance; teachers, scout leaders, coaches, and employers will all have their input. But in the end, each child must make up his or her own mind as to the kind of person he or she will be. As children mature, they will decide what values to adopt, what behaviors to engage in, what attitudes to hold, and what religious faith to accept. *Teaching for moral growth* while the child is in the home is not the whole picture, nor does it come with a lifetime guarantee. But it does give the child a start in the right direction and, if coupled with ethical teaching in the school and church, is more likely to bring about a morally mature adult who knows what is right, has the will to act in accordance with that knowledge, and puts that knowledge into practice in everyday life.

NARRATIVE AND PSYCHOLOGY

Psychologists, unlike parents and religious leaders, are trained to be scientific in their approach, so traditionally there has been little room for storytelling or narrative in their discipline. "The world of science, almost by definition, accepts only those relationships that occur at non-chance levels as discovered through experimentation" (Kassinove & Eckhardt, 1992, p. 10). Psychology is the study of animal and human behavior and of the forces that account for that behavior. Observations are made under controlled conditions with a sufficiently large number of subjects (animals or people) that the findings can be applied to other subjects. For example, if we find that students who make good grades in high school also make good grades in college, we can predict how well high school students will do in college even before they get there. There are some exceptions but by and large we know about what to expect. If we would observe only one student and write an interesting account of her experiences in high school, what courses she took, and what grades she received, and then follow her to college and do the same, we could not generalize from her story to other students in school. We would not know if she were typical or if she might be an exception. We would have to observe other students as well before we could apply our findings to the majority of high school subjects.

Scientific observation is important and no one should underestimate its worth. Without it we would not have gotten very far in our quest to understand the world in which we live. However, within the past few years, there has become an increasing realization among some psychologists that we may have put so much emphasis on research and so little on individual stories that we have tipped the scales too far in the direction of controlled experimentation and too little in the direction of concrete human and interpersonal relationships. Jerome Bruner (1986), in an invited address to the American Psychological Association, spoke of "two modes of thought, each providing distinctive ways of ordering experience, of constructing reality" (p. 11). One is the logical world of the researcher complete with well-formed arguments based on formal empirical truth, hypothesis testing, and consistent noncontradictory facts. The other is a good story with concern for the human condition, including the particulars of individual experience set in time and place. One appeals to logic and consistency, the other to empathy and individual intentions. "Efforts to reduce one mode to the other or to ignore one at the expense of the other inevitably fail to capture the rich diversity of thought" (p. 11). David Berliner (1992) in the *Educational Psychologist* speaks to the same issue when he says that "the methods of naturalistic inquiry, a form of inquiry dependent on the telling of a good story, need to be learned along with the traditional quantitative methods. It is the human predilection for stories, as much as anything else, that has made qualitative inquiry so popular in recent years" (p. 159).

Psychoanalysts, in contrast to most psychologists, have always preferred stories to experimentation. The client tells of events in his or her life that appear to be problem areas, and the therapist interprets these events in accordance with analytic theory. These individual stories then become case studies which psychoanalysts share with each other, explaining the details of the case and the methods of therapy that appear to be effective. M. Scott Peck's (1983) *People of the Lie* and Robert Coles' (1989) *The Call of Stories* are popular examples of this approach.

It is precisely because psychoanalysts have not used the scientific approach that they have received criticism from those who favor controlled experimentation. But the tide seems to be turning in favor of using narrative as well as experimentation. This is especially true as it relates to mental health. The whole realm of counseling (which is presently growing at such a rapid pace that in some people's minds the sole purpose of psychology is to help people with their personal problems) uses the stories of clients as the basis for therapy. Without narrative there would be no way for the clinician to know where to begin.

Other psychologists have also begun to think seriously about using stories as well as science in a variety of settings including that of teaching the child what is right and what is wrong. "A very effective way to introduce children to the moral life . . . is to have them hear, read, or watch morally challenging narratives" (Vitz, 1990, p. 716). This is because children's understanding of moral issues is "interpersonal, emotional, imaginistic, and story-like" (p. 711). Stories are now presented in the classroom for the purpose of having children discuss the moral dilemma within the story. (See chapter 9 for how this type of story is used at different grade levels.) The moral dilemma story method is favored by psychologists who emphasize the cognitive or thinking processes of the child.

SELF-NARRATIVE

Telling one's own story takes place not only in therapy but in other contexts as well. We tell bits and pieces of our story to the people we meet, so they will know something about us. They do the same with us, so we will begin to know them. If we like each other's stories, we become friends; if we don't, we will probably go our separate ways.

Stories bind us together in understanding and concern. Whether in a secular or a religious setting, we form a kinship with those persons whose stories we know. The story may come from the neighbor next door, be written in a letter by a missionary overseas, be printed in the local newspaper, or be given in a testimony service at church. It matters not the source. What matters is that once we know the person's story, we know the person. Stories and people cannot be separated.

> Stories bind us together in understanding and concern. Whether in a secular or a religious setting, we form a kinship with those persons whose stories we know.

Self-narrative for the purpose of moral growth is being increasingly lauded by some educators as the method to use in the context of the school. When students author their own stories, they come to see that they must take responsibility for their own thoughts, feelings, and actions. Authoring one's story means to "authorize" and gives new meaning to the term "know thyself."

Mark Tappan and Lyn Brown (1989) suggest that the teacher begin by saying to students, "All people have had the experience of being in a situation where they had to make a decision, but weren't sure of what they should do. Would you describe a situation when you faced a moral conflict and you had to make a decision, but weren't sure what you should do?" (p. 195) Younger children tell their story orally whereas high school students write what they wish to relate. The story should include the details of the situation, what the conflict was, what the student thought should be done, what was actually done, whether the action was considered the right thing to do, what emotions were experienced, what might have been a better action to take, and why this was a moral problem. "Teachers must listen carefully, respectfully, and responsively to such stories, thereby supporting and encouraging the emergence of each student's own authority and sense of self-authorization" (Tappan, 1991, p. 21). Narrative provides a powerful vehicle for understanding our own moral experiences.

We will return to the use of stories in a later chapter, especially as narrative relates to *teaching for moral growth* in the context of the classroom. But let us turn our attention first to other traditional methods that have stood the test of time. We will examine a biblical approach and then look at the character education method that has been in place since before the turn of the century.

NOTES

1. I once observed my three-year-old putting rocks from the driveway into his fireman's handkerchief. When asked what he was doing, he responded: "I'm David and the next person to come along is Goliath." Approaching on the sidewalk was a very proper looking woman who probably did not wish to be pelted with rocks and would interpret the act as coming from a very undisciplined child, rather than from the hero he imagined himself to be. Fortunately for the woman (but unfortunately for the creative development of the child), identification with a Bible character was not permitted under these circumstances.

2. Each issue of *Christian Parenting Today* in a section called "Mindwatch" has reviews of books, music, and videos that teach children moral and spiritual truths. Examples of books are *The toddlers activity Bible* by Betty Aldridge (Thomas Nelson), *Sometimes you win, sometimes you don't* by Ginger Fulton (Moody Press), *Little people in tough spots* by Gilbert Beers (Oliver Nelson), *Shadows and shining lights* by Ann Hubbard (Focus on the Family), *The toddlers bedtime story book* by Gilbert Beers (Victor Books), *Jenny and Grandpa: What is it like to be old?* by Carolyn Nystrom (Lion Publishing), and *Journey to nowhere* by Judy Baer (Bethany House). *You and God and me together* by Jan Kempe (Discovery House) has twelve moral dilemma stories with Scripture.

3. Stories are not the whole picture of God's revelation to the human race. Narrative must be coupled with Bible-based theology and Christian doctrine in order for people to understand the attributes of the Deity and how He relates to His created beings. As Donald Bloesch states it in *A theology of Word & Spirit* (Downers Grove, IL: InterVarsity, 1992), "With the rise of narrative theology, the emphasis has shifted from exploring the metaphysical implications of the faith to investigating the story of a people

on pilgrimage. While reflecting certain biblical concerns, this development is nonetheless fraught with peril. Theology can ill afford to ignore the issue of truth, for it is truth that gives narrative its significance. Revelation brings us not only insight into the human condition but also foresight into the divine plan for the world" (p. 133).

Older children and adults are able to comprehend a more systematic approach whereas younger children cannot. This is why narrative is especially important for those who because of age are less mature in their understanding of the Christian faith.

REFERENCES

Bennett, W.J. (1991). Moral literacy and the formation of character. In J.S. Benninga (Ed.), *Moral, character, and civic education in the elementary school* (pp. 131–138). New York: Teachers College Press.

Berliner, D.C. (1992). Telling the stories of educational psychology. *Educational Psychologist, 27,* 143–161.

Bruner, J. (1986). *Actual minds, possible worlds.* Cambridge, MA: Harvard University Press.

Coles, R. (1989). *The call of stories: Teaching and the moral imagination.* Boston: Houghton Mifflin.

Kassinove, H., & Eckhardt, C. (1992, Summer). Religious involvement and behavior therapy training: Student conflicts and ethical concerns. *Psychologists Interested in Religious Issues Newsletter, 17,* pp. 1, 10–12.

Nelson, L.L. (1990). Narrative theology and storytelling in Christian education with children. *Christian Education Journal, XI(1),* 95–104.

Peck, M.S. (1983). *People of the lie: The hope for healing human evil.* New York: Simon & Schuster.

Ryan, K. (1991). The narrative and the moral. *The Clearing House, 64,* 316–319.

————. (1993, May 19). Helping shape children's values. *USA Today,* p. 7D.

St. John, E.P. (1918). *Stories and story-telling in moral and religious education.* Boston: Pilgrim Press.

Tappan, M.B. (1991). Narrative, authorship, and the development of moral authority. In M.B. Tappan & M.J. Packer (Eds.), *Narrative and storytelling: Implications for understanding moral development* (pp. 5–25). New York: Jossey-Bass.

Tappan, M.B., & Brown, L.M. (1989). Stories told and lessons learned: Toward a narrative approach to moral development and moral education. *Harvard Educational Review, 59,* 182–205.

Vandenplas-Holper, C. (1990). Children's books and films as media for moral education: Some cognitive-developmentally oriented considerations. *School Psychology International, 11,* 31–38.

Vitz, P.C. (1990). The use of stories in moral development: New psychological reasons for an old education method. *American Psychologist, 45,* 709–720

TWO

A Biblical Approach

The theme of the Bible is the greatness, magnitude, and righteousness of God. It speaks of One so holy that sin cannot be tolerated in any form. It is a message that says that what we consider to be good cannot be compared to the goodness of God. It is a revelation that the distance between where we are and where God is is so vast there is no way we can reach Him, that God must come to us if we are to know what He is like.

This is no better illustrated than in the story of Job as recorded in the Old Testament. By human standards, there was no one as good as Job. He used his vast wealth to care for the poor, feed the hungry, and provide for the orphans. He prayed for his children and offered sacrifices to God. Job was so moral that he caught the attention of God who said to Satan, "Have you considered my servant Job? There is no one on earth like him; he is blameless and upright, a man who fears God and shuns evil" (Job 1:8).

After Job's wealth and all his possessions were taken from him, and he was so miserable he wanted to die, his one request was that God would speak to him and tell why all this had happened to him. How could bad things happen to good people? And God heard his request and came to him. He told Job that no one knows what God knows, no one sees what God sees, no one understands how God works in the heavens and in the earth, and no one is good when compared to the goodness of God. Then Job realized how little he was in comparison, and he didn't try to tell God about all the good things he had done before he got so sick, nor did he feel that he deserved anything because he hadn't cursed God when everything was taken from him. In God's presence, Job no longer felt important. He even said he despised himself when he saw how much better God was than he was.

God was pleased that Job had learned what he was supposed to learn, that there is a wide gulf between the goodness of people and that of God. We read that God gave Job back as much as he had before, and Job lived until he was very old, enjoying his children and grandchildren.

The message that Job received directly from God is one recorded in Scripture for our edification. It says that no matter how moral we may be, no matter how kind our deeds, no matter how good our intentions; all are of little significance when compared to the goodness of God. The gulf between human beings and God is so vast that there is no comparison. God may be pleased with what we do even as He was pleased with what Job did, but until we recognize who God is — that He alone is the Creator and Redeemer and in Him alone resides goodness and justice — we cannot find favor with Him nor are we able to understand a morality that transcends our own finite minds.

AN UPSIDE — DOWN WORLD

Not only does Scripture contrast God's goodness with that of the human race, it also shows that the values of the kingdom of God are very different from those of this world. Let us begin with first century Palestine.

In Jesus' time, prestige came from being adult rather than child, male rather than female, strong rather than weak, whole rather than deformed. It was also important to come from the right lineage (in this case, Jewish), to hold a prestigious position (such as membership in the Sanhedrin), to be known as a good person (in this case, conformity to the religious laws of the Old Testament), and to have wealth.

Having wealth took on special significance because wealth was associated with God's favor. Again and again, God promised to bless those who followed Him by increasing their lands, cattle, servants, and crops. They were assured of a long life, many children to carry on the family name, and recognition for generations to come. It was generally accepted that wealth was a special blessing from God to signify His pleasure. Turning the equation around was thus equally valid. Namely, those lacking in material possessions or offspring to perpetuate their lineage were without God's favor. Had the rich young man who asked Jesus about inheriting eternal life given up his wealth and followed Christ, he would have lost not only his possessions but also the status he enjoyed as being one of God's favored people. For him, the cost was too great. His enviable position of being a good person in the eyes of his contemporaries meant more than the promise of eternal life to come.

VALUES TURNED ON THEIR HEAD

It was said of Jesus' followers that they turned the world upside down (Acts 17:6). They had learned from their Master, for this is exactly what Jesus had done. The values of the time were turned on their head by the one who was God incarnate. To Jesus, being an adult did not take precedence over being a child. He told the disciples that unless they would become like little children, they would never enter the kingdom of heaven (Matt. 18:3-4). Being male was not more prestigious than being female, and being Jewish did not bring more favor with God than being Gentile. Witness Jesus' example of talking to a Samaritan woman even though the custom of the day forbid a man to talk publicly with a woman or a Jew to speak to a Samaritan (John 4:9). Being strong was not necessarily best either, for "God chose the weak things of the world to shame the strong. He chose the lowly things of this world and the despised things — and the things that are not — to nullify the things that are" (1 Cor. 1:27-28).

Having wealth could work against a person as well. As the rich young man walked away, Jesus commented that it was "easier for a camel to go through the eye of a needle than for a rich man to enter the kingdom of God" (Mark 10:25). Jesus told a parable of one who was "dressed in purple and fine linen and lived in luxury every day" (Luke 16:19). At his gate was a beggar "longing to eat what fell from the rich man's table" (16:20). Upon their deaths, the rich man went to hell and the poor man to heaven. You can imagine how surprised Jesus' listeners must have been. This was not the way the story should end. Rich men didn't go to hell and poor men didn't go to heaven.

OLD TESTAMENT LAW NO LONGER THE PINNACLE OF MORALITY

Furthermore, Jesus made it plain that conformity to Old Testament law was not sufficient to make someone a good person. Obedience to the law was only a beginning. Jesus said that He came not to abolish the law but to fulfill it (Matt. 5:17). Fulfillment included the emotions of the heart and the understanding of the mind, as well as what the person did. By stating the intent or precept behind the law, Jesus gave a better interpretation of what the law meant. "Do not murder" is the law; "do not be angry" is the state of mind. "Do not commit adultery" is the law; "do not look on a woman to lust after her" is the intent of the will. The washing of the hands is the law; the cleansing of the heart is the purification of the inner being. "In the Sermon on the Mount Jesus stresses that we must be far beyond a morality that stops at mere obedience to a few rules. . . . Christian morality goes down to the level of our character as well as our habits; to love as well as action" (Barclay, 1978, p. 148).

Jesus also told the disciples that the meek would inherit the earth, they should love their enemies as well as their friends, and they should rejoice when they were insulted because of their relationship with Him. And, unless their righteousness surpassed that of the Pharisees and the teachers of the law they would not enter the kingdom of heaven (Matt. 5:20). Blessing would come upon those who mourned, who were peacemakers, who were merciful, and who were "poor in spirit" (Matt. 5:3). "To be 'poor in spirit' is to acknowledge our spiritual poverty, indeed our spiritual bankruptcy, before God. For we are sinners, under the holy wrath of God, and deserving nothing but the judgment of God. We have nothing to offer, nothing to plead, nothing with which to buy the favour of heaven" (Stott, 1978, p. 39).

JESUS AND HIS FOLLOWERS TO BE FIRST IN THE KINGDOM

Jesus' message to the disciples was the same as that given by God to Job: human ideas of goodness and morality do not begin to fathom the meaning of righteousness as seen in God Himself and in the Scripture.

How strange this must have sounded to all who heard it. How strange is still sounds to us today. We want so much to believe that we are capable on our own of deciding what is right and wrong, what is good and evil. But we, like first-century citizens, are products of a society that is warped by sin and often incapable of seeing its many injustices. We, like them, continue to measure success by wealth and power, values that were considered by Christ to be hindrances to the message of the Gospel.

Jesus was an enigma to all who knew Him and a constant embarrassment to His disciples. He scorned those at the top of the social ladder, but was kind and gentle to those at the bottom. Those in power came to hate Him and tried to have Him killed, and those who were powerless and without status grew to love Him and with changed lives worshiped Him. He said this is the way it would be — that in the kingdom the last would be first and the first would be last (Matt. 19:30). "The new heroes were the throwaways of institutionalized religion. They were the repentant sinners and publicans, the tax collectors and harlots. And what of the old heroes, the scribes and the priests, the Pharisees and Sadducees, the guardians of the old sacred way? They now were the villains, dethroned, brought low" (Kraybill, 1990, p. 72). Money, power, prestige — those things considered desirable both in Jesus' time and today no longer have value in comparison with being a disciple of Jesus Christ. Jesus turned the world upside down and asks that we, His followers, understand the meaning of this message and make it a part of our very being.

A BIBLICAL APPROACH TO MORAL AND SPIRITUAL GROWTH

We have seen what the Bible says about being a good person and learned that goodness as interpreted in Scripture differs from the definition offered by the human race. Goodness in the Bible is perfection, found only in God and revealed to us in the person of Jesus Christ. It is imputed to believers by virtue of their becoming members of the family of God.

We will now turn to ways that moral and spiritual growth may take place. Again we will use the Bible as our guide. First, we will note that *conflict* contributes to moral and spiritual growth. Without conflict we would be content to remain as we are, thus negating any felt need to change or develop. We will also see how our *actions* are important. Those of us who call ourselves Christians need to consider how we can follow in the steps of the one whose name we bear, engaging in those behaviors that are honoring to Him. Next, we will note that moral and spiritual growth include becoming mature in the *knowledge* of God. We who are believers seek for wisdom, understanding, and insight so that we may know better the ways of righteousness. Last, the Scriptures acknowledge the tremendous *potential* within each of us that comes not from ourselves but from the creative and redemptive power of God.

For each of these four ways of growing morally and spiritually — conflict, action, knowledge, and potential — we will use examples from Scripture. The Bible is the Christian's guide to faith and practice and has stood the test of time. There can be no better tradition for understanding moral growth than to look into God's Word.

MORAL AND SPIRITUAL GROWTH INVOLVE CONFLICT

Conflict comes in a variety of forms. It comes when we want to reach a goal but circumstances keep us from doing so. It comes when we are faced with a problem we cannot solve. And it comes when we are in emotional turmoil over events beyond our control and do not know how to cope. All of us face conflict in our daily lives.

Picture yourself in a situation in which you must choose between two courses of action, both of which you find to be desirable. How do you decide which is better? You feel you should attend that special service at church but you also feel you should make the necessary preparations for the next day's work. There is not time for both. Sociologists and psychologists call this an *approach-approach conflict* because whichever way you go you have done something you wanted to do and knew to be important. It may be hard at the time to decide but this is the easiest type of conflict because you always end up with something you want. Many of the decisions we make are not between good and evil but rather between the better of two actions, both of which are good.

A second type of conflict is having to choose between two events, neither of which is to your liking. You don't want to lie to your friend, but neither do you want to hurt her feelings. Again, how do you decide? You have to say something to her which will result in either lying or hurt feelings. This is known as an *avoidance-avoidance conflict* because whichever way it turns out you are unhappy with the results. Subsequently, this type of conflict will put more pressure on you than the approach-approach type. Some decisions we make mean choosing the lesser of two evils.

A third type of conflict takes place when something you want and something you don't want are so closely tied together you either have to take both or you can't have either. You may want to witness to others about your faith, but you know you will be embarrassed if you do so. Again, how do you decide? Do you witness and suffer the embarrassment or not witness and not be embarrassed? This is known as an *approach-avoidance conflict*. The closer you come to witnessing the more you anticipate the embarrassment. The more you put off witnessing the less embarrassment you feel. However, you remind yourself that you have not done what you know you should, and the cycle begins again. Your friends who witness, and probably suffer little if any embarrassment, will tell you to think about how important it is to share the good news of the Gospel with others. The research on approach-avoidance conflict, however, indicates that you will be more apt to witness if you can reduce the fear associated with being embarrassed. Increasing the desire to approach (in this case witnessing) is not as effective as decreasing the need to avoid (in this case embarrassment). Reducing the embarrassment may come by observing how others witness and then practicing their method. Or it may come by a process called role-playing in which you and a Christian friend practice witnessing to each other. Practice makes a difficult task much easier.

We see, then, that conflict occurs when a choice must be made. But without choices, where would we be? We would accept things the way they are, thus negating the opportunity for moral and spiritual growth.

Approach-Approach Conflict in Scripture
The children of Israel wanted both the true God, Yahweh, and the false gods of their heathen neighbors. This way they could cover all bases, so to speak. They would have Jehovah's help when needed, and they would not offend their neighbors. But Joshua reminded them that this proliferation of deities was not acceptable. They would have to decide which way they would go and to whom they would give their allegiance. At this point they were faced with an approach-approach con-

flict. Joshua was quick to remind them that it was Yahweh who had helped them reach the Promised Land. "Now fear the Lord and serve him with all faithfulness. Throw away the gods your forefathers worshiped beyond the River and in Egypt, and serve the Lord" (Josh. 24:14). Then the people answered, "Far be it from us to forsake the Lord to serve other gods. . . . And the Lord drove out before us all the nations, including the Amorites, who lived in the land. We too will serve the Lord, because he is our God" (vv. 16, 18).

The Amorites did not have a conflict. How they would live and what they would worship was predetermined. They were not called upon to decide between their idols and Jehovah. It was only those whom God called His people, those whom God was dealing with and whom He asked to be "holy" (Deut. 7:6) who experienced the inner turmoil that comes with making such a decision. C.S. Lewis (1960) used the term "dismay" to describe this turmoil.

> Of course, I quite agree that the Christian religion is, in the long run, a thing of unspeakable comfort. But it does not begin in comfort; it begins in the dismay I have been describing, and it is no use at all trying to go on to that comfort without first going through the dismay. In religion, as in war and everything else, comfort is the one thing you cannot get by looking for it. If you look for truth, you may find comfort in the end; if you look for comfort you will not get either comfort or truth — only soft soap and wishful thinking to begin with and, in the end, despair. (p. 39)

And so it has been for generations. Those who know and follow their natural inclinations or subscribe to the lifestyle of those around them do not have to face a decision as to how they will act or who they will be. They know no other way than the one they already adhere to. They can be no one other than who they already are. There may be no Joshua to tell them there is more than one option and that a choice should be made. Or, if a Joshua does appear, the subsequent conflict is often short-lived for they do not understand the true destiny of the human race or the purpose for which it was created.

Avoidance-Avoidance Conflict in Scripture

Not only does approach-approach conflict appear in Scripture but we see a number of examples of avoidance-avoidance conflict as well. After fleeing from Egypt, the Israelites found themselves between Pharaoh's advancing army and the waters of the Red Sea. No matter which way they turned they faced certain death. To cite other examples, Jacob found that living with his father-in-law had become intolerable but going back home to his brother Esau might be even worse. He was between a rock and a hard place. Elijah faced either starvation or Jezebel's wrath. Peter had to choose between denying Christ or being scorned.

In the case of the Israelites, God chose to intervene and perform the miracle of dividing the waters. Esau's attitude changed over the years so that Jacob was not harmed. An angel brought food to Elijah to strengthen him. And Peter, grieving over the enormity of what he had done by denying his Lord, was offered forgiveness for his failures. Avoidance-avoidance conflict may be so devastating that God in His mercy steps in and performs a miracle on our behalf, changing circumstances or attitudes, including our own, or promising wisdom and strength as we make the difficult decision, or offering forgiveness when we have made the wrong choice.

Approach-Avoidance Conflict in Scripture
The third type of conflict, namely that of approach-avoidance, is inevitable in the life of the believer. As Christians we have two natures: a sinful nature inherited from Adam and a spiritual nature inherited from Christ. "For if, by the trespass of the one man, death reigned through that one man, how much more will those who receive God's abundant provisions of grace and of the gift of righteousness reign in life through the one man, Jesus Christ?" (Rom. 5:17) The Apostle Paul struggled with this problem and revealed his anguish in a letter to the Romans. "When I want to do good, evil is right there beside me. For in my inner being I delight in God's law; but I see another law at work in the members of my body, waging war against the law of my mind and making me a prisoner of the law of sin at work within my members. What a wretched man I am!" (7:21-24) The closer a person is to God, the greater the realization of the forces that would keep one from being godly. Given this truth, it is understandable why Paul and other devout Christians through the ages have had such a moral and spiritual struggle.

MORAL AND SPIRITUAL GROWTH INVOLVE ACTION

In 1896, Charles Sheldon began writing a story entitled *In His Steps,* which he read a chapter at a time to the young people in his congregation in Topeka, Kansas. By 1935 it had been printed in twenty-one languages and by sixty-six publishers. A single printer sold over 3 million copies of one edition in the streets of London. This highly readable book is a fictional account of what happened in one congregation when the pastor and members pledged not to do anything for a year without first asking the question, "What would Jesus do?" and then endeavoring to follow Jesus as closely as each one knew how, no matter what the result might be.

They soon discovered that doing what Jesus would do made them distinctly unpopular with employers, family, and friends. Opportunities for career and advancement were adversely affected and loss of employment and property resulted. Yet, even with the reverses, each one who was willing to follow "in His steps" found that God's grace was sufficient. Together they had the joy of relieving human suffering, winning souls to Christ, and encouraging other Christians to new discipleship. A miraculous change came into their own lives and to the congregation as a whole.

Few Christians have ever tried to do what Sheldon's characters did. Is this because the cost would be too great, one's lifestyle would have to change, and friends would question stability and judgment? Perhaps so. But if we call ourselves Christians, that is, followers of Christ, we must accept the invitation to go with Him, to learn His teachings, to let Him lead us, if not literally, at least in spirit and in truth.

Even as He humbled Himself (Phil. 2:8), we are to humble ourselves (James 4:10). As He became a servant (Phil. 2:7), we too must serve (Gal. 5:13). As He cared for the poor and helpless (Luke 4:18), we also must seek to help those who can do nothing for us in return (14:13-14). As He confronted the religious leaders who interpreted the Scripture to their own advantage (Luke 11:46), we may be called upon to confront religious leaders today who seize upon certain biblical passages that put them in positions of power or authority. Jesus did not follow the status quo. He judged those who were not used to being judged (11:43) and did not condemn those whom society said should be condemned (John 8:11).

Personal Morality or Social Morality?
The Scriptures place great stress on the behavior of those who belong
to God, and what people do is an indication of their relationship to the
Lord. Israel, as a covenant nation, was constantly reminded of this, and
worshipers presenting themselves at the gate of the temple would hear
the question:

> Lord, who may dwell in your sanctuary?
> Who may live on your holy hill?
> [And the answer:]
> He whose walk is blameless
> and who does what is righteous
> who speaks the truth from his heart . . .
> who does his neighbor no wrong . . .
> who despises a vile man
> but honors those who fear the Lord. (Ps. 15:1-4)

Time and again, God told the Israelites that if they would follow His
commandments, He would do great things for them. But if they disobeyed, destruction would be their lot. God was concerned with both
personal morality and social responsibility. Speaking through the
Prophet Amos, the Lord chided the people for such affluent behaviors
as lounging on couches, dining on choice lambs, drinking by the bowl-
ful, and using the finest lotions (Amos 6:4-6). But the main thrust of
the message of Amos was the lack of concern for those less fortunate.

> You trample on the poor
> and force him to give you grain. . . .
> You oppress the righteous and take bribes
> and you deprive the poor of justice in the courts. (5:11-12)

Because of this God tells them:

> I hate, I despise your religious feasts;
> I cannot stand your assemblies.
> Even though you bring me burnt offerings and grain offerings,
> I will not accept them. (5:21-22)

Personal morality and social morality (what John Stott, 1975, calls "micro-ethics" and "macro-ethics" in *Balanced Christianity*) are integrated in the New Testament as well. James, writing to the "brothers," asked for such personal virtues as patience, stability, thankfulness to God for His gifts, humility, and a dependence on God's will (James 1). This request is coupled with the overarching social mandate of visiting the fatherless and the widows and converting sinners from the error of their ways.

Some of us were reared in homes where great stress was placed on personal morality. We were not to lie, steal, deceive, cheat, or swear. We were to respect authority, take responsibility, and be self-disciplined. If we did these things we were considered to be good persons. Little was said, however, of the social problems that plague much of the world. The immorality of hunger, the sin of racial prejudice, the evil of sexism, the outrage of pollution were not topics that seemed relevant. It was almost as though these ills are present and no one was responsible for them. The cry for justice by Amos and other Old Testament prophets took second place to the Ten Commandments, and Jesus' egalitarian stance and show of concern for every person seemed less important than Paul's admonition for right living.

On the other hand, some believers today have become so involved in such social issues as abortion, war protests, welfare programs, politics, or penal reform that they ignore God's commands for sexual purity, control of temper, honest dealings with others, and a life of prayer. They readily see the sins of society but seldom acknowledge any wrongdoing of their own.

But both aspects of moral behavior, the personal and the social, are important. When the young man who wondered what he could do to inherit eternal life told Jesus that he had kept the commandments, Jesus recognized that the social aspect of moral behavior had been neglected in his life and said, "One thing you lack. Go, sell everything you have and give to the poor" (Mark 10:21). However, when Judas objected to Mary's act of pouring expensive perfume on Jesus' feet and said that the perfume could have been sold and the money given to the poor, Jesus responded that Mary's act of worship was of greater significance. "You will always have the poor among you, but you will not always have me" (John 12:8).

Jesus and Social Action

The Apostle Matthew records a time when Jesus and His disciples were together on the Mount of Olives, and Jesus was asked what would happen at the end of the age. He answered:

> When the Son of man comes in his glory, and all the angels with him, he will sit on his throne in heavenly glory. All the nations will be gathered before him, and he will separate the people one from another as a shepherd separates the sheep from the goats. He will put the sheep on his right and the goats on his left.
>
> Then the King will say to those on his right, "Come, you who are blessed by my Father; take your inheritance, the kingdom prepared for you since the creation of the world. For I was hungry and you gave me something to eat, I was thirsty and you gave me something to drink, I was a stranger and you invited me in, I needed clothes and you clothed me, I was sick and you looked after me, I was in prison and you came to visit me."
>
> Then the righteous will answer him, "Lord, when did we see you hungry and feed you, or thirsty and give you something to drink? When did we see you a stranger and invite you in, or needing clothes and clothe you? When did we see you sick or in prison and go to visit you?"
>
> The King will reply, "I tell you the truth, whatever you did for the least of these brothers of mine, you did for me." (Matt. 25:31-40)

It is interesting to note that the separation of the "sheep" and the "goats" depends on numerous small acts of kindness—the social aspects or "macroethics" of Christian behavior. Those chosen by the King are those who are sensitive to the needs of others and act to relieve human suffering. Being a part of God's family means growing morally not only in our personal lives but also in our dealings with others. Right action, both private and public, is necessary for moral and spiritual growth to occur.

MORAL AND SPIRITUAL GROWTH INVOLVE KNOWLEDGE

After David died and Solomon had been crowned king, the Lord appeared to Solomon in a dream and asked him to state the one thing he wanted most (1 Kings 3:5). Solomon's response was given in humility. He said that he was God's servant, a little child in understanding compared to the magnitude of the task of ruling a large nation. He asked that God give him discernment so he could govern fairly, so he could distinguish between right and wrong. God was pleased with Solomon's answer and said: "Since you have asked for this and not for long life or wealth for yourself, nor have asked for the death of your enemies but for discernment in administering justice, I will do what you have asked. I will give you a wise and discerning heart" (3:11-12).

A wise and discerning heart meant far more than the acquisition of information. Wisdom to Solomon was more than the 3,000 proverbs and 1,005 songs for which he was credited. It was more than his knowledge of botany and biology (1 Kings 4:33), meteorology and geology (Ecc. 1), life stages and the fleeting nature of human existence (Ecc. 12). It was, to put it in the words of the text, "very great insight, and a breadth of understanding as measureless as the sand on the seashore" (1 Kings 4:29). Wisdom, insight, and understanding are components of the intellect that surpass the kind of knowledge we have when we acquire information for a specific purpose, only to forget it when it is no longer needed.

> A wise person understands that all he or she is derives from God. I am wise if I understand that God is God and I am not. The wise person is righteous, in that he or she walks after God's ways, knowing that those ways are the ways that the Creator established for human flourishing. With this knowledge of God and God's ways, the wise person has the framework to acquire discernment and good judgment; this individual will not be taken in by ephemeral and illusory pleasures, because his or her experience is not merely an experience of fact but includes a discernment of what has enduring value. (Evans, 1992, p. 113)

The words "wisdom" and "knowledge" are often used interchangeably in Scripture and have a common meaning. "The fear of the Lord is the beginning of knowledge, but fools despise wisdom and discipline" (Prov. 1:7). "For the Lord gives wisdom, and from his mouth come knowledge and understanding" (2:6). Both knowledge and wisdom in the Bible have a moral component. If we fear the Lord and if we are wise, we will weigh what is right and what is wrong and endeavor to follow the right path.

Knowledge Linked with Conduct

Knowledge and wisdom are linked with conduct as well. David asked God for understanding, "and I will keep your law and obey it with all my heart" (Ps. 119:34). Jesus told the disciples after He had washed their feet and explained the spiritual significance of this ordinance that if they understood the things He was telling them, they would be blessed if they would do them (John 13:7). Paul told the Philippians that what they had "learned or received or heard," they were to put into practice (Phil. 4:9); and James wrote that "the wisdom that comes from heaven is . . . peace-loving, considerate, submissive, full of mercy and good fruit, impartial and sincere" (James 3:17). John Stott (1972) in *Your Mind Matters* expresses it this way:

> Knowledge is indispensable to Christian life and service. If we do not use the mind which God has given us, we condemn ourselves to spiritual superficiality and cut ourselves off from many of the riches of God's grace. At the same time, knowledge is given us to be used, to lead us to a higher worship, greater faith, deeper holiness, better service. What we need is not less knowledge but more knowledge, so long as we act upon it. (p. 60)

The link between knowing and doing finds its greatest expression in the life of Jesus. The mind of God was revealed not only in the natural world of creation but in the spiritual world of revelation through Jesus Christ. Jesus came to do His Father's will, and this will was the fulfillment of a plan in the mind of God to regenerate humankind, to bring people again into fellowship with God. Both the revelation in nature and the revelation in Christ speak to our minds. Without intelligence neither would be known. Without the Bible to explain to us the significance of the Creator, without whom the creation would not be, and the attributes of the Redeemer, without whom there would be no salvation, we would be like those who are "without hope and without God" (Eph. 2:12).

Knowledge Linked with Creation

God made us in His own image, and a part of that image is the rational component of the personality. He created us with the ability to make sense of the world around us and yet with a yearning to understand more than our present world, to understand the deeper issues of life and of the One who created that life. "The knowledge of God differs from all other knowledge in that man can have this knowledge only as far as God reveals it. If God did not initiate the revelation of Himself, there would be no way for man to know Him. Therefore, a human being must put himself under God who is the object of his knowledge. In other scholarly endeavors, the human being often places himself above the object of his investigation, but not so in the study of God" (Ryrie, 1986, p. 26).

Again, we are humbled as we see the great gap between our thoughts and God's thoughts, between our ways and His ways. But we are encouraged because He invites us to use our minds—to reason, to think, to judge. "Come now, let us reason together" (Isa. 1:18) is the invitation. "Incline your ear to wisdom, and apply your heart to understanding" (Prov. 2:2, NKJV) is the admonition. God expects us to use our intellect. Without rationality there would be no fellowship with God. Without a knowledge of him there would be no understanding of how we can grow morally and spiritually. "A mind is a terrible thing to waste" is the slogan of the United Negro College Fund. A mind is indeed a terrible thing to waste, as this is the only way God has chosen for us to know Him and His plan for our lives.

> **God made us in His own image, and a part of that image is the rational component of the personality.**

MORAL AND SPIRITUAL GROWTH INVOLVE POTENTIAL

When we think of potential we consider those abilities that reside within the person and will be manifested at the proper time when the opportunity arises. Potential is realized in all areas of development; the physical with an increase in size, the intellectual with a growth in understanding, the social with the augmenting of interpersonal relationships, and the emotional with distress (or delight) in infancy turning into feelings of jealousy, fear, and anger (or affection, joy, and elation) as the child matures.

Children have the longest period of dependency in comparison with the young of any species. They also have the greatest potential. How long it takes for an organism to reach maturity is directly related to the extent of that organism's potential. Dogs and cats have greater potential than flies and mosquitoes, which is one of the reasons they make better pets. But when compared with humans, canines and felines are strictly limited in what they can do even when fully grown. They cannot plan their day, communicate their thoughts, or read a book. Nor are they capable of developing morally or spiritually. We impute human characteristics to them because we want to think of them in this way, but in our more rational moments we know our inferences are in our imaginations and not in reality.

The tremendous potential of the human species in comparison with all other life forms has led some people to say that we can do anything we want to do and be anything we want to be if we try hard enough and have sufficient confidence in ourselves. There is no doubt that hard work and an adequate self-concept are advantageous to most tasks, but they are not the whole picture. Although many of us never realize our full potential, that does not mean our powers are limitless or our thoughts capable of turning into self-fulfilling prophecies. When we compare ourselves with the Creator and Redeemer we see how small we really are, that all that we have or hope to be come as gifts from Him rather than being generated from within ourselves.

> **We acknowledge that the human race as created by God and made in His image takes precedence over all other forms of life.**

Potential As Seen in Creation

We acknowledge that the human race as created by God and made in His image takes precedence over all other forms of life. The uniqueness of this species "man" came not only from the ability to communicate with God and to govern the earth but from a potential to be "like God, knowing good and evil" (Gen. 3:5). Moral and spiritual potential is a function of knowing the difference between what is right and wrong, a knowledge known only to God until the time of the Fall in the Garden of Eden. But the Fall does not mean we no longer have worth. Sin did not make humans into nonhumans. The very essence of being human means that the image of

God remains and sets people in a higher position than any other created being.

The distinction of being human is most meaningfully represented in the life of Jesus Christ. God, in His infinite love, chose to become one of us, to take on human form, to be truly man even as He is truly God. That the Creator of the universe, the One in whom all things consist (Col. 1:17), should clothe Himself in the form of humankind is an amazing fact. But it is precisely because of this that the human race has a dignity and a potential that far exceeds all imagination. The capacity to accept our humanity and the humanity of others is related to God's love for us in that Christ came "in human likeness" (Phil. 2:7).

Potential As Seen in Salvation

The enormous worth and importance given to humankind and the moral potential that humans share with no other creature is a consequence not only of the creative will of God and the fact that God chose to be clothed in human form, but also of what is sometimes referred to as the saving will of God or the process of redemption. Counts (1973) emphasizes this point: "But man's importance because he is at the center of God's plan of creation is almost overshadowed because he is also at the center of God's plan of redemption. Man's value is now also calculated in terms of his status as one for whom Christ died" (p. 41).

The Creator is also the Redeemer. The fellowship between God and man that was lost due to disobedience is possible once more. God made the human race for a special reason, and the reason as revealed through the written Word and the Incarnate Word is that we should become more like Him. The potential for moral and spiritual growth is through Jesus Christ, and lest anyone think that it is possible to be like God without divine alliance, Jesus set the matter straight in the illustration of the vine and the branches.

> I am the true vine and my Father is the gardener. He cuts off every branch in me that bears no fruit, while every branch that does bear fruit he trims clean so that it will be more fruitful. . . . Remain in me, and I will remain in you. No branch can bear fruit by itself; it must remain in the vine. Neither can you bear fruit unless you remain in me. (John 15:1-4)

48

Spiritual growth comes to fruition only through unity with Jesus Christ and is not to be confused with self-deification. Our growth is a function of our relationship with God: a God who created us, a God who redeems us. "Those who put themselves in His hands will become perfect, as He is perfect — perfect in love, wisdom, joy, beauty, and immortality" (Lewis, 1960, p. 175).

Even as all the capabilities of the fully functioning adult are wrapped up within the newborn child, all that the Christian can be as an heir of God and a coheir with Christ (Rom. 8:17) is potentially within him or her upon arrival into God's family. But the process of development takes time. "As newborn babies, crave pure spiritual milk, so that by it you may grow up in your salvation" (1 Peter 2:2). Peter also admonished those "who through the righteousness of our God and Savior Jesus Christ have received a faith" (2 Peter 1:1) to "grow in the grace and knowledge of our Lord and Savior Jesus Christ" (3:18). Paul wrote that "we . . . are being transformed into his likeness with ever-increasing glory, which comes from the Lord, who is the Spirit" (2 Cor. 3:18). Being in Christ means we can say with the psalmist, "The Lord will perfect that which concerns me" (Ps. 138:8, NKJV). Perfection is the ultimate in moral and spiritual growth, and the potential for perfection is given to us as members of the family of God.

A BIBLICAL APPROACH AND PSYCHOLOGY

Each of the major psychologies we will be examining in this book emphasizes one of the four expressions of morality: *conflict, action, knowledge,* and *potential.* By contrast, the Bible stresses all of them, thus presenting a more complete picture of what it means to be a moral person. The struggles we face along the way, what we do, how we think, and all that we can be through our rela-

> **Psychologists, as scientists, do not study the realm of the spiritual, for this is the province of the theologian. But psychologists do study moral growth. Therefore, it is within the realm of the moral that the two disciplines of theology and psychology find a common ground.**

tionship with Christ is laid out for us in Holy Scripture.

Psychologists, as scientists, do not study the realm of the spiritual, for this is the province of the theologian. But psychologists do study moral growth. Therefore, it is within the realm of the moral that the two disciplines of theology and psychology find a common ground. Twenty years ago, Mansell Pattison (1972) wrote, "This issue of morality may prove to be the most vital of all in the dialogue between psychology and theology. . . . The contemporary concern over morality in both psychology and theology may open the doors to collaboration in the most vital enterprise of our society" (pp. 200-201).

Since that time, numerous theoretical statements have been made and research studies conducted to ascertain what this relationship is. We will be looking at a number of these, especially as they relate to what we as teachers, parents, and pastors can do to encourage moral growth in the young people entrusted to our care. As was mentioned in the Introduction, a person does not have to be a follower of Christ to appreciate the moral quest, for believers and nonbelievers alike share an interest in morality as it relates to personal conduct, strength of character, and social conformity. But for those of us who are Christians, we would agree with Mark Oordt (1991) that: "From a Christian viewpoint, the maturity of one's moral-decision making cannot be separated from the maturity of one's spiritual development. A Christian would hardly deny that morality is related in a significant way to one's relationship with God" (p. 356).

Before we go to the psychologies that explain how moral growth takes place, we will look at a third traditional approach to morality, namely that of *character education*. In chapter 1 we took up the case for storytelling. In this chapter we looked at a biblical approach. Next, we will see that character education has also stood the test of time. However, character education today is not the same as it was at the turn of the century. We will see what changes have been made and what they mean to those of us who teach in the school, the home, and the church.

REFERENCES

Barclay, O. (1978). The nature of Christian morality. In B. Kaye & G. Wenham (Eds.), *Law, morality, and the Bible* (pp. 125–150). Downers Grove, IL: InterVarsity.

Counts, W.M. (1973). The nature of man and the Christian's self-esteem. *Journal of Psychology and Theology, 1*(1), 38–44.

Evans, C.S. (1992). Developing wisdom in Christian psychologists. *Journal of Psychology and Theology, 20*, 110–118.

Kraybill, D.B. (1990). *The upside-down kingdom.* Scottdale, PA: Herald Press.

Lewis, C.S. (1960). *Mere Christianity.* New York: Macmillan.

Oordt, M.S. (1991). The role of empathy in moral judgment and its application to psychotherapy. *Journal of Psychology and Christianity, 10*, 350–357.

Pattison, E.M. (1972). Psychology. In R.W. Smith (Ed.), *Christ and the modern mind.* Downers Grove, IL: InterVarsity.

Ryrie, C.C. (1986). *Basic theology.* Wheaton, IL: Victor Books.

Sheldon, C.M. (1896). *In his steps.* New York: Grossett & Dunlap.

Stott, J.R.W. (1972). *Your mind matters.* London: Inter-Varsity.

————. (1975). *Balanced Christianity.* Downers Grove, IL: InterVarsity.

————. (1978). *Christian counter-culture: The message of the sermon on the mount.* Downers Grove, IL: InterVarsity.

THREE

Character Education

On my desk is a little book entitled *Fifty Hints and Helps in Character Education.* It was written by Edith King and published on Friday, June 12, 1931. I was immediately attracted to it because it reminded me of what my teacher emphasized when I was in kindergarten several decades ago.

In it is the same chart she had called "Clean Hands Honor Roll." The pupils' names are listed down the left hand column and the days of the week — Monday through Friday — across the top. Each child with clean hands received a star in the appropriate square. I remember she would seat us in a circle and then proceed to look closely at our hands, first the back with careful scrutiny to fingernails, then the palms. If we passed inspection we got the star, if not we received a scolding. One child never passed, which told the rest of us that he was clearly deficient and not the kind of child we should be friends with.

Cleanliness is listed in this book as one of thirty-one qualities that make for a good character. It is suggested that the teacher select three or four a month so that all can be covered during the year. For example, in September she can stress cleanliness, honesty, health, and kindness. In October she can take up reliance, courtesy, promptness, and order; in November, cheerfulness, cooperation, patriotism, and peacefulness; in December, courage, truthfulness, obedience, and thoroughness. Character is defined as "what God and the angels know you are . . . the sum total of ideas, aspirations, attitudes within the brain, mind, and Spirit which crystallize into thought and action" (p. 6).

Older children can make their own character charts and score themselves. The teacher also keeps a record, so that student and teacher can discuss their respective ratings. Another suggestion is that roll be taken by each child giving a safety rule when his or her name is called. Appropriate responses would be, "I will play on the playground, not on the pavement," "I will cross the street only at the intersection," "I will walk only on the left hand side of pavement," and "I will step off the pavement when cars pass me" (p. 32). Thrift is taught by learning such maxims as, "A penny saved is a penny earned," "Put not your trust in money but put your money in trust," "Waste not, want not," and "To him that hath shall be given." Music also has its place, for "singing fortifies the health, widens culture, refines intelligence, enriches the imagination, makes for happiness, and endows life with added zest" (p. 17).

No child wants to be a "Goop." The Goops "are a family of folks who live in a tumble-down house, eat very poor food, and have no good clothes, no toys or playthings" (p. 37). This obvious discrimination against the poor fortunately does not translate to the poems that follow that show character failings of Goops rather than a lack of this world's goods.

Tidiness

Little scraps of paper,
Little crumbs of bread,
Make a room untidy
Everywhere they're strewed.

Do you sharpen pencils
Ever on the floor?
What becomes of orange peels
And your apple core?

Teaching for Moral Growth

Can you blame your mother
If she looks severe?
When she says, It looks to me
As if the Goops were here.

There are poems on honesty, borrowing, tardiness, generosity, and Miss Manners, each one telling the child what to do so as not to be Goop. Then there is teasing:

Teasing

Tease to linger longer
When your mother bids you go.
Tease to have a story
When your father answers no.
Tease to have a story
When your Uncle doesn't please.
That is the way to be a Goop—
— Tease, tease, tease.

Hint about the carriage
When there's only room for three,
Hint about the toys you like
And every doll you see,
Hint about the candy,
You're fond of peppermint,
That's the way to be a Goop,
— Hint, hint, hint.

In Hygiene or Gymnasium class, the child is to make out a "Perfect Day Program." This includes what is done throughout the day and how much time is spent for each activity. This can be quite detailed down to the specifics of "number of deep breaths taken" and "amount of water drunk." Even sports are not exempt: "Instructors, coaches, and others in charge of groups should have and keep before their students the idea of emotional control. The wild yelling, the hysterical actions of men and women at some of the big baseball games of the country are a blot on our country's reputation" (p. 42). Bible stories should be read and Scripture passages should be memorized (many from the Book of Proverbs) to enhance character development. Dramatization of stories and plays, making a book that cites heroic acts, and the art of letter writing are also encouraged.

King's delightful book is fairly typical of the character education approach used in the schools earlier in the century. It was a direct method of telling children what is right and what is wrong, and the child was to behave accordingly. There are rules to be learned, and conformity is important. Character education goes with the common sense idea that training in such habits as cleanliness, obedience, care of property, truthfulness, and dependability is important to a child's development and can be expected to last for a lifetime. Children are instructed in these virtues and given rewards for compliance and punishment for infractions.

This monitoring of the child's actions as a way of teaching morality has been used more widely than any other method. It is based on the universally accepted premise that adults know better than children what is proper. Furthermore, directions and guidelines are essential not only for the development of the young but also for the smooth functioning of the home or the school. It appears to be the most natural way we have to teach for moral growth and one that is still used daily by both parents and teachers.

HOW EFFECTIVE IS CHARACTER EDUCATION?

In the mid-1920s, Hugh Hartshorne and Mark May (1928-1930) were funded by the Institute of Social and Religious Research to conduct a study which came to be known as the Character Education Project. The study took five years and produced three volumes, all published by Macmillan under the title, *Studies in the Nature of Character.* Almost 11,000 students, ages eleven through sixteen, in both public and private schools were tested for "behavioral tendencies that can be labeled 'character' " (Weeren, 1989).

These tests included situations in which the children had a chance to cheat, lie, and steal. Mark May described examples in each of these categories in an interview in 1973 with Lisa Kuhmerker (1988). With cheating, "We told the kids to take a piece of paper and draw circles on it. We said, 'Now close your eyes and put an X in each one' — can't be done — and if a kid comes in with X's in his circles, you know . . . he cheated" (p. 12). With lying, questions were asked such as "Did you ever say anything behind someone's back that you wouldn't say to his face?" "Do you read your Bible every day?" These questions dealt with things that people feel they ought to do but don't really do. "When you get to the end of this thing you know perfectly well that the person is lying through his teeth" (p. 12). With stealing, coins were put into a box and the children were asked to solve a puzzle in which the total would add up to the same amount vertically, horizontally, and diagonally. "We told the kids to write in each circle the coin they would use. . . . We put in the right number of coins in the box but also added a fifty-cent piece. . . . It was a dirty trick, but it worked" (p. 13).

There were many other tests as well; altogether, over 17,000 were given. The purpose was not to counter any student as to his or her behavior, but rather to ascertain for the group as a whole what variables are correlated with a good character. In the days before calculators or computers, this must have been a massive undertaking.

Hartshorne and May discovered that almost all children are dishonest under some circumstances but not under others. A child might cheat on a math test but not on a spelling test. A child who would lie by saying, "I always smile when things go wrong" or "I always obey my parents cheerfully" might not steal the fifty cents from the coin box. Behaviors tend to be specific to the situation in which the child finds himself or herself to be in. We cannot group children into two categories, honest and dishonest.

Some children, of course, are more honest than others. As a group, the more honest ones were higher in intelligence and came from homes that were better off socioeconomically. They attended more progressive schools and their siblings were also more honest, a seeming reflection on the home. By contrast, honesty was not related to either the sex or the age of the child. Nor were children who participated in organized programs of religious education or other groups emphasizing character development more honest than children without this opportunity.

This last finding must have been quite a blow to Hartshorne and May. It certainly was not what they expected nor what the funding agency would have wanted. But good researchers report their findings accurately, and this is what Hartshorne and May did. They could not have known at the time that their study would be cited again and again by those who say that character education programs are ineffective and should not be used in the context of the school. This conclusion was not completely accurate, though, as there was one school that placed great emphasis on character, including the use of a daily record of good deeds in which children could advance from rank to rank and were rewarded for doing so. Also, in this school pageants were performed that portrayed virtues, there was an active Junior Red Cross, opening exercises were directed toward ideals, and the principal took an active interest in each child. Weeren (1989) reports that, "the children in this school were found to be the least deceptive of the sub-sample" (p. 19).[1]

The Hartshorne and May study does serve, however, to remind us that more is needed than just telling a person what is right and what is wrong. Knowing the good and doing the good are not the same. Those who do not act morally may know as well as anyone what the standards of behavior are, but they simply choose not to abide by them or do not see why they are obligated to please others. This very important piece of information meant that if character education programs were to continue, methods other than direct instruction would need to be implemented.

SOCIAL ADJUSTMENT

The social adjustment approach seemed to be the logical answer. If children could get along with peers, teachers, and family, they would develop into the kind of people who were good neighbors and respected citizens and would be a credit to themselves and their country. A preponderance of such well-adjusted adults would assure the kind of democratic living so highly prized. But how was this to be done? What should the schools do so children would internalize these values?

Social adjustment was already a part of character education. Such qualities as kindness, courtesy, promptness, cheerfulness, unselfishness, cooperation, adaptability, justice, friendliness, and generosity (King, 1931) could not be separated from one's relationship with others. Edward Sisson (1910) in *The Essentials of Character* wrote that honesty and justice are among the oldest and most admired virtues and that "the deepest of all truths in human life is the essentially *social nature of man*" (p. 133); and Harry Emerson Fosdick (1923) believed that magnanimity, which he defined as not "collecting grudges" or being jealous or resentful or prejudiced, was one of the twelve tests of character.

But in the forties, fifties, and sixties, social adjustment came to mean not only a person's relationship with others but also one's own mental health and feeling of well-being. Many educators and psychologists believed the two could not be separated. You could not feel good about others until you felt good about yourself. You could not help others until you helped yourself. Nor could you appreciate the feelings of others until you understood your own feelings. A good self concept became the key to becoming a good citizen.

Parents were told that every child had the right to unconditional love, and this was to be communicated to the child on a regular basis. "I may not like what you do but I'll always love you" was as important to psychological health as good food was to physical health. Schools began implementing programs that would make every student feel capable, attractive, and secure. Telling the child what was right or wrong was no longer in vogue; this was for each child to decide on his or her own. Guilt feelings were counterproductive to a healthy mind. Misbehavior signified an emotional problem, not a moral one. Doing what others wanted you to do was sometimes stifling; doing what you wanted to do was liberating. This did not mean that we should not try to please others even as we wanted them to please us, but if there was a conflict between the two; others and ourselves, our first responsibility was to ourselves even as their first responsibility was to themselves.

On the surface it might seem that the emphasis was on self-adjustment rather than social adjustment, but the philosophy of many educators at the time was that the first would lead naturally to the second. Programmed within every child is the desire to grow up, to mature, to develop. This is part of the "biological given" and applies not only to an increase in physical size, but also to a better understanding of the world in which we live in the development of personality, in emotional maturity, and in getting along with others. The child does not have to be told how to act, what to say, or how to feel. This will come naturally as the child comes to terms with his or her own needs and interacts in a real world with others. Cooperative learning within the school will facilitate the child's natural striving for moral growth as long as the teacher is careful not to communicate that some choices are right and other choices are wrong. Besides, is it not unfair to fault children for their behaviors if they are told what to do? If they have no voice in the decision-making process, how can they be held responsible for their actions? Children must understand why certain values are important in order for them to be internalized. And if values are not internalized, they are meaningless.

A two-day conference, sponsored by the U.S. Department of Education's Office of Educational Research and Improvement, met in 1987 in Washington, D.C. to discuss issues and research questions on the topic "Moral Education and Character." Scholars from such disciplines as history, philosophy, sociology, psychology, literature, and education joined in examining the range of practices and problems central to moral education and the development of a good character. The social adjustment approach was one of a number of approaches discussed and was referred to as the "psychological solution" which "focuses on sensitivity to the self-esteem and well-being of the students. This strategy is especially careful about the sensitivities of students and encourages students to express unpopular viewpoints" (Pritchard, 1988, p. 8).

This stance of leaving moral decisions up to each person was in keeping with the increasing separation of church and state. One of the criticisms of character education was that it was often taught in the context of religious education, especially Christian education. Given the growing plurality of cultural and religious ideologies, this was no longer acceptable especially in the context of the public school. Any group that would indoctrinate, insist on conformity to traditional content or methodology, resist the development of new ideas and information, or adopt the attitude of there being nothing better for one's children than what had been taught in the past, was considered to impede quality education which encouraged each student to pursue learning in an open-minded fashion.

The significance of personal decision-making was also considered to be compatible with the American emphasis on individual autonomy and the free enterprise system. We pride ourselves on living in a nation where each person matters, where all are equal under the law. We cherish our freedoms and the right to come and go as we please. We encourage independence in our children, from putting a spoon in a toddler's hand so she can feed herself to asking the teenager to decide what he wants to major in when he goes to college. We prefer an occupation where we are allowed input as to how things are done, and we expect to be treated with dignity and respect. The natural hierarchy of any institution is based on one's responsibilities, not on one's worth. It follows, then, that children have rights too, that the decision of the child as to what is good and what is bad, what is right and what is wrong, may be as valid as the decision of the adult.

HOW EFFECTIVE IS SOCIAL ADJUSTMENT?

There are many commendable features about the social adjustment approach, as we will see in a later chapter, but there have been problems connected with its use, as well. Some have linked it to an increase in social irresponsibility and the rise in "me-ism." Goble and Brooks (1983) wrote that a "relativistic, value-free point of view . . . is not realistic and leads to increasing crime and violence and other costly manifestations of social disintegration" (p. 88). Pritchard (1988) stated that the " 'psychological solution' . . . can degenerate into a relativistic endorsement of any belief whatsoever, the view that anything is right just as long as you believe it to be so" (p. 8); and Lickona (1991b) stated that the "personalism" of the 1960s and 1970s which gave rise to "values clarification" programs in the schools "spawned a new selfishness" (p. 9) and a general rebellion against authority figures that included parents and teachers.

Books such as Christopher Lasch's (1979) *The Culture of Narcissism* and Karl Menninger's (1973) *Whatever Became of Sin?* appeared to warn people of the dire results of the psychology of one's right to self-fulfillment.

Whether these accusations are completely fair is a matter of debate. It would not be out of line, though, to say that communicating to a child that there are no moral absolutes, that the difference between good and bad is a subjective choice, and that guilt is not a sign of wrongdoing does not provide a firm foundation by which decisions can be made nor does it reckon with society's expectation of stable, responsible citizenship. Without a standard of behavior agreed upon by all civilized countries, an understanding of virtue as penned by philosophers, or a respect for the opinions of recognized authorities such as parents or ministers, a person regardless of age will be at a loss. We need something to tie our morals to that is bigger than ourselves.

It is true that children want to grow up. They see that getting bigger means they will be given greater freedom and more privileges. But does it also follow that children want to grow up in every other way as well? Some children have a keen desire to be cooperative, please their parents, and fit into the group. As they grow older, they enjoy helping those outside the family, have a conscience that is tender toward God, and make moral judgments that are characterized by maturity. Other children are quite the opposite, engaging in selfish, immature actions and attitudes, and getting older does not seem to make them more trustworthy or honest. The desire to become mature morally does not appear to be universal. As parents and educators we cannot count on a natural inclination on the part of children to be good persons to produce the kind of citizens society needs.

> **The desire to become mature morally does not appear to be universal. As parents and educators we cannot count on a natural inclination on the part of children to be good persons to produce the kind of citizens society needs.**

WHERE DO WE GO FROM HERE?

If the direct approach, what Robert Hall (1979) called the *hard line* approach of indoctrination was not effective in getting children to internalize moral values and thus change their behavior, and if the non-direct approach, the *soft line* approach of letting the child decide for himself or herself has not led to greater social adjustment as it was supposed to do, then where do we go from here?

The answer may be in what Hall called the *middle way,* "an approach which neither forces young people to accept one set of moral rules nor gives them the impression that decision-making is all a matter of personal opinion or whim" (p. 14). The *middle way* avoids both the didactic element of the *hard line* and the values-free disposition of the *soft line* while encompassing the merits of both positions, namely, the transmittal of moral values that have acquired societal consensus and the free-dom to decide for oneself what values are meaningful. The *middle way* is more difficult to implement as it sets up a creative tension between the two. But this is what the newer programs in character education are trying to do. Let us look at how this is being implemented.

Almost all programs now include a presentation of those values that have been agreed upon by the larger society. These are sometimes referred to as "fixed values" because they are not subject to change, or "core values" because they form the core or center of the program. The "consensus solution" was the term used by participants of the Moral Education and Character Conference. As they put it, "There is a con-sensus about central moral concepts and values such as respect and responsibility that can be conveyed to children without hesitation" (Pritchard, 1988, p. 7). Teachers do not have to be neutral or apologize for these values or imply that they are relative to personal interpretation.

It may start with a few rules in the classroom based on the right of every person to be safe and to be treated with respect. At the lower elementary level, the rules must be put into behavioral terms so chil-dren know exactly what is expected of them. "For example: I shouldn't steal another kid's milk money; I should do my own work on a test; I shouldn't bully a smaller child on the playground; I should keep a promise to go somewhere with a friend even when a better offer comes along" (Lickona, 1991a, p. 76). Children can participate in the making of the rules, but the basic principle of respecting the rights of others remains intact.

William Bennett (1991), U.S. Secretary of Education during the Rea-gan administration, called for "moral basics" to be taught in the schools:

> We should teach values the same way we teach other things: one step at a time. We should not use the fact that there are indeed many difficult and controversial moral questions as an argument against basic instruc-tion in the subject. We do not argue against teaching physics because laser physics is difficult, against teaching biology or chemistry because gene splicing and cloning are complex and controversial. . . . So the moral basics should be taught in school, in the early years. The tough issues can, if teachers and parents wish, be taken up later. (p. 137)

The American Institute for Character Education, which developed the Character Education Curriculum, bases its program on "a worldwide study of value systems" and has identified fifteen basic values "shared by all major cultures and world religions" (Goble & Brooks, 1983, p. 88). These values are courage, conviction, generosity, kindness, helpfulness, honesty, honor, justice, tolerance, the sound use of time and talents, freedom of choice, freedom of speech, good citizenship, the right to be an individual, and the right of equal opportunity.

Another organization, the Association for Supervision and Curriculum Development, formed a panel (ASCD Panel on Moral Education, 1988) to respond to the growing alarm over the materialistic and "me-first" attitudes of many young people today. The panel submitted six major characteristics of the morally mature person "derived from universal moral and democratic principles" (p. 5); namely, someone who respects human dignity, cares about the welfare of others, integrates individual interests and social responsibilities, demonstrates integrity, reflects on moral choices, and seeks peaceful resolution of conflict. Under each of these are several statements as to what is included. For example, the person who integrates individual interests and social responsibilities will become involved in community life, share in community work, fulfill commitments, develop self-esteem through relationships with others, and display the virtues of self-control, diligence, fairness, kindness, and civility.

HOW SHOULD "CONSENSUS VALUES" BE TAUGHT?

The problem for the teacher, then, is how to translate these desirable personality characteristics to learning and activities that will enable students to understand what it means to be moral and act in moral ways. Without an operational plan, educators have little more than a nice sounding list of traits. "The major problem with lists is that they do not provide such clear guidelines for behavior as many character educators would lead us to believe" (Lockwood, 1991, p. 247). Setting up guidelines is not impossible, but it is time-consuming. Becoming involved in and sharing in community life and work, for example, may take a variety of forms depending on the age of the students. As the classroom is a community that bridges the smaller community of the home and the larger community of the society, the classroom is a good place to begin. Younger children will enjoy a discussion of how each member of the class can advance the happiness and well-being of the class as a whole. The child is given the freedom to consider his or her own individual interests as these contribute to being a socially responsible person. Discussion also can include the privileges and responsibilities of being a member of a family and the interdependence of everyone in the larger society. The lesson of interdependence must be put in tangible form: "the clothes I wear come from the work of others; the tools my grandfather used were made by someone else" (Vasconcellos & Murphy, 1987, p. 72).

Older children have opportunities for community service that extend beyond the classroom. Helping others may range from assisting the neighbor next door to being involved in nonprofit agencies such as hospitals, nursing homes, day-care centers, or homeless shelters. There is no better way to teach adolescents the values of altruism, compassion, courtesy, generosity, and responsibility than to give them opportunities to help others. Teenagers need to see that they can make a difference in the lives of others, contribute to the neighborhood in a positive way, be appreciated and needed, and have a vital part in making the world a better place in which to live. Terry Anderson (1988) reported that in 1984 the Atlanta public school system began requiring high school students to perform 75 hours of community service as part of the requirements for a diploma. The results were very positive. Anderson also mentioned other programs used throughout the United States, including a program in San Marcos, California in which values were stressed. Educators in San Marcos reported that within three years test scores were up 26 percent for eighth-graders and 29 percent for high school seniors. There was a 65 percent decrease in drug suspensions and a 90 percent drop in teen pregnancies. The dropout rate was 1.9 percent compared with the state average of 21.2 percent.

Other characteristics of the morally mature person also need to be put into operational terms so students learn what it means to act in these ways and understand why doing so is better for them and for others. Seeking "peaceful resolution of conflict" is one that can be practiced every day. Some teachers and administrators feel that much of their time is spent working on this one alone. Letting students have input into how this can be done is often quite effective. Through discussion or role playing of real or imagined conflict, students learn how to better handle their aggression. Telling students not to hit, kick, or pull hair or engage in name calling is not as effective as giving them the opportunity to think of optimal ways to solve their own interpersonal problems. Seeking a peaceful resolution to conflict is a "given" not subject to negotiation; how it is done takes many forms.

It is unrealistic to expect teachers to know how to implement all this on their own. Most educators have been trained in specific subject matters, but not in the strategies of moral decision-making. Needed are programs that teachers can understand and follow. Also necessary is acceptance by the community and the support of administrators and the school board.

One such program is the Heartwood Project developed for children in kindergarten through sixth grade in the Pittsburgh Public Schools. Classic children's stories from around the world present seven universal values: courage, loyalty, justice, respect, hope, honesty, and love. The children hear a story read aloud, then discuss its contents and their reactions to it. A teacher guide and color-coded (a different color for each virtue) activities cards give suggestions for implementing the virtues both at home and at school. This literature-based, multicultural approach includes vocabulary, defining the virtues, learning to say the seven virtue words in another language, art, and story writing. By the third grade, 80 percent were able to correctly define the virtues, and 87 percent were able to tell stories representing each of the virtues (Kuhmerker, 1992).

It is best if the whole community is involved in the moral education of students. This occurred in 1982 in Baltimore, Maryland where a task force representing different religions, ages, races, and income met to decide what common core of values should be taught in the 148 schools of Baltimore County. The U.S. Constitution and the Bill of Rights were selected as the basis for the values to be implemented. Upon approval by the local PTAs, the teachers' association, the school board, church organizations, and the American Civil Liberties Union, copies of the program were given to all parents. Teachers joined together to determine implementation in the classroom and students also became actively involved. "In every building, prominent displays and announcements emphasize important values selected by that school. Every student, from the severely handicapped to the gifted and talented, participates in learning values in some way. School projects have addressed topics such as computer ethics in the schools, the role of coaches as examples for students, academic honesty in a highly competitive high school, and the search-for-truth incentive in science" (Saterlie, 1988, p. 47).

The Child Development Project in northern California (Battistich, Watson, Solomon, Schaps & Solomon, 1991), the Ethical Quest Project in Tacoma, Washington (Sullivan, 1979), and the Colorado Springs School Study (Laven, 1982) are other programs designed to integrate the teaching of societal values with input from students as to how these values can be understood and implemented in everyday life. It is what Battistich et al. (1991) call a "hybrid" view that combines a traditional model of social and moral values with a developmental model of "commitment to autonomous moral principles based on the development of social understanding through reciprocal peer interactions" (p. 25). Clark Power (1991) puts it well when he says that "schools must both bear tradition and stimulate critical inquiry if our society is to flourish as a democracy" (p. 331).

HOW EFFECTIVE IS THE NEW CHARACTER EDUCATION?

Measuring the success of the more recent programs in character education is difficult because of the many factors involved. Evaluation is often in the form of testimonials which are positive. A battery of assessment procedures used after four years into the Child Development Project consistently found more spontaneous prosocial behavior on the part of students in the Project than students in comparison classrooms. These children also demonstrated greater perspective-taking skills, showed more consideration of other persons' needs, and were more apt to consider the consequences of actions (Battistich et al., 1991). Other programs offer similar optimistic results.

It is still too soon to know how effective these programs will be. In the twenty-first century we will be in a better position to evaluate the "hybrid" approach. Also, only a few schools have a character education program in comparison with the number of schools that either have no syllabi for *teaching for moral growth* or use a different approach than character education. However, from the way it looks now, a combination of consensus values and opportunities for children to engage in participatory decision-making appears to hold great promise.

CHARACTER EDUCATION BEGINS IN THE HOME

Sheldon and Eleanor Glueck (1974), criminologists at Harvard Law School, studied the characteristics of over 2,500 male offenders in reformatories, correctional schools, jails, and prisons; matching them with nondelinquent boys and men by age, ethnic origin, intelligence, and place of residence. They wanted to see how the two groups differed. The kind of homes the men grew up in appeared to be the most important factor. "If one is looking for a point of impact in which a multiplicity of criminogenic influences are involved, it will be found in the household, in parent-child relationships . . ." (p. 234). The Gluecks found over fifty differences that were highly significant in the home, the most prominent of these being the discipline of the boy by the father, the supervision of the boy by the mother, the affection for the boy by the parents, and the cohesiveness of the family.

Delinquents and criminals tend to come from homes in which discipline is overstrict or erratic, supervision is unsuitable, neither parent shows warmth or love, and there is little or no closeness of family members. Nondelinquents are more apt to come from homes in which discipline is firm but kindly, supervision is suitable, parents show affection for the child, and the family does many things together. The Gluecks were able to predict which children would become delinquent and which would not long before the children were old enough to have gotten into trouble with the law. This was done simply by looking at the kind of homes they were born into. Predictions made by the Gluecks were found to be amazingly accurate some fifteen years later.

A study like this always brings up the question of control. What can be done to reduce the population of our penal institutions? What can be done so children grow to be moral? The Gluecks took the position that no "pill" can cure delinquency nor does presenting moral principles help because mere knowledge is not adequate. Furthermore, they found that even the most advanced forms of psychotherapy will not help some criminals. Nor is the hard approach of greater punishment or the soft approach of saying the offender can't help it effective in getting him to change his behavior. What is needed is the structuring of an integrated personality and wholesome character "especially during the plastic formative years of early childhood" (p. 227), and this is accomplished largely in the home.

As was mentioned, in comparison with noncriminals very few criminals come from homes in which the discipline is "firm but kindly." Research in the area of child development shows that "firm but kindly" is optimal. Diana Baumrind (1970), in a ten year study of parent-child relationships, found that *authoritative* parenting in which the parent exerts firm control without hemming the child in with too many restrictions is more apt to produce a motivated, friendly, moral, and cooperative child than either *authoritarian* parenting in which the parent attempts to shape, control, and evaluate all the activities of the child, or *permissive* parenting in which few demands are placed upon the child who is permitted to do whatever he or she pleases. The authoritarian parent works from a position of power encouraging little independent thinking or individuality on the part of the child; the permissive parent works from a position of reason not insisting on responsible or orderly behavior. The children of authoritarian parents tend to be discontented, distrustful, and lacking in warmth, while the children of permissive parents tend to be the least self-reliant and self-controlling of all three groups. Children reared permissively are often said to be "spoiled" and may become tyrants who rule their own parents. Contrary to popular opinion, child psychologists do not advocate permissive child rearing.

Psychologists do, however, advocate authoritative child rearing that uses a combination of both power and reason. Authoritative parents use a unique combination of high control and positive encouragement of the child's autonomy and independence. There is no question but that the parent is in charge. Guidelines and rules are given within which the child must operate, and standards for future conduct are set. But parents share their reasons for the rules and encourage verbal give-and-take on the part of the child. Both the rights and interests of the parents and the rights and interests of the child are taken into consideration. "Authoritative control can achieve responsible conformity with group standards without a loss of individual autonomy or self-assertiveness" (Baumrind, 1970, p. 105). Like the character education programs in the schools that combine values that are agreed upon by the society with student input as to how these values can be implemented, the authoritative parent combines rules that are for the good of the child with a respect for the child's growing independence, allowing the child opportunity for decision-making within the boundaries set by the rules.[2]

CHARACTER EDUCATION AND THE CHURCH

Robert Coles (1986) of Harvard University has spent years studying the moral life of children; rich and poor, black and white, religious and nonreligious. Coles found that the majority of children and adolescents today have no firm moral code or religious orientation to guide them in the decisions they must make. They receive little instruction or guidance in the home or at school, relying instead on peer influence or what seems to work best in a given situation. Coles firmly believes that in order for moral development to take place, traditional values such as a religious faith and a respect for authority are necessary. Young people must understand why an attitude of "me first" and "winning at any cost" is unacceptable.

Coles found that both affluence and poverty adversely affect character development. Adolescents with money faced the greatest uncertainty of all teenagers when confronted with such questions as to whether it is all right to have an abortion and what to do when pressured to drink at a party. Those from the poorest homes felt the greatest pressure to take drugs, disobey authority, or join a gang. "Almost 20 percent of the junior and senior high schoolers from the poorest circumstances agreed with the statement: 'Suicide is all right, because a person has a right to do what he wants with himself' " (Coles & Genevie, 1990, p. 46). This is in contrast with just 8 percent of others of the same age who agreed that suicide is all right. However, poor black children in the South who had religious teaching in the home and a social life within the church fared far better than wealthy white children in New England who did not have the advantages of a faith that communicated to them that they are children of God who should seek to follow His plan for their lives. As Coles (1986) stated in *The Moral Life of Children,* "In home after home I have seen Christ's teachings, Christ's life, connected to the lives of black children by their parents. . . . Such a religious tradition connects with the child's sense of what is important, what matters" (p. 34).

Teachers and ministers within the church can help children and adolescents sort out values and religious traditions that are fixed and agreed upon by the church community from values and personal choices that are relative to the individual and therefore subject to change. Fixed values may be the Ten Commandments or the teachings of Jesus; relative values may be hairstyles or the kind of music a teenager enjoys. Fixed values such as "thou shalt not kill" or "thou shalt not steal" (Ex. 20:13, 15, KJV) or "swear not at all; neither by heaven . . . nor by earth" (Matt. 5:34-35, KJV) may be discussed as to how they can best be implemented in a variety of contexts, but the commandments remain normative and unalterable. By contrast, individual values are personal, providing freedom of expression. Young people do not have a right to resist fixed values that are for the good of everyone, but they do have the right to resist interference in adopting values that affect only themselves such as occupational choice or the kind of clothes worn. Teachers and youth ministers within the church need to model this ability to differentiate one from the other by accepting choices made by youngsters that reflect individual preferences while not accepting choices that harm others or violate a law. If pastors are as judgmental of teenage males wearing earrings as they are of teenagers shoplifting or swearing, they can hardly expect the young people they lead to discriminate between those behaviors you have a right to choose for yourself and those behaviors you must reject because they harm others or are forbidden in Scripture.

Many religious communities have their own list of do's and don'ts

> **Teachers and ministers within the church can help children and adolescents sort out values and religious traditions that are fixed and agreed upon by the church community from values and personal choices that are relative to the individual and therefore subject to change. Fixed values may be the Ten Commandments or the teachings of Jesus; relative values may be hairstyles or the kind of music a teenager enjoys.**

that become the fixed rules for anyone who is a member. What is included on the list and how long it is differs from one church to another. Young people who match personal values with church values will not create problems for themselves or for the faith community. Other adolescents, however, identify with the church community as well as with groups outside its realm. Consequently, they are forced to sort out differing expectations, coming to terms with their own sense of what is right and wrong. These are the adolescents who are most in need of patience and understanding. They need to think through the consequences of their choices, keeping in mind the well-being of others and what is taught in Scripture as well as what is significant to themselves. An attitude of open-mindedness on the part of youth leaders within the church and a willingness to discuss moral issues without being quick to give the "right answer" will help young people resolve the conflicts they face.

NOTES

1. Vitz (1990) agrees that the critique of the Hartshorne and May study is inaccurate, and gives as evidence the findings that "certain high morale schools and teachers did produce students who behaved better . . . and teacher ratings of trustworthiness did correlate with behavioral measures of honesty" (p. 717). Emler (1983) questions if the tests used by Hartshorne and May were good measures of moral conduct: "the forms of dishonesty they allow are trivial" (p. 189). "The very fact that an adult gives a test in which cheating is apparently so easy tells the child that this adult cares little whether cheating occurs or not. Such tests also involve a serious moral ambiguity in that the test giver must lie and cheat in order to catch out the test taker lying and cheating" (pp. 189–190).

2. Books, audios, and videos are available that entertain as well as instruct the child in character traits. Among them are the *I can choose* and *Andrew can* paperbacks designed by Pacific Press for the preschooler in which choices are made in such areas as responsibility, safety, obedience, and sharing; "book-azines" by Zoomer & Company for children eight to twelve years that teach about feelings, "solid Christian values," and self-esteem; the *McGee and me* video series produced by Tyndale House for children under twelve that teach Christian values; and the *Adventures in odyssey* audio series available from Focus on the Family (age not specified) that teach such character traits as integrity, purity, loyalty, and wisdom.

REFERENCES

Anderson, T. (1988, November 23). Schools plant seeds to cultivate kids with character. *USA Today*, Sec. D., p. 6.

ASCD Panel on Moral Education. (1988). Moral education in the life of the school. *Educational Leadership, 45*(8), 4–8.

Battistich, V., Watson, M., Solomon, D., Schaps, E., & Solomon, J. (1991). The Child Development Project: A comprehensive program for the development of prosocial character. In W.M. Kurtines, & J.L. Gewirtz (Eds.), *Handbook of moral behavior and development: Vol. 3. Application* (pp. 1–34). Hillsdale, NJ: Lawrence Erlbaum.

Baumrind, D. (1970). Socialization and instrumental competence in young children. *Young Children, 26,* 104–119.

Bennett, W.J. (1991). Moral literacy and the formation of character. In J.S. Benninga (Ed.), *Moral, character, and civic education in the elementary school* (pp. 131–138). New York: Teachers College Press.

Coles, R. (1986). *The moral life of children.* Boston: Atlantic Monthly Press.

Coles, R., & Genevie, L. (1990, March). The moral life of America's schoolchildren. *Teacher Magazine,* pp. 43–49.

Emler, N. (1983). Moral character. In H. Weinreich-Haste & D. Locke (Eds.), *Morality in the making* (pp. 187–211). New York: John Wiley & Sons.

Fosdick, H.E. (1923). *Twelve tests of character.* New York: George H. Doran Company.

Goble, F.G., & Brooks, B.D. (1983). *The case for character education.* Ottawa, IL: Green Hill Publishers.

Glueck, S., & Glueck, E. (1974). *Of delinquency and crime: A panorama of years of search and research.* Springfield, IL: Charles C. Thomas.

Hall, R.T. (1979). *Moral education: A handbook for teachers.* Minneapolis, MN: Winston Press.

Hartshorne, H., & May, M.A. (1928–1930). *Studies in the nature of character: Studies in deceit* (Vol. 1); *Studies in self-control* (Vol. 2); *Studies in the organization of character* (Vol. 3). New York: Macmillan.

King, E.M. (1931). *Fifty hints and helps in character education.* Painesville, OH: Educational Supply Company.

Kuhmerker, L. (1988). Dialog: Mark May talks with Lisa Kuhmerker. *Moral Education Forum, 13*(1), 9–13.

———. (1992). Curriculum review: The Heartwood Project, an ethics curriculum for children. *Moral Education Forum, 17*(1), 17–19.

Lasch, C. (1979). *The culture of narcissism: American life in an age of diminishing expectations*. New York: Warner Books.

Laven, W. (1982). Democracy in the independent school: The Colorado Springs School study. *Moral Education Forum, 7*(4), 9–17.

Lickona, T. (1991a). An integrated approach to character development. In J.S. Benninga (Ed.), *Moral, character, and civic education in the elementary school* (pp. 67–83). New York: Teachers College Press.

———. (1991b). *Educating for character: How our schools can teach respect and responsibility*. New York: Bantam.

Lockwood, A. (1991). Character education: The ten percent solution. *Social Education, 55*, 246–248.

Menninger, K. (1973). *Whatever became of sin?* New York: Hawthorn Books.

Power, C. (1991). Democratic schools and the problem of moral authority. In W.M. Kurtines & J.L. Gewirtz (Eds.), *Handbook of moral behavior and development: Vol. 3. Application* (pp. 317–333). Hillsdale, NJ: Lawrence Erlbaum.

Pritchard, I. (1988). *Moral education and character*. Washington, DC: U.S. Department of Education.

Saterlie, M.E. (1988). Developing a community consensus for teaching values. *Educational Leadership, 45*(8), 44–47.

Sisson, E.O. (1910). *The essentials of character*. New York: Macmillan.

Sullivan, P. (1979). A school rules unit designed to foster moral development in the elementary school. *Moral Education Forum, 4*(3), 21–28.

Vasconcellos, J., & Murphy, M.B. (1987). Education in the experience of being citizens. *Educational Leadership, 45*(2), 70–73.

Vitz, P.C. (1990). The use of stories in moral development: New psychological reasons for an old education method. *American Psychologist, 45*, 709–720.

Weeren, D.J. (1989). Hartshorne & May revisited. *Moral Education Forum, 14*(4), 16–19.

PART II

PSYCHOLOGICAL APPROACHES
TO MORAL GROWTH

FOUR

Moral Growth by Moral Conflict: A Psychoanalytic View

When we read a novel and agree with the author that a character's strange behavior is really an expression of an inner, unconscious need, we acknowledge the insights of Sigmund Freud. If we forget an appointment and wonder if perhaps we may have wanted to forget, we are reflecting post-Freudian thought. If our spouse is orderly, obstinent, or frugal and we believe our mother-in-law is responsible, we are accepting Freud's claim that early childhood experiences are important in shaping a person's subsequent behaviors throughout life. When we awaken and question what our dream *really* meant, we are recognizing Freud's findings that what is dreamed is only a surface manifestation of hidden urges and desires.

The popularity of psychoanalysis has given not only mental health professionals but people in all walks of life the idea that unconscious components of the personality are emotional in nature, comprised of feelings such as anxiety, fear, hate, and lust. Freudian terminology has also become a part of our vocabulary and we use it freely. We call it *regression* when a five-year-old begins wetting her pants after the baby is born, *compensation* when a physically unattractive acquaintance develops a charming personality, *denial* when a neighbor sets a place at the table for her deceased husband, and *rationalization* when the child who spent hours on the telephone says he did not do his homework because he had to clean his room. Shrouded from conscious awareness, the reasons for these defensive behaviors must remain disguised in order to be effective. This is why it is easier to recognize them in others than in ourselves. But do we not engage in the same defensive procedures when we alleviate stress by cuddling up to something soft and warm — a favorite quilt or a person we love, or when we wear clothes that hide our defects, or when we "forget" we had a quarrel with our spouse, or when we have our own excuses for work left undone?

We may hum or whistle a tune which reflects our mood before we have made a conscious decision to do so. We may substitute one word for another and be embarrassed because this "Freudian slip" reveals an interest we scarcely were aware of ourselves. We may return to the kitchen several times to check on the stove when we know full well that a single check is sufficient. Or, like Archie Bunker in the TV series "All in the Family," we may attribute to others those very characteristics we dislike yet are present unrecognized in ourselves. Freud believed such behaviors can be explained by looking deep within the unconscious portion of the personality. Emotions preceding thought, slips of the tongue, compulsive actions, and projection of our traits to others are but a few of the ways in which we endeavor to cope with our needs and with the world around us.

SIGMUND FREUD (1856–1939)

The name of Sigmund Freud has become a household word. Founder and father of psychoanalysis, Freud was born in Freiberg, Moravia (now Czechoslovakia) and was well recognized for his accomplishments by the time of his death. A precocious young man, he graduated *summa cum laude* from medical school where he specialized in neurology. He became increasingly interested in the effect of the mind on disorders of the central nervous system, and by using the method of hypnosis with patients in a hospital setting found that depression, anxiety, and hysteria stem from psychological disturbance rather than from physical disease. This discovery opened a whole new area of investigation in the makeup of the personality. Later, using the method of free-association, in which the patient says whatever comes to mind, Freud developed the theory of "psychic determinism," a view that all behavior, including dreams, fantasies, and even slips of the tongue, are determined by psychic forces rather than by unlawful or random dispositions.

Freud's father, Jacob, was a Jewish merchant and his mother, Amalia, was Jacob's third wife. She was twenty years younger than her husband. Freud was their first-born and was named Sigismund Schlomo at birth. (One of his half-brothers was older than his mother and Freud was younger than his nephew.) The family was poor and moved to cramped quarters in Vienna when Freud was three years old. Six siblings followed — five girls and a boy. Freud did not like Vienna and longed for the days when he was in Freiberg and his mother's only child.

In many ways Freud was favored. His parents believed he would someday be great and gave him his own room while the other eight members of the family crowded into three bedrooms. Freud's room was full of books where he read constantly, slept, often ate by himself, and received his friends who studied with him. A piano purchased for his sisters to play was immediately removed when young Freud complained that the noise disturbed him.

In 1882 Freud met Martha Bernays. Within two months they were engaged but did not marry for another four years. It was expected that Freud be able to make a living for them first. They wrote to each other almost every day but seldom saw each other as he was too poor to make the trip. Freud was often moody, depressed, domineering, and jealous. He smoked cigars and tried cocaine, which he felt were substitutes for not being with the one he loved. In September of 1886 he married the woman he called "Princess" and their first child, a daughter, was born a year later. Five more children were to join the family before it was complete, the youngest being a girl named Anna who was her father's favorite and who became a well-known psychoanalyst in her own right.

As Freud listened to his patients discuss their lives, he became increasingly convinced that sexual factors were the basis of their problems. This idea was not accepted by either the psychiatrists he worked with or by the genteel folk who read his books. *The Interpretation of Dreams* was published in 1900, received unfavorable reviews, and sold only 600 copies in eight years. Undaunted, Freud continued to write and analyze his patients. Each new book brought further revelations and applications of his theory to a variety of topics, including literature, law, religion, war, and art.

After the turn of the century his fortune began to change. He was given an appointment at the University of Vienna which gave him prestige. A group of young men gathered every Wednesday to learn from him, forming the nucleus of the Vienna Psychoanalytic Society. In 1908 he was invited to lecture in the United States, and in 1910 the International Psychoanalytic Association was formed.

A cancerous growth was removed from Freud's mouth when he was in his late sixties. An habitual cigar smoker, Freud suffered the consequences until his death sixteen years later. Successive operations removed large portions of his jaw, yet he refused to take anything but an occasional aspirin as he said he wanted his mind clear to do his writing.

In 1938, the year before his death, Freud left Austria accompanied by his wife and Anna, to escape the Nazi regime. Permission to leave was granted only after Princess Marie Bonaparte raised thousands of dollars to pay the Nazi leaders. President Franklin D. Roosevelt also intervened on his behalf. Freud said good-bye to his four sisters who were all later killed in the concentration camps. Freud was well-received in London and died in his sleep at the age of eighty-three.

Without the insights and writings of Sigmund Freud we would be at a loss to understand and describe human behavior. Peter Gay (1985), Sterling Professor at Yale University, in *Freud for Historians* states it this way:

Psychoanalytic vocabulary has become common coin in our time. . . . The less technical among psychoanalytic terms — conflict or projection or repression, even ambivalence — have almost acquired the status of platitudes. . . . No one can dispute . . . that psychoanalytic concepts have become part of ordinary discourse, and that Freud's ideas . . . have entered the collective consciousness and become part of what most of us regard as "commonsense." (pp. 17–18)

PSYCHOANALYSIS AS THEORY

Psychoanalysis is both a theory and a form of therapy. As a theory, emphasis is placed on unconscious processes that come in conflict with the demands of a real world. Instinctive, irrational, pleasure-seeking impulses present at birth and seething with sexual and aggressive energy are thwarted by societal restrictions and taboos. The result is a constriction of sensuality and a demand for behaviors deemed appropriate by a civilized world.

The consequences to the developing person are frustration and defense. Feelings of guilt for noncompliance, a fear of parental rejection for hating as well as loving, and underlying anxiety for lack of impulse control all take their toll on the child. Growing up is difficult and fraught with danger, for growing up means conflict — a conflict between instinctive forces within and social restrictions without, between a desire for pleasure and a desire to live in a world that limits pleasure, between what one wants and what one can have. Growing up may result in the development of moral character, or it may result in the acquisition of neurotic traits, or perhaps both character and neuroses will be the outcome. But whatever the final state, the process of development from the depraved condition of the newborn to the mature disposition of the adult is fraught with tension and compromise.

COMPONENTS OF THE PERSONALITY

Freud saw the personality as composed of three parts: The *id* consisting of irrational passions and instincts and oriented to pleasure, the *ego* encompassing rational and cognitive components of the personality and oriented to the world of reality, and the *superego* embodying societal values and attitudes and oriented to matters of right and wrong. The id is present at birth; the ego and the superego develop later. Freud believed that all three components should be well formed by the age of six.

Id

The id is a seething mass of energy demanding immediate and direct expression of its needs. As the inherited portion of the personality it is composed of animal-like drives and instincts that are largely sensual and aggressive in nature. The id has no mind, no consciousness, and no awareness of anything other than its own desires.

Within the id are two classes of instincts, the *eros,* or life instinct, having to do with self-preservation, and the *thanatos,* or death instinct, having to do with self-destruction and aggressive tendencies toward others. The *libido* is the energy of the life instinct and is usually associated with sexual pleasure, which may be expressed either directly in

78

sexual intercourse or indirectly in warm and pleasant relationships with others. The death instinct is destructive, finding release by turning against the self as in self-mutilation and suicide or by turning against others as in sadism and murder. Life and death, love and hate, preservation and destruction are part of the id and constitute one's heritage as a member of the human race. These conflicting forces are destined to remain throughout life, seeking release and working at cross-purposes with each other.

Ego

Sometime during the first year of life the infant becomes aware of an external physical and social environment, a world of reality that will not permit the total gratification of id impulses. If the child is to survive he or she must take into consideration not only the world of pleasurable states, but also the real world of the external. In order to cope with this situation, part of the id is changed into a rational structure oriented to reality and becomes the "I" or ego portion of the personality.

The ego functions as a decision-maker, guiding perceptions and behaviors and protecting the person against both the dangers of an external world and the harm that would come if id desires remained unchecked. The ego is primarily conscious, having awareness of self and its decisions. Being intelligent and prudent, it weighs the consequences of action in accordance with the situation, provides control of emotion, and generally serves the best interests of the person. By diverting the energy of the id to its own use, the ego is empowered to reconcile the biological demands of the id with the external pressures of a real world. The ego continues to develop through middle and late childhood and even into the adult years, but as reality changes and new problems arise, increased intellectual capacities must be brought to bear and the person must alter perceptions to meet life's challenges and to reckon with the consequences of behavior.

Superego

The superego, which contains both conscious and unconscious elements, begins to develop as early as two or three years of age as part of the ego changes to a new structure that incorporates adult attitudes and values. The process is called *introjection* because the child is introjecting

79

or putting within the self the expectations and normative demands of the society.

There are two subsystems operating within the superego, one called the *ego ideal*, which is the self-image of what the person feels he or she should be, and the other called the *conscience*, which is a self-criticizing agent that produces feelings of guilt when parental demands are not met. The ego ideal is positive, creating feelings of esteem and pride when the standard is met; the conscience is negative, bringing punishment for infractions from within the individual. Both the ego ideal and the conscience are important for moral growth, the ego ideal developing when the child is praised and the conscience developing when the child is punished. Unlike the ego, which gains in power and importance after the child starts school, the superego is less apt to develop after the early years, making the first few years of life the critical period for the cultivation of internal controls. Without the stability and trustworthy behavior that accompanies inner restraints, society as we know it could not survive.

MECHANISMS OF DEFENSE

Repression

Some of the desires of the id are so out of keeping with what society will allow that they are not permitted into consciousness. The person is not even aware of having these desires. This is known as *repression*. Repression occurs because the ego, or "I" portion of the personality, is so threatened by what would happen in the real world if instinctual urges were given free expression that these urges are relegated to the realm of the unconscious rather than being recognized and dealt with in a rational way. "Repression does not rid us of the bad objects we have taken in. They are out of sight but not out of mind" (Jones, 1991, p. 15).

Freud had much to say about the effects of repression on the personality. He believed that socially unacceptable passions and instincts do not go away simply because the person does not know about them. Instead, they remain within the individual, generating fear and anxiety and feelings of guilt, and seeking outlets of expression in some disguised form such as dreams or neurotic behavior. "The psychology of the neuroses has taught us that, if wishful impulses are repressed, their libido is transformed into anxiety. And this reminds us that there is something unknown and unconscious in connection with the sense of guilt. . . . The character of anxiety that is inherent in the sense of guilt corresponds to this unknown factor" (Freud, 1913/1952, p. 79).

A case in point is the child of four or five years of age who has an incestuous desire for his mother (Freud believed that boys this age feel that way about their mothers). But the child is thwarted in his desire because of the presence of his father. Dad is bigger and stronger than he and already has mother. Furthermore, the child develops castration anxiety for he fears his dad will castrate him if he knows of his intentions. So, like the mythical Greek figure, Oedipus, he grows to hate his father and would like to kill him. But society takes a dim view of boys killing their fathers and having sexual relations with their mothers, so these instinctual desires are not allowed into consciousness but remain rather at the unconscious level, creating feelings of anxiety and distress. Not understanding the turmoil within him, the child knows only that he wants to be near his mother and that he does not wish to share her with anyone.[1]

Freud believed that the successful resolution of the Oedipus complex takes place when the child learns to identify with the parent of the same sex. The boy must identify with the father who is feared and hated. In this way, even though he cannot have mother directly, by being like the one who does have mother, he too vicariously has mother. Being masculine, like dad, makes him less anxious and helps to satisfy sexual and aggressive urges. The counterpart of the Oedipus complex in boys is the Electra complex in girls. Suffering from "penis envy," the girl of four or five years of age desires her father and is jealous of her mother. Freud held that the girl wishes to compensate for the loss of the penis by having a child by her father. By six or seven years of age she will have resolved the unconscious turmoil by identifying with her mother.

Sublimation

A second mechanism of defense is *sublimation*. Sublimation takes place when the psychic energy of the id is transferred to the ego so that the person's behavior can be monitored and gradually changed to activities that are considered by the society to be creative and culturally beneficial. Helping others in times of trouble, expressing oneself in writing or in the arts, and engaging in religious exercises are ways in which sublimation may take form. Unlike repression in which sexual impulses are not admitted into consciousness, sublimation allows for an awareness of primitive drives but mandates that these drives be desexualized.[2]

Pearson (1954) gives the example of a small child who wishes to play with his feces but sublimates this desire and plays in the mud instead. In time, the child learns to play in sand and then to collect rocks, arranging the rocks in attractive patterns. Little by little his behavior is being changed to socially more acceptable forms. The original sexual impulse of playing with his own excrement has been turned in the direction of a nonsexual art expression that is pleasing both to himself and to others. He may become a great artist and receive recognition for his accomplishments. The sublimated desire, rather than being kept at the unconscious level, has been given opportunity for demonstration, thus enabling the person to remain psychologically healthy. The energy of the libido is released to the ego so that the individual is free to create and to engage in culture-building activities.

Regression
Sometimes a person will revert to an earlier pattern of behavior or mental functioning, usually during a period of stress. This is known as *regression*. A nine-year-old sucks her thumb whenever she is scolded; an adult sleeps in a fetal position when he hears he may lose his job. Regression may be so severe that the person must be cared for as an infant, or it may be so mild as to go unnoticed. Mild forms of regression are visible all around us if we are but tuned as to what to see. Adults, as well as children, need "security blankets" to ease the pressure of everyday living. We find that inner tensions are released when we play a game with a child or rock back-and-forth in our favorite rocker. But regression is more apt to refer to extreme behaviors that indicate a return to primitive and infantile ways of adjusting to conflict. Used in this sense, regression is an unhealthy mechanism for dealing with stress for it renders the person ineffectual both to the self and to others.

Projection
Another protective device employed by the ego to deal with emotional conflict is *projection*. Sometimes when people have thoughts or feelings

that are unacceptable, they may unwittingly attribute these characteristics to someone else but remain unaware that they possess them themselves and that their behavior is affected by them. When this occurs, projection is used. If we say that someone does not like us, it often means that we do not like that person although we are reluctant to admit our own feelings in the matter. A wife who would like to engage in extramarital sex may accuse her husband of infidelity while thinking of herself as pure and noble. The young woman who is claustrophobic believes that others are fearful while riding in elevators but that she is able to cope quite well.

Another example is the small boy, already mentioned, who is at the Oedipal phase of psychosexual development and suffers from castration anxiety. His own unconscious hostility for the father is attributed to the father so that he believes it is the father, not himself, who wishes to inflict pain. Freud wrote that projection is a "defensive procedure, which is a common one both in normal and in pathological mental life" (Freud, 1913/1952, p. 61). It helps us to like ourselves better if we attribute our undesirable traits to others rather than recognizing them in ourselves. Although positive attitudes and feelings also may be projected, the term generally is not used in this way.

Introjection

The counterpart of projection is *introjection*. Whereas in projection people believe that their own characteristics are more descriptive of others than of themselves, in introjection they introject, or put within themselves, the qualities and characteristics of others. As was mentioned, introjection is the mechanism used in the development of the superego. Introjection begins as soon as the child learns the difference between self and non-self, between what is a part of one's own body and what is external. The infant incorporates milk from the mother and it becomes a part of the self, but the mother remains distinct from the self. Yet, because she brings great pleasure and the child would like to be assured that she will always be nearby, she becomes both the object and the subject of the child's affections. As object, she is to be possessed; as subject, she is to be imitated. The child knows her first as object, as the instrument by which needs are satisfied; the child knows her later as subject, as the one whose attitudes and expectations for conduct become a part of one's own personality. By introjecting her attributes and demands, she becomes in the best sense of the word a part of the self.[3]

Freud (1937/1957) writes that introjection also accounts for the depression a person feels after losing a loved one. "Another such instance of introjection of the object has been provided by the analysis of melancholia. . . . A leading characteristic of these cases is a cruel self-depreciation of the ego combined with relentless self-criticism and bitter self-reproaches. . . . The shadow of the object has fallen upon the ego." To lose someone we love is to lose a part of ourselves. "Melancholias . . . show the ego divided, fallen into two pieces, one of which rages against the second. This second piece is the one which has been altered by introjection and which contains the lost object" (p. 187). To love deeply is to experience great pleasure, both of possession and of identification, but to lose that love is to experience great pain for only the shadow remains to haunt and darken our lives.

Other Defense Mechanisms

Other mechanisms used by the ego to satisfy conflicting demands include *rationalization* in which socially acceptable explanations are given for actual, less honorable motives; *compensation* in which success in one area is substituted for weakness in another; *escape* which may be either physical or mental; *denial* or a turning away from reality by ignoring or disavowing its existence; and *reaction formation* in which the behavior exhibited is the exact opposite of the behavior the individual would like to pursue. In every case, the mechanism used enables the person to deal in some way with threat so that inner tensions are released while outbreaks of anxiety are prevented. The defensive maneuver protects the self from instinctual demands within and environmental restrictions without, from a developing superego that brings a sense of guilt and the censorship of acquaintances that would stifle individualism and creative expression.[4]

The ego must remain strong for the person to be psychologically healthy. The ego's job is to mediate between opposing forces and defend itself against the conflicts that would destroy it. "The healthy person is the one who has good ego-strength. Destructive impulses exert less pressure on the individual so that he or she is increasingly able to make responsible decisions about how to deal with the tasks of everyday living" (Jones & Butman, 1991, p. 71).

Are Defense Mechanisms Helpful or Harmful?
There are both healthy and unhealthy ways of dealing with stress, the end result depending on which defense mechanism is used, how often it is used, the way in which it is used, and the age of the person using the defensive procedure. Freud (1937/1957) considered repression to be unhealthy, for it "ramifies like a fungus . . . in the dark and takes on extreme forms of expression" (p. 90). Repressed desires are not allowed into consciousness where they can be dealt with in a rational manner but are kept out of mind, thus rendering the individual unable to recognize and face the problems of life and placing him or her in a vulnerable position should repressed urges find an avenue for direct expression. By contrast, sublimation is healthy for it is at the conscious level, at least in part, making possible a compromise between the individual's own interests and society's insistence that the finished product be of value. In sublimation the energy of the id is used by the ego to pursue a variety of options, thus allowing for creative expression and altruistic contribution.[5]

> **Defense mechanisms are used by people who are normal and by people who are abnormal, but the way in which they are used and the extent to which they are used will differ. It is normal to escape reality by daydreaming; it is abnormal to escape reality by a psychotic detachment from the world.**

Other mechanisms of defense also may be deleterious or beneficial depending on the mechanism used. Denial is unhealthy for it does not allow the acknowledgment of reality. Compensation is healthy for it encourages the cultivation of socially desirable traits and behaviors. Projection is unhealthy, for as fears and hates are attributed to others, the person becomes paranoid, suspicious, and resentful. Introjection, the counterpart of projection, is healthy for by its use we put within ourselves the expectations and normative demands of the society so that we can live harmoniously with others.

85

MECHANISMS ARE USED BY EVERYONE

Defense mechanisms are used by people who are normal and by people who are abnormal, but the way in which they are used and the extent to which they are used will differ. It is normal to escape reality by daydreaming; it is abnormal to escape reality by a psychotic detachment from the world. It is normal to be dependent on others; it is abnormal to regress to the point where we expect others to take complete care of us. It is normal to put our best foot forward; it is abnormal to rationalize by making constant excuses for our behavior. It is normal to say we are fine when we feel poorly; it is abnormal to engage in reaction-formation by washing our hands for hours because we have an unconscious urge to be dirty. Normal uses of defense mechanisms enrich and strengthen the ego for they alleviate stress, allow compromise, and maximize one's interests and potential. Abnormal uses of defense mechanisms impoverish and weaken the ego for they contribute to paranoia, obsessional neuroses, and psychotic withdrawal, thereby limiting the person's ability to enjoy life and to cope with its challenges.

The age of the person also makes a difference. Freud believed that defense mechanisms are necessary for young children but should be resorted to less and less as the person matures. Healthy development calls for replacing unconscious mechanisms which produce anxiety and fear with methods of control that are under the direction of the conscious ego. "Freud's assumption that during the period of the ego's formation the defense mechanisms function as protective devices and may therefore have favourable influences upon its adequate development does not, of course, contradict his other assumption that when they persist in adults they should be regarded as pathogenic" (Sjöbäck, 1973, p. 279). By adulthood people should have mature egos that are able to understand the nature of instinctual demands, the press of conviction, and the coercion of outside constraints; and they should be able to achieve a balance between these forces so that they can go about their daily lives as productive and satisfied persons. However, many adults are not able to do this and continue to use defense processes.

PSYCHOANALYSIS AS THERAPY

As a form of therapy, psychoanalysis brings into consciousness fantasies, ideas, feelings, and events that have been repressed and kept at the unconscious level. "The unconscious mind is the storage place for all our problems and is also the place that must be reached for curing disorders of the mind" (Elchoness, 1988, p. 4). The usual method is "free-association," so called because the patient, after being made comfortable by lying on a couch, freely says whatever comes to mind while the therapist takes the memories, hopes, and dream world of the patient and analyzes their hidden meanings. By bringing into awareness unconscious processes, analyst and patient together can deal with the problems. It is expected that with free-association "more and more significant unconscious material will emerge" (Jones & Butman, 1991, p. 74). "By extending the unconscious into consciousness the repressions are raised, the conditions of symptom-formation are abolished, and the pathogenic conflict exchanged for a normal one" (Freud, 1920/1949, p. 377).

Other methods for bringing the unconscious into the light of day are dream analysis, hypnosis, word associations, jokes, and some forms of art (Edelson, 1988). Avstreih and Brown (1979) write that movement and art therapy provide "the vital tools with which we can extend the work of psychoanalysis into the nonverbal sphere. Body and visual imagery may well be the only viable way in which we can reach that imagistic, preverbal netherworld where words fail; it may form a link or bridge facilitating the emergence of these images in the verbal sphere, allowing further conceptualization" (p. 67). The use of movement and other art forms does not preclude verbal communication, but serves to provide the analyst with cues as to where the problems may lie. This is especially important with children who may need another medium of expression and with neurotic adults with rigid defense mechanisms.

The purpose of therapy is to strengthen the ego's defense system so that it emerges victor over both the animal-like urges of the id and the idealistic but impossible demands of the superego. Freud saw the analyst as coming to the aid of the patient, for it is only with the analyst's help that the patient is able to take charge of his or her own life.

Our plan of cure is based upon these views. The ego has been weakened by the internal conflict; we must come to its aid. The position is like a civil war which can only be decided by the help of an ally from without. The analytical physician and the weakened ego of the patient, basing themselves upon the real external world, are to combine against the enemies, the instinctual demands of the id, and the moral demands of the superego. We form a pact with each other. The patient's sick ego promises us the most complete candor, promises, that is, to put at our disposal all of the material which his self-perception provides; we, on the other hand, assure him of the strictest discretion and put at his service our experience in interpreting material that has been influenced by the unconscious. Our knowledge shall compensate for his ignorance and shall give his ego once more mastery over the lost provinces of his mental life. This pact constitutes the analytic situation. (Freud, 1949/1970, p. 430)

A strong ego, then, is the mark of good mental health, for only the ego has the consciousness and ability needed to understand the complexities of life and to appreciate its ambiguity. "The analytic therapist aims not only to help clients feel better and function better but also to extend their perspective—the view of reality—and to recognize and accept that even with improvement, life is inevitably a mixture of comic, ironic, romantic, and tragic elements" (Messer & Winokur, 1980, p. 824). Patients must be set free, not to do whatever they please, but to understand themselves and to appreciate the vicissitudes of the human condition. By strengthening the ego, old conflicts are worked through and new conflicts are challenged. The end result is not so much a feeling of equanimity as one of competency to deal with both the self and with the society in which one lives.[6]

Psychoanalysis should not be thought of as a catchall term for any kind of psychotherapy, for it represents only one type of therapy, namely, one based on the teachings of Sigmund Freud and used by him or a recognized follower. Psychiatrists who are psychoanalysts have gone through psychoanalysis as part of their own training and only those psychiatrists specifically trained in psychoanalysis are in a position to employ such techniques. The method is not usually available to other trained professionals such as counselors, neurologists, ministers, or educators. Even other psychotherapists and physicians schooled in ways of helping people are not in a position to "psychoanalyze" their patients, an expression used far too loosely by laypersons to include any method whereby one tries to understand the hidden meaning of another's speech or behavior. Extensive training is needed for the therapist to learn how to interpret the underlying significance of what patients say when they recall their dreams or relate whatever comes to mind during a period of free-association.[7]

It has been said, perhaps facetiously, that psychoanalysis is only for the rich and idle. In a sense this is true. The services of a medical doctor carefully trained in an area of specialty command a price, and sessions may take place daily over a period of several years. Furthermore, the arrangement usually involves only two people, analyst and analysand (the name given to the patient in psychoanalytic literature) working together. Group therapy, so popular today, in which expenses are shared and peers as well as therapist have a role in the healing process, is not the preferred method although it is increasingly being used.[8] The format for reporting in journals and books what takes place during the therapy session is the case study — an in-depth look at one patient and the changes that take place in that patient as therapy proceeds. In this way psychoanalysts share their insights and sustain the dialectic between theory and practice.[9]

PSYCHOANALYSIS AND MORAL GROWTH

In Freudian psychoanalysis, moral growth is an integral part of the total process of personality development. The same forces that bring a person to social maturity bring a person to moral maturity. As children we incorporated within ourselves the dictates and demands of an external world as interpreted to us by our parents, making societal standards a part of our own personalities. As adults, we pass them on to our children knowing that they, in turn, will do the same when they become parents. In this way the culture is perpetuated from generation to generation.

Mental health and moral health cannot be separated. Karl Menninger (1973), founder of the famed Menninger clinic in Topeka, Kansas, states it well in *Whatever Became of Sin?*

> I am a doctor, speaking the medical tongue with a psychiatric accent. For doctors, health is the ultimate good, the ideal state of being. And mental health — some of us believe — includes all the healths: physical, social, cultural, and moral (spiritual). To live, to love, to care, to enjoy, to build on the foundations of our predecessors, to revere the constant

miracles of creation and endurance, of "the starry skies above and the moral law within" — these are acts and attitudes which express our mental health. (p. 230)

A look at the basic assumptions of psychoanalytic thought with regard to moral growth will enable us to understand better the process by which this development takes place.

BASIC ASSUMPTIONS

Unlike other psychologies that hold that children are born neither good nor evil (note chap. 6), or that children have within themselves the desire for moral understanding (note chap. 8), or children are goodly creatures with great potential for moral self-actualization (note chap. 10), the psychoanalytic approach fastens on the darker side of the human condition. *The original nature of humankind is one of depravity.*

> **The optimal time for moral growth to occur is between two and six years of age. One of Freud's greatest contributions was to emphasize the importance of the early years. This is no better illustrated than in the area of morality.**

Born with irrational passions and instincts and desiring only the satisfaction of one's own needs, the person is animalistic, seeking gratification of sensual and aggressive impulses and void of moral direction or desire. In the original state humans are not fit to live with others for they are crude, insensitive, and arrogant. Intervention must take place if a child is to become a moral individual.

Moral growth occurs when the child internalizes the expectations and normative demands of the society as interpreted by the parents. The helplessness of human infants puts them in a vulnerable position. Left to themselves they would die. The dependency on the parents for life itself brings about an imitation of parental actions as a way of keeping the parents close. Later, children will identify with parental attitudes and beliefs as well. Children try to be like their parents because this makes them feel more grown up, and growing up is something every child wants very much to do. As representatives of the society, those of us who are parents constantly explain the "shoulds" and "should nots" of the social order to our children, using a variety of methods to assure that conformity will take place. It is in this way that our children learn to accept the demands of the culture and to make these an integral part of their own personalities.

The optimal time for moral growth to occur is between two and six years of age. One of Freud's greatest contributions was to emphasize the importance of the early years. This is no better illustrated than in the area of morality. Even before the child's first birthday he or she is aware of a world outside that brings pleasure or pain. Pleasure is associated with doing what is good, and pain is associated with doing what is bad. By the age of two, children have begun to imitate the actions of those around them, and by age four or five they are well on their way to adopting parental standards. Good and bad, right and wrong, moral and immoral are interpreted for them by the same people who satisfy their personal needs. For the normal preschooler, the world of reality and the world of right and wrong have become an integral part of daily life, and the baser passions inherent at birth are now subjugated to meet these new demands. Never again will the influence of parents be so strong. Never again will the child be so close to someone who meets both physical and psychological needs while at the same time demanding behaviors considered appropriate by the society.

Moral growth may continue after the early years but takes on a different form. As the child becomes less dependent on parents and enters the larger world of other adults and peers, ideas of what is right and wrong begin to change. Baby-sitters and teachers will take on some of the authority of the parents, and peers may demonstrate the importance of mutual interdependence, but the child does not rely on teachers or agemates for survival, nor does he or she live with them during the early formative years. Consequently, the variety of influence is less related to an internalization of standards that are normative for every occasion and more related to the consequences of behavior that differ from one circumstance to another.

Furthermore, stages of moral growth correspond with certain chronological ages and are related to the "task achievement" (Tice, 1980) of that stage. In early childhood the task is to identify with parents, whereas in later childhood tasks include "being able to take a moral point of view more effectively over a wide range of experience" and "further attainment of moral values, rules, principles and ideals" (Tice, 1980, p. 191). As each stage of moral development includes remnants of earlier stages, children who have not developed a strong sense of right and wrong during the early years will be hampered in moral stability at a later time. Middle childhood, adolescence, and adulthood are all important in the development of morality, but each age has its roots in previous ages and as such is contingent on the success or failure of the earlier periods.

Moral growth takes place in a context of conflict and defense. The emotional conflict generated by the battle between the natural desire to please self and the external pressure to conform to the society makes for inner turmoil and feelings of guilt. The focus of psychoanalysis is on passion rather than intellect, desire rather than reason. Yet, without this conflict there would be no moral progress. Psychopaths are so named because they do not have a conscience, nor do they experience feelings of guilt. Their pathology stems from a lack of anxiety over their behavior and an unwillingness to adopt cultural standards. Not having experienced the inhibitions that arise when societal restrictions are internalized, they continue their infantile ways of caring only for themselves with no concern for the well-being of others. At the other extreme are neurotic individuals who find the conflict overwhelming, and because they cannot cope, they suffer acute anxiety and distress.

Normal individuals also experience conflict, but unlike neurotics they are able to deal with the tensions. Being psychologically healthy, they turn the distress into opportunities for creative and culture-building activities. Nevertheless, the line between neurotic and healthy is not always clear, and for both groups the process of moral growth is painful and fraught with danger and compromise. "Conflict is intrinsic to human nature and forms the core of our being. The key psychic drives inevitably conflict because the aggressive and erotic drives do not naturally complement each other. The structures conflict also: id and superego battle, like two powerful horses, with the relatively impotent ego astride them both. Consequently, conflict is as much a part of normalcy as it is of pathology" (Jones & Butman, 1991, p. 72).

Because of the emotional turmoil and distress that accompanies conflict, Freud believed that *becoming a moral person benefits the society more than it does the individual.* "We can demonstrate with ease that what the world calls its code of morals demands more sacrifices than it is worth" (Freud, 1920/1949, p. 377). Yet Freud recognized that the code is essential for without it would be unleashed "a savage beast to whom consideration towards his own kind is something alien" (Freud, 1930/1961, p. 59). The aggressive nature of human beings emerges wherever it finds an outlet—in lust and killing as well as in revolution and war. Society as we know it could not exist without repressive forces keeping its members in line. "Not only must we measure up to the hopes generated by an early but increasingly challenged narcissism, to the dreams and values of the best side of our parents, to the grand and noble pieties of a more social nature—national imperatives, ethnic or racial slogans—we must also deal with the hundreds of no's, many intimidating indeed, which gradually make us run for various covers or learn to take (adroitly or truculently) a stand" (Coles, 1986, p. 32).

But in the long run society does not win either. "This conflict is not resolved by helping one side to win over the other" (Freud, 1920/l949, p. 375). For both the person and the social order there are only compromises, adjustments, and concessions. Nor will it ever be different. The human race will continue to experience the consequences of its own depravity, and the society will continue to make its rules, written and unwritten, only to find them broken time and again. The person becomes the victim-spectator of greed and lust, tragedy and oppression, and the social order becomes the tyrannical overseer torn by insurrection and strife. This shadow-side of the human race is oppressive and pessimistic, but it is, nevertheless, an aspect of humanity we cannot dismiss. Readily visible all around us are the manifestations of evil. The plight of humanity is described in Holy Writ and found in the musings of great philosophers and poets. Without an acknowledgment of sin and its consequences, we deceive ourselves, choosing to look only at the brighter side of life rather than to gain a total picture of the human condition.

COMPONENTS OF THE PERSONALITY AND MORAL GROWTH

As we have seen, those who follow Freud's teachings believe that the infant is helpless and depraved. Every child is born as an id, or an it, with irrational instincts and passions. In order for the child to become a better person an ego that relates to reality and a superego that relates to matters of right and wrong must be formed. The ego and the superego become part of the personality, working to help the child become a moral person. The role of the ego is to produce mechanisms of defense against the id so as to keep in check sexual and aggressive impulses that would destroy the person and the society in which one lives and to keep the superego from bullying the person to the point of neuroticism. Later, the ego will use more conscious methods of control to keep the id and the superego in their proper places (see, e.g. Lee, 1948; Lorand, 1972; Pattison, 1968). Wallwork (1991) also writes of the importance of ego functioning.

> Morality is normally impossible without an ego that identifies conflict situations in a real world, thinks about normative standards, evaluates which standards are applicable, and chooses the course of action believed to be right. . . . Thus, even ideals, standards, rules, and prohibitions that originated as primitive authoritarian introjections can be subjected to the more rational scrutiny of the mature ego. (p. 224)

The role of the superego, by contrast, is to hold before the person an ideal to strive for and a conscience that condemns when the ideal is not reached. By internalizing the superego, the child incorporates the standards of the society and as an adult passes them on to the next generation.

Psychoanalysts would say, then, that the amoral infant becomes capable of morality as he or she develops an ego that relates to the world of reality and a superego that relates to a world of good and evil. An optimal balance between ego and superego is essential for moral development, and achieving this balance is a constant struggle throughout one's life.

Psychoanalysts would say, then, that *the amoral infant becomes capable of morality as he or she develops an ego that relates to the world of reality and a superego that relates to a world of good and evil. An optimal balance between ego and superego is essential for moral development, and achieving this balance is a constant struggle throughout one's life.* The ego provides flexibility and vision; the superego provides stability and purpose. Both are needed for moral maturity to be realized.

Some professionals who refer to themselves as social learning psychologists have borrowed heavily from psychoanalytic theory and have also emphasized the place of the ego as well as the superego in moral development.[10] They feel that both a world of reality and a world of right and wrong must be considered and a healthy balance between them attained if one's conduct is to be moral. The consequences of behavior as well as the press of conviction should be contemplated before a course of action is taken. Adopting the best of both components of the personality, namely, the flexibility of the ego to vary as the situation demands and the stability of the superego to stand firm on matters of principle is essential for moral action to take place. If the ego is present without the constraints of the superego, one's conduct will be opportunistic and unpredictable and may lead to delinquency. If the superego with an overdeveloped conscience is dominant without regard for the consequences of behavior in a real world, the personality will be constricted and life will have little to offer by way of pleasure and creative expression. An ego without a superego is mundane and superficial; a superego without an ego is oppressive and damaging to self and others.[11] Like the id, the ego is interested in what is best for one's self without concern for ethical standards. Also like the id, the superego is blind, unintelligent, and demanding. And so, the ego needs the superego to give it consistency and depth, and the superego needs the ego to give it sight and understanding. Consequently, social learning psychologists emphasize that a balance between ego and superego, reality and ideal, intelligence and conscience is more moral than a preference for one apart from the other.

But a balance between consequences of behavior in a real world and standing firm on matters of principle is not easy to achieve, and the conscientious person who tries to weigh both will find that conflict is inevitable.[12] Yet, without this conflict there would be no growth, and the individual would be relegated either to the superficial life of the here and now or to the tyrannical world of impossible ideals and feelings of guilt. So, the struggle continues—a struggle between the life and death instincts within the id, between the id and the real world of the ego, between the ego and the dictates of the superego. The id says "I want," and the superego says "thou shalt" or "thou shalt not," and the ego which serves as mediator says "I will" or "I won't" or "I will but only in this socially acceptable way."

The methods or mechanisms used by the ego to make concessions to the id and the superego while keeping them both in line are also a part of moral growth. It is to a consideration of how these mechanisms enhance or deter morality that we now turn.

MECHANISMS OF DEFENSE AND MORAL GROWTH

As was mentioned, Sigmund Freud held that defense mechanisms contribute to the development of morality especially when used by children who are younger than five or six years old. After the age of six, the mechanisms are less effective in producing moral character and when employed by adults may result in neuroses rather than in socially desirable personality characteristics.[13] The mechanism of introjection is especially important for young children, for it is when children introject societal standards as interpreted to them by their parents that they begin to act in socially acceptable ways. Their conduct stabilizes into trustworthy and acceptable patterns even though adults are not present to monitor their actions. Identification with the parent of the same sex (the resolution of the Oedipus complex) plays a significant role for it allows for a repression of aggressive and sexual impulses which if left unchecked would destroy both the person and the society.

Sublimation also is effective in contributing to moral growth for it allows children to express themselves in socially acceptable ways without constricting the personality and creative endeavors. By sublimating id impulses, young people learn to paint pictures, play musical instruments, or engage in religious activities which bring pleasure both to themselves and to others.

Interestingly, unhealthy mechanisms sometimes play a role in moral development, and healthy mechanisms if used in excess are harmful to the formation of character. For instance, repression keeps sexual and aggressive impulses in check so the person can live with others; denial ("I don't believe this is happening to me") alleviates the trauma of disaster which would render the individual incapacitated; and projection paves the way for an empathic understanding of others and their concerns. On the other hand, sublimation "can become a compulsion, a counting compulsion, for example" (Pearson, 1954, p. 186); compensation may cover up the less attractive characteristic rather than acknowledge one's shortcoming; and introjection can lead to "obsessional neuroses, a gratification of sadistic tendencies and of hate" (Freud, 1937/1957, p. 132). Obviously, the way the mechanism is used as well as which mechanism is used determines whether it contributes to or detracts from the development of a wholesome personality.

Without the conflict that comes when defense mechanisms are employed, the child would not become a moral adult. Adults in our society who have no conscience and who are therefore sociopathic,[14] have little conflict for they have not introjected the demands of the social order, nor have they repressed sexual and aggressive urges nor sublimated the desires of the id. Consequently, they have weak egos and underdeveloped superegos. Neurotics, on the other hand, have a disproportionate amount of conflict. Unduly concerned about what others think of them and fearful that at any time they may have more anxiety than they can cope with, they introject what they perceive the attitudes of others to be, repress thoughts and feelings that would make them free and creative beings, and sublimate their individualities to oppressive consciences. Neurotics have weak egos and dictatorial superegos.

Healthy adults have come to terms with all three components of the personality: a demanding id, a watchful ego, and an overbearing superego. As children they made use of defense mechanisms to internalize societal demands, but as they matured the repressive forces gave way to more conscious methods of control. Ego and superego have developed together, each fulfilling its purpose and each continuing in a balanced relationship with the other, the ego serving to protect the individual in a world of reality and the superego guarding the mores and standards of the social order. The conscious, rational ego and the unconscious, restrictive superego both have a place in the formation of a healthy personality and a wholesome character.

How Moral Are Adults?

Although Freud believed that the final state of the person is preferable to the depraved condition of the newborn, he did not have good words for adults, either, as seen in a letter written in 1918 to a minister of religion. "I have found little that is 'good' about human beings on the whole. In my experience most of them are trash, no matter whether they publicly subscribe to this or that ethical doctrine or none at all. . . . . If we are to talk of ethics, I subscribe to a high ideal from which most of the human beings I have come across depart most lamentably" (Freud, 1963, pp. 61-62). Even after a lifetime of conflict, the person still is not moral, according to Freud. The tension, inhibitions, and restraints have made the person more palatable to others, but he continues to be victim both of his own passions and of the restrictions placed upon him by the society.

The pessimism of Freudian psychoanalysis is great and is not shared by all psychoanalysts, yet the shadow side of the human race is a fact of life and should not be taken lightly by those who would understand the nature of the human condition. In psychoanalytic theory, people are born sinful and will remain sinful all their lives. Improvement is in the offing with the formation of the ego and the superego, but even so, humankind cannot be said ever to become moral in the full sense of the term.

So, the struggle continues — a struggle to be a better person and to live in a better world. It is a struggle that knows no end, yet, without that struggle, life would be empty and void of meaning. Humanity has no choice but to go on, doing the best that it can in the face of incredible odds.

PROBLEMS

As with any psychological theory, problems arise relative to the validity of the theory and to the methodology employed. Let us look at several of these problems as they relate to Freudian psychoanalysis.

Is Psychoanalysis Scientific?

One of the major criticisms of psychoanalysis is that it does not lend itself to scientific inquiry. Freud presented many of his ideas in such a way that they can neither be verified nor falsified, leaving the student who is committed to an experimental approach at a loss to know what to accept and what to reject. How can it be determined, for example, that the small boy has an incestuous desire for his mother if he has no awareness of this desire? How can any repressed desire be investigated, for that matter? Is it sufficient to take the word of the therapist, trained in psychoanalysis, that the Oedipus complex is indeed present and represents one of Freud's greatest insights? Unless a person already is oriented to psychoanalysis, the answer probably will be negative.

Another concept difficult to measure is that of reaction-formation. If one's behavior is sometimes the same and sometimes the opposite of what the person would like it to be, how can the underlying motive really be known? And, again, if different motives produce the same behavior, how can one know what motive is present? Is the person clean because she wants to be or is it because of an unconscious wish to be dirty? Psychoanalysis is a closed system for it has a built-in method of explaining away any evidence that is contrary to it. As such, it is empirically unsound and methodologically weak. Data gained from therapy sessions add little, for therapy is clinical rather than systematic in nature, each case being unique, making the information obtained of questionable value when applied to people in general.

Take another example, this one closer to our search for an understanding of how morality develops. Suppose that the small child has acquired a strong superego by identifying with the parents and imitating their behaviors. But as the child grows older, parental influence decreases while peer influence increases, the ego-ideal and the conscience making up the superego become less important while the ego that looks to the consequences of behavior in a real, external world takes on greater significance. Does this mean that the child is becoming more moral or less moral? How can we tell? Are there measuring instruments to aid us in our search for the answer? What criterion should we use in deciding what it is we want to measure? Shall we look at overt behavior to see if it lines up with agreed upon social norms? Shall we test for emotional stability and mental health? Shall we gauge the strength of the superego by listening to confessions and feelings of guilt? Do we need a longitudinal approach whereby the person is tested at different age periods to see what changes take place at different times in his life? Psychoanalytic theory does not provide us with the answers, nor is it stated in such a way that the answers are forthcoming.

This is not to imply that Freud's ideas have not generated considerable research, for indeed they have. The large number of doctoral dissertations and journal articles on Freudian concepts attest to this fact. Several volumes (Eysenck & Wilson, 1973; Fisher & Greenberg, 1977; Hook, 1959; Pumpian-Mindlin, 1952; Sarnoff, 1971; Sears, 1943) also have been published and represent the conclusions of both supporters and critics of Freudian thought as related to experimental investigation. The supporters say that psychoanalytic concepts can be tested scientifically and argue for "the fruitfulness of a marriage between psychoanalytic concepts and experimental research" (Sarnoff, 1971, p. ix). The critics say just the opposite. "There is not one study which one could point to with confidence and say: 'Here is definitive support of this or that Freudian notion' " (Eysenck & Wilson, 1973, p. 392). Most authors and editors make an effort to show that some of Freud's ideas can be supported by the research, whereas other ideas cannot be supported. The topic of how psychoanalysis relates to science is sufficiently detailed and so filled with controversy that interested students will find more than enough material to keep them busy for some time.

Rather than arguing for "a marriage between psychoanalytic concepts and experimental research," some supporters defend psychoanalysis as being above the trappings of the so-called scientific method with its gathering of facts and use of numbers. They argue that the great insights given to a few great minds as to the nature of humankind and the world in which we live cannot be put into empirical molds and judged in accordance with how well they fit those molds. It is a travesty even to suggest that psychoanalytic theory can be cut into pieces and the pieces subjected to operational definitions designed by experimenters who understand numbers better than they understand genius. Erich Fromm (1980), a psychoanalyst, put it like this: "If one tries to study one aspect of the personality apart from the whole, one has to dissect the person—that is to say, destroy his wholeness. Then one can examine this or that isolated aspect but all the results one arrives at are necessarily false because they are gained from dead material, the dissected man" (pp. 13-14).

Be that as it may, most psychologists think of themselves as scientists and tend to take a jaundiced view of any theory that does not lend itself to objective scrutiny. Consequently, psychoanalysis does not have the level of support from academicians that many psychologies enjoy. This does not detract, however, from its acceptance by the educated lay-person, by clinicians trained in its methodology, or by other intelligent people in disciplines not oriented to scientific verification.

ARE EMOTIONS GIVEN TOO MUCH EMPHASIS?

A second criticism of psychoanalysis is that the affective nature of human beings is emphasized at the expense of other important charac-teristics of the personality. In Freudian psychoanalysis, emotion takes precedence over reason, passion over intellect, and the volitional nature of the person is given no significant role. Like the learning theory view (see chap. 6) that people have little to say about what they do or become, Freud saw the person as the victim of oppressive forces, the product of a destiny beyond one's control. But unlike the learning view that sees the restrictive forces as only from without, the psychoanalyst views the pressures as coming from within the individual as well as from the social order. Irrational passions and instincts present at birth war against each other, making the person fearful and anxious. Later, the society bombards the person with its demands, thereby providing a double assault upon the organism. As the victim of two warring fac-tions, one from within and the other from without, the person's only available response is one of strong emotion. Reason and free will have little to contribute in such a context. Conflict is basic to our very existence and constitutes our heritage as members of the human race.

Even so, the emphasis on emotion takes away from the dignity of people as thinking, autonomous beings. If reasoning is but a facade, self-determination an illusion, and morality a product of a dictatorial superego adopted early in life, there is little to commend the human race. Freud saw people as basically hedonistic, naturally aggressive, and seeking pleasure wherever it may be found. Nor do people show an interest in a life based on ethical principles. Whether infant or adult, there is little good to be said about the human condition. Health comes when the ego is in control for the ego contains an element of rationali-ty, but for many people that desirable state never will be attained, and they are destined to live out their lives in frustration and defense.

In the area of moral development, especially, an emphasis on the affective without regard for the cognitive renders the person incapacitat-ed. As guilt feelings emerge with the advent of the superego, provision must be made for intellectually dealing with those feelings, or one is left helpless and confused. Nor can people be held accountable for wrong-doing if they are subjected to forces beyond their rational control. For this reason, social learning psychologists and neo-Freudians have put more emphasis in recent years on the ego components of morality and less on the superego variables in an effort to resolve this problem.

WAS FREUD RIGHT ABOUT THE OEDIPAL COMPLEX?

Not only did Freud stress emotion at the expense of other components of the personality, but males were given precedence over females, children over adults, and sexual interests over other desires. Whether these emphases constitute a problem depends on one's perspective, but a number of writers, including some psychoanalysts, are critical of Freudianism with regard to these issues. Granted that males historically have been dominant, that childhood is the critical period for emotional development, and that people are sexual beings, this is not to say that females suffer from penis envy, that the personality cannot change after age six, and that every wish and every object have sexual connotations. Yet Freud's writings would imply this, so that an acceptance of his ideas would relegate women to an inferior position, negate the efforts of educators and others who work with children after the age of six, and direct one's attention to the sexual aspect of all events and all relationships when other factors may have greater meaning. Erich Fromm (1980) speaks to this last point as it relates to the Oedipus complex.

> Freud in his discovery of the Oedipal tie to the mother discovered one of the most significant phenomena, namely man's attachment to mother and his fear of losing her; he distorted this by explaining it as a sexual phenomenon and thus obscured the importance of his discovery that the longing for mother is one of the deepest emotional desires rooted in the very existence of man. (p. 30)

Fromm goes on to explain that even the most intense sexual relationship will not last if it is without affection and that "to assume that men should be bound to their mothers because of the intensity of a sexual bond that had its origin twenty or thirty or fifty years earlier is nothing short of absurd considering that many are not bound to their wives after even three years of a sexually satisfactory marriage" (p. 29).

WAS FREUD'S METHODOLOGY SOUND?

A third problem with Freudian psychoanalysis is that Freud attributed characteristics found in neurotic patients in a clinical setting to all people everywhere. There is reason to question the validity of a theory in which the abnormalities of a few are made normative to the population as a whole. Applying insights derived from disturbed people to the behavior of the rest of the population is dubious at best; at worst it is deceptive, presenting a picture that highlights the less desirable features of the human condition rather than giving a more accurate portrayal that includes both favorable and unfavorable traits. Furthermore, Freud seldom studied children directly. Instead, he took many of his ideas of what children are like and the difficulties that they face by listening to adult neurotics tell of their childhood memories. One wonders how accurately these early experiences were recalled and the extent to which they can be applied to normal children. During therapy sessions Freud noted that patients often spoke of their relationships with family members and other acquaintances in such a way that the sexual component appeared to be dominant. From this Freud surmised that children go through a series of stages that are psychosexual in nature and that healthy personality development is dependent on the timing and sequence of each stage. Whether one accepts Freud's ideas of what children are like as insightful or rejects them as misconceived, the methodology by which Freud reached his conclusions leaves much to be desired.

WILL THE REAL DR. FREUD PLEASE STAND UP?

The final problem is that any interpretation of Freudian thought, either by supporters or by critics, is subject to error for a variety of reasons. First, Freud's thinking changed on a number of issues over the course of his lifetime. What he wrote early in his career and what he wrote in his later years varies, so that the scholar must determine what should be taken at face value and what should be relegated to a lesser position by virtue of when it was written.

Second, supporters accuse the critics of only a superficial understanding of what Freud meant by what he said, and they proceed at length to elaborate on what Freud really meant by this or that idea, leaving the inquirer to think that whereas the critic may err on the side of superficiality, the supporter errs on the side of reading too much into Freud's statements. Derek Wright (1971) may be right when he says that "any account that goes beyond a series of quotations from Freud's work is bound to be in some degree an individual interpretation" (p. 31).

Third, Freud emphasized some ideas in an effort to counterbalance what he felt to be lacking in the understanding of people at the time. Had he lived in another era his writings might have fastened on other concerns. The importance of early childhood, the sexual nature of human beings, and the psychological basis of neurotic behavior were needed concepts to offset misunderstandings prevalent during the early twentieth century. For instance, in response to criticisms that he over-emphasized the shadow side of human nature, Freud (1920/1949) wrote: "We dwell upon the evil in human beings with the greater emphasis only because others deny it, thereby making the mental life of mankind not indeed better, but incomprehensible" (p. 131). Freud thus saw his ideas as providing a balance to the misconceptions of the day.

If it appears that Freud wavered with regard to the consequences of moral development, at times stressing the ills of fear and repression and at other times condoning the social system as a necessity, it was because he saw it both ways. The need to live life freely and the need to submit to civilizing forces are both viable, even though having to accept both only adds to one's conflict. Yet conflict is necessary for moral development. Freud believed that without anxiety, fear, and disequilibrium one cannot become a better person.

Whether the criticisms in this section indicate that Freud's contribution to an understanding of human nature and moral development is not as great as generally thought or whether it means that Freud's teachings need more careful study in order to be fully appreciated and understood is left to the judgment of the reader. The lack of scientific rigor, the emphasis on emotion apart from reason and volition, the stress on early childhood and on the sexual nature of human beings, the generalizing from the abnormal few to the normal many and from adults to children, and the difficulty of interpreting Freud's writings are more disturbing to some people than they are to others.

But regardless of one's leanings, all would agree that Freudianism has had a noticeable impact on child-rearing procedures and on an understanding of the importance of the affective component of a person's life. Sigmund Freud was one of those few pioneers whose ideas have significantly changed the way in which we view ourselves, our families, our friends, and our world. His conclusions have permeated our culture and given us a vocabulary with which to discuss human behavior.

It is to an application of psychoanalysis in the Christian community that we now turn. In the next chapter we will look at ways in which Freud's ideas and those of other psychoanalysts have impacted the world of teachers, parents, and pastors.

NOTES

1. After his baby brother was born, my five-year-old said to me on more than one occasion, "Let's you and me run off and get married and we'll leave daddy home to take care of the baby." Does this mean that Freud was right—that my child harbored unconscious incestuous desires? I think not. A more rational explanation is that he did not wish to share my attention with the baby.

2. A number of years ago, a student told me that one of my colleagues gave the following example of sublimation to the students in his psychology class. "When I see a pretty girl, my id says 'rape her'—but I merely wink." She reported that she and some of the other female students felt a bit uncomfortable when, on occasion, he would look at one of them and wink.

3. Freud believed that male homosexuality occurs when the Oedipus complex continues until after puberty, at which time "mother as object" becomes "mother as subject," and the teenager begins looking for a new object to love. Because he still identifies with mother rather than with father, the object of his affection will be male rather than female. Freud (1937/1957) put it this way: "The genesis of male homosexuality in a large class of cases is as follows. A young man has been unusually long and intensely fixated upon his mother in the sense of the Oedipus complex. But at last, after the end of his puberty, the time comes for exchanging his mother for some other sexual object. Things take a sudden turn: the young man does not abandon his mother, but identifies himself with her; he transforms himself into her, and now looks for objects which can replace his ego for him, and on which he can bestow such love and care as he experienced from his mother" (p. 186). In J. Rickman (1957), (Ed.), *A general selection from the works of Sigmund Freud*, Garden City, New York: Doubleday.

4. Scholars disagree as to the number and designation of Freud's defense mechanisms.

For an in-depth discussion on this topic, see M. Sjöbäck (1973), *The Psychoanalytic theory of defensive processes,* New York: John Wiley & Sons.

5. Stanley Leavy (1988), in *In the image of God: A psychoanalyst's view* (New Haven: Yale University Press), states that "sublimation is good because it permits higher culture to take place as energies are redirected from the passions to the creative and spiritual, but it is bad because it may deplete the resources and leave nothing for bodily satisfaction" (p. 34).

6. For information on the extent to which psychoanalytic therapy is used in the United States, see L. deMause (1979), New developments in applied psychoanalysis, *Journal of Psychohistory, 7,* 163–173.

7. This is not to imply that every psychoanalyst accepts all of Freud's ideas or conducts the therapy session in precisely the same way as Freud. Neo-analysts, or neo-Freudians as they are sometimes called, however, do hold to many of the basic teachings of Freud, and therapy sessions are conducted in a way that is commensurate with those teachings. Among the more prominent psychoanalysts are Erik Erikson, Carl Jung, Alfred Adler, Karen Horney, Erich Fromm, Bruno Bettelheim, and Robert Coles.

8. By 1986, three nonmedical psychoanalytic institutions, two in New York and one in Los Angeles, had been accepted into membership by the International Psychoanalytic Association. Group psychoanalysis has also increased in favor, reducing the cost of individual sessions and providing clients with the support of others with similar difficulties. In some cases clients are invited to prepare for the session by approaching the unconscious — voluntarily or involuntarily — through dreams and active imagination. (See R.A. Johnson, 1986, *Inner work: Using dreams and active imagination for personal growth,* San Francisco: Harper & Row.)

9. Now, more than fifty years after Freud's death, the emphasis on unconscious processes continues to dominate psychoanalytic therapy. The areas of interest range from revealing multiple personality disorders to providing a nurturing environment for clients with low self-esteem; from psychopharmacologic approaches to dealing with eating disorders; from the use of hypnosis to uncover covert ego states to looking at unconscious rage that triggers spouse and child abuse. Enabling the client to achieve insight into his or her problems brings relief of immediate symptoms and in time results in a reconstruction of the personality.

10. Ego psychologists stress moral understanding and the changes that occur during middle and late childhood, believing that ego variables play as great a part in determining the moral behavior and attitudes of adults as does the formation of the superego during the early years. For a closer look at ego morality in psychoanalysis, see R.S. Lee (1948), *Freud and Christianity,* London: James Clarke & Co.; S. Lorand (1972), Historical aspects and changing trends in psychoanalytic therapy, *The Psychoanalytic Review, 59,*

Moral Growth by Moral Conflict: A Psychoanalytic View

497–525; E.M. Pattison (1968), Ego morality: An emerging psychotherapeutic concept, *The Psychoanalytic Review*, 55, 187–222; and E. Wallwork (1991), *Psychoanalysis and ethics*, New Haven: Yale University Press.

11. The following account was related to me by a medical missionary from Nigeria and illustrates the damaging consequences of an inflexible superego. In the fall of 1966, soldiers were coming in and slaughtering the Biafran people. Another missionary working in Kano, Nigeria was asked by a soldier if a certain man was an Ibo. Feeling that he could not tell a lie, the missionary responded in such a way that the man was killed by the soldier. The next morning when several missionaries got together to discuss the incident, some said that the missionary had done the right thing because, after all, the murdered man was only a native, not one of their fellow Christians.

12. It becomes increasingly apparent in looking at the actual behavior of believers that a healthy balance between ego and superego is difficult to achieve. It may be that sometimes decisions are made one way, sometimes another. David, the Psalmist, on one occasion feigned madness (1 Sam. 21:13) and ate the shewbread which was not lawful in order to preserve his own life, a behavior which rather than being condemned by our Lord was used to explain His own actions (Matt. 12:3-4). On another occasion, David placed himself in a situation in which he could have lost his life because he was unwilling to go against his conscience in raising his hand against Saul, the Lord's anointed (1 Sam. 24:6).

13. "Psychoneuroses result from heightened conflict between sexual and aggressive drives or their derivatives; they are attempts to control and limit the expression of such drives. This struggle is not based on a realistic appraisal of the current situation with its opportunities for gratification under the reasonable restraint of the normal superego. . . . Freud grouped hysteria, phobia, and obsessive-compulsive neurosis in the category *transference neuroses.* . . . Patients afflicted with melancholia and schizophrenia. . . . Freud termed these entities *narcissistic neuroses*" (Psychoneurosis. 1990. In B.E. Moore & B.D. Fine (Eds.), *Psychoanalytic terms and concepts,* pp. 154–155, New Haven: The American Psychoanalytic Association and Yale University Press.)

14. *The Diagnostic and statistical manual of mental disorders* (3rd ed. — better know as DSM-III-R.), (1987), Washington, DC: American Psychiatric Association, describes the sociopath as having a personality disorder. "The essential feature of this disorder is a pattern of irresponsible and antisocial behavior beginning in childhood or early adolescence and continuing into adulthood. . . . These people fail to conform to social norms and repeatedly perform antisocial acts that are grounds for arrest, such as destroying property, harassing others, stealing and having an illegal occupation. . . . They generally have no remorse about the effects of their behavior on others."

REFERENCES

Avstreih, A.K., & Brown, J.J. (1979). Some aspects of movement and art therapy as related to the analytic situation. *The Psychoanalytic Review, 66,* 49–68.

Coles, R. (1986). *The moral life of children.* Boston: Atlantic Monthly Press.

Edelson, M. (1988). *Psychoanalysis: A theory in crisis.* Chicago: University of Chicago Press.

Elchoness, M. (1988). *Sigmund says: A lighter look at Freud through his id, ego, and super-ego.* Sepulveda, CA: Monroe Press.

Eysenck, H.J., & Wilson, G.D. (1973). *The experimental study of Freudian theories.* London: Methuen & Co.

Fisher, S., & Greenberg, R.P. (1977). *The scientific credibility of Freud's theories and therapy.* New York: Basic Books.

Freud, S. (1949). *A general introduction to psychoanalysis* (J. Riviere, Trans.). New York: Perma Giants. (Original work published 1920)

_____. (1952). *Totem and taboo* (J. Strachey, Trans.). New York: W.W. Norton. (Original work published 1913)

_____. (1957). Group psychology and the analysis of the ego. In J. Rickman (Ed.), *A general selection from the works of Sigmund Freud* (pp. 169–209). Garden City, NY: Doubleday. (Original work published 1937)

_____. (1961). *Civilization and its discontents* (J. Strachey, Ed. and Trans.). New York: W.W. Norton. (Original work published 1930)

_____. (1963). The letters of Sigmund Freud to Oskar Pfister. In H. Meng & E.L. Freud (Eds.), *Psychoanalysis and faith: The letters of Sigmund Freud and Oskar Pfister* (E. Mosbacher, Trans.). New York: Basic Books.

_____. (1970). The technique of psychoanalysis. In V. Comerchero (Ed.), *Values in Conflict* (pp. 429–38). New York: Appleton-Century-Crofts. (Formerly published in *An outline of psychoanalysis,* 1949, New York: W. W. Norton.)

Fromm, E. (1980). *Greatness and limitations of Freud's thought.* New York: Harper & Row.

Gay, P. (1985). *Freud for historians.* New York: Oxford University Press.

Hook, S. (1959). *Psychoanalysis, scientific method, and philosophy.* New York: New York University Press.

Johnson, R.A. (1986). *Inner work: Using dreams and active imagination for personal growth.* San Francisco: Harper & Row.

Jones, E.M. (1993). *Degenerate moderns: Modernity as rationalized sexual behavior.* Harrison, NY: Ignatius.

Jones, J.W. (1991). *Contemporary psychoanalysis and religion: Transference and transcendence.* New Haven: Yale University Press.

Jones, S.L., & Butman, R.E. (1991). *Modern psychotherapies: A comprehensive Christian appraisal.* Downers Grove, IL: InterVarsity Press.

Leavy, S.A. (1988). *In the image of God: A psychoanalyst's view.* New Haven: Yale University Press.

Lee, R.S. (1948). *Freud and Christianity.* London: James Clarke & Co.

Lorand, S. (1972). Historical aspects and changing trends in psychoanalytic therapy. *The Psychoanalytic Review, 59,* 497–525.

Menninger, K. (1973). *Whatever became of sin?* New York: Hawthorn Books.

Messer, S.B., & Winokur, M. (1980). Some limits to the integration of psychoanalytic and behavior therapy. *American Psychologist, 35,* 818–827.

Pattison, E.M. (1968). Ego morality: An emerging psychotherapeutic concept. *The Psychoanalytic Review, 55,* 187–222.

Pearson, G.H.J. (1954). *Psychoanalysis and the education of the child.* New York: W.W. Norton.

Pumpian-Mindlin, E. (1952). *Psychoanalysis as science.* Stanford, CA: Stanford University Press.

Sarnoff, I. (1971). *Testing Freudian concepts: An experimental approach.* New York: Springer.

Sears, R. (1943). *Survey of objective studies in psychoanalytic concepts.* New York: Social Science Research Council.

Sjöbäck, M. (1973). *The psychoanalytic theory of defensive processes.* New York: John Wiley & Sons.

Tice, T.N. (1980). A psychoanalytic perspective. In M. Windmiller, N. Lambert, & E. Turiel (Eds.), *Moral development and socialization* (pp. 161–99). Boston: Allyn & Bacon.

Vitz, P.C. (1993). *Sigmund Freud's Christian unconscious.* Grand Rapids: Eerdmans.

Wallwork, E. (1991). *Psychoanalysis and ethics.* New Haven: Yale University Press.

Wright, D. (1971). *The psychology of moral behavior.* Harmondworth, Middlesex, England: Penguin Books.

FIVE

Guidelines from Psychoanalysis for Teachers, Parents, and Pastors

P rior to the time of Freud it was generally thought that young children were mindless creatures, more like animals than humans, and that whatever happened to them before the age of six or seven was of little consequence compared with later life experiences. Children also were thought of as innocent beings having neither an interest in sex nor a propensity to engage in sex-related activities. The role of parents was to take responsibility for the physical care of children to assure survival and to keep them in line so that they could learn to conform to an adult world. There was little reason to believe that what parents said and did related to the intellectual development of one so young or affected the emotional well-being of the child years later when maturity was reached (Aries, 1962).

Teachers received the child when it was assumed that the child was ready to learn. Traditionally, the teacher's role was to inculcate the skills that the child needed to know in order to take his or her place in society. Learning was considered a cognitive endeavor, the affective component taking a back seat in an understanding of how knowledge is acquired. Consequently, the method used to teach, whether severe or gentle, was of little importance. Teachers were hired to teach, not to understand individual differences or to be concerned with the feelings of students.

It was in this milieu that the works of Sigmund Freud fell like a bomb. Freud's ideas were so explosive to educated and lay public alike that his writings were received both with fascination and rejection. Freud wrote that many of the problems seen in adults stemmed from experiences that occurred during the first few years of life. Time and again, Freud noted that his patients would recall events that took place in early childhood—events so traumatic they were affected by them all their lives. It became increasingly clear that children are not mindless, emotionless, sexless beings but are aware of what goes on around them and sense keenly the quality of interpersonal relationships. Freud (1913/1968) reiterated the saying, "The child is father to the man" (p. 183), meaning that the adult personality is determined by the experiences one has as a child.

This emphasis on the early years, as well as Freud's teachings on infant sexuality, the death instinct, the importance of the unconscious, and the role of psychic determinism, made for profound changes in the attitudes of people toward others. Parents began to see that they were responsible not only for the physical care of the child, but also for the emotional health of their young. Teachers, as well, were told that learning would be enhanced if they became familiar with the defense mechanisms used by children. Repression, regression, and projection are utilized by students to compensate for conflicts within their personalities, and a recognition of this fact and an understanding of behaviors that accompany these mechanisms would aid the teacher in being more sympathetic with students and thus would increase learning in the classroom. As Freud's ideas became more widely accepted, the roles of educators, parents, and others who work with youth came to have greater significance.

Freudian psychoanalysis is often referred to as classic psychoanalysis whereas the theories and interpretations of Freud's followers are more apt to be known by such designations as post-Freudian, neo-Freudian, or contemporary psychoanalysis. We will use both classic and contemporary ideas in our application to the work of teachers, parents, and pastors.

GUIDELINES FOR TEACHERS

One of the first writers to address the issue of how a knowledge of psychoanalysis is beneficial to the educator was Freud's daughter, Anna, who applied her father's ideas both to the rearing of children in the home and to the teaching of children in school. Although Anna Freud (1935) did not deal specifically with the manifestations of the ego and the superego in school-age children, she did maintain in her book *Psychoanalysis for Teachers and Parents* that psychoanalysis does three things for "pedagogy."

> In the first place, it is well qualified to offer a criticism of existing educational methods. In the second place, the teacher's knowledge of human beings is extended, and his understanding of the complicated relations between the child and the educator is sharpened by psychoanalysis, which gives us a scientific theory of the instincts, of the unconscious and of the libido. Finally, as a method of practical treatment, in the analysis of children, it endeavors to repair the injuries which are inflicted upon the child during the process of education. (p. 106)

STUDENTS' EMOTIONAL NEEDS COME FIRST

Anna Freud's criticism of education is that there is too much "decorum and convention" in the schools. Pressure is put upon children to conform, and when they do conform it is considered an educational success. But the price children pay may be too high. "These educational successes are too dearly bought. They are paid for by the failures with those children who are not fortunate enough to reveal symptoms of suffering" (A. Freud, 1935, p. 109). Anna Freud believed that as educators we should show more interest in the child who is suffering and less interest in what society considers to be proper. Meeting the emotional needs of our students takes precedence over getting them to act in conventional ways.

AS EDUCATORS WE SHOULD KNOW OURSELVES

With regard to the second point that a knowledge of psychoanalysis will help teachers understand the student and their relationship to the student, Anna Freud's opinion was that as teachers we need to understand ourselves first and then we will be in a better position to understand our students and the nature of our relationship with them. She held that being psychoanalyzed is a necessary prerequisite to understanding oneself, and therefore she recommended that educators go through psychoanalysis before beginning a teaching career. This would be a hard one for most of us to follow through on, but let us hear her out.

She tells the story of a young woman who had an unhappy childhood and left home to become the governess of three boys, the second of whom was not as favored as the other two in either appearance or ability. This young woman gave the second child extra attention and tutoring until he was able to do as well as his brothers and was accepted and appreciated by his parents as were the others. Then a strange thing happened. The feeling of love she had for this child turned to hate, and although she was greatly desired by the family, the animosity between herself and the boy became so great she was forced to leave. It was not until she had undergone psychoanalysis some fifteen years later that she discovered the reason for what had occurred. Being an unloved child herself she unconsciously had identified with the boy and had given him the love and attention she felt she should have had as a child. When he became successful and won the favor of his parents she no longer could identify with him, but rather became jealous and hostile. Had she been aware earlier of the source of her feelings she could have dealt with her emotions in a rational way, thereby alleviating the strain that came between her and the boy.

> As educators we need to be aware that there is an underlying reason for the student's fantasies, that slips of the tongue and witty comments have psychic meaning, that instinctive forces play a part in their emotions, and that each person is a sexual being interested in exploring his or her own body and in finding his or her role as male or female.

REALIZE THERE IS A REASON FOR WHAT STUDENTS DO AND SAY

Other writers who apply psychoanalysis to the school also stress Anna Freud's second point of the relationship between teacher and student.

Few teachers, though, have either the money or the time to be psycho-analyzed, so less is said in the literature about psychoanalysis as a form of self-understanding for teachers, and more is said about psychoanaly-sis as knowledge to be applied to an interpretation of students' behav-ior in the classroom. By knowing how the id, the ego, and the superego combine to effect actions and attitudes, we can appreciate the use of defense mechanisms in children. As educators we need to be aware that there is an underlying reason for the student's fantasies, that slips of the tongue and witty comments have psychic meaning, that instinctive forces play a part in their emotions, and that each person is a sexual being interested in exploring his or her own body and in finding his or her role as male or female. Although we are not trained as analysts or therapists, we should know how to bring about a positive transference between ourselves and the students and how to encourage students to adopt a value system that will satisfy all three components of the personality—the id, the ego, and the superego. Children with deep-seated problems need to be encouraged to communicate their feelings and thus bring into consciousness unconscious fears and anxieties so that these emotions can be dealt with in a rational, issue-oriented way.

Deal with Specific Problems in the Context of the School

The third way, according to Anna Freud, that psychoanalysis may be applied to pedagogy is in the area of repairing the damage done to the child during the process of being educated. Teachers today are con-cerned not only with problems the child may have incurred while going to school, but also with those that stem from the home and subse-quently affect performance in the classroom. School phobia and test anxiety are two such problems.

School Phobia

School phobia (not to be confused with truancy, especially when ob-served in younger pupils at the elementary grade level) is not so much a fear of what may happen at school as it is a fear that something terrible will happen to mother when the child is not with her. The psychoana-lytic explanation (Kelly, 1973) is that the school phobic child has an overprotective mother who has not resolved her own need for depen-dency and consequently looks to her child to meet this need. She may

114

say that she wants her child to go to school and she believes that this is so, but unconsciously she wants the child to stay with her. This is the mother who takes great pleasure in doing things for her child, distrusts the ability of anyone else to care for the child, feels uncomfortable whenever the child is out of her sight, and is quick to accept the child's complaint of not feeling well as an excuse to keep the child home.

The result is a symbiotic relationship that feeds on itself, making the mother increasingly solicitous and the child increasingly dependent. The problem may not be evident until a specific incident such as the mother's not being home when the child returns from school, a robbery occurring in the neighborhood, or the child's becoming ill at school, triggers the phobic reaction within the child. From then on, the thought of going to school makes the child sick, and recovery occurs only when it becomes obvious that he or she has won another day of reprieve. School phobic children are not faking, they are truly ill. Obviously they need help, but if therapy is to be successful it must include the parents, and especially the mother. Without getting to the source of the difficulty, little will be accomplished.

The well known psychoanalyst Bruno Bettelheim (1987) agrees that school phobia is an unconscious fear of a loss of contact with the mother but adds that the child also may have an unconscious wish not to grow up, "to remain forever his parents' little child" (p. 65). If there are younger siblings at home, "illness becomes a way not only to stay home, and thus make sure that one will not be forgotten, but also to get even more of the mother's attention" (p. 66). He recommends a period of home schooling after which the child will voluntarily return to school. However, he acknowledges that this remedy may not always work, thereby necessitating the use of other ways of assuring the child of one's affection.

Test Anxiety

Test anxiety is another problem some children face. The way the term is used in the literature, text anxiety refers not so much to the uneasy feeling all of us have experienced at one time or another in a testing situation, but rather to the crippling fear some people sustain whenever they are called upon to take a test. In the test-anxious person, the magnitude of the response is out of all proportion to what would be expected in that situation. Test-anxious students may become so frightened they are unable to answer even the simplest questions, or so perturbed at the thought of taking a test that they are incapacitated. They complain of feeling nauseous and are too sick to remain in the classroom. The solution is not to stop giving tests in school, for tests have always been used to evaluate the performance of students. Rather, it is imperative that children learn to live with tests and to overcome this handicap so they can function in a normal way.

A psychoanalytic interpretation of test anxiety has been given by Sarason, Davidson, Lighthall, Waite, and Ruebush (1960) in a book entitled *Anxiety in Elementary School Children: A Report of Research*. These scholars, all from Yale University at the time the book was written, wrote that test anxiety stems from a conflict between the unconscious internal world of the child and the conscious external reality that the child faces. Internally, test-anxious children feel hostility toward their parents for demanding more of them than they feel they can deliver. Externally, they have a high positive regard for their parents and want to please them. The test is a tangible reminder that they cannot meet parental expectations, thus signaling the conflict within, a conflict between hate and love, between anger and wanting to make parents happy. These children feel guilty, and in order to keep their feelings of hostility at the unconscious level, they derogate their own worth and lessen the turmoil within themselves by becoming too ill to take the test. This withdrawal from emotional involvement and retreat from situations that are psychologically threatening allow them to cope in the only way they know how. As Sarason and the others put it:

> The most obvious manner in which our thinking has been influenced by psychoanalysis will be seen in our conception of the anxious response as a conscious danger signal associated not only with an external danger but also with unconscious contents and motivations the conscious elaboration of which is inhibited or defended against because such elaboration would place the individual in an even more dangerous relation to the external world. (Sarason et al., 1960, p. 6)

Children with test anxiety can be helped if they have an understanding teacher. The Yale scholars suggest that the teacher take a low-key approach to testing situations so as not to be perceived by these children as being like their parents. If we as teachers have a test-anxious child in our class, we should convey the message that a test is a natural event, not a momentous occasion that marks one for life or portrays one's worth to the world. The less we say about tests, the better. The atmosphere of the class and of the school should be sufficiently relaxed that the anxiety felt by these children while in a testing situation will not generalize to other situations. The problem only becomes worse if children become anxious about their role in playing games at recess time or if they begin to dislike their classmates who do well on tests. We need to give test-anxious children a lot of external support, thus easing their fears that they are not doing what is expected of them. Test anxiety can be overcome, but only when the conflict within the child is lessened by an understanding adult.

ACADEMIC SUCCESS LINKED WITH SUPEREGO STRENGTH

Bruno Bettelheim (1970) links the desire to study and to learn in school with superego development. In a lecture at Harvard University, Bettelheim said that children from lower-class homes often do poorly academically because they have not learned to postpone gratification, a superego characteristic. What brings pleasure at the moment (id) and what seems to work best for them in the world of reality (ego) takes precedence over the conviction that learning in school is a good thing to do and will be of benefit at some future time. Studying is not nearly as exciting as many other things these children could be doing, so unless they have a conscience that says that doing their best is right and anything less is wrong, they will not be sufficiently motivated to learn. "Fortunately for education as it now exists, most middle-class children still enter school with a very strong superego and . . . with the ability to postpone pleasure over long stretches of time well established . . . but . . . their number is constantly declining" (p. 96).

Bettelheim saw the reason for the decline in motivation among middle-class children as being due in large measure to the emphasis today on material possessions rather than on teaching the child to act in ways that would guarantee eternal salvation. "The image of the affluent society plays havoc with the puritanical virtues" (p. 97). Furthermore, parents believe they must assure the child of their love regardless of the child's behavior. Taken together, the stress on money and what money can buy, plus the promise of unconditional love, provide the reason for why today's child does not have a strong conscience. If the child has all that is needed now, and if the child has nothing to fear from either God or the parents, then from the child's perspective there is no reason to engage in the difficult task of studying as a way of gaining respect or of

BRUNO BETTELHEIM (1903–1990)

Born in Austria of affluent Jewish parents, Bettelheim completed his studies with Sigmund Freud and received the Ph.D. from the University of Vienna in 1938. Shortly after, he was arrested by the Nazis and spent a year at Dachau and Buchenwald. At the request of Eleanor Roosevelt, who had heard of his work with psychotic children, he was released and brought with his wife, Gertrud, to the United States. He found work at Rockford College and then became a professor at the University of Chicago where he spent twenty-six years heading the Sonia Shankman Orthogenic School, the university's residential school for schizophrenic and autistic children. He and his wife raised three children, two girls and a boy.

Bettelheim's interests were many and varied. He studied children's reading material in the schools, wrote a book about fairy tales (for which he won the National Book Critics Circle Award), applied insights from his experience in the concentration camps to therapeutic interventions for autistic children, expressed his views on sex education, movies, and parenting, and interpreted Freudian psychoanalysis in *Freud and Man's Soul* (1982).

After Gertrud's death in 1984, Bettelheim became greatly discouraged. "As long as we are in love with somebody, we try to stay alive to be with them. It's as simple as that," he told a writer for the Los Angeles Times Magazine. A stroke in 1987 impaired his ability to write, although he still maintained a schedule that permitted him to collaborate on a book and supervise therapists. By 1989 he became increasingly confused and often talked of dying. The next year, after moving out of his fifth-floor Santa Monica apartment overlooking the ocean and into a retirement home in Washington, Bruno Bettelheim, at age eighty-six, joined the increasing number of elderly people who take their own lives.

being assured of a better life to come. Bettelheim believes that middle-class children today are too comfortable and fear nothing. "My contention is that for education to proceed children must have learned to fear something before they come to school. If it is not the once crippling fear of damnation and the woodshed, then in our more enlightened days it is at least the fear of losing parental love (or later, by proxy, the teacher's) and eventually the fear of losing self-respect" (Bettelheim, 1970, pp. 97-98).

Bruno Bettelheim's explanation of why children are not motivated to learn may seem a bit harsh, even as Anna Freud's application of psychoanalysis to an understanding of the child may seem too permissive. Nevertheless, we must admit that children who are desirous of doing well in school and who consistently try to do their best often have strong internal controls that make them feel guilty when their homework is not done, when they are late for school, or when they do something that displeases the teacher. Unless there is guilt and a sense of apprehension stemming from a religious conviction that one has not pleased God or from the feeling that the bond of love with the parent has been broken and will not be mended until confession is made and behavior changed, it may well be that the motivation to learn and to do well in school is impaired.

Some children who may not have superego strength will identify with a particular teacher who gives them special attention and will in turn want to please that teacher. This identification with an adult is less apt to occur at school than in the home, but we all know of cases where this has happened and students have acted in more acceptable ways — doing homework, not lying or stealing, obeying the rules — in order not to break the bond of friendship the student feels with the teacher. In rare cases superego strength forms after the critical period, and we as teachers should at least be aware that this is a possibility.

A CASE STUDY APPROACH

Joseph and Joseph (1977) have applied Bettelheim's ideas to children with learning and behavioral deficits. Using the case-study approach, they tell of Larry who could not learn because he was interested only in immediate pleasure, of Paul who also was an academic failure and had been involved in incidents of vandalism and smoking marijuana, of

Kathy who was a clever shoplifter and was often truant, and of Bob who was so undisciplined and disruptive that the teacher was relieved when he did not come to school. By describing each child and his or her background, the authors gave a clear picture of what the child was like. Suggestions were given as to how each child could be helped in the context of the school and how psychoanalysis explained the difficulties each child faced. Larry needed help in developing an ego so he could feel better about himself and could learn to postpone gratification; Paul should receive positive attention whenever he did his work at school so that he would be less apt to seek attention in socially unacceptable ways; Kathy "needs the teacher to function as a superego for her" (p. 118) helping her sort out what is right and what is wrong; and Bob, who seldom got enough to eat, could be worked with by meeting his basic id needs for survival so that he, like Larry, might begin to develop an ego. By using case studies, Joseph and Joseph (1977) showed how psychoanalysis may be applied to the school both as a theory to account for behaviors and as a form of therapy to enable teachers to assist those children with moral and motivational problems.

ERIKSON'S SENSE OF INDUSTRY

Psychoanalyst Erik Erikson (1980) of Harvard University has an eight-stage theory of personality development that extends from birth to old age. Like Freud, he stressed the early years as being the most important and saw conflict arising from both biological development and societal expectations; but unlike Freud he put more emphasis on social interactions and less emphasis on sexual needs and desires.

According to Erikson, at each stage of life there is a problem that must be met in order for the child to go to the next stage with confidence. The infant must develop a sense of *trust*, the toddler a sense of *autonomy*, the preschool child a sense of *initiative*, the school-age child a sense of *industry*, the adolescent a sense of *identity*, the young adult a sense of *intimacy*, the mature adult a sense of *generativity*, and the elderly a sense of *integrity*.

If, when a child starts to school, he or she has found the world to be a trustworthy place, has been given opportunities to make decisions for oneself, and has initiated many activities that teach about both a world of reality and a world of fantasy, then the child is ready for the experi-

120

ences that will develop a sense of industry.

A sense of industry includes good relationships with peers, school tasks that are completed successfully, and a feeling of competence as a member of the society. "This is socially a most decisive stage: since industry involves doing things beside and with others, a first sense of division of labor and of equality of opportunity develops at this time" (Erikson, 1980, p. 93). Teachers, especially during the elementary grades, must be ready to recognize the efforts and accomplishments of the child. Otherwise, a feeling of inferiority or inadequacy will develop that will hinder the child from continuing on to the next stage of healthy personality development.

A Sense of Identity

Erikson views adolescence as a transition period between childhood and adulthood in which the adolescent is searching for identity. The teenager asks himself or herself such questions as: "Who am I?" "Where did I come from?" "Am I heading toward some kind of understandable future?" "What is life all about?" The goal is to harmonize one's past and future, achieve self-certainty, come to terms with sexual identity, and develop an ideology or set of beliefs. "The adolescent is in a kind of no man's land between childhood and adulthood. . . . There was security in childhood; there is the promise of some security in adult life. In the meantime there is the insecurity of feeling you don't belong in either world" (Hague, 1986, pp. 102-103). One's ideology is confirmed by fidelity or commitment to others, ritualization of everyday habits that make for balanced stable living, and taking an independent stance. Most adolescents abandon some of the values set by parents while accepting others. They must learn to set their own vocational goals.

Some high school students are not successful in achieving a sense of individual identity. They are uncomfortable with their appearance, their uniqueness as persons, and their lack of connectedness to others in the surrounding society. Erikson would say they are suffering from role confusion. They do not know who they are, where they came from, or where they are headed. They may be isolated or directionless, or in some cases, they accept without question the roles others impose upon them.

121

Youth after youth, bewildered by some assumed role, a role forced on him by the inexorable standardization of American adolescence, runs away in one form or another; leaving schools and jobs, staying out all night, or withdrawing into bizarre and inaccessible moods. Once "delinquent," his greatest need and often his only salvation, is the refusal on the part of older friends, advisers, and judiciary personnel to type him further by pat diagnoses and social judgments which ignore the special dynamic conditions of adolescence. (Erikson, 1980, p. 97)[1]

Secondary school teachers have the opportunity of helping teenagers accept or improve their appearance, use role playing to practice social skills, achieve a masculine or feminine role, and prepare for a vocation. Teachers also can assist students in acquiring a set of values and an ethical system with which to guide behavior. The teacher is in a key position, along with parents, to transmit not only the knowledge of the culture, which has been handed down from generation to generation, but also the values of the culture that have stood the test of time. This must be done in the context of a rapidly changing technological society, making the task more difficult but increasingly urgent.

ATTITUDES TOWARD SEXUAL CONDUCT

One area in which values are especially important for junior high and high school students is that of sexual behavior. The conflict between the instinctual desires of the id and the social mandates of the real world as interpreted by the ego is especially difficult during the teen years. Adolescents are physically capable of bearing children, but they are neither emotionally nor economically prepared to rear them. In our complex society where adolescence extends for a period of six or more years, young people are expected to put sexual drives on hold while they expend their energies preparing for the adult tasks of a career, financial independence, and social maturity. "Some professions require study till the individual is in his late twenties or early thirties. Because of this long dependent status as a student, it is difficult for an identity to emerge" (Miller, 1978, p. 241).

Adolescents must come to terms with their own identity before they are ready for *intimacy* (Erikson, 1980), and intimacy takes time — lots of time. Intimacy means intimacy with oneself, with friends, and finally with a special person with whom one wishes to be intimate in a unique way. Erikson believed that this special relationship provides the foundation for marriage which in turn establishes a secure base for the children born of that union. Teenagers simply have not had the time to go through the necessary psychological stages to be good parents.

In the light of this psychological unpreparedness, the figures on teen pregnancy are startling. Each year more than a million American teenagers become pregnant, four of five of them unmarried. In some families, the cycle of teen pregnancy is repeated time and again, the babies of unwed teens becoming parents in their own right within twelve to sixteen years (Wallis, 1985).

Behaviors cannot be divorced from attitudes, and although there is not a one-to-one correspondence between what a person thinks and what a person does, thought and action are often related. In January of 1989, Market Facts, Inc. polled 2,046 teenagers, half male and half female, as to their attitudes on sex, religion, school, family, and future plans. The results were reported in *Seventeen* magazine (Chace, 1989). Forty-four percent of the girls and 54 percent of the boys agreed with the statement, "There's nothing wrong with premarital sex" (p. 103).

Some studies show that religious youth are more likely to abstain from sexual intercourse than less religious youth (e.g., Mahoney, 1980; McCormick, Izzo, & Folcik, 1985; Woodroof, 1986). However, in a summary article for *Christian Parenting Today,* Sheppard (1989) reported that "research shows little difference between the sexual behavior of Christian teens and a cross section of American adolescents" (p. 68). This statement is based on a survey conducted during the summer of 1987 with 1,438 young people, ages twelve through eighteen attending eight evangelical denominations. The survey was commissioned by the Josh McDowell Ministry with assistance provided by the Barna Research Group of Glendale, California.

In other research, Jensen, Newell, and Holman (1990) found attitude toward sexual permissiveness to be a better predictor of sexual behavior than religious practice. They studied the frequency of sexual intercourse of 423 single students enrolled in family relations classes at Cameron University in Lawton, Oklahoma and at the University of Wisconsin-Stout. A five-way analysis of variance design included the variables of church attendance, age, state, gender, and attitude toward sexual permissiveness. Attitude toward sexual permissiveness was the only significant predictor although it interacted with church attendance in that nonpermissive males and females who attended church had the lowest frequency of sexual behavior but permissive subjects who also attended church every week had one of the highest frequencies of sexual intercourse. Attitudes, then, appear to be a good predictor of sexual behavior. Religious practice may or may not be related.

The *Gallup Report* (1987, August) stated that in 1969 Protestants and Catholics were about even in their disapproval (70 percent and 72 percent respectively), but by 1987 only 50 percent of Protestants and 39 percent of Catholics disapproved of premarital sex. It would appear from these figures that the picture in many people's minds of premarital sex being approved by adolescents and adults who are not affiliated with the Christian religion but not approved by those who are affiliated with Christianity is not accurate.

To place "blame" on the adolescent's peer group and not upon the society as a whole is unfair. "A high percentage of young people do experiment with drugs, alcohol, and cigarettes and become sexually active early, but they are apt to be more influenced in this by prevailing social values in the adult world than by an oppositional 'youth culture' " (Russell, 1990, p. 4). The worlds of advertising, TV programming, and popular culture communicate that sex is all right for any physically mature person and can be engaged in strictly for pleasure. "In the course of a year the average viewer sees more than 9,000 scenes of suggested sexual intercourse or innuendo on prime-time TV" (Wallis, 1985, p. 81).

What can the teacher do? Does sex education help? If so, what should be included in the program?[2] If not, what are other options? In another context (Clouse, 1991) I have reviewed the research in this area. Literally hundreds of studies have been conducted in an effort to answer these questions. The teacher in a Christian school may have an advantage, especially if students come from stable, intact families in which traditional parental attitudes have been conveyed, and if the students are *young* — that is — either preteen or in early adolescence. "Just say no" programs probably have little effect on teenagers who already are sexually active. The best time for training in decision-making skills is before they are needed.

Freud wrote in the foreword of a book on delinquency that the purpose of education is "to guide the child on his way to maturity, to encourage him, and to protect him from taking the wrong path" (Aichhorn, 1925/1963, p. v). As teachers we are expected to guide, encourage, and protect the student and keep the student from going in the wrong direction.

GUIDELINES FOR PARENTS

Freud's emphasis on the early years means that the parent plays a greater part in what the child becomes than does any other adult. This is especially true as it relates to moral growth. Both the ego and the superego are in the process of forming before the child starts to school. What happens to children before the age of six or seven will have an effect on them the rest of their lives. Parents are the society's first and most important teachers.

PSYCHOSEXUAL STAGES

Freud believed that each person goes through a series of stages that are psychosexual in nature, each stage corresponding to a particular chronological age and forming the basis for the stage that follows. The infant is at the *oral* stage, so named because the mouth serves as the erogenous zone with its functions of breathing, crying, and incorporating milk from the mother. The toddler is at the *anal* stage, an appropriate term considering that children universally are toilet trained at this age. The *phallic* stage is entered when children are approximately four years of age and constitutes the time when the Oedipus and Electra complexes occur, forcing the child to identify with the parent of the same sex in order to resolve the conflict brought on by an erotic desire for the parent of the opposite sex.

The child enters *latency* about the time he or she starts school and remains at this stage during the elementary years. The term latency implies that sexual interests are latent or dormant, and the child is ready to settle down to learn more about a real world and to form close friendships with peers of the same age. Puberty ushers in the *genital* stage, a time when the genital area becomes the erogenous zone, and the young person enters another period of emotional turmoil in preparation for taking on an adult role.

PARENTS AND PSYCHOSEXUAL STAGES

The quality of care given to the child at each stage of development has a profound impact on social and moral growth and will leave an indelible imprint on the adult personality. During the oral stage parents should recognize the dependency needs of the infant, willingly provide for these needs, and encourage a sense of trust. Most parents do this quite naturally. During the anal stage, they need to be aware of the child's strivings for independence, appreciate these as an indication of growing up, and provide an optimal balance between autonomy and control. During the phallic stage, we can help the child come to terms with his or her own sexual identity by exhibiting sex appropriate behaviors and modeling socially desirable husband-wife relationships in the home.

Latency brings a respite from inner turmoil and is a time when social values and practices are conveyed by peers and teachers as well as by parents. During the genital stage the problems of the first three stages again appear; and as some of us who have raised teenagers know far too well, this may be the most difficult period of all as we help our child work anew to resolve the issues of dependence, independence, and identity.

The ego begins to form during the oral stage as soon as the infant is able to differentiate between self and non-self. The superego appears in rudimentary form during the anal stage when the child begins to understand that some behaviors are "good" and other behaviors are "bad." We can actually observe the process of *introjection* taking place when, for example, our toddler turns away from an object he or she has been told not to touch or when our two-year-old says "I a good boy" because he sits quietly in church, picks up his toys, or whatever else he knows to be acceptable behavior. The internalization of social and parental standards results in children being able to monitor their own behavior and to experience feelings of guilt when that behavior is not in conformity with expected demands. The ego and the superego both continue to develop throughout childhood and even into adulthood, but Freud believed that the most sensitive or critical period for their formation occurs before the age of five or six.

AS PARENTS WE ENCOURAGE MORAL GROWTH

It is to the social learning psychologist who has studied how the conscience develops that we owe much of our understanding of how psychoanalytic theory can be applied to the rearing of children. The investigations of Robert Sears (1960) and others within the social learning framework have shown that the superego or conscience is more apt to occur if we as parents are accepting of the normal dependency needs of our child, if we take the time to reason with the child regarding the consequences of behavior, and if we use love-oriented techniques of discipline. Let us look at each of these in turn.

We Accept the Dependency Needs of Our Children
The dependency needs of children take on many forms. Wanting to be near us, touching us, engaging us in conversation, insisting that we watch while they perform some type of task, and fussing or crying until attention is received are all expressions of dependency well known to those who have children. If we as parents are accepting of these needs, if we are not unduly irritated or impatient when these needs are expressed, a close relationship usually will be established with our children, thus laying the foundation for the identification process in which our children incorporate within themselves our attitudes and expectations for behavior.

Accepting parents tend to be warm and loving and are quite happy to have the child nearby to talk with her, watch her antics, and respond to her needs. This does not mean that parents can meet the dependency needs of the child at all times for this would be physically impossible and emotionally exhausting. Furthermore, we would be hard pressed to argue that it would be healthy for a child to receive such attention constantly. But it does mean that if we as parents enjoy being with our children, we are more apt to establish a bond of influence with them than if we are cold and disinterested.

> **Reasoning with children regarding the consequences of behavior enables them to see cause-effect relationships between what they do and what happens as a result.**

We Reason with Them about the Consequences of Behavior
Reasoning with children regarding the consequences of behavior enables them to see cause-effect relationships between what they do and

what happens as a result. Sometimes called consequence-oriented discipline, it involves talking with children about what they have done or plan to do and the effect of their behavior on others as well as on themselves. This technique is an effective means of getting children to feel a growing responsibility for the outcome of their actions and capitalizes on their capacity for empathy. Saying, "You will hurt his feelings if you say that," "Don't run or you may drop it and it will break," "How would you feel if everyone in the family yelled 'shut up' at you like you just did to your brother?" will help children see that even as it matters to them what others do, it matters to others what they do as well. The use of reasoning enables children to think before they act, to hold in check their impulses, and to take into consideration the rights of others.

We Use Love-Oriented Techniques of Discipline

Love-oriented techniques of discipline tend to make for a strong superego whereas thing-oriented techniques of discipline often result in inadequate conscience development. An explanation of terms is in order. Love-oriented techniques involve the giving or withdrawing of either physical or psychological manifestations of love. If the child behaves in a way pleasing to the parent, reward may come in the physical form of hugging or picking the child up, or it may come in the psychological form of letting the child know how proud you are of her, how much she means to you, or how glad you are to have her. Parents who are warm and accepting of the child tend to use the orientation of love to reward the child for behavior deemed desirable. Children find this bond of warmth and affection a most advantageous one and become quite unhappy whenever they feel they have done something to cause a breach in this relationship.

If children are disobedient or act in some other unacceptable way, parents who use love-oriented techniques temporarily withdraw their affection. This physical or psychological separation from the parent prevents the child from getting the amount of attention and affection to which he or she is accustomed. The parent expresses disappointment with the child and conveys that the pleasant relationship they usually have cannot continue under the circumstances. The child may be sent to another room or the parent may "get tears in her eyes and turn away" (Sears, 1960, p. 104), thus reducing or eliminating for a time the conversation between them.

This withdrawal of affection makes children miserable. They feel guilty and ashamed, and in an effort to get back into the good graces of the parent, they will be more willing than before to identify with the values, attitudes, and behaviors expected of them. Not wanting this gap to occur, they begin to resist the temptation of doing those things that are not acceptable. Love-oriented discipline arouses anxiety over losing the parent's love, and to reduce this anxiety the child learns to control unacceptable impulses. Withholding love intensifies the child's need for approval. This technique appears to work, however, only in homes where the parent is basically warm and loving and accepting of the child's dependency. Mothers and fathers who are cold, who normally do not give much love, cannot by lack of attention and affection produce a strong conscience in their children. Apparently one cannot withdraw what is not already there. And, like all forms of discipline, love-oriented techniques will lose effectiveness if used in excess.

Thing-oriented techniques of discipline involve the use of tangible rewards for desirable behavior and physical punishment or deprivation of privileges for undesirable behavior. If the child pleases the parents, the reward comes in getting extra money, toys, or permission to do something generally forbidden, such as staying up at night to watch the late show. If the child displeases the parents he or she is spanked or deprived in some way such as not getting an allowance or going to bed without supper.

All of us who are parents use some combination of love-oriented and thing-oriented techniques. To use one method or the other exclusively would be impossible. There probably are as many combinations of both kinds of discipline as there are homes in which children are being reared. Thus, the comparison is not between homes that are only love-oriented as opposed to those that are only thing-oriented, but rather between homes in which the major controlling factor for keeping the child in line is the love relationship between parent and child as opposed to those in which physical punishment, deprivation of privileges, and tangible rewards are used.

Love-oriented parents will at times use thing-oriented techniques. They may spank or not let the child go out to play. They will find physical punishment effective *on occasion* and deprivation of privileges and tangible rewards productive of desirable results, but this will not be their usual method of discipline and certainly not their preferred method. Children find it natural and easy to identify with love and will generally want to please the parent who is kind and warm. A child growing up in a thing-oriented household, however, will find identification with the parent a more difficult task. It is not natural to identify with someone who often brings pain and unhappiness or who, when pleased, gives money rather than time and favorable attention. Material objects cannot substitute for the companionship of parents.

Why Love-Oriented Techniques Work

The rationale for the effectiveness of love-oriented techniques as opposed to thing-oriented techniques includes such elements as the kind of model provided by the parent, the timing of the punishment, the emotion generated in the child, and the reaction of the child to the punishment. Love-oriented parents model socially desirable behaviors, whereas thing-oriented parents often display the very behaviors they find repugnant in the child. For example, love-oriented parents control their tempers and expect the child to do the same. Thing-oriented parents lash out when irritated and yell or hit, actions they do not wish to see in their children.

The timing of the punishment also makes a difference. Love-oriented procedures take place over a longer time-span than do thing-oriented procedures. Love-withdrawal gives the child time to think about what he or she has done, to engage in a critical evaluation of oneself. A spanking, however, obviates the need for self-punitive thoughts, for the misdeed already has been paid for by suffering physical pain. Moreover, love-withdrawal is terminated when the child engages in the corrective act, such as confession, restitution, or reparation. Physical punishment, by contrast, is more likely to occur and terminate at the time of the deviant act and prior to any corrective act.

The emotion generated when the child in a love-oriented home has done something wrong is usually that of guilt, whereas the emotion generated in the child in a thing-oriented home is usually that of fear. Guilt brings the child to the parent to confess; fear sends the child in the other direction to escape detection. Love-oriented procedures attempt to change the child's behavior by inducing internal forces toward compliance; thing-oriented procedures are more conducive to an orientation based on fear of punishment and less on changing the behavior from unacceptable to acceptable forms. Thing-oriented discipline also is an affront to the child's growing sense of autonomy and may leave the child frustrated and angry.

Observation tends to confirm that when parents accept the normal dependency needs of the child, reason with the child regarding the consequences of behavior, and use love-oriented techniques of discipline, the child is more apt to identify with the parents and with their values. Granted that these procedures are time-consuming and that they lose effectiveness as the child grows older, nevertheless, the development of internal controls must begin early, or they may never form at all. Having a strong conscience or superego is essential for a moral life and should not be left to develop by chance.

CHILDREN WITHOUT A SUPEREGO
BECOME ADULTS WITH A CHARACTER DISORDER

Sadly, some children never develop a superego. They relate only to what will bring pleasure (id) and to what they can get from a world of reality (ego). Not having the internal controls that monitor behavior when no one is present, they cannot be trusted. As adults, they continue to be opportunistic and unpredictable. They exhibit poor judgment and planning, project blame onto others when things go badly, and are unable to form deep and persistent attachments to other persons. If they display these characteristics in extreme form they are called psychopaths, sociopaths, or "moral imbeciles." They are viewed as having a character disorder for they seem to lack anxiety or distress over their behavior and do not see why they are obligated to follow the rules of society. This attitude, coupled with the long-standing nature of the pathology (usually from early childhood), makes therapy virtually impossible. Interestingly, people with a character disorder often create a favorable first impression. They are intelligent, know how to glad-hand others, and have a salesperson type personality. But they also are impulsive, feel no concern over the rights and privileges of others (although they act as if they do), and are masters at saying whatever is necessary to get others to satisfy their desires.

We all know people like this for they are in every walk of life. In some cases it can be shown that as children they were neglected or mistreated, but in other cases no detectable reason can be found, leaving the possibility that constitutional factors may play a part in the pathology. If the problem is not environmentally based, it is most unfair to hold parents accountable for the child's lack of moral development, although since the advent of Freud, parents usually are the ones who are blamed if the child does not become an upstanding member of the community.

IS THERE SUCH A THING AS TOO MUCH SUPEREGO?

At the other end of the continuum are people who are so overcome by anxiety and feelings of guilt that they are unable to enjoy life. Rather than lacking a superego, as is the case with the sociopath, they seemingly have too much superego. They are miserable and afraid, and sometimes to alleviate their distress they will seek therapy.

> Trained to think rigidly about right and wrong, convinced of one's own imperfections and incompetence, fearful of failures or punishment . . . these people are constantly plagued with guilt feelings. These guilt feelings come not because of sorrow for sin or regret over law-breaking. They are signs that the person is preoccupied with a fear of punishment, isolation, or lowered self-esteem. To bolster oneself, such people often are rigid, critical of others, unforgiving, afraid of making moral decisions, domineering, and inclined to assert an attitude of moral superiority . . . they are angry, unhappy people who need help and understanding more than criticism. (Collins, 1980, p. 121)

For such individuals, the ego needs to be strengthened so that a healthy balance between a world of reality and a world of right and wrong will occur. The ego variables of intelligence, an adequate self-concept, and the ability to plan for the future play a role in moral decision-making, as do the superego variables of guilt, confession, and resistance to temptation. Parental standards should not be so high that the child can never succeed, nor should parents withhold love to the point where the child feels continuous blame.

There are times, of course, when guilt feelings are appropriate and even desirable. Guilt is healthy when it brings about a change in behavior from unacceptable to acceptable forms, but guilt is unhealthy when it renders the person anxious and afraid with no change in conduct taking place. As parents we need to know when to praise and when to reprove, when to overlook and when to call attention to the child's actions. What we do and say is crucial to the development of a conscience within the child. To become truly moral, our children's sense of well-being must be tied to the authority of the superego, an authority adopted as their own from the restrictions and beliefs we have given to them.

As we have seen, the psychoanalytic position is that morality develops within children as they internalize the expectations and normative demands of the culture as interpreted to them by the parents; and the critical time for this to occur is between the ages of two and six years. Both ego and superego take shape at this early age, and both ego and superego must grow together, each in harmony with the other, if children are to someday take their place within the society as responsive and responsible adults.

A GOOD ENOUGH PARENT

Bruno Bettelheim (1987) in his book A Good Enough Parent calls for empathy and understanding on the part of the parent. He writes that everyone at times engages in behaviors that are socially unacceptable and for which at the moment there is seemingly no explanation. Many years later, something may trigger in that person's mind the reason why he or she said or did what was done. He gives examples of episodes in his own life when neither he nor his parents understood his actions but it all became clear to him later in life.

It follows, then, that when a child acts in ways that parents label as wrong, there may be very good reasons for the behaviors if only it were known what lay in the unconscious part of the mind. As parents we should exercise patience and not be too quick to judge these actions. If we are aware that we too engage in behaviors that are not always rational or approved of by others, and that unconscious forces are operating within us as well, we will be more apt to be understanding of others. The better we know ourselves, the better we can know our child. "Freud spoke of the sympathy that exists between the unconscious of one person and that of another, suggesting that we can understand another person's unconscious only through our own. One cannot adequately explain what is involved in love, anger, jealousy, or anxiety, nor can words really convey what one feels in depression or elation. But if one has experienced these states of being one knows what another person is likely to be feeling" (Bettelheim, 1987, p. 89).

A good enough parent is comfortable with himself or herself as a person, is not unduly anxious about doing everything right for the child, follows his or her own intuition in child rearing before taking the advice of experts, is aware of the importance of early experiences ("the earlier the experiences are, the more emphatic their influence," p. 11), and has a deep respect for the child's unique personality. A good enough parent is aware that the child passes through stages of development and will make allowances for behaviors typical at each stage of growth. These include "the slow move from living by the primitive pleasure principle, which induces him to try to satisfy desires immediately without any regard for consequences, toward the reality principle, based on the realization that he is often much better off if he modifies some of his desires . . . and the internalization of these demands in the form of the superego" (p. 11).

Bettelheim also says that a good enough parent knows the importance of play and the delicate balance between play and reality. Play helps the child learn about the world and experience a feeling of mastery over it. And a good enough parent is aware of the problems that come in the young person's search for identity and will provide a supportive environment. This is especially difficult "when our adolescent child suddenly and without apparent reason throws a tantrum the way he did as an infant; becomes dirty and as messy as he was years ago; stuffs himself silly, or refuses to eat at all" (p. 156). But the teenager must regress to an earlier time, traveling again through all the stages he has known up to this point, in order to progress to the next stage, namely that of identity.

And always there is conflict. Like all psychoanalysts, Bettelheim emphasizes the constant struggle deep within the personality. "Man will always be beset by deep inner conflicts resulting from the discrepancies between what he is by nature and what he himself—or his parents and educators—wish him to be; that he unavoidably has to struggle against selfish, aggressive, asocial tendencies which are as much part of his evolutionary inheritance and his personal makeup as are his desires to form close emotional attachments; that the egoistic drive for self-preservation is often in painful conflict with altruistic tendencies" (p. 10). The good enough parent, more than anyone else, can provide the environment necessary to help the growing child in his or her struggle to face this inevitable conflict. A deep respect for each child's unique personality is of paramount importance.

GUIDELINES FOR PASTORS

Sigmund Freud likened the church to the army, both being highly organized groups protected from dissolution by the strength of the leader, the camaraderie of the members, and the threat of a foe. In both the church and the army the leader is charged with the welfare of the members, offering protection from forces that would war against the group, and providing direction for the organization as a whole. In the church the leader is Christ; in the army it is the commander-in-chief. "Each individual is bound by libidinal ties on the one hand to the leader (Christ, the Commander-in-Chief) and on the other hand to the other members of the group" (Freud, 1923/1970, p. 444). The stronger the emotional ties of members to the leader and to each other, the stronger the group's chances for survival. The loss of the leader constitutes one of the gravest dangers any organization may face.

Freud gave as examples a general being killed in battle and the soldiers fleeing, and Christ being portrayed as less than divine ("Joseph of Arimathaea confesses that for reasons of piety he secretly removed the body of Christ from its grave.") and therefore unfit to be the head of the church (p. 446). The loss of the leader creates panic because the relationship of members to each other is based on the relationship of each member to the leader. "There is no doubt that the tie which unites each individual with Christ is also the cause of the tie which unites them with one another" (p. 443).

Although the group offers both protection and companionship, it also subjects its members to a common ideology and to a set pattern of behavior. Individuality is not encouraged, nor can it be condoned. Freud saw both the church and the army as authoritarian, each pressuring its members to conform to a standard of conduct determined by the leader. Members cannot have their own ideas of right and wrong and act upon them as this would weaken the structure, bringing diversity and making the organization less effective in fighting a common enemy. Nor are members free to leave the group at will. If they do try to leave, they will be scorned and ridiculed and cast in the role of the adversary, for nothing is more threatening to a group than for its own members to defect. "A religion, even if it calls itself the religion of love, must be hard and unloving to those who do not belong to it" (Freud, 1923/1970, p. 445). Religious groups that are tolerant were seen by Freud not as showing "a softening of human manners," but as indicating "the undeniable weakening of religious feelings and the libidinal ties which depend upon them" (p. 447).

What Is the Christian Church?

Freud by his own confession was not a believer in Christ. Consequently, he viewed the church differently than do those of us who are a part of that great company of believers called the Christian church. Freud saw religious worship as a compulsive act engaged in to relieve one's feelings of guilt. To him, God was nothing more than a glorified father complex stemming from childhood. Furthermore, he believed that science one day would replace religion, for as people come to know more about the world and are better able to control the forces of nature they no longer will be terrified of the elements and seek a deity to provide protection from the unknown.

Such a view, of course, is incompatible with the Christian faith. Those of us who are followers of Christ believe that religious worship is a chosen act, not a compulsive act. We confess our *guilt* to God, not our *feelings* of guilt. God is the great I AM, the one who always was and is and always will be. We did not create Him through the wish for a father figure, but He created us in His own image. Nor can we know Him except as He chooses to reveal Himself to us. Moreover, science will never take the place of faith for only God can control the forces of nature, and we would know nothing about the world and the forces within it apart from an intellect which He has given us.

Is the Church Like an Army?

Freud's likening the church to the army provides an interesting analogy, however, for we read in Scripture that Christians are to be like soldiers ready for battle. We are to put on the full armor of God: the belt of truth, the breastplate of righteousness, the shield of faith, the helmet of salvation, and "the sword of the Spirit, which is the word of God" (Eph. 6:17). And for what purpose? "So that you can take your stand against the devil's schemes" (Eph. 6:11). A good soldier is willing to endure hardship, wants to please his commanding officer, and will not allow himself to be distracted by civilian affairs (2 Tim. 2:3-4). We are told to be good soldiers of Jesus Christ.

WHAT IS THE ROLE OF THE PASTOR?

We also are told to honor those who are placed in a leadership role over us. These lesser leaders when compared to Christ, bear His name, are chosen for their qualities, and are ordained by God to care for the local church (1 Tim. 3:1-10). They serve in many ways — as preachers and teachers, as models of good behavior, and as holding "the deep truths of the faith with a clear conscience" (v. 9). They are deserving of respect for they have chosen "a noble task" (v. 1).

The Pastor as Therapist

The work of the pastor today is much the same as it was in the time of the Apostle Paul. The one who leads the congregation is to preach the Word, visit the sick, and encourage the faithful in the things of the Lord. Pastors are to help those who are troubled, strengthen those who are weak, and bring aid to those in need. Yet pastors today often are assigned another task, namely that of counselor or therapist. In many churches they are expected to function in the role of a psychologist in addition to all the other duties of the clergy. It is thought that pastors should advise on all matters, not just those pertaining to the religious.

But what is not so readily understood is that it takes training to operate in this capacity. One must be educated to recognize the difference between anxiety and conviction, depression and guilt, abreaction and conversion, sickness and sin. If pastors consider all problems brought to them as being spiritual in nature and are unable to sort out the psychic ramifications of a parishioner's disturbance, they may advise in ways that will aggravate the condition, causing irrefutable harm. On the other hand, if they see only the psychological manifestations of the turmoil but do not recognize the spiritual needs of the parishioner, they may prostitute their calling as ministers of the Gospel by glossing over sin and by saying little about the readily available redemption provided for the one who has sinned.

> The pastor or church leader who takes on the role of therapist should be prepared to handle any situation that may arise. This includes knowing what to do if the church member "falls in love" during therapy sessions. Even as it is not uncommon for a client to develop strong feelings of love or hate for the therapist, it is not uncommon for the parishioner to develop strong feelings of love or hate for the minister.

The pastor or church leader who takes on the role of therapist should be prepared to handle any situation that may arise. This includes knowing what to do if the church member "falls in love" during therapy sessions. Even as it is not uncommon for a client to develop strong feelings of love or hate for the therapist, it is not uncommon for the parishioner to develop strong feelings of love or hate for the minister. Psychoanalysts are trained in such matters. They consider the *transference* between themselves and the patient a normal phase of the therapeutic process and are prepared to resolve any conflicts that may arise before sessions are terminated. But the clergy is not trained in this way, and some ministers have become so traumatized by a parishioner's feelings of intense love that they have behaved indiscreetly or have refused to see the person again. In some cases scandal has ensued, and the minister has had to leave the church.

The Pastor as Preacher
The clergy's desire to know more about the field of psychology in an effort to help those within the church who are suffering from emotional stress is to be commended. Other things being equal, the pastor who is knowledgeable in psychotherapy will be in a better position to counsel those who have emotional needs than the pastor without this knowledge. Nevertheless, the Christian minister should remember that the principal calling of the clergy is to faithfully

preach the Word of God, not to perform the duties of a psychothera-
pist. Karl Menninger (1973) has made a case for the preaching of
repentance as being more therapeutic than the practice of counseling.
He says this is so because preaching reaches a larger number of people
and also serves to inhibit the kind of life that contributes to mental
illness. As he put it in *Whatever Became of Sin?*:

> Some clergymen prefer pastoral counseling of individuals to the pulpit
> function. But the latter is a greater opportunity to both heal and prevent.
> An ounce of prevention is worth a pound of cure, indeed, and there is
> much prevention to be done for large numbers of people who hunger
> and thirst after direction toward righteousness. Clergymen have a golden
> opportunity to prevent some of the accumulated misapprehensions,
> guilt, aggressive action, and other roots of later mental suffering and
> mental disease.
>
> How? Preach! Tell it like it is. Say it from the pulpit. Cry it from the
> housetops.
>
> What shall we cry? Cry comfort, cry repentance, cry hope. Because
> recognition of our part in the world transgression is the only remaining
> hope. (p. 228)

The Pastor as Friend

For those within the church, Karl Menninger's comments surely are
valid. But what about those who are not members of the church and do
not feel at home within its walls? What if they hear the preaching of the
Gospel, feel convicted, and confess their sins, but no one in the church
befriends them and the pastor never follows up to see if they are
growing in the Lord? What if there are no hands to sustain, no hearts to
love, no prayers to uphold them before the throne of grace? Will they
be able to change their ways and live Christian lives because they have
heard the minister preach? Will the feelings of guilt and the overt
expressions of confession be enough to make them new persons, moral
persons before God?

For some the answer may be in the affirmative, but for others it is
not. Psychologist Joseph Hunt (1938) gives an account of several young
men for whom more than preaching was needed. He writes of talking
with an adult patient on the psychiatric ward of St. Elizabeth's Hospital
in Washington, D.C., who informed him that five of his neighborhood

gang of fifteen were confined to that institution. When hospital records confirmed this high percentage, Hunt became interested. He asked the informant, identified as Ww, to tell as much as he could remember about each of the boys. Ww described the neighborhood as poor, alcoholism was common, and the boys received little or no parental guidance. By the time most of the gang were in their teens they were introduced to homosexuality by the laborers at a slaughterhouse and to bestiality by the men who kept the barns where race horses were wintered. The boys often visited these places and regularly engaged in the perversions.

In the same community was a church where frequent revival services were held. Some of this group attended the services and experienced intense feelings of guilt over their perversions. Ww mentioned that one evening he went forward four times, crying each time, and was informed that once each evening was sufficient. After these times of guilt and confession, the boys who went forward would tell each other that they were not going to return to the perversions. But when sexual tensions would mount and they were teased by other members of the gang who did not attend the revival services, they would break their resolves and return to their former behavior. Ww reported that by the time they were in late adolescence, they were almost continuously miserable. They quit school, did odd jobs, and drank heavily. There was seemingly no way to escape the conflict between the sexual perversions and the religious values. The guilt not only did not deter them from immoral behavior, but also served to intensify their unhappiness. Hunt noted that of the seven who frequented both the slaughterhouse and the church, five were committed to the hospital. Those who indulged in the perversions but did not attend the revival services and those who went to the revival services but did not frequent the slaughterhouse or barns were not hospitalized.

In the case of these young men, the church had preached the consequences of sin and the need to confess, but this message had not sustained them in the hour of temptation. As boys growing up they needed to be with Christians, to see how Christians live, to be befriended by the young people and the pastor of the church who had values different than their own. But this did not take place and, although they repented of their sins, they did not have the power to follow through on their resolves. In *psychoanalytic* terms, Ww and the others who went to the revival services fluctuated between a superego that condemned and an id that demanded gratification. At no time was the ego, that component of the personality that makes rational decisions and carries them through, operating on their behalf. In *theological* terms, these young men had strong feelings of guilt, but the guilt did not bring them to salvation. They experienced a "worldly sorrow" rather than a "godly sorrow" and so were unable to change their behavior (2 Cor. 7:10).

THE PASTOR AS YOUTH MINISTER

Erik Erikson's writings on the psychosocial stage of identity has been of considerable interest to those who work with teenagers and young adults. James Marcia (1980) has extended Erikson's sense of identity to describe four identity types: identity diffusion, moratorium, identity achievement, and foreclosure.

Identity diffusion types tend to be aimless, disorganized, and opportunistic. They give little thought to past or future, play different roles depending on who they are with, and generally have poor self-concepts. In school they take the easiest classes and do not care what others do as long as they are allowed to do whatever they please. Family relations are often poor with a father who takes an authoritarian approach to child rearing. Identity diffused adolescents seemingly have no desire to join the adult world with its responsibilities and values. Ww and his friends were probably identity diffusion types who happened to wander into the church where revival services were being held because they had nothing more interesting to do at the time.

Moratorium types are aware that they must come to terms with occupation, sex role, and values but they are not prepared to make these decisions while in their teens or early twenties. They need a period of experimentation in which they change majors, try different jobs, go from one intense relationship to another, and convert to a succession of ideologies or religions. They tend to be anxious, extreme in their views, independent, competitive, and quite unpredictable. Because a period of moratorium is a luxury working youths cannot afford, moratorium types are more visible among college students who have been raised by permissive parents. Moratorium types may show a strong commitment to their faith and be leaders in the youth group at church.

But then they are gone to embrace another view or philosophy, only to move on again to still another in the months or years that follow. Moratorium types usually settle down in time, taking their place as responsible adults.

Identity achievement types tend to be stable and mature, consistent in behavior and attitudes, and effective in interpersonal relationships. They often have a firm commitment to occupational choice and are comfortable with their religious values. They know who they are and where they are going. If all goes well, there is little identity crisis. If, however, doors are closed to their chosen profession, or they are jilted by their boyfriend or girlfriend whom they intend to marry, or their religion does not meet their scrutiny, identity achievement types are thrown into a time of searching for what went wrong. Given their desirable personality characteristics and a supportive family, they usually come to terms with alternatives and make a satisfactory adjustment. Compared with the other types, these young people have a distinct advantage. Identity achievement young people are the "straight arrows" who are desired in any church and can be counted on to enhance the work of the Lord in the years to come.

Foreclosure types also know what occupation they wish to pursue, the kind of person they will marry, and the religious faith they espouse. However, these aspirations come directly from the parents and are accepted without question. The young woman who becomes a hairstylist like her mother and gets her training at the same school is probably an example of foreclosure, that is, if she has always understood that this is what she will do. Foreclosure types are often working youths who marry early and raise a family. They seem not to go through the identity crisis seen in their peers. Studies show, though, that they are more vulnerable to criticism, more accepting of traditional values, and more inclined to do what they are told by authority figures (Marcia, 1967). They usually come from families in which the father is controlling but not harsh. Of the four groups, they are lowest in autonomy and highest in need for social approval (Orlofsky, Marcia, & Lesser, 1973). If their place of work closes, their spouse leaves, or the pastor of their church is involved in a scandal, foreclosure types find it more difficult to pick up the pieces and get on with their lives. Foreclosure young people are the "good kids" who seldom get into trouble, cause their parents no pain, and can be counted on to be the backbone of the church. However, they need constant praise and encouragement to have a feeling of worth.

The pastor as youth minister will have all four identity types in the church. Identity diffused teens are seldom there unless accompanied by the parent. They have little desire to be in a religious service and come only when they are made to do so. There are more interesting places to be and more interesting things to do. All of us have observed these young people. They may be the children of our best friend, the deacon, the pastor himself, or even our own children. In each case, the caring parent is hoping for a "miracle" whereby this teenager will have a change of heart and become a completely different type of person. A charismatic pastor or youth minister who develops an exciting program of activities may be able to keep the identity diffused youngster interested long enough to communicate that the future makes sense for those who trust God. Reaching these youngsters who tend to drift aimlessly is more apt to occur during the early adolescent years while they are still in church than when they are older and on their own.

Moratorium types need patience. It does little good to try to get them to settle down before they are ready. They must make their own decisions in their own good time as to occupation, beliefs, and values. The period of experimentation may last into the late twenties or thirties, but they are learning a great deal in the meantime and will in the end make a contribution to the society and perhaps to the church as well.

Identity achievement and foreclosure types are what most parents and pastors prefer. These young people have either arrived at self-chosen commitments or have accepted the goals and values of their families. Either way, they know what they want and are preparing for their life's work. They provide a stable, dependable nucleus within the church and can be counted on to become leaders within the parish as they mature. It is important to both types that they, in turn, can count on the pastor to be the kind of person who is worthy of his calling and who is upright and honest in every aspect of life. Immorality in any form will cause the work of the Lord to be hindered.

IN CONCLUSION

Teachers, parents, and pastors who embrace the Christian faith will not agree with Freud that we create God out of our own imagination and that our image of God is based largely on our interactions with parents — especially as these interactions relate to the resolution of the Oedipal complex. But we do agree with Freud that religious faith comes early in the child's life, and this faith has an affective component that resides at the unconscious level even before an understanding of faith takes place.

Teachers and pastors continue the work begun by parents. If parents are not believers, the Christian teacher or pastor may play the role of the parent in introducing the child to the Christian faith. "The close relationship of God concept with self-concept brings the religious education task close to the general task of child-rearing" (Meadow & Kahoe, 1984, p. 79). Our responsibility to the next generation is great and one to be taken seriously. That internal monitor of behavior called the conscience or superego is essential for moral growth to take place. And it comes, not from heredity but from the interactions of significant people in the child's life, ready to be passed down to the next generation when the child becomes an adult. In this way our influence extends long past the time we are actively engaged in the process of Christian education. We have the promise that "from everlasting to everlasting the Lord's love is with those who fear Him, and His righteousness with their children's children" (Ps. 103:17).

NOTES

1. There has been an alarming proliferation in recent years of private mental hospitals that encourage parents to commit their difficult teenager to their care. In a special report by Patti Jones (1990, October), "Don't put me away, mom, please!" *Redbook*, pp. 140–148, it is stated that the typical patient is white and between fifteen and seventeen years of age. Private health insurance pays the bill. These institutions exploit parents' fears and, driven by the need for profit, may create an artificial demand. Some offer free examinations and increase the salary of employees who recruit patients. It is estimated that less than 40 percent of teenagers committed by their parents are psychotic, on drugs, or have some other disorder that would warrant their being in a hospital. The rest exhibit behaviors that are irritating to parents yet fall under normal adolescent personality traits.

2. Sex education programs fall into two major categories: those that encourage abstinence and those that encourage responsible decision-making. Among the programs that

encourage abstinence are "Family values and sex education," available from *Focus on the Family* in Colorado Springs, CO; "Teen sexual behavior: A leader's resource of practical strategies with youth" from *American Alliance for Health, Physical Education, Recreation and Dance* in Reston, VA; and "Why wait" from *Josh McDowell Ministry* in San Bernardino, CA. Among the programs that encourage responsible decision-making are "Take charge of your life," a workbook sponsored by the California State Department of Health Services and used by the Salvation Army; "Safe sex," a booklet written by Verne Becker (1988) and distributed by InterVarsity Press; "OCTOPUS — A church-based sex education program for teens and parents" (*Adolescence, 19,* 757–783, 1984) that includes nurses, educators, counselors and ministers.

REFERENCES

Aichhorn, A. (1963). *Wayward youth.* New York: Viking. (Original work published 1925)

Aries, P. (1962). *Centuries of childhood: A social history of family life* (R. Baldick, Trans.). New York: Alfred A. Knopf.

Bettelheim, B. (1970). Moral education. In N.F. Sizer & T.R. Sizer (Eds.), *Moral education: Five lectures* (pp. 84–107). Cambridge, MA: Harvard University Press.

————. (1987). *A good enough parent.* New York: Alfred A. Knopf.

Chace, S. (1989, October). My generation. *Seventeen,* pp. 99–106.

Clouse, B. (1991). Adolescent moral development and sexuality. In D. Ratcliff & J.A. Davies (Eds.), *Handbook of youth ministry* (pp. 178–213). Birmingham, AL: Religious Education Press.

Collins, G.R. (1980). *Christian counseling: A comprehensive guide.* Waco, TX: Word Inc.

Erikson, E.H. (1980). *Identity and the life cycle.* New York: W.W. Norton.

Freud, A. (1935). *Psychoanalysis for teachers and parents* (B. Low, Trans.). New York: Emerson Books.

Freud, S. (1968). The claims of psycho-analysis to scientific interest. In J. Strachey (Ed. and Trans.), *The standard edition of the complete psychological works of Sigmund Freud* (Vol. 13, pp. 163–190). London: Hogarth. (Original work published 1913)

————. (1970). Two artificial groups: The church and the army. In V. Comerchero (Ed.), *Values in conflict* (pp. 442–447). New York: Appleton-Century-Crofts. (Original work published 1923)

Gallup Report. (1987, August). More today than in 1985 say premarital sex is wrong. Report No. 263, p. 20.

Hague, W.J. (1986). *New perspectives on religious and moral development.* (Report No. ISBN-0-88864-939-8). Edmonton, Alberta, Canada: University of Alberta. (ERIC Document Reproduction Service No. ED 272 407)

Hunt, J. McV. (1938). An instance of the social origin of conflict resulting in psychoses. *American Journal of Orthopsychiatry, 8,* 158–164.

Jensen, L., Newell, R.J., & Holman, T. (1990). Sexual behavior, church attendance, and permissive beliefs among unmarried young men and women. *Journal for the Scientific Study of Religion, 29,* 113–117.

Joseph, D.A., & Joseph P.B. (1977). Teaching children with deficient value systems. In L.J. Stiles & B.D. Johnson (Eds.), *Morality examined: Guidelines for teachers* (pp. 105–119). Princeton, NJ: Princeton Book Company.

Kelly, E.W., Jr. (1973). School phobia: A review of theory and treatment. *Psychology in the Schools, 10,* 33–42.

Mahoney, E.R. (1980). Religiosity and sexual behavior among heterosexual college students. *Journal of Sex Research, 16,* 97–113.

Marcia, J.E. (1967). Ego identity status: Relationship to change in self-esteem, "general maladjustment," and authoritarianism. *Journal of Personality, 35,* 119–133.

_____. (1980). Identity in adolescence. In J. Adelson (Ed.), *Handbook of adolescent psychology* (pp. 159–187). New York: John Wiley.

McCormick, N., Izzo, A., & Folcik, J. (1985). Adolescents' values, sexuality, and contraception in a rural New York county. *Adolescence, 20,* 385–395.

Meadow, M.J., & Kahoe, R.D. (1984). *Psychology of religion: Religion in individual lives.* New York: Harper & Row.

Menninger, K. (1973). *Whatever became of sin?* New York: Hawthorn Books.

Miller, J.P. (1978). Piaget, Kohlberg, and Erikson: Developmental implications for secondary education. *Adolescence, 13,* 237–250.

Orlofsky, J.L., Marcia, J.E., & Lesser, I.M. (1973). Ego identity status and the intimacy vs. isolation crisis of young adulthood. *Journal of Personality and Social Psychology, 27,* 211–219.

Russell, A. (1990, Winter/Spring). Adolescence: Path to a productive life or a diminished future? *Carnegie Quarterly, 35,* 1–13.

Sarason, S.B., Davidson, K.S., Lighthall, F.F., Waite, R.R., & Ruebush, B.K. (1960). *Anxiety in elementary school children: A report of research.* New York: John Wiley & Sons.

Sears, R. (1960). The growth of conscience. In I. Iscoe & H.W. Stevenson (Eds.), *Personality development in children* (pp. 92–111). Austin: University of Texas Press.

Sheppard, S. (1989, November/December). The case for chastity: 7 ways to help your teen save sex for marriage. *Christian Parenting Today,* pp. 67–71.

Wallis, G. (1985, December 9). Children having children. *Time,* pp. 78–90.

Woodroof, J.T. (1986). Reference groups, religiosity, and premarital sexual behavior. *Journal for the Scientific Study of Religion, 25,* 436–460.

SIX

Moral Growth by Moral Behavior: A Learning View

How do our words relate to our actions? In an innovative study, a group of students at Princeton Theological Seminary were asked to prepare a short talk to be delivered at another building on campus. Some were assigned the Parable of the Good Samaritan; others were to speak on the vocational interests of seminarians. Preparation time was short, some students having only the few minutes it took to walk between the two buildings to decide what they would say while others were given a little more time before they were to make their presentation. The researchers (Darley & Batson, 1973) used the path between the buildings as their own version of the road from Jerusalem to Jericho. Slumped along the way they placed a shabbily dressed person with eyes closed, coughing and groaning. Which seminarians would help the "victim"? Would the topic to be addressed make a difference? Would time constraints be a factor?

The results showed that it made no difference what the talk was about. "Indeed, on several occasions, a seminary student going to give his talk on the parable of the Good Samaritan literally stepped over the victim as he hurried on his way" (p. 107). How much time the student had, though, was important. Those who were told they were already late were significantly less apt to offer aid than those who were not so rushed.[1]

It is one thing to talk about compassion; it is quite another to engage in compassionate behavior. What we say or what we think or how we feel does not affect others as directly as what we do. It is our actions that speak louder than words. It is our overt expression of kindness or generosity or caring that makes the difference in other people's lives.

All psychologists, regardless of orientation, recognize that for psychology to be a science, what is studied must be open; that is, any topic must be publically verifiable and expressed in a way that can be measured. "A commitment to scientific method continues to distinguish psychology from philosophy, a view from which few psychologists would dissent" (Chiesa, 1992, p. 1298). But what sets learning psychology apart from the other psychologies is its almost exclusive emphasis on an inductive approach that fastens on the behavior itself and on the events within the environment that increase or decrease that behavior. By studying overt behaviors (called responses) and environmental events (called stimuli) researchers can note cause-effect relationships and supply information that is more accurate than information obtained in any other way. The deductive method of hypothesis testing and theoretical formulation used by many psychologists is not one that learning psychologists find to be attractive.

The area of morality is no exception. We may say that what we do stems from the ideas of right and wrong we internalized from our parents (see chap. 4), from our own reasoning about what is good and what is bad (see chap. 8), or from our naturally wanting to be good persons (see chap. 10); but the learning position is that we do not need to study feelings, thoughts, or other internal conditions to explain morality. Nor do we need to speak of innate goodness or innate depravity in accounting for why we do the things we do. Although not totally denying the realm of emotions or the life of the mind, or even the existence of their own souls, learning psychologists insist that it is only as psychology uses the method of science, linking environmental events with observable behaviors, that humankind is in a position to control its world and understand its conduct. The environment is all important to what a person does.

Psychologists who look at behavior as having been learned from the environment go by a variety of names including those of "behaviorists" because they emphasize overt behaviors, "associationists" because they show the relationship of one stimulus to another, "S-R psychologists" because they link stimuli and responses, and "learning psychologists" because they believe that people learn to be whatever they become. But whatever the name, these men and women comprise one of the largest groups of American psychologists and their record over the years is impressive. Beginning with salivating dogs and proceeding to cats in puzzle boxes and rats running mazes, learning psychologists have extended their studies upward along the phylogenetic scale to show that many of the laws operative in animal learning are applicable to complex kinds of human behaviors as well.

The learning approach, then, adopts the position that people start out neutral and learn to be whatever they are made to be by the environment. Our personalities, interests, temperaments, and motivations are the result of our experiences. We learn to be pleasant or disagreeable, happy or sad, aggressive or helpful, capable or ineffective. And we learn to be moral — or immoral, as the case may be. If we grow up in a good environment we learn to be good. If we grow up in a bad environment we learn to be bad. Most of us are both good and bad, good when we are with good people and bad when we are with bad people. And, as we said, whether we are good or bad depends on what we *do*, on how we behave.

There are three major areas in learning psychology; namely, classical conditioning, instrumental (operant) conditioning, and social learning. We will look at these in turn, noting how each relates to moral growth.

CLASSICAL CONDITIONING

People have been interested in psychology for hundreds of years, but it was not until Wilhelm Wundt, son of a Lutheran pastor, founded the first psychological laboratory in Germany in 1879 that psychology could be said to have become a science. Later, around the turn of the century, a Russian physiologist by the name of Ivan Pavlov, using methods similar to Wundt's, made an interesting discovery. Pavlov noticed that dogs in the laboratory would salivate to the sound of a bell if they associated the bell with getting food. Pavlov called salivating to the bell a psychic secretion to differentiate it from the unlearned physical reaction of salivating to food. Pavlov did not consider himself a psychologist, but the word "psychic" used in the experiment seemed to stick, and today "psychology" is often used to mean the study of animal and human behavior and seldom to mean the study of the "psyche," or soul, as its literal interpretation would imply.

WATSON'S LITTLE ALBERT

The conditioning method used by Pavlov was adopted in the 1920s by an American psychologist named John B. Watson, who, with his assistant, Rosalie Rayner, conditioned an eleven-month-old child to fear a white rat. "Little Albert," as he is known in psychological circles, liked to play with furry creatures, but he did not like loud noises. Earlier studies made Watson believe that infants have a fundamental or unlearned fear of loud noises, so when Albert reached for the white rat, Watson sounded a loud noise behind him. After several pairings of the rat (the conditioned stimulus) with the noise (the unconditioned stimulus), Albert reacted to the rat in the same way that he did to the noise. Just seeing the rat made Albert cry and try to crawl away (Watson & Rayner, 1920).

Pavlov had found that dogs would salivate not only to the original conditioned stimulus of the bell but to other bells as well. How much salivation occurred depended on how close in tone a second bell was to the original bell. This phenomenon is known as *stimulus generalization,* which means that the learner will generalize from the original conditioned stimulus to other stimuli similar to it. Watson saw this with Little Albert as well. Not only did Albert learn to fear the rat but he also learned to fear objects resembling a rat. Albert became afraid of a white rabbit, a sealskin coat, a Santa Claus mask, and Watson's hair. Albert even showed a reaction to cotton, although cotton was too far removed in similarity to the rat to produce much of a response. Albert showed no fear of blocks and other objects that did not resemble a rat (Harris, 1979).

The significance of Watson's study is apparent. He had shown that the emotions people experience may be learned by pairing one stimulus with another. No longer need one look for mentalistic explanations or internal forces to account for human responses. What was needed was to identify the observable conditions that influence behavior. In order to control behavior one had only to supply the proper stimuli at the proper time. Here was a science of psychology unhampered by introspective techniques and deductive assumptions. Here was a cause-effect relationship between stimuli and responses, between the environment and what one does (Watson, 1931).

Watson was so pleased with the results that he said he could take any healthy infant and by controlling the infant's environment he could make the child into any kind of specialist he might select—a doctor or a lawyer, a merchant or a chief, and even a beggar or a thief. It was the environment that made people what they are, not their ancestry or temperament or any special innate abilities. To Watson the environment and the behaviors resulting from the environment were the proper subjects for psychology. "For Watson, the road to progress in psychology was to follow after the natural sciences in dealing only with empirically verifiable constructs (i.e., behavior); thus behavior was understood through its material and causal relationships to other behaviors and environmental events" (Jones & Butman, 1991, p. 147).

Watson did not have the opportunity to continue his studies. He became involved in a divorce scandal and was dismissed from his post. Unable to find another position in the academic world because of the incident, Watson left the field of psychology and became a businessman. His influence, nevertheless, continued and is still felt today. Known as a behaviorist because he emphasized overt behaviors and the environment that produced those behaviors, Watson's ideas were readily received by Americans who wanted to believe that heredity means little and environment means a great deal.

CLASSICAL CONDITIONING IS EVERYWHERE

The effects of classical conditioning are all around us. We see it in animals as well as in our own behavior. The family cat comes running and meowing when she hears the electric can opener. The sound of the can opener (a conditioned stimulus) has been associated with getting food (an unconditioned stimulus). Her meowing awakens the dog who comes running to see if there is food for him. The cat's conditioned response of meowing becomes the dog's conditioned stimulus to come, the dog previously having associated a meowing cat in the kitchen with getting food. Horses also are trained by the process of classical conditioning. Both "giddap" and "whoa" (conditioned stimuli) have been associated with natural stimuli that unconditionally produce the response of going or the response of stopping.

As a labor-saving device, ranchers in southwestern Japan are putting beepers (conditioned stimuli) on cows to call them to their chow (unconditioned stimuli). At the Shimane Prefectural Animal Husbandry Experiment Station in Japan "the cows learned to respond to the pagers during a week of Pavlov-inspired training, when they listened to beepers while they chewed wheat husks at the feed lot" (Rancher using pocket beeper to summon cows for chow, 1992).

At the human level, as well, all of us have experienced seeing someone we have never seen before and having an immediate emotional reaction. If we are drawn to this person, we may tell ourselves it is "love at first sight." If we are repulsed, we turn the other way. In classical conditioning terms, stimulus generalization has occurred. The person reminds us of someone we already know. Even if we cannot remember who the original person (conditioned stimulus) is, we know immediately whether our reaction to the original person was favorable or unfavorable by our reaction to the one just seen. The emotion remains even though our knowledge of the original conditioning may not.

In one of my graduate classes I had two students by the name of Sandra. One Sandra insisted that I call her Sandy, the other wanted to be called by her given name. Upon inquiry I found what I had suspected; namely, in each case "Sandra" was linked with an unconditioned stimulus that was unfavorable in the case of Sandy and favorable in the case of Sandra. Sandy associated her name with a father who yelled "Sandra" whenever he was angry with her; Sandra associated her name with a father who used it when he was pleased with what she did. Years after leaving their respective households, they both responded to their names on the basis of events that had occurred many years before.

CLASSICAL CONDITIONING AND THE HIGHER MENTAL PROCESSES

Over the years conditioning studies have become more sophisticated so that now very complex kinds of human behaviors may be attributed to classical conditioning. As was mentioned, words are conditioned stimuli that have been paired with concrete referents (unconditioned stimuli). These words, in turn, may be associated with other words, resulting in "verbal habit-families" (Staats, 1961) and bringing about higher mental processes, such as language acquisition, concept formation, and problem-solving. Both the emotions generated by words and the meaning of words have been explained by classical conditioning.

When people react in different ways to the same word, as in the case of "Sandra," it is because they have learned the words in different settings. "Each language has a history of development within a cultural context. Peoples who were scattered over the earth developed language patterns that reflect their way of experiencing life in particular regions and the development of their cultures" (Steensma, 1977). Words like *communism, humanism, Christianity,* and *Buddhism* evoke varying reactions. One man's meat is another man's poison. The learning psychologist would say that if we were raised in the same environment and had the same experience as the people we disagree with, and if they had been raised as we had been, we would have their attitudes and they, ours. Recognizing this should make us less judgmental of others when their ideologies conflict with our own.

INSTRUMENTAL CONDITIONING

All learning does not take place by a process of classical conditioning. Some learning occurs because the consequence of behavior results in the behavior being repeated. This is known as instrumental conditioning. It differs from classical conditioning in that instrumental conditioning is based on what follows the response rather than on what has preceded it. A dog lopes down the road, turning left at the intersection. A baby lies in a crib making baby noises. A man whistles while he works. A student types a term report. Unlike the reflexive act of salivation or the emotion felt when seeing someone who reminds us of someone else, these behaviors occur because the organism is capable of making the response and has found the response to be useful or instrumental. The dog finds food to the left rather than to the right or straight ahead. The baby receives attention from the mother. The man enjoys the sound of his whistling. The student gets a better grade with a typed report. In each case, it is the consequence of the behavior rather than a prior stimulus that determines its continuance.

Instrumental conditioning, unlike classical, usually involves responses that are spontaneous. The responses seem to emanate from the learner and are said to be emitted. Emitted behaviors are called operants because they operate on the environment to produce results. Often when we say we have learned something we are talking about a change in behavior that has occurred due to instrumental conditioning. Motor skills such as walking or writing a letter, intellectual skills such as saying the Gettysburg Address or memorizing the multiplication tables, and moral behaviors such as telling the truth or helping another person would be examples of learning by a process of instrumental conditioning.

B.F. SKINNER'S OPERANT CONDITIONING

The fact that living beings, both animal and human, respond to the consequences of their behavior has been known for centuries, but it was not until B.F. Skinner of Harvard University wrote *The Behavior of Organisms* in 1938 that the position now known as instrumental (operant) conditioning was formalized. His later works (1953, 1971, 1983) clarify and expand the position. Skinner did not deny the existence of mental processes, but like other learning psychologists he took the view that if psychology is to explain behavior it must of necessity look at overt responses and at the environment that accompanies those responses.

Skinner further believed that it is truly the environment with its reinforcers and punishers that determines human behavior, not mentalistic desire or choice. People are not free agents governing their own lives, but rather they are the products of environmental contingencies. A person may speak of willpower or of self-control, but these terms are misnomers. No one is free; all are controlled by the environment. We may say we are free, usually when we are fortunate in having a favorable environment, but we are only fooling ourselves, making it more difficult to understand why we act as we do. We feel not free when our lives are filled with noxious or painful events, yet we are no more free when we feel free than when we do not. Reinforcers are as important as punishers in determining behavior, and our awareness of environmental effects or lack thereof in no way changes the facts.

In *Beyond Freedom and Dignity* (1971), Skinner explained his position.

Man's struggle for freedom is not due to a will to be free. . . . The literature of freedom . . . has been successful in reducing the aversive stimuli used in intentional control, but it has made the mistake of defining freedom in terms of states of mind or feelings, and it has therefore not been able to deal effectively with techniques of control. . . . It is unprepared for the next step which is not to free men from control but to analyze and change the kinds of control to which they are exposed. (pp. 41-42)

Attitudes, as well as feelings, are not reliable guides. In 1987, he wrote that if we want a change in behavior we will look not at attitudes but at what happens within the environment.

If I turn off unnecessary lights and appliances in my home, it is not because I have a "positive attitude" toward conservation, but because doing so has had some kind of reinforcing consequence. To induce people to conserve energy, one must change contingencies of reinforcement, not attitudes. No one should try to beat a "path from information to action," because action is the problem and contingencies the solution. (Skinner, 1987, p. 785)

B.F. SKINNER (1904–1990)

Considered by many to be America's most influential psychologist, Burrhus Frederic Skinner was active in experimental psychology for a span of sixty-three years. He majored in English while in college, intending to become a novelist, but decided against it when he found, as he put it, he "had nothing to say." He applied to Harvard to become a scientific psychologist and received the doctorate in 1931. Following a period of research at Harvard, he accepted a teaching appointment at the University of Minnesota in 1936, the same year he married Yvonne Blue. He chaired the psychology department at Indiana University from 1945 to 1948, returning to Harvard in 1948 where he remained until his death.

Fred Skinner was born in Susquehanna, Pennsylvania into a warm and stable family. His only sibling, a younger brother, died suddenly of a cerebral aneurism at the age of sixteen. Mary Graves, his teacher for eight grades in a one-room school, had a profound influence on him, introducing him to the world of books. He loved school, often begging the janitor to let him into the schoolhouse before anyone else arrived. He lived in the same house all through childhood and went to the high school his parents attended. When he wasn't studying, he spent his time building things — wagons, merry-go-rounds, and rafts; reading a variety of materials, especially Francis Bacon; playing the piano and saxophone; and writing poems and stories. His parents were quite religious, and his grandmother once impressed upon him the concept of hell by showing him the glowing bed of coals in the parlor stove. By the time he left home to go to college he no longer accepted his parents' faith.

Skinner's inventiveness often took a practical turn. (He had built a flotation device while in high school to separate ripe from green elderberries.) So, when he and his wife decided to have a second child and she said she didn't mind bearing children but that the first two years were very difficult, he decided to build an air crib — a clean, roomy, glass-enclosed structure in which warm air circulated through a tightly stretched sheet. Being climate controlled, baby Deborah needed only a diaper even in the cold of winter. The crib was used as any crib would be, namely, to give the infant a safe place to sleep and play. She was often taken out for interactions with the family. The vicious rumors of Deborah being psychologically damaged by the experience simply were not true.

Walden Two was published in 1948 and sold more than a million copies in paperback. Written in seven weeks, it describes a fictional community in which operant conditioning principles are applied to every aspect of personal and social life. Inspired by its message, communes began springing up in the 1960s across the continent, Twin Oaks in the foothills of Virginia being one of the best known. Although the communities have since folded, plagued by economic problems and the exodus of some of its more capable members, the controversy generated by Walden Two continues between those who adore Skinner as a messiah and those who abhor him as a menace.

Professor Skinner received numerous awards including the American Psychological Association's Distinguished Scientific Award in 1958 and the Gold Medal Award of the American Psychological Foundation in 1971. He was diagnosed with leukemia in November of 1989 and told he only had a few months to live. "I'm not religious," he said in a 1990 interview with a National Public Radio correspondent, "so I don't worry about what will happen after I'm dead. . . . The only thing that touched me was the thought that I will have to tell my wife and my daughters. You see, when you die, you hurt people. Because they love you. And you can't help it. . . . That bothered me" (p. 12).

On August 10, 1990, eight days before his death, he accepted in person a Citation for Outstanding Lifetime Contribution to Psychology at the 98th Annual Convention of the American Psychological Association in Boston. He was lauded as "a creative scientist . . . a pioneer in psychology . . . an intellectual leader . . . a citizen of the world."

B.F. Skinner continued to be productive until the time of his death. He would rise every morning at a quarter to five (as he had for the past 30 years) have a cup of coffee, and be at his desk by 5:00. His most productive hours were from 5:00 to 7:00. After that he did what he pleased, which included listening to Wagner at full volume. He sustained a close relationship with his wife of fifty-three years and was very fond of his two daughters, one of whom took a leave from her family and work as a psychologist to be with her father during his final days. Of his last days he observed, "I've had a very good life. . . . I'm enjoying these last months as well as I ever enjoyed life" (p. 12).

Trudeau, M. "An introspective discussion with B.F. Skinner." *Science Briefs*, Oct./Nov., 1990, pp. 10-12.

Even the word "mind" is misunderstood. "Often, however, 'mind' means little more than 'do.' . . . Those who 'speak their mind' say what they have to say. We are cautioned to avoid falling by 'minding our step' in the sense of noticing it. Students 'mind their teachers' in the sense of obeying them, and teachers 'mind their students' in the sense of watching them" (Skinner, 1989, p. 17). And on the evening before his death, Skinner (1990) penned these words: "The history of psychology is informative. It began 100 years ago, with an introspective search for mind. Watson attacked introspection in his behavioristic manifesto of 1913, and for that or other reasons introspection was essentially abandoned. Behaviorists turned to the study of behavior for its own sake. . . ." (p. 1210)

REINFORCERS AND PUNISHERS

In instrumental conditioning the controls are called reinforcers and punishers. There are two types of reinforcers, positive and negative. A positive reinforcer is any stimulus which, when added to the situation, increases the probability of the response. Positive reinforcers for a child would be consumables, such as candy or pop; manipulatables, such as trinkets or toys; social, such as a smile or a compliment; or the use of the Premack method.

The Premack method was named after David Premack (1965) who wrote that high probability behavior may be used to reinforce low probability behavior. High probability behavior for a child may be playing Nintendo™ games, and low probability behavior may be studying. If playing Nintendo™ games means the child does not get studying done, then playing them may be contingent upon having completed a specified amount of studying first. The idea, of course, is not new. Mothers for years have told their children, "Take out the garbage and then you can go play." But being aware of the seemingly endless possibilities of the Premack method increases the alternatives for dealing effectively with ourselves and with others.

A negative reinforcer is any stimulus which, when *removed* from the situation, increases the probability of the response. The stimulus removed should be negative, or undesirable, in order for its removal to be reinforcing. For instance, we tend to avoid people who constantly complain about how they feel. Listening to them talk about their aches and pains is irritating. We also put on sunglasses to remove the sun's glare, and we dodge potholes in the street when we are driving. All these behaviors we find reinforcing because they remove unpleasant events. Negative reinforcement is also exemplified in the old saying that we like to sit on a hot stove because it feels so good when we get off. Getting off the hot stove is reinforcing because it removes a painful stimulus. Having been negatively reinforced for such behaviors, we will continue to avoid complainers, put on sunglasses, dodge potholes, and jump off hot stoves.

There are two types of punishers, Type I and Type II. Even as positive and negative reinforcers *increase* the probability that a response will occur, punishers *decrease* the probability that a response will occur. Reinforcers (negative as well as positive) are desirable or rewarding to the learner; punishers of both types are undesirable or noxious to the learner.

A Type I punisher is any stimulus which, when *added* to the situation, decreases the probability of the response. Type I punishers include being spanked, scolded, and threatened. Any stimulus that is noxious or aversive may be used as a punisher. A Type II punisher is any stimulus which, when *removed* from the situation, decreases the probability of the response. The stimulus removed should be desirable or rewarding in order for its removal to be punishing. Not letting children watch their favorite TV show or taking away their allowance when they have done something wrong are examples of Type II punishers. Losing one's job would be punishing to many adults.

Reinforcers and Punishers Are Associated with the Giver
We tend to like people who provide reinforcers and dislike people who administer punishers. Police officers are usually thought of as meting out punishers. They are more likely to apprehend offenders than to help small children and elderly persons across the street. For this reason police officers get more than their share of criticism. Rather than giving us a positive reinforcer such as a package of M & M's™ candy or a twenty-dollar bill when they see us driving in a safe manner or providing a negative reinforcer such as recommending that the potholes in front of our house be filled, they wait until we break the traffic laws and give us a ticket (a Type I punisher) and remove our money (a Type II punisher).

> **Whether a stimulus is reinforcing or punishing depends on whether it increases or decreases the response, not on whether the one providing the stimulus considers it to be reinforcing or punishing.**

Reinforcers and Punishers Are Defined by Their Effects
Whether a stimulus is reinforcing or punishing depends on whether it increases or decreases the response, not on whether the one providing the stimulus considers it to be reinforcing or punishing. A teacher may think Johnny is being rewarded when his writing paper is put up on the board. But if Johnny begins to write poorly, he has been punished instead. A closer look may reveal that Johnny's best friend does not write well or that Johnny is teased on the playground for being "teacher's pet." The teacher may scold Suzie for being out of her seat and threaten to send her to the principal's office. If Suzie continues out-of-

seat behavior, it may be that the attention she receives from the teacher and the grins and looks she gets from her peers is reinforcing. To the teacher the scolding and threat are punishers, but to Suzie they provide an environment in which she receives the attention she wants.

A stimulus may be reinforcing to one child and punishing to another. Jimmy, in kindergarten, likes a gold star on his picture. Jerry, in eighth grade, would find the gold star demeaning. Michelle is pleased when the teacher puts her writing paper on the board, even though Johnny is not. Michelle does not care if the kids call her teacher's pet.

THORNDIKE'S LAW OF EFFECT

Whereas Watson leaned heavily on the studies of Pavlov, "Skinner's work now is commonly considered an extension of Thorndike's Law of Effect" (Iversen, 1992, p. 1326). Edward Lee Thorndike (1913), an American researcher and appropriately called the father of educational psychology, observed both animals and people in problem-solving situations and concluded that whenever a response is followed by a satisfying state of affairs, the connection between the stimulus and the response is strengthened (a cat in a puzzle box will get out sooner the second time in the box). If, however, a response is followed by an annoying state of affairs, the connection between the stimulus and the response is weakened.

Before 1930, Thorndike held that the effects of satisfiers and annoyers are equal and opposite, but after 1930, with continued experimentation, he changed his mind and concluded that satisfiers (rewards) are more powerful than annoyers (punishment). For example, he found that students learned Spanish words more quickly if told when they were right than if told when they were wrong. Although it may be questioned whether being told you are wrong constitutes a punishment, if Thorndike's conclusions are correct, the social implications of his work are immense.

Skinner and others who have built upon Thorndike's truncated "law of effect" and have conducted their own research on this issue say that even though punishment is very effective at the time the learner is being punished, there are side effects that must be considered, and in the long run the results of punishment may be worse than the original inappropriate behavior for which the learner was punished. Whenever we are in a situation that we associate with punishment, we become anxious and fearful. We try to escape physically, to leave the scene. If this is not possible, we try to escape mentally by daydreaming or sleeping. If mental diversion is not allowed, a whole complex of aggressive behaviors comes into play. We become belligerent and strike out verbally or physically. If we cannot turn our anger against the one who perpetrated our discomfort, and usually we cannot, we will lash out at anything or anyone around us. Sometimes we turn the aggression inward against ourselves, deprecating our abilities and our personalities. In extreme cases, people have taken their own lives.

This means that it is better to reinforce desirable behavior than to punish undesirable behavior. Although punishment is necessary at times, it has been used in many situations in which it was not needed. Parents and teachers and others in power use punishment because the press of the moment seems to demand it, and they cannot separate immediate results from long-range effects. Rewarding a competing, socially acceptable behavior may be as effective as punishment and has the further advantage of not being detrimental to personal happiness or hindering interpersonal relationships.

INSTRUMENTAL CONDITIONING IN OUR EVERYDAY LIVES

The effects of instrumental conditioning are constantly with us. We know what will produce pleasure and what will produce pain, what will work and what will not, what will bring attention and what will be ignored. Teaching pets and circus animals to do tricks is accomplished by instrumental techniques. Much of human behavior, as well, has been acquired by operant means.

Learning to talk is a case in point. Even as the meaning of words is learned by classical conditioning, the pronunciation of words is learned by instrumental conditioning. The baby lies in the crib making baby noises which sound something like "ma-ma-ma-ma" or "da-da-da-da." As these sounds approximate the words "mama" and "daddy," the infant receives favorable attention, and the parents gradually shape the infant's speech by reinforcing closer and closer approximations to saying the sound "ma" or "da" just twice rather than several times. As the child matures, he or she will learn to say "mommy" and "daddy," or whatever the parents wish to be called, only to change to "mom" and "dad" after the child starts to school and is told by peers that "mommy" and "daddy" are only for "kindergarten babies." Saying words also enables the child to get what he or she wants, and in this way the child soon learns that language is useful or instrumental.

SOCIAL LEARNING

A third way that learning takes place is by imitating the behavior of other people. We learn to talk like the people around us, to adopt their dress styles, and even to rise to our feet at a concert when we see others doing so. Studies show that we are more apt to copy the behaviors of people we perceive as being similar to ourselves, those of the same socioeconomic class, race, sex, and occupation. Advertisers make use of this fact by featuring models with whom we can readily identify. We also take into consideration the place and the occasion, and even the time of day.

From early childhood we have been taught that appropriate behavior is often specific to the situation. Had we lived in another age or in another culture our mannerisms and appearance would be quite different. Pictures of our parents when they were young strike us as quaint, and a visit to a foreign country shows us that customs vary from place to place. In some parts of the world men wear dresses, and in other parts of the world one is expected to give a loud belch after a meal as a compliment to the hostess.

Learning psychologists have different names for imitative behavior including observational learning, matching behavior, incidental learning, and vicarious learning. But the term usually given is "social learning."[2] Social learning is so much a part of our lives that it would seem to be almost contagious. It begins early in life with the toddler cocking his head to one side just like dad, sitting in a rocker with a book in his lap just like grandmother, and saying "uh-oh" with the same tone of voice as older brother.

Peer influence begins early, as parents know who have observed their own fairly well-behaved youngster acting like a regular hellion when visiting relatives or friends whose children are allowed to do whatever they please. By the age of three, most children copy what they perceive to be sex-appropriate behavior; for example, boys will play with toy cars, and girls will serve tea to their dollies. Even in homes where parents disdain sex-role differences and model this by both working outside the home and both taking physical care of the children, the influence of the larger society is evident. A four-year-old boy in nursery school will not continue to play with dolls if he is teased by the other children for doing so. He finds he must restrict his activities or be punished by his peers.

REINFORCERS IN SOCIAL LEARNING

In order for social learning to be put within the framework of learning psychology, three elements must be present. There must be a stimulus, a learner, and a response. The stimulus acts upon the learner, and the learner makes the response. The response is then linked to a reinforcer that assures the continuance of the response until a habit pattern is formed. In social learning the stimulus is the model, the learner is the person who copies the behavior of the model, and the response is the behavior imitated. Any event within the environment following the response that makes the learner more apt to respond in the same way is called a reinforcer. A person will not copy the behavior of another person unless he or she feels rewarded or reinforced in some way for doing so.

The reinforcer may come directly from the model, as in the case where dad thinks it is cute when his young son cocks his head, and grandmother says he is "such a good boy" when he sits in a rocker with a book in his lap. The attention they give the child makes him eager to engage in these behaviors again. Or, the reinforcer may be built into the behavior itself. If the child says "uh oh" after spilling his milk, his mother thinks he feels bad about the incident and is less apt to scold; and when he asks for more milk (a verbalization he learned by copying the speech of others) he is more apt to be given the milk and is reinforced by its good taste.

A third type of reinforcer is vicarious in nature, that is, the imitator sees the self as receiving the same rewards as the model. For young children, models include not only parents and peers but community helpers, sports figures, detectives, cowboys, and cartoon characters seen on television. When the child imitates these personages the child imagines that he or she is being given all the attention and praise and recognition that they receive.

THE MODEL IN SOCIAL LEARNING

It matters not to children whether the model is real or imaginary, for in their minds they become whatever they pretend to be. If they are garbage collectors they will do with toy garbage trucks exactly what they see real garbage collectors do with their truck. If they are cowboys they will dress like cowboys, practice roping, and their pets become "doggies" out on the range. If they are a cartoon figure seen on Saturday morning television, they are at that moment the hero and accept as their own all the glory and prestige befitting one who is so brave and daring as to fight "the bad guy" and rescue an innocent victim in distress.

Teenagers are notorious for copying the behavior of friends. Witness junior-high students on their way to school — all wearing the same kind of sneakers, the same style of jeans, or the same type of T-shirt. Even socks must be a certain color and length, and verbal expressions must be up-to-date. Senior highers get up early to shampoo and blow-dry their hair. If the hair does not look just right, back it goes in the water for another try. Hair must be styled like everyone else's. And then they are off to school (hairstyle gone with the first gust of wind) in a car equipped with stereo, speakers, an equalizer booster, and the right cassette "jammin" at high volume. When asked by the parent why this is necessary, the answer is, "Because that's the way it is." Young people wonder that their parents are so naive as not to understand that to be different is to be ostracized by the group. Parents, in turn, wonder why their children talk about being free and doing their own thing when "doing your own thing" turns out to be just like everyone else's "thing."

ALBERT BANDURA'S IMITATIVE BEHAVIOR

Research in social learning abounds. In a typical study, a group of subjects will be exposed to models who act one way while another group of subjects will be exposed to models who act another way. The subjects are then watched to see if their behaviors differ depending on which models they observed. For example, a child may be told not to touch the candy in the room where he or she is playing. A second child is sent into the room having been told there is some special candy waiting there for him. Does the presence of the candy-eating peer mean the first child is more apt to eat the candy than would be the case if the second child had not come into the room or if the second child were instructed not to touch the candy and did not do so?

Albert Bandura, well-known for his work in the area of social learning, showed children a film in which an adult was seen hitting and punching an inflated Bobo doll. When these children were placed in a room with Bobo (and observed through a one-way mirror) they were more apt to hit and punch the doll than were children who had not seen the film (Bandura, Ross, & Ross, 1963). Albert Bandura (1965) of Stanford University also found that children who see an adult model praised after engaging in an aggressive act are more apt to imitate the aggressive act than are children who see the adult model scolded for the behavior. However, if children think they will be reinforced for acting aggressively, they will do so regardless of the consequences of the same action to the model.

There are occasional instances of animals imitating people and of people imitating animals, but this is relatively rare. For this reason social learning is generally thought of as a human phenomenon. Social learning also has the distinction of accounting for a larger repertoire of behaviors than does either classical conditioning or instrumental conditioning. Language acquisition is a case in point. Whereas the meaning of words may come about by classical conditioning and the pronunciation of words may take place by instrumental conditioning, social learning provides for a complete behavioral sequence of verbal expression. A person may reproduce a sentence or even several sentences by imitating the speech of others and in this way eliminate the need for the pairing of each word (conditioned stimulus) with its concrete referent (unconditioned stimulus) as in the case of classical conditioning, or the reinforcement of each word in a chain of words that makes up a sentence as in the case of instrumental conditioning. With imitative behavior, meaning is given to the sentence as a whole, and reinforcers accompany the total unit of speech.

Bandura (1986) recognizes the role of both classical conditioning (e.g., "In the initial stages of speech acquisition . . . children . . . have to learn the referents to which the words apply," p. 505) and instrumental conditioning (e.g., "children find language useful in explaining their own behavior to themselves and others," p. 510). But social learning goes further in that modeling provides for the child patterns of speech that include judgmental skills and generalizable rules. Bandura explains that modeling an activity while describing that activity in words is an effective form of communication (p. 506). Without language we would be at a loss to relate to others in a complex society.

LEARNING PSYCHOLOGY AND MORAL GROWTH

Learning psychology has its roots in the philosophy of British associationist John Locke, who held that we are born as a *tabula rasa,* or blank tablet. Nothing is written on the tablet until we interact with an external world. It is our circumstances, not heredity, temperament, or choice, that determine what is inscribed upon us. It is the experiences we have that determine the kind of persons we will be. Control the experience, and you control whether we are moral or immoral.

Moral behaviors, then, are learned responses, and the learning does not differ in kind from the learning of all other behaviors. Moral behaviors are learned when we are in a good environment. A good environment is one in which we have adequate models of moral behavior and are reinforced for socially desirable conduct and punished for socially undesirable actions. The learning psychology answer to moral growth is that *children become capable of morality by training, example, reward, and punishment. By imitating the actions of appropriate models and by being reinforced for behaviors deemed good by the society and punished for behaviors deemed bad, we learn to be moral persons.* Consistent and extensive training in good behaviors will result in good habits that persist for a lifetime.

> **Learning psychology has its roots in the philosophy of British associationist John Locke, who held that we are born as a tabula rasa, or blank tablet.**

A reiteration of the basic ideas of learning psychology will enable us to see how learning psychology may be applied directly to the way in which moral growth occurs.

BASIC ASSUMPTIONS

The learning psychologist believes that the society determines what is right and what is wrong, what is good and what is evil. Society takes as its highest priority its own survival, and thus the preservation of the social order becomes the greatest good and its destruction the greatest evil. A good person is a responsible citizen, complying with the mandates of the social group to which he or she belongs. *To be moral is to act in ways that benefit society; to be immoral is to act in ways that harm society.* If people conform to the behavioral standards of the group, they are moral for they are responding to the environment in a way that will enhance the well-being of others. If people reject such standards, they are immoral for their response has a deleterious effect on others.

The emphasis of learning psychology, then, is on overt behavior, not on what a person says or thinks, for what we do more directly affects others than any other type of response. People who are immoral need to change their behavior, not their temperament or their motives or their thought processes. Once the behavior is changed, the problem is solved. A child who tells lies, for example, needs to learn to tell the truth, for lying is harmful to others. When the child stops lying and speaks truth, the problem no longer exists and the child is conforming to the expectation of the group. Rather than trying to find some hidden reason for the lies, such as innate depravity, a weak will, or a devious mind, learning theorists would say that lying is the problem. Lying is an external problem with external consequences. Deal with the consequences and you have dealt with the problem.

Moral (or immoral) behavior does not just happen; it is a product of environmental conditioning. None of us starts out moral or immoral, nor do we happen to become one way or the other. Rather, moral behavior like all behavior is learned. Learning is defined as a change in behavior as the result of experience. Experience comes from living in an environment composed of thousands of stimuli that act upon the learner in such a way as to produce a variety of responses. B.F. Skinner (1974), the leading spokesman for learning psychology, wrote:

A behavioristic analysis rests on the following assumptions: A person is first of all an organism, a member of a species and a subspecies. . . . The organism becomes a person as it acquires a repertoire of behavior under the contingencies of reinforcement to which it is exposed during its lifetime. . . . It is able to acquire such a repertoire under such control because of processes of conditioning. (p. 207)

The relationship between "contingencies of reinforcement" and "processes of conditioning," to use Skinner's words, results in moral or immoral behavior, even as it results in other kinds of behavior. Furthermore, this relationship is not capricious but is the very stuff of which science is made. A basic tenet of scientific research is that there is order in the world, that certain events bring about certain responses, that future behavior can be predicted on the basis of past behavior, and that there are commonalities between members of a particular species so that information gathered from some members may be generalized to others. Learning theorists do not need to observe every child to know what most children will do in a given set of circumstances. Psychologists who are interested in the area of morality and hold to the learning approach look for correlations between environmental events and overt behaviors to understand better the nature of the relationship between them.

Classical Conditioning and Moral Growth

The term *classical,* as was mentioned, comes from Pavlov's classic experiment in which he found that dogs learned to respond to the neutral (conditioned) stimulus of a bell if the bell previously had been paired or associated with the natural (unconditioned) stimulus of food. The sound of a bell does not ordinarily produce activity of the salivary glands, but food in the mouth does. By pairing the bell with the food, the dogs would salivate to the bell in the same way that they would salivate to the food.

Although it is a giant step from salivating dogs to moral behavior in humans, some studies indicate that moral or immoral behavior may be learned by pairing a stimulus that would not naturally produce the behavior with a stimulus that does produce the behavior. For example, a child who comes when called engages in the moral act of obedience. The word *come,* like all words, is a conditioned stimulus, for it has no meaning apart from its association with natural events. As a toddler the child may have associated "come" with outstretched arms, smiles, and good food. It is because of this association that the child will come when called even though the natural unconditioned stimuli of favorable attention and good food may not be present. The child has been conditioned to obey.

Hans Eysenck (1960) took the position that children will learn to fear situations in which aggressive or cheating behaviors, for example, have been associated with slaps, withdrawal of privileges, or shamings. The pain (unconditioned stimulus) associated with the punishment produces a natural (unconditioned) response of avoidance. When the pain is paired with a situation (conditioned stimulus) in which the child wants to aggress or wants to cheat, the child will associate the desire with the pain and tend to avoid that situation. In other words, if aggressive or cheating behavior is associated with punishment, the child will learn to avoid situations in which he or she is likely to aggress or cheat.

The tenor of most learning psychologists today is that it is better to precede a socially desirable behavior with a pleasant stimulus than to use punishment as a warning to the child not to engage in a socially undesirable behavior. Both methods are effective, though, and most parents use some combination of the two.

Learning psychologists also play down individual differences, insisting that it is the environment that makes each of us different. Eysenck takes exception to a strict environmentalism and says that differences in the ease with which children are acculturated into the society may be accounted for by differences in their nervous systems. Extroverts are harder to condition than introverts. At the extrovert extreme is the psychopath, who, in spite of adequate intelligence and a good upbringing, is devoid of moral sense. At the introvert extreme are neurotics who make themselves miserable by suffering feelings of guilt over behaviors few people would consider wrong. Eysenck (1960) has demonstrated that psychopaths, compared with normal people, need many more pairings of conditioned and unconditioned stimuli before any effect is seen. Neurotics, with "a conscience much more tender than the average person" are "particularly easy to condition" (p. 15).

Instrumental Conditioning and Moral Growth

Unlike classical conditioning in which two or more stimuli are associated prior to the response, instrumental conditioning looks at what happens after the response. It is the consequence of the response that determines whether the response is strengthened or weakened. If something pleasant (called a reinforcer) happens after a response, the response is more apt to occur again. The response is instrumental or useful to the one making the response. If something painful (called a punisher) happens after a response, the response is not instrumental and is less apt to occur again. Also, if nothing happens after a response, it is not useful to the organism to have made the response, and the response is less apt to be repeated.

Moral or immoral behavior is strengthened when reinforced and weakened when punished or ignored. If a moral act like telling the truth is praised or an immoral act like stealing means more money, these acts have been reinforced and are more apt to occur again. If, however, telling the truth means a spanking or stealing means getting caught and jailed, these acts have been punished and are less apt to reoccur. When "good" behavior like playing quietly is disregarded or "naughty" behavior like throwing a temper tantrum is ignored, these behaviors are not instrumental or useful and are less apt to be repeated. Moral behavior, then, is learned when the child associates socially acceptable responses with rewards and socially unacceptable ones with punishment.

Behaviors may be followed by both immediate and long-range consequences. When this occurs, immediate reinforcers and punishers take precedence over the long-range reinforcers and punishers. "The behavior [the organism] exhibits at any moment is under the control of a current setting" (Skinner, 1974, p. 207). If we overeat we do so because the immediate reinforcers of good taste in the mouth and pleasant fullness in the stomach take priority over the more remote punishers of poor health, less energy, and a less attractive appearance. A student who finds studying to be unpleasant probably will do very little of it. The punishers accompanying studying behavior take precedence over the more distant reinforcers of good grades and the promise of a better income. In the same way, *moral (or immoral) behavior is more apt to be learned if reinforcers and punishers occur immediately following the behavior than if they occur at a later time.*

A young child may need reinforcers every few minutes, whereas an older child may need reinforcers every hour. The learning psychologist believes that if reinforcers are delivered immediately following the behavior and if they occur with sufficient frequency, the learning of the behavior is assured. The same applies to the learning of moral behavior. But unfortunately, we underestimate the number of reinforcers necessary for optimal functioning, and our timing in providing punishers and reinforcers is so far removed from the behavior exhibited as to lose maximal effectiveness. We ignore behaviors that should be reinforced (e.g., the child is supposed to be good), and extend the punishers (e.g., "You'll get a spanking when your dad gets home") and the reinforcers (e.g., "If you don't get a grade less than a C you'll get a bicycle for Christmas") past the time of their greatest usefulness. We would do well to analyze how we respond so that we and others will learn to be moral.

Social Learning and Moral Growth
Moral (or immoral) behavior may be learned by imitating the behavior of another person. Learning to be good or learning to be bad by imitating a model is called social learning. Social learning theorists emphasize the importance of incidental learning, that is, learning that takes place incidentally, or without instruction. The child learns more by percept than by precept, more by watching and imitating the behaviors of others than by following their directions and rules. The parent who says, "Do what I say, not what I do," is not reckoning with the way learning takes place. The principal who tells the student while paddling him, "This will teach you not to hit people," is providing a model of aggression that may have more effect on the child than the pain inflicted. Good habits are formed by imitating the good behaviors of others. Bad habits are formed by imitating those behaviors that are detrimental to the society.

> **Moral (or immoral) behavior may be learned by imitating the behavior of another person. Learning to be good or learning to be bad by imitating a model is called social learning.**

Some expectations of conduct are universal, being found in all cultures, whereas other expectations vary from culture to culture or from place to place. All societies, however mandate some standard of honesty and dependability to assure the survival of the group. Yet immigrants to a new land, for example, must make many adjustments before they feel at home in their new surroundings. Even if one moves from one social class to another, as in the case of prolonged unemployment or unexpected affluence, changes in behavior will undoubtedly accompany the move. Middle-class norms, including moral strictures, are predominant in our Western society, but they differ, nonetheless, from both lower-class and upper-class expectations.

Even within a social class, children may find that their parents have one view of right and wrong while their peers have another. When this occurs, children will act one way when with their parents and another way when with their friends. Flexibility and adjustment are terms used to connote the positive aspect of this capacity to change, whereas instability and opportunism are the negative counterparts of this phenomenon.

Learning psychologists would say, then, that morality is not a fixed entity to be applied to all situations and to all people. Rather, morality is a relative concept. Nothing is good in and of itself to be accepted and uniformly applied to every situation. Rather, morality changes as the occasion changes. A behavior may be moral in one situation but not in another. When in Rome, one does as the Romans; when not in Rome, one simply does something else. Each culture, society, and group must determine what is good and what is bad, what is moral and what is immoral. The moral person is the one who picks up on the cues (stimuli) within the environment and responds in such a way that his or her behavior is supportive of the goals and aspirations of the surrounding group.

This does not mean there are no criteria by which to judge what has value and what is of little worth. One has only to compare the consequences of some standards with the consequences of others to see that some behaviors promote optimal functioning of the group whereas other behaviors destroy the very fabric of the society, and even result in its demise. Brotherhood and kindness promote the health of any group; divisiveness and aggression eat into the society like a cancer. Learning to be moral means that children will acquire through imitation behaviors that profit others, and they will inhibit those behaviors that are detrimental to those around them. Each individual is a member of the groups to which he or she belongs, and in this sense each one is part of his or her own destiny, a part of whether we live in a moral or an immoral world.

PROBLEMS

Learning psychology has been presented up to this point in a relatively uncritical way, but the perceptive reader probably is aware that there are a number of problems inherent in the position. We will look at some of the objections given in the literature to see what the critics have to say.

IS MORALITY RELATIVE TO THE SITUATION?

One problem is that the learning approach provides no theoretical basis for deciding what is right and what is wrong. As such, it gives little direction as to which of many behaviors one should choose in order to be a moral person. Without a philosophy or theology that transcends the present culture, one can never be sure of what is the right thing or how to choose the good over the evil. There are so many opinions, so many models, so many views of what is right and what is wrong. How does one know which opinion to listen to, which model to imitate, which view is best? If the only guideline for what is good and what is bad is what benefits the society or harms the society, and if societies change from time to time or do not agree among themselves as to what is beneficial or harmful, the result is confusion. Truth becomes relative to the occasion, and one is left with what is often referred to as "situation ethics." Each of us is a member of several groups or sub-groups at the same time, and without guiding principles we are hard pressed to know to which of these groups we should give our allegiance.

Suppose, for example, that a child and several friends have devised a method for cheating on a test. At test time the child is a member of the group composed of cheaters, a member of the class as a whole, a member of the entire school, and also a member of the community. Which of these groups has the right to say whether cheating is right or cheating is wrong? The child's friends say it is right if it means a higher grade. Other children in the class say it is wrong because the child may get caught or because it violates a rule. The teacher may say that children who cheat are only cheating themselves. People in the larger community may not care, but some will say that cheating is at cross-purposes with what we are trying to teach our children. Who is to decide? To which of these groups of people does the child listen?

174

Some adults who would criticize a child for cheating on a test will misrepresent their earnings for income tax purposes and feel justified in doing so because their friends approve of the action and it will mean a more comfortable life for their families. So, who is to determine whether falsification of records is good or bad? Does it depend on who is doing the lying? Should the extent of the misrepresentation be considered? Does it matter who is being lied to? Does one's motive make a difference? Is every situation different, each occasion to be determined on its own merits? Without anchorage in a philosophy that supersedes the event, one is hard-pressed to answer these questions.

Is the Underlying Reason for Moral Behavior Important?

A second problem is that moral behavior is a superficial way of looking at morality. It is superficial in that the emphasis is on overt behavior rather than on internal qualities that produce the behavior. One is not moral because one acts in moral ways. Rather, one acts in moral ways because one is moral. Good deeds are a manifestation of goodness, not goodness itself. This is made abundantly clear when we see that people are good for a variety of reasons. Some possess integrity and strength of character, and the goodness is a natural consequent of an inward condition. Others are good because they perceive it to be in their best interests to be that way, but given another time or a different situation, the good behavior no longer is present. Unless a view of morality includes other components of the moral process, such as reasoning that sees beyond the benefits of the moment, emotional states of empathy and love that enable a person to put self in the place of others and be concerned with their well-being as well as with one's own, or a religious commitment that holds that all humankind is made in the image of God and therefore befitting of dignity and respect, morality as moral behavior is shallow and unfeeling. By focusing on the external, the development of internal controls is lost sight of. By limiting morality to the study of stimulus-response connections, much of the significance of what it means to be a good person is forfeited. Moral behavior is only a part of what it means to be moral, a surface manifestation of an inward state, which in some people is a reflection of a true sensitivity to moral concerns, and in others nothing more than the opportune response at the moment.

ARE WE PERSONALLY RESPONSIBLE FOR OUR ACTIONS?

Another problem or criticism is that the uniqueness of the human race as thinking, feeling, creative beings is not recognized. Humans are seen as an extension of the phylogenetic scale and, like other animals, seek only to avoid pain and increase pleasure. We become mere pawns or puppets of environmental contingencies, passive organisms to be manipulated by others, the objects rather than the subjects of psychological study. We have no choice, no free will, no autonomy. Consequently, we have nothing to say about our behavior, including our moral behavior. Nor are we in a position to construct a value system based on our interests and tastes.

As infants we were like all other infants. It was the environment—not heredity or maturational processes, not temperamental predisposition or cognitive potential, not decision-making or any desire on our part—that made us what we are today. Not even our enthusiasm, plans, aspirations, and hard work have played a role except as these were programmed by an external world. All the characteristics that give us as human beings a special place in the universe and elevate us to a position superior to other life forms have been largely ignored in learning theory. Even religious views come from external sources, the joys of heaven and the sufferings of hell being used as reinforcers and punishers to encourage appropriate behaviors and discourage actions society does not want.

If we have no say in what we become, is it not unfair to hold us responsible for the kind of persons we are? How can we be praised or blamed for our interests, our personalities, our motivation—or lack thereof? We did not make ourselves intelligent or unintelligent, fascinating or dull, moral or immoral. Nor should we be held accountable if we lack appropriate models to imitate. It also follows that we should not hold ourselves responsible. We did not get ourselves into the mess we are in, nor can we get ourselves out. How can we rise above our environment and be anything other than what we have learned to be? If we are mean or abusive toward others or alcoholic or homosexual, we are in no way to blame. We did not make ourselves this way, nor can we change. If others want us to be different, it is up to them to make it worth our while. They can provide reinforcers and punishers to get us to comply with their way of doing things, or they can provide socially acceptable models for us to emulate.

This stance of not holding others or ourselves responsible is understandably attractive to many people. It marks us as nice people not to judge others whose circumstances differ from our own, and it certainly is more pleasant to blame someone else for our difficulties than to take the blame ourselves. But an unwillingness to assume any role in the kind of people we are lets us off the hook, so to speak, much too easily. It is generally understood that all of us have something to say about who we are and what we do. We make decisions all day, every day. It begins with "mind over mattress" first thing in the morning and continues with what we wear and what we eat and what we say to our spouse and to our children. And many of the decisions we make are moral in nature because they directly affect others. To say we are not accountable for what we do or what we are militates against the common understanding of what it means to be a member of the human race, a good or a bad person. A morality without personal responsibility is a morality lacking an important ingredient.

DOES CONTROL TODAY MEAN MORAL GROWTH TOMORROW?

Still another criticism is that learning psychology confuses means and ends. Reinforcing a child for appropriate behavior today may or may not result in desirable behavior tomorrow. If the only reason for not swearing is to avoid punishment, the child will not swear when in the presence of the punishing adult but will swear when out of earshot. Short-term control does not always mean long-term results. Behaviorists say that if a child is consistently reinforced for acceptable behavior and punished for unacceptable actions, the child will develop good habits that persist into adulthood; as the twig is bent, so grows the tree.

Obviously, there is an element of truth to this, but the problem comes when we see that though some individuals continue the behaviors they were taught as children, others go in very different directions. Siblings are usually treated in much the same way in the home, yet they turn out differently. Granted, no two people have exactly the same environment, and siblings will choose different friends and have different school situations; even so, it does not appear that the environment alone accounts for such discrepancies in their lives. There is reason to believe that all the variables that relate to moral behavior are not external; some components must come from within. Even as external and internal are not to be confused, neither should means and ends be. Process and product relate to each other, but one is not the same as the other. Means must be appropriate to the valued ends, but each remains separate from the other, to be considered together and individually for an understanding of how moral development occurs.

Do Adults Model the Behaviors They Want in Children?

Adults may not be suitable models. Learning psychologists are aware of this, but it remains, nevertheless, a problem in their approach. As parents we say one thing then do another. We say we want quiet and yell at our children. We say we want honesty but do not always deal honestly with them. We say we want industry but sit on the sofa watching TV while they are to do their homework. We may even expect our children to be more emotionally mature than we are. They are not to fuss or cry, but we feel justified when we complain about what happened at work or give an accounting of our latest aches and pains.

The inconsistency between what we expect of our children and our own behavior is often glaring, and it seems to be greatest in homes where the parent takes the attitude that by virtue of being a parent one can do no wrong. Whatever the parent decides is right and should be accepted without question. The reason is not that the parent's decision or performance is necessarily best for the child, or even for the household in general, but rather that as the one in charge the parent has the authority to make the decision and therefore should be given respect.

Even if we agree that parents do indeed have the right to demand performance from their children that differs from their own, the fact remains that children learn more by what they see than what they are told. Copying another's behavior comes naturally, obeying authority does not. Yelling calls for yelling, dishonesty brings dishonesty, and laziness results in laziness. And if punitive measures are such that children cannot exhibit these behaviors when with the parent, they will exhibit them in nonpunitive environments or when they are old enough that the parent no longer can control them physically. There are always exceptions, of course, but usually a child will take on the characteristics of the parents. It is sobering to see ourselves reflected in the behavior of our children. If we truly care for them we will be willing to change our own actions in an effort to become more suitable models.

WHO CONTROLS THE CONTROLLER?

The last problem we will consider has to do with the ethics of control. Some learning psychologists speak to this issue while others show little concern. Whenever the desire to control others and the satisfaction of one's own need for power becomes more important than the best interests of the one being controlled, there is reason to believe that the one in charge is not acting in a moral or ethical way. The controller should be as concerned with the ethics of his or her own behavior and the reason for wanting to be in charge as with the ethics of the behavior of the one being controlled. This is especially important when those controlled are in a dependent position — children, students, employees, or prisoners — and are either unaware of the ways in which they are being manipulated or are unable to leave the scene in which they find themselves.

It is not unusual for persons in charge to begin their leadership with the best interests of those in their care in mind, but as time goes by and they are reinforced by increasing adulation, they change from ethical administrators to vindictive tyrants interested only in making life easier and more glorious for themselves. The adage "power corrupts" is no better illustrated than in the horror of the mass suicide at Jonestown. Yet it is seen on a small scale all around us, making us aware that we need checks along the way to be sure that, whether we are controlling or being controlled, we do not fall into the trap of exalting authority for the sake of authority alone. Those in power must recognize that they are not somehow a different breed of humankind or better than those they command. Compassion, accountability, and humility are necessary ingredients for ethical leadership.

It would be inaccurate to say that these problems apply to the ideas of every learning psychologist. There are many variations on the learning theme that have not been touched on. Only the major ideas of classical conditioning, instrumental conditioning, and social learning have been dealt with, and there are varieties within each of these. Also, care must be exercised not to take a theory to its extreme conclusions, thereby creating a caricature rather than an accurate portrayal. But in the realm of morality there appears to be a deficit in the learning position. By fastening attention only on observable responses and on the external events that strengthen or weaken those responses, much of what is generally thought of as morality is excluded. Behavioral conformity is an important component of the moral condition and affects other people more directly than any other aspect, but it is, nevertheless, only one part of the total picture and by itself stands bare and incomplete. Morality as moral behavior finds its greatest expression in relationship with other components of morality so that together a totality is formed that imposes upon the parts a certain organization and yet is above or distinct from the parts.

Whether we accept or reject learning psychology as a philosophy, the fact remains that we are constantly modifying the behavior of those around us, even as they are modifying our behavior. We can do it unconsciously with unknown and often unhappy results, or we can do it consciously and deliberately, programming our actions so as to develop desirable qualities in others. Learning techniques work. Furthermore, they are easily understood and readily applied. By knowing the problems we are in a better position to avoid the pitfalls.

In the next chapter we will consider ways in which learning psychology provides guidelines for teachers, parents, and pastors concerned with the moral growth of those committed to their care.

NOTES

1. Of the forty subjects, sixteen (40 percent) offered some form of aid to the victim. Only 10 percent in the high-hurry group offered aid as compared to 63 percent in the low-hurry group. The Parable of the Good Samaritan would indicate that high religiosity does not in itself predispose a person to help someone in need. Darley and Batson (1973) interpreted the findings to mean that the seminarians had a conflict between helping the victim and doing what they believed was their duty in following the directions of the researcher. "Conflict, rather than callousness, can explain their failure to stop" (p. 108).

2. Social learning includes within its perimeters not only learning psychology but also psychoanalysis. The learning theory concept of imitation and the psychoanalytic concept of identification (presented in chap. 4) are closely related, the two developing simultaneously in the young child. Theoretically speaking, however, they are far apart. Imitation emphasizes overt responses learned when a person copies the behavior of another, whereas identification stresses the internalization of normative demands and the adoption of the ideas and attitudes of the model. Imitation results in the acquisition

of good habits; identification brings about the development of a conscience or superego.

For an in-depth discussion of the way in which social learning spans the distance between these two disparate psychologies and includes portions of both within its scope, see Hoffman, M.L. (1970), Moral development, in P. Mussen (Ed.), *Carmichael's manual of child psychology*, Vol. 2, New York: John Wiley & Sons; Kohlberg, L. (1963), Moral development and identification, in H.W. Stevenson (Ed.), *Child psychology: 62nd yearbook of the National Society for the Study of Education*, Chicago: University of Chicago Press; and Woodward, W.R. (1982), The "discovery" of social behaviorism and social learning theory, 1870–1980, *American Psychologist*, 37, 396–410.

REFERENCES

Bandura, A. (1965). Influence of model's reinforcement contingencies on the acquisition of imitative responses. *Journal of Personality and Social Psychology, 1*, 589–595.

————. (1986). *Social foundations of thought and action.* Englewood Cliffs, NJ: Prentice-Hall.

————., Ross, D., & Ross, S. (1963). Imitation of film mediated aggressive models. *Journal of Abnormal and Social Psychology, 66*, 3–11.

Chiesa, M. (1992). Radical behaviorism and scientific frameworks: From mechanistic to relational accounts. *American Psychologist, 47*, 1287–1299.

Darley, J.M., & Batson, C.D. (1973). "From Jerusalem to Jericho": A study of situational and dispositional variables in helping behavior. *Journal of Personality and Social Psychology, 27*, 100–108.

Eysenck, H.J. (1960). The development of moral values in children: The contribution of learning theory. *British Journal of Educational Psychology, 30*, 11–21.

Harris, B. (1979). Whatever happened to Little Albert? *American Psychologist, 34*, 151–160.

Iversen, I.H. (1992). Skinner's early research: From reflexology to operant conditioning. *American Psychologist, 47*, 1318–1328.

Jones, S.L., & Butman, R.E. (1991). *Modern psychotherapies: A comprehensive Christian appraisal.* Downers Grove, IL: InterVarsity Press.

Premack, D. (1965). Reinforcement theory. In D. Levine (Ed.), *Nebraska symposium on motivation* (pp. 123–180). Lincoln: University of Nebraska Press.

Rancher using pocket beeper to summon cows for chow. (1992, July 11). *The Terre Haute Tribune.*

Skinner, B.F. (1938). *The behavior of organisms: An experimental analysis.* New York: Appleton-Century-Crofts.

_____. (1953). *Science and human behavior.* New York: Macmillan.

_____. (1971). *Beyond freedom and dignity.* New York: Alfred A. Knopf.

_____. (1974). *About behaviorism.* New York: Alfred A. Knopf.

_____. (1983). *A matter of consequences.* New York: Alfred A. Knopf.

_____. (1987). Whatever happened to psychology as the science of behavior? *American Psychologist, 42,* 780–786.

_____. (1989). The origins of cognitive thought. *American Psychologist, 44,* 13–18.

_____. (1990). Can psychology be a science of mind? *American Psychologist, 45,* 1206–1210.

Staats, A.W. (1961). Verbal habit-families, concepts, and the operant conditioning of word classes. *Psychological Review, 68,* 190–204.

Steensma, G.J. (1987). Language. In G.J. Steensma & H.W. VanBrummelen (Eds.), *Shaping school curriculum: A biblical view* (pp. 62–71). Terre Haute, IN: Signal Publishing.

Thorndike, E.L. (1913). *The psychology of learning.* New York: Teachers College.

Watson, J.B. (1931). *Behaviorism.* London: Routledge & Kegan Paul.

Watson, J.B., & Rayner, R. (1920). Conditioned emotional reactions. *Journal of Experimental Psychology, 3,* 1–14.

SEVEN

Guidelines from Learning Psychology for Teachers, Parents, and Pastors

No formal training is needed to apply learning psychology to our everyday lives. Perhaps this is because we already engage in learning practices, and by becoming familiar with the principles of the learning approach, we can understand better what is taking place when we interact with others. Both direct intervention, as seen in behavior modification, and indirect mediation that comes with imitation and modeling are included in learning psychology. A knowledge of behaviorism clarifies what we are doing and shows ways we may have erred in the past and how we can do a better job in the future.

The learning psychologist would say that none of us is good or bad in and of ourselves. Rather, we become what we are made to be by the environment. Faulty behavior reflects a faulty environment, not a faulty person. We should not think of ourselves and others as moral or immoral in the sense of some inherent quality. Instead, we should look to our actions to see if we are exhibiting the kind of behavior that will make for the continuance of the society rather than the kind of behavior that will bring about the destruction of the social order.

If faulty behavior is indeed a consequence of a faulty environment, recent studies would indicate that young people today live in such an environment. An example of such a study is one done by the Joseph and Edna Josephson Institute of Ethics in which 7,000 students ages fifteen to thirty were surveyed as to their behaviors in school. Some of the findings were that "61 percent of high school students and 32 percent of college students said they had cheated on an exam during

ENJOYING OLD AGE

When B.F. Skinner was in his seventies, he began writing and speaking on ways to enjoy old age. He believed that problems of the elderly are often shortcomings in the environment. As one ages, the environment must change. For example, a young person is fatigued, takes a vacation and returns refreshed; an old person is fatigued, takes a vacation, and returns feeling worse. What was once reinforcing is now punishing. Vacations, if taken, must be altered. Perhaps less time away from home with less planned for each day will work out better. Poor vision, faulty hearing, and difficulty in walking means glasses, hearing aids, and a cane are added to the environment. If forgetting is a problem, you write down what you want to do. Better yet, do it at the time you think of it. Hang the umbrella on the door knob if you want to take one with you.

Retirement makes things worse. You think others will praise you as they continue your work but this is not so; they will go on as though you were never there. Remain with those who have your same interests; they will keep you thinking. Living in the past with your memories doesn't help, either. You can continue to be productive if you look to the future rather than to the past. However, you will need to go on a structured variable-ratio schedule. By this Skinner meant that as you grow older you must be content with fewer productive hours per day. Yet these hours can be very reinforcing. It's like the difference between comics and good literature. Youth is more like the comics when you are reinforced every few minutes but soon forget what made you laugh. Old age is like good literature in which it may take considerable time to read something that grabs your attention but once read, it is meaningful and you don't forget it.

the past year; 33 percent of high school students and 16 percent of college students said they stole something in the last year; more than a third of all students said they would lie on a resume or job application" (Wike, 1992, p. 1).

The learning position is advantageous in that those of us in charge of dependent children need not shrug our shoulders and say that nothing can be done to help the child or adolescent who has already learned socially undesirable conduct. The idea of a critical period beyond which there is little hope has no place in the learning framework. To be sure, older children are less apt to change their behaviors than younger children due to years of previously conditioned responses. But age is not the important variable. As long as there is an environment sur-rounding the person — and always there is that — he or she can change. Students who cheat, steal, or lie can learn not to engage in these behaviors.

As teachers, parents, and pastors we are not only invited to control, we are obligated to control. We are to provide appropriate reinforcers for desirable behavior and appropriate punishers for the undesirable. We are to be good models for children to observe and imitate as well. The learning psychology answer to moral growth is encouraging to those of us who work with others regardless of their ages.

Let us turn our attention first to ways in which teachers may use learning psychology to foster moral behaviors in the children in the school, and then we will look at ways learning psychology may be applied to the home and to the church.

GUIDELINES FOR TEACHERS

The behavioral approach to morality is the one taken by school children when asked to determine what is proper. The following list (with spell-ing errors uncorrected) was given by sixth-graders in response to their teacher's request to write "class standards."

> Listen to the teacher when she is talking or yelling.
> Keep your shoes on in school.
> Don't say shut up if the teacher doesn't like it.
> Don't stay in the restroom all day.
> Don't go to the bathroom all the time.

The bathroom isn't a meeting place and classes aren't held there.
Don't hide in the bathroom on hot days.
Don't play with thing.
Leave your treshures at home.
Stand when you walk into class.
Be ploite to all the teachers, not just yours.
Don't be a taital tail.
Don't lend back of your chair.
Don't scrap your chair.
Stay in your set.
Stay in your sit.
Try not to hit your classmates.
Be good to the little people.
Don't ride on another girl's back, you could get hurt.
No pooping bags at lunch.
Don't spit on the playground.
If the teacher says something funny, don't pound on your desk.
Don't bother the Princeble.
Use your time wisley.
Four people don't have to take one hurt person to the office.
Don't fall out of your chairs.
Dont' crew gun or candy.
Don't crawl on floors.
Witch your mouth.
Wash your language. (Amory, 1971, p. 10)

Children are very serious about providing rules for conduct but think a separate rule must be given for each behavior. The list becomes so long that no one could remember it all. Adults realize that only a few regulations should be given at any one time and so will state a rule in such a way that a number of behaviors will be included, such as: "Follow directions." "Complete all assignments." "Do not leave the classroom without permission." "Keep hands, feet, objects to oneself." "Work independently." Both classical and instrumental techniques are helpful in conditioning the child to adjust to the stated demands.

THE TEACHER'S USE OF CLASSICAL CONDITIONING
Classical conditioning develops habits in the child that make for the smooth functioning of the institution. Children learn that the bell

means to put their books in their desks and line up for recess or that recess is over and it is time to get in line and go back in. The bell is a conditioned stimulus that provides a cue for what the child is to do.

Classical Conditioning and the School Phobic Child

Classical conditioning may be used by the school psychologist to help the school phobic child. The phobia probably developed by stimulus generalization, that is, the child has generalized from one unpleasant event that occurred at school to all events associated with going to school. Consequently, the child shows a fear reaction to events that normally would not bring about a fear response. Even thinking about school can make the child ill. The child needs to be reconditioned so the phobic reaction does not continue.

This is done by pairing stimuli or events that remotely resemble the original conditioned stimulus (the event that caused the fear) with pleasant rather than unpleasant unconditioned stimuli. This process is called systematic desensitization because as the child is systematically introduced to conditioned stimuli that are closer and closer to the original conditioned stimulus on which the fear reaction took place while at the same time experiencing pleasure, he or she is desensitized to the phobic reaction.

Suppose, for instance, that we were to recondition Watson's Little Albert. We would begin by showing Albert some white cotton while giving him good food or an interesting toy. When Albert no longer showed a fear of cotton, a Santa Claus mask would be paired with the food or the toy—then a stuffed Easter rabbit, a fur coat, and so on, until finally a live rat would be presented. The child would now associate the rat with the food or the toy rather than with the loud noise, and the fear reaction would be extinguished. School phobia is dealt with in the same way. If it has emerged full blown (not the occasional reluctance to go to school, in which case the child is marched off to school anyway), the phobic child is gradually given more and more exposure to the school situation until he or she is able to go for a full day.

Classical Conditioning Techniques Used by Classmates

Desensitization methods are also used by peers to change the child who does not conform to their way of behaving. The first-grader who has temper tantrums at home may not have them at school because such action is labeled as infantile by his or her classmates; and a junior-high student displaying normal behavior for one's age may be quickly acculturated into a delinquent group by being hardened, systematically, against actions the larger society considers to be decent and right. Delinquent teenagers link a concern for others and a respect for authority with weakness and effeminacy, whereas starting a fight or shoplifting is considered daring and clever. Parents and teachers are understandably concerned when they see a child from a good home spending time with peers who engage in antisocial acts, for they know it is only a matter of time before this child will talk and act in the same way. Stability of behavior tends to be maintained when a person remains in an environment that does not demand such change, and realizing this, parents may seek a school for their child that will continue the expectations of behavior established in the home. Proponents of Christian day schools give this as a major reason for the establishment of church-supported educational institutions.

Classical Conditioning Explains Our Likes and Dislikes

All of us can list the subjects we liked in school — and the ones we did not like. We may have liked reading but not math, music but not art, biology but not history. Each of us has a different list. How did we come about making our lists? What were the circumstances?

When we talk about the subjects we liked, we feel good inside and remember the reading teacher who took a special interest, the applause of the audience at a first piano recital, the excitement of dissecting a frog. But when we think of the subjects we did not like we become tense and would like to forget the "dummy" math class we were assigned to in high school while our friends took algebra and geometry, the embarrassment of a painting so poorly drawn that the teacher in amazement could only say "tell me about it," and a history class that threatened a scholarship because it skewed our grade point average. In each case the emotions and memories occur because of circumstances we experienced years before. We associate the subject studied (conditioned stimulus) with other events (pleasant or unpleasant) that produced the same reactions in the past that we feel today when we recount what happened.

The same is true in the matter of whether we wanted to please the teacher and do what we were asked or be as devious as possible just to get even. If we liked the teacher it was all coming up roses; if we didn't it was tacks in her chair and everyone in the class coughing at ten minutes after the hour.[1] All teachers tell students what they should and should not do. Whether students listen and how they respond depends in large measure on how they feel about the one in charge.

The personality of the teacher, then, and whether he or she has established rapport with students will make a big difference in how effective instruction will be in the matter of what behaviors are socially desirable and what will not be tolerated. It is only natural to want to please some people and not others. If children perceive that a teacher really likes them, it is easier for them, in turn, to engage in the behaviors expected of them. An association of a pleasant stimulus (the teacher) with desirable conduct is effective not only at the moment but sometimes for years to come.

THE TEACHER'S USE OF INSTRUMENTAL (OPERANT) CONDITIONING

Behaviors are learned not only by associating stimuli or events prior to the response, as in classical conditioning; behaviors are also learned by what happens after the behavior has taken place. This is known as instrumental or operant conditioning. If good things happen after a response is made, the response is reinforced and is more apt to occur again; if bad things happen after a response is made, the response is punished and is less apt to be repeated.

Behavior Modification

The method used is often referred to as behavior modification. Behavior modification, in the broadest sense of the term, is a modification of behavior regardless of the technique employed, but its usual meaning in psychological literature is an application of instrumental (operant) conditioning procedures to changing one's behavior. Behavior modification strategies demand the manipulation of environmental conditions so that good things happen after socially acceptable behaviors and bad things happen after socially unacceptable behaviors. By arranging the consequences of a person's acts, desirable behavior is strengthened and undesirable behavior is weakened or extinguished.

There are a series of steps to be followed to assure that behavior modification will occur, and although it is not essential that every step be taken, doing so provides order and direction to the procedure.

The first step is to decide who the subject will be. The subject is the person whose behavior will be modified. It may be oneself, a friend, the whole class, or just one child.

The next step is to note a specific undesirable behavior the subject engages in on a fairly regular basis. This is not hard to do. Talking out of turn, being late, swearing, complaining, not doing homework, hitting, repeated sharpening of pencils, staring out the window, plus a hundred more, are all possibilities.

Third, the baserate is taken. Baserate is the number of times within a specific period that the undesirable behavior occurs naturally before behavior modification begins. In obtaining baserate, the behavior must be broken into overt responses that can be observed and tallied. If the undesirable behavior is talking out of turn, the teacher will count the number of times the student talks without being called on during a thirty minute lesson. If the undesirable behavior is not doing homework, the teacher has only to mark how many days of the week the student comes to class without the homework assignment completed. If the undesirable behavior is swearing, the teacher will tally the number of times swearing occurs in a typical day. If these behaviors differ for the student from one class to another or from one time of the day to another, then baserate should be taken in each situation. Although it is not always essential to take baserate, without it we would not know how much improvement had taken place after behavior modification was implemented.

The fourth step is to determine the reinforcer for the undesirable behavior. Learning psychologists say there is always a reason why people do what they do. One of the tenets of operant conditioning is that a subject (animal or human) will not continue a behavior that is not instrumental or useful, and behavior is useful when the organism gets something it wants by engaging in that behavior. The reinforcer for talking out of turn may be the attention received from the teacher. The reinforcer for not doing homework may be that the child has more time to play. The reinforcer for swearing may be the smiles of friends and the good feeling one has when hostility is released in this way.

Meacham and Wiesen (1970) tell of a first-grade teacher who tried to decrease fighting behavior on the playground of several boys in her class. The more she attended to this, the more the fighting seemed to increase. She went to the counselor who first engaged the boys in "play therapy." He would take them out of the classroom at specific times for a period of special play at which time he would endeavor to establish a good relationship with them. The result was that the fighting increased even more than before. Apparently, the boys knew why they were being singled out to receive this special time with the counselor. The counselor then hit on an idea. The teacher was to observe the children during recess and if a child fought, his name was to be written on the board in the classroom. When the counselor came to get youngsters to spend time with them, he chose only from those children whose names did not appear on the board. Playground fighting soon ceased.

A similar incident was reported by Sulzer and Mayer (1972). Each time a child would push or hit, the teacher would say simply but firmly, "You cannot push. You must leave." The child was then placed on a chair in the hall outside the classroom for five minutes. This seemed to be effective for awhile, and then the hitting and pushing returned. Upon investigating the teacher found that the principal was stopping to give the youngster a pep talk on the importance of getting along with other people. "Having never in the past received any attention from the principal, the child's undesirable behavior was probably being reinforced by the well-intentioned, kindly toned lecture" (p. 157). A conference between teacher and principal cleared up the situation. The principal no longer stopped to chat, and hitting and pushing diminished.

After the reinforcer is determined, step five is to set up a program so the reinforcer does not follow the behavior (a Type II punisher). The teacher ignores the child who talks out of turn. The parent agrees that homework will be done before the child is allowed to play. The child who swears is seated in the classroom so he or she cannot see the reaction of friends.

Whenever the reinforcer is removed, as in the examples given, the response will not continue. But sometimes there are several reinforcers and we may not be able to name and remove them all. Also, some teachers seem unable to ignore undesirable behavior, parents may refuse to cooperate, or the child may be so used to hearing parents swear that profanity will continue even without the attention of friends. When this occurs, the undesirable behavior is followed by an aversive or painful event, known as a Type I punisher.

Each semester I have the students in my undergraduate psychology classes go through a behavior modification exercise using themselves as the subject. The behaviors mentioned most often by my students are faulty eating habits, smoking, and swearing. Most students will try a Type II punisher first. A Type II punisher for overeating may be taking away the good taste of the food. This can be done either by pretending that the food is unpalatable (the spaghetti is worms and the meatloaf is dung) or by adding something to the food that makes it taste terrible. Whether by imagination or by adding a noxious stimulus, the food no longer tastes good and the reinforcer has been removed.

The student who smokes sees each cigarette as a deprivation of oxygen, another nail in the coffin. The smoker pictures himself in a coffin suffocating and gasping for breath as each "nail" is pounded in. The one who swears will turn from others so as not to receive their attention, or she may tell herself how wrong it is to swear, thus removing the good feeling one normally would have after swearing.

If this is not effective, then a Type I punisher must follow the behavior. A Type I punisher for overeating might be, to put it in the words of my students, "looking at a picture of a girl in a string bikini who weighs 260 pounds" or "doing twenty sit-ups" or "running the stairwell." For smoking, the aversive stimulus might be "having friends tell you how bad it is for you" or "telling yourself it stinks" or "trying a different brand that has an unpleasant taste." For swearing, it might be "putting a quarter in a jar each time you swear" or "pinching yourself hard." One student carried a surgical mask that he wore for five minutes each time he swore. The punisher, either Type II or Type I, must have sufficient intensity for the undesirable behavior to be weakened or extinguished.

For obvious reasons, punishers are best applied to oneself. Care should be taken in using punishers with someone else, although it is generally considered permissible to use some types of punishers with dependent children in the context of the home or the school. If punishers are used, schools are now more apt to go to Type II punishers such as depriving the child of recess, a good grade, or a popcorn party on Friday afternoon. The Type I punisher of a paddling is used less and less.

At the same time the undesirable behavior is being punished, a desirable competing behavior is selected. This is step six of the behavior modification program. A desirable competing behavior is any socially acceptable behavior that cannot occur at the same time as the undesirable behavior. One does not eat modestly and overeat at the same time, nor does one refrain from smoking and smoke at the same time, nor can one be silent and swear at the same time. A person may substitute celery for pastries, sugarless gum for cigarettes, and kind words for swear words.

This step of selecting a desirable competing behavior is followed by the seventh step of using either the original reinforcer or another reinforcer to strengthen the desirable behavior. A reinforcer for not overeating may be feeling better physically or shopping for new clothes. The reinforcer for not smoking may be using the money formerly spent on cigarettes to buy cassettes for the car stereo. The reinforcer for not swearing may be getting the attention of others one likes, as in the case of the student who wore the surgical mask so that a girl he wanted to date who did not like swearing would go out with him.

Sometimes a person will decide to skip the fifth stage of punishment, going directly to the sixth and last stages of selecting a desirable competing behavior and reinforcing that behavior. It is undoubtedly more pleasant for all concerned if punishment is not used, and in some cases it is best not to punish. However, research and observation tell us that combining both a punisher for the undesirable behavior and a reinforcer for the desirable competing behavior increases the effectiveness of the technique and shortens the length of time needed for conditioning to take place.

Behavior modification procedures work. They are efficient and the steps are easy to understand and to implement. Anyone who says the method does not work either has not proceeded through all the steps or has not found adequate punishers for undesirable behaviors or adequate reinforcers for desirable behaviors. Even those with a bias against operant techniques, if trained in their use, have to admit that they do work.

A case in point is the Butler County Area Vocational-Technical School, north of Pittsburgh, which has been giving prizes for perfect attendance (Kelly, 1992). For perfect attendance "kids get a crack at daily drawings for fast-food dinners, monthly drawings for power tools . . . an annual drawing for the top prize — one of six cars, donated by local car dealers and refurbished by the kids in the auto body shops" (p. 1D). The six cars sit in a grassy area by the school for all to see. Other schools give out coupons for fast-food (donated by Pizza Hut™, McDonald's, Wendy's™, Long John Silvers, etc.), compact discs at music stores, and dinner dates in limousines (the limos being donated by local funeral homes). Still other schools let good students skip the final exam or have their choice of privileges. If some call this bribing, the schools call it "positive reinforcement." And it works! "In 1991-92 alone, there was an 86 percent increase in students with perfect attendance" (Kelly, p. 2D).

Programmed Instruction
Another application of instrumental (operant) conditioning in the schools is the use of programmed materials. When Skinner's daughter was in elementary school in the 1940s he studied the assignments she brought home and was concerned that the lessons were confusing, often having no specific goal. There was a substantial time interval before the lesson was graded (a teacher with a full class simply could not let every child know immediately if an answer was right or wrong), and the lesson seemed oriented to negative consequences (that is, his daughter would do an assignment so as not to be embarrassed). Skinner felt there must be a better way. Material to be learned should be programmed to assure a high level of success, each child could learn at his or her own rate, the teacher could monitor each student's progress, and there would be immediate feedback as to the correct response.

Teaching Machines
Teaching machines and programmed booklets were developed based on operant techniques. They provided for units of study being presented in small steps with immediate feedback as to whether the student's answer was right or wrong. Not only was there the advantage of not having to wait for the teacher to grade the lesson, but each problem or frame was

based on the one preceding so there was a sequence of steps in learning the lesson. Children progressed at their own rate, and teachers, whether or not they lacked formal training in the subject matter, could supervise a whole class at a time.

The greatest enthusiasm for teaching machines and other programmed approaches came in the 1950s and early 1960s when a number of studies indicated that children learned more in a given period of time by using programmed materials than when they were taught by traditional methods. But the excitement was short-lived. The materials were expensive and the machines often needed repair. Also, good programs were difficult to write and seemed to be the exception rather than the rule. Later studies showed that the rapid learning reported earlier did not continue over the long run, perhaps because the novelty had worn off and children became bored. Furthermore, the materials were appropriate only for certain subjects like mathematics, in which there was one right answer. They tended not to lend themselves to other subjects like social studies in which class discussions were of value. Reasoning, creativity, insight, and the sharing of ideas are difficult to program into a machine, yet these abilities play a vital role in the education of the child.

One of the heaviest uses of programmed materials at the present time is in Christian day schools using Accelerated Christian Education (A.C.E.) materials. Advertised by its founder and president, Donald Howard (1979), as "the most completely Christian curriculum on the market" (p. 10), A.C.E. is in booklet form and each packet "quotes Scriptures and is carefully planned to glorify God and to teach and encourage Christian living" (p. 10). Students set their own goals as to how many pages they will do that day and begin the next day where they left off. "Pupils work independently in their 'offices' (which have partitions high enough to discourage talking) throughout most of the day. . . . Incentives are offered by means of an elaborate, but effective, system of rewards and privileges, which include field trips and trophies" (Wiggin, 1981, p. 44).

Now called the School of Tomorrow, A.C.E. programs "provide complete curriculum for preschool through high school. . . . Approximately 7,000 schools in 106 countries around the world currently use A.C.E. curriculum to meet the educational needs of their children"

(Howard, 1993). Parsons (1987) states that roughly a third of all Christian schools in the United States operate with the A.C.E. curriculum (p. 64).

Public schools still make use of programmed materials, but to a lesser degree than was true twenty or twenty-five years ago. At times the programmed approach is appropriate for it adds interest and variety to the educational process, but it has been shown that its effectiveness diminishes when employed on a large scale. Programs need to be selected carefully and used only for certain types of materials. Nor should such lessons be used as a substitute for the well-trained teacher. Being educated is far more than knowing one correct answer to a question. Being educated means being creative, learning to get along with others, preparing for a career, appreciating the world in which we live, and acting in socially acceptable ways — skills that tend not to lend themselves to programmed instruction.

Computer Assisted Instruction
Computers now have taken the place of programmed booklets and teaching machines, and are being used on a grand scale in many school districts. Computer assisted instruction (CAI) is typically used at the elementary level and relies on drill and practice of material presented earlier by the teacher or a textbook. There are also tutorial programs in which new information is given. Problem-solving ability may be called for, often taking the form of games or simulations. Some programs deal with attitudes and values, moral concerns to the humanistic psychologist (Biehler & Snowman, 1993). Accelerated Christian Education also makes use of computer technology (Rowe, 1990).

Studies show that CAI provides interest and motivation, especially for students who may not do well with more traditional methods of instruction. But, like the mechanical teaching machine, the computer is only as effective as the quality of its programs. Good programs sometimes take thousands of hours to produce and therefore entail considerable expense, and the more interesting games and simulations may distract more than they teach. Used as supplemental classroom instruction, however, computer assisted instruction can be quite effective. Given the fascination with computers that many educators and students have, it appears that computer assisted instruction is here to stay.

THE TEACHER'S USE OF SOCIAL LEARNING

Morality and immorality, like other behaviors, are learned by observation and imitation. Both good and bad habits are formed when we copy the actions of people around us. We learn to be good by imitating people who are good; we learn the opposite when we imitate people who are bad. And, according to the learning psychologist, good and bad depend on what we do, not on internal states of thinking or feeling.

The Teacher As Model

As teachers we need to be reminded that many pairs of eyes see what we do and many pairs of ears hear what we say. Younger children are more apt to imitate the mannerisms and speech of the teacher; older children are more aware of the teacher's lifestyle and feel it unfair to be criticized for engaging in the same behaviors they see exhibited in their instructor. A lesson on personal cleanliness or physical fitness is less effective when taught by someone with oily hair or obese proportions, and teenagers feel it most unjust to be penalized for an activity such as smoking when the one who punishes them slips off to the furnace room several times a day to have a smoke. "Moral education does not just refer to students, but must encompass all other aspects of the educational environment. In an important way, teacher morality and the moral character of teachers influence the moral education that students receive. Teachers are not just facilitators or leaders of moral discussions or Socratic midwives, but serve as models for students" (Sichel, 1988, p. 225).

"Are you modeling honesty in your high school classroom?" is the question asked by Brian Keane (1984). A checklist is provided

> As teachers we need to be reminded that many pairs of eyes see what we do and many pairs of ears hear what we say. Younger children are more apt to imitate the mannerisms and speech of the teacher; older children are more aware of the teacher's lifestyle and feel it unfair to be criticized for engaging in the same behaviors they see exhibited in their instructor.

including an examination of the motivation and methodology behind the teacher's rules of order and of honesty. It is important to differentiate between rules that make for the smooth functioning of the classroom such as being quiet and staying in one's seat and rules that deal with issues that are in the realm of the moral such as not cheating, showing respect, and fair play. Are we as teachers vindictive, overly punitive, too permissive? Do we follow the policies and perform the duties expected of us in the particular school system in which we are employed? Do we "cut corners" when other adults are not looking? Students readily pick up on even our more subtle behaviors and soon learn whether we are genuine and sincere. "The personal stance of the teacher . . . is crucial, since students will derive their attitudes toward honesty, values and all of morality from the atmosphere with which they are surrounded" (p. 38).

Peers As Models

Hanshaw Middle School is one of five junior high schools in Modesto, California. At Hanshaw, the student population which is largely Hispanic is divided into seven "houses" which are essentially schools within a school. The 60 to 100 students in each house take all their classes together. Instead of naming the schools after colors or letters or animals, the principal came up with the idea of linking each school with one of the California State University campuses within a few hours' drive of Modesto. Arrangements are made for students to visit their namesake universities, where they are hosted by minority students. Some junior-high students wear T-shirts bearing the name of their school. The idea is simply for "the youngsters to picture themselves as college students someday" (Gursky, 1992, p. 33). Presently, only 3 percent of California State University graduates are Hispanic. Using college students of the same ethnic background as models, junior high youngsters hopefully will identify with them and will plan to imitate their behaviors when they complete high school.

Story Characters As Models

What kind of stories are children and young people reading in the context of the school? The content of basal readers and books on library shelves is receiving increased attention as concerned citizens find that many of the characters depicted in these books are unworthy role models for the child.[2] Children and teenagers are influenced by exemplars in stories as well as by real people. If they read of people who act and talk in dishonorable ways and yet receive no criticism or punishment for these behaviors, it only stands to reason that they, in turn, will be inclined to engage in similar activities. Lying may be condoned in a story as long as everything turns out all right, and outwitting a younger or less intelligent child may be pictured as entrepreneurial and shrewd. The pros and cons of censorship of classroom materials have been hotly debated, but the fact remains that our major responsibility is to our children and to their moral and spiritual development. Counteracting worldly influences is not easily done, nor do we wish to shelter our sons and daughters more than is necessary, yet a steady diet of the literature found in some classrooms will not result in the kinds of behavior we wish to see in the next generation.

Should We Return to the McGuffey Reader?
Some educators have advocated a return to the type of story read by children at the turn of the century. Interestingly, Graney (1977) found little difference in the overt behaviors of children depicted in McGuffey's Readers and the behaviors of children depicted in more recently used readers. He did find, however, that the model of authority had changed from individual figures in McGuffey to a combination of individualistic and collectivistic authority figures in modern readers and that the characters in McGuffey's Readers were more inner-directed, whereas the exemplars in modern readers were more inclined toward being in harmony with the peer group. Parents and teachers who feel there are times when the child should not go along with the crowd have reason to be concerned with some of the messages given in textbooks today.

GUIDELINES FOR PARENTS

Whether parents use classical conditioning, instrumental conditioning, social learning, or some combination of the three, the emphasis is on control. If we can control the environment, we can control the behaviors of our children. The control may come by pairing a neutral stimulus (e.g., the word "yes") with a natural stimulus (e.g., a hug) as in classical conditioning; ignoring, reinforcing, or punishing responses as in instrumental conditioning; or providing appropriate models for children to imitate as in social learning. But whatever the method, the focus is on manipulating the environment in such a way that overt behaviors are altered from socially undesirable to socially desirable forms. We know that behavior changes as circumstances change, and an understanding of how this takes place puts us in an advantageous position for modifying the behaviors of the children entrusted to our care.

> **Whether parents use classical conditioning, instrumental conditioning, social learning, or some combination of the three, the emphasis is on control. If we can control the environment, we can control the behaviors of our children.**

THE PARENT'S USE OF CLASSICAL CONDITIONING

Classical conditioning has a variety of uses in the home. We will mention but a few.[3]

Dealing with Unnecessary Fear

Parents may use classical conditioning to alleviate fear responses in children. By the time youngsters are four or five years of age, they are capable of imagining all kinds of terrible things happening to them. They fear the dark, the sound of a toilet flushing, wild animals in their bedroom at night, or someone who is strange in appearance.

When our older son was four and the neighbors would come home at night the lights from their car would create shadows on the wall of his room, frightening him as he was going to sleep. Shadows (conditioned stimuli) were linked in his mind with monsters (unconditioned stimuli) that could harm him. What was needed was a plan of action on our part to link shadows with pleasant rather than unpleasant unconditioned stimuli.

This was easily done. For several days, we had fun making shadow pictures on the wall. We got a children's book on shadows which we read to him. We would go for walks at night and jump on each others' shadows while at the same time trying to keep other family members from jumping on our own. It wasn't long before our son was no longer afraid of shadows. To put what happened in learning psychology terms, we had arranged the environment so that the emotion generated by shadows became one of pleasure rather than one of fear.

A similar approach may be used if we want the child not to be afraid of electrical storms. By taking the child to the window when a storm approaches, and holding the child close, we can talk about the beauty of the lightning and the deep tones of the thunder. By associating the storm with our warmth and pleasure, the child will come to appreciate one of the wonders of nature.

Establishing a Close Relationship with the Child
Classical conditioning begins at the time of birth. Infants have a need for nutrients and contact comfort. These needs are met when they are given the breast or the bottle and held close in their mothers' arms. The tension that arises from hunger or being alone is reduced by the food and by body contact with another human being. In classical conditioning terminology, the food and body contact are unconditioned or natural stimuli that result in the unconditioned or natural responses of sucking the nipple and of fingering the mother's breast or hair. As the child is fed, other stimuli also present are associated with these unconditioned stimuli and take on importance for the child. The sound of the mother's voice as she talks or sings to her baby, her facial expressions, the way she holds the baby, and even odors and colors, are associated with the meeting of the child's basic needs.

These conditioned stimuli (so called because they have significance only as they relate to or are conditioned on unconditioned stimuli) take on importance in their own right, and infants will come to desire the presence of the mother even when she is not directly meeting their needs for sustenance and contact comfort. They will make sounds to bring her to them, and when they are old enough to get around they will follow her, making sure she is close by. Her gestures and words begin to take on special significance, a nod or a yes telling them what they are doing is all right and a shake of the head or a no telling them to stop whatever they are doing and to go no further. In the classical conditioning paradigm all words are conditioned stimuli for they have no meaning apart from their concrete referents. So a mother who takes good care of her little ones, staying close by to meet their needs, will have a profound effect on their behavior as she communicates with them.

CLASSICAL CONDITIONING LINKED WITH SPIRITUAL TRUTHS

Further stimulus generalization, often referred to as higher order conditioning, occurs when the conditioned stimuli of the mother's presence and her words are linked to other conditioned stimuli. For example, you may tell your children of a heavenly Parent who loves and cares for them. Even as you as their earthly parent approve or disapprove of their actions, a Heavenly Father approves or disapproves of their behavior; and even as they are to listen to and obey you, they are to listen to and obey God.

There are times when these higher order conditioned stimuli may be linked directly with unconditioned stimuli, thereby strengthening the bond between the fulfilling of spiritual needs and the meeting of primary drives. Bible stories may be read to the small child when the child is sitting on the parent's lap, or the whole family may read the Scriptures together while enjoying a good meal or while sharing interesting experiences. As the child grows older and influences outside the home play a larger part in his or her behavior, it becomes increasingly difficult for parents to stamp in associative bonds, so it is important that this be done on a regular basis during the first few formative years of the child's life. A cohesive family in which members continue to engage in activities together will sustain the early influences of classical conditioning for a longer period of time.

RESPONSE GENERALIZATION LINKED WITH APPROPRIATE BEHAVIOR

Not only does stimulus generalization occur, but response generalization also takes place. For example, children who learn to act properly at home are more apt to act properly when away from home. If they cooperate with parents, they will probably cooperate with others. Response generalization, also called habit generalization or response tendencies, means a person acquires behaviors that become so automatic he or she engages in these practices even without thinking about them. Saying please and thank you and sharing toys and interests are examples of such desirable response tendencies. Frequently we do not have time to think through what we should do in a given situation, so it becomes important that these reflexive responses considered to be good and right by the society become part of our automatic response repertoires.

CUING AND MORAL BEHAVIOR

Conditioned stimuli are cues linked with unconditioned stimuli to alert the child as to the appropriate response. As has been mentioned, all words are conditioned stimuli and are used by parents to tell the child what should or should not be done. Sometimes, however, we find ourselves using the same words and phrases over and over, creating unpleasantness for everyone. If we hear ourselves saying to our child, "I'm sick and tired of telling you . . ." or "If I've told you once, I've told you a hundred times . . ." this is a good indication that cues other than words may be more suitable.

Krumboltz and Krumboltz (1972) tell of eleven-year-old Alan who was given the responsibility of feeding his dog and turtle. Constant reminders from his mother were a source of mutual aggravation. She then devised the plan of hanging a reversible cardboard sign each morning and evening where Alan could see it. On one side the sign said, "Alan, we're hungry. Woofer and Humpback." The other side read, "Now we're full. Thanks. Woofer and Humpback." When Alan fed the pets he turned the sign over himself (pp. 80-81). A cardboard sign proved to be a more suitable cue than verbal reminders.

Taking responsibility for the welfare of pets is one of the ways we teach our children to develop dependable and caring behavior. In time, Alan will remember to tell himself that the pets must be attended to, and the cardboard sign will not be needed. Through this seeemingly simple activity Alan is learning to act in moral ways.

EMOTIONAL GENERALIZATION AND MORAL BEHAVIOR

Classical conditioning also reveals how emotions develop, and even though the focus of learning psychology is on overt behaviors rather than on affective responses, the two cannot be separated entirely. "Acceptance of the relationship of reinforcement and emotion makes necessary the systematic study of classical conditioning. . . . Psychologists who consider learning and behavior in their work need access to a theory that treats emotions and behavior . . . in a unified framework" (Staats, 1988, p. 748). Without classical conditioning the learning psychologist would be at a loss to link the affective and the behavioral.

Emotional generalization is as relevant to an understanding of how moral behaviors are learned as is stimulus generalization and response generalization. The feelings of our children toward us and their pride in being members of the family relate directly to their behavior. Conditioning children to act morally should be done in the atmosphere of the home. It is the most natural and effective place for the development of dependable and responsible actions.

THE PARENT'S USE OF INSTRUMENTAL CONDITIONING

Considerably more has been written about the application of instrumental (operant) conditioning in comparison with classical conditioning. Even so, most of the information on instrumental methods applies to the school rather than to the home. An exception to this is Gerald Patterson's *Living with Children* (1976), written in a style most parents will find easy to understand and to use. The ideas presented were pretested with over a hundred families, and thousands more have profited from their use. The down-to-earth language and programmed approach of the book make it an informative guide to handling problems adults often have with their children. All parents would do well to be familiar with steps to take to deal with such behaviors as disobedience, whining, not wanting to go to bed at night, bedwetting, and temper tantrums. Changing unacceptable responses to acceptable responses is what behavior modification is about.

Using Instrumental Conditioning with Children Who Steal

There is a section in this small volume on children who steal. As stealing is categorized in all societies as immoral, it is interesting to note ways parents may weaken or extinguish stealing by rearranging the child's environment. First, the parent must count "(a) when he borrows things without asking; (b) money missing from your purse; (c) when anyone says they saw him steal; (d) when he shows up with some new item he says he found or was given to him" (Patterson, p. 105). The parent should not try to prove the child stole something, as the child will argue, thereby setting a trap for the parent.

Let the child know he is being monitored and that at the end of the week if there are points against him, he must put in an extra hour of work. This he will do even if you can't prove he stole. More points mean more hours. If he took something from outside the home, he must not only work but return the item and offer to work for the one who owned the item. If this is done consistently, the child will learn in time to avoid not only stealing but situations in which he could be accused of stealing.

Patterson states that stealing is usually related to lying and to having time to wander. "A lie costs 5 points. Work out how long it should take for him to get home from school. Give him 2 points for getting home on time and letting you know" (p. 107). Any time he leaves home he must ask permission, saying where he is going, who he will be with, and what he is going to do. He is then told when he must be home. If he is late, he loses points. If he returns on time, he is given points. The behaviors of each day are put on a chart, so the child can see where he stands. As he becomes more responsible and stays out of trouble, he is given more time away from home. But always the parent has a right to know where he is, who he is with, and what he is doing. The parent must be consistent or behavior modification will lose its effectiveness.

Using Instrumental Conditioning with Children Who Fight
Another source of information is Rodger Bufford's *The Human Reflex: Behavioral Psychology in Biblical Perspective* (1981). In a chapter entitled "Application of Behavioral Approaches to Child Rearing," Bufford has given a detailed account of how parents can systematically shape the behavior of the child in areas such as getting dressed, toilet training, table manners, and body hygiene. "From a behavioral perspective, moral behavior is believed to develop in the same ways that other forms of behavior develop: through the principles of respondent and operant conditioning" (Bufford, p. 170).

Aggressive behaviors such as hitting and kicking are considered by many people to be wrong for they harm others. Bufford gives the example of a mother using operant techniques to reduce fighting in her sons. Whenever they would hit, kick, shove, or scratch, she would make them go to separate rooms for a specified number of minutes. A period of sharing and cooperation would be followed by her approval along with an invitation to have a snack of juice or cookies.

Many of us as parents have tried similar techniques. Others wait until the fighting and noise get beyond the point of toleration and then step in and punish children by scolding or spanking. Whether we separate our children or use a punisher, we will get the desired results. But in the long run we are working against what we want to accomplish if we model the very behavior we do not wish to see in our children, namely, using aggressive means to stop aggression. Granted that the parent has the right to scold and spank; that is not the point. The point is that children imitate what they see. In homes where parents use physical punishment as the major way or the only way of keeping children in line, there is considerably more aggression between siblings than is the case where parents use nonagressive techniques. We will pursue this thought in greater depth when we look at the topic of social learning in the home.

BEHAVIOR MODIFICATION

Parents may go through the same behavior modification steps with their children as was outlined for the teacher. First, we decide if the subject is one child or more than one child in the family. Second, we decide what undesirable behavior our child engages in that needs to be reduced or eliminated. Third, we count how often our child engages in this undesirable behavior. Fourth, we try to find the reason our child engages in this behavior; in other words, what is reinforcing the undesirable behavior? Fifth, how can we remove the reinforcer so the behavior does not continue? Sixth, what is a desirable competing behavior that our child can do instead? Seventh, how can we reinforce the child for the desirable behavior so it occurs more often?

One of my graduate students used these steps with his children when the family went on an extended vacation trip. The undesirable behaviors the children engaged in were complaining about the length of the trip, being thirsty, being hungry, and saying they had to go to the bathroom. He did not keep a record of how often these behaviors occurred but assured me it happened "all the time." The reinforcer for the behaviors was apparently telling the children the trip was not that much longer and stopping for soda pop, food, and restroom breaks. The competing desirable behavior was for the children not to complain about their discomfort. But how could this be done? How could he reward them for not complaining? Scolding only made the situation more unpleasant.

My student then hit on a good idea. Before the trip he gave each of his children five dollars worth of quarters to be spent however they wished after they reached their destination. But there was a catch. Any time a child would ask, "When are we going to get there?" or "I have to go to the bathroom" or "I'm thirsty" that child had to forfeit a quarter. Any complaints about giving up a quarter meant forfeiting another quarter. The reinforcer for not complaining was having more quarters to spend while on vacation. There were ample opportunities during the trip for eating, drinking, and going to the bathroom; so no mistreatment was involved. It was my student's way of arranging environmental contingencies so the trip would be a pleasant one rather than an unpleasant one. Even his children liked it better.

Is Behavior Modification a Form of Bribery?
Criticisms may be leveled against any form of control, but behavior modification seems to have received more than its share. Opponents say that the child is supposed to be good and therefore should not be bribed to behave. Yet, a question must be asked. How many adults would continue to go to work each day and do a good job if they knew they would never receive another paycheck? Is getting paid bribery?

Also, the charge is made that no one has the right to exercise that much control over another human being. But the fact remains that all of us are controlling each other all the time anyway. Parents control their children and children control their parents. It is a two-way street. Is it unethical to know what we are doing so we can do a better job? When we think of the many people who are unhappy because they have unconsciously trained family members to complain, act rude, or be lazy, it would seem that they owe it to themselves and to each other to be aware of what they are doing and program their behaviors to produce optimal results.

Does Behavior Modification Contribute to Self-Interest?
The objection is often raised that children will learn to play the game and will act badly unless they are externally reinforced for every task completed. The attitude of "make it worth my while" is not acceptable in a family in which members must cooperate with each other. If I ask my son to mow the lawn and he responds, "What are you going to give me, Mom?" my answer will be, "Tell you what, son, I'm going to give

you supper and a place to sleep tonight." This is followed with a lecture on being a part of a family unit in which we all do things for each other without monetary rewards.

One of the guidelines of contingency management is that the one in charge will reinforce children in such a way that in time children will learn to provide their own reinforcers. Children who take responsibility in the family and do their share of the work have better self-concepts. They know they are of value and are appreciated by others within the family unit.

When Is It Best Not to Use Behavior Modification?
Some tasks may be so difficult that tangible reinforcers are necessary at the *beginning* of the learning process. Children who find reading frustrating and painful, for example, may do a great deal of it if they are given money (or extra TV time or staying up later at night) contingent upon the amount read. The parent will pair the money with the social reinforcer of praise so that the child will receive both reinforcers at the same time. In time the tangible reinforcer is no longer needed, and the social reinforcer of praise is paired with the child's pride in doing something that is hard to do. The child also is gaining favor in the eyes of the teacher and classmates. The object is to get the child to read well enough that reading no longer is frustrating and painful and he or she can enjoy the story for itself. But some children will never get to that place unless they first are given a tangible reward.

By contrast, one would not tell a child who loves to read that a reward will be given when the book is finished. That is going the wrong direction and is at cross-purposes with behavior modification principles. Behavior modification does not appear to be needed once the desirable behavior is well established and the behavior contains within itself its own reinforcer.

THE PARENT'S USE OF SOCIAL LEARNING
Parents not only condition the child to act as he or she does, they also are the child's first example of how people are supposed to behave. Parents should not be held completely responsible for what the child becomes, but they are, nonetheless, the salient influence during the early years when habits are formed. Imitating parental behavior is usually

208

indirect, inasmuch as neither parent nor child is aware of the extent to which it occurs. Studies indicate that children see the parent as having more privileges and greater power, so they are reinforced by the thought that they too will have these advantages if they act in the same way.

Direct and Indirect Forms of Modeling
Modeling also may have a direct or didactic function when used to teach a specific skill. "Watch what I do and then you do it the same way" is a familiar phrase. Learning to tie shoelaces, prepare a meal, swim, or drive a car may be acquired by consciously imitating a model. Language acquisition involves both indirect and direct forms of modeling. The child imitates the speech of the adult and also puts words together in grammatically correct patterns when instructed to do so. In a similar fashion, parents who talk about the Lord and spend time reading the Scriptures may observe the same behaviors in their children. And if they direct their children to engage in Bible reading and prayer, the results are even more visible.

The indirect approach may not be sufficient in and of itself to obtain the desired results. When this occurs, the direct approach also must be used. All of us have seen parents who were kind and considerate of their children and who assumed that their children would automatically treat them in the same way. When this did not happen, they wondered what went wrong. The direct approach of giving specific instructions as to the behavior expected, along with reinforcers for appropriate actions and punishers for inappropriate actions, is needed as well. But, as we have said, parents should keep in mind when reinforcing or punishing not to exhibit behaviors they do not wish to see in their children. This is not always possible, but at least we should make the effort.

Aggressive and Nonaggressive Behaviors Are Imitated
Sears, Maccoby, and Levin (1957) interviewed 379 mothers of kindergarten-age children asking them how they had raised their children from birth. Mothers who reported the least amount of aggression in their children were mothers who did not allow the child to act aggressively, and when the child did begin an aggressive act, the mother would stop the child in a nonaggressive way. For example, if the child tried to hit her (as all small children do from time to time) she would catch the

child's arm tightly, but without hurting the child, and would tell the child in a calm but firm voice that this was something she must *never, never* do.

Mothers who reported considerable meanness or aggression in their children used a different pattern of control. Children were allowed to act aggressively after which they would be punished for the act. If they hit her, she would hit them back. They could be abusive to other members of the family and show their anger in other ways, but it was only when the quarreling, loud noise, door slamming, or whatever made the mother sufficiently uncomfortable occurred, that she would step in and stop them, often with loud scolding and slaps. In this way, children developed patterns of aggressive behavior and also observed aggressive actions on the part of the parent.

Parental Aggression Linked with Delinquency in Children
We live in an aggressive society, and the home is one of the least safe places for many people to be. More than 2.5 million cases of child abuse were reported in the United States in 1990, and more than 1,200 children died from abuse-related incidents. As noted in chapter 3, Glueck and Glueck (1974) found that most delinquents and criminals came from homes in which discipline was overstrict or erratic. By comparison, few offenders came from homes in which discipline was firm but kindly. Both overstrict and firm parents punish their children, but the difference lies in the severity of the punishment, the fairness with which it is administered, and the extent to which it is used in comparison with less aggressive ways of keeping the child in line.

Dozens of studies have been conducted on this topic since the Gluecks reported their findings. Hotaling, Straus, and Lincoln (1990) in a review of the literature found that "it appears that children assaulted by parents are more violent toward brothers, sisters, parents, and persons outside the family. They are also more likely to be involved in property crime, to have adjustment difficulties in school, and to be involved with the police" (p. 458).

Other Models in the Home
Other influences in the home also play a part in whether the child will act in moral or immoral ways, and the parent would do well to exercise control in these areas. The books the child reads, the magazines looked

at, the pictures and plaques hung on the walls, the programs watched on television, the CDs and tapes listened to — all are a part of the environment of the home. And all serve as models for the child.

Televised Violence and Aggressive Behavior
The effect of television alone is enormous. By the time children complete high school, they will have watched 22,000 hours of TV — 11,000 more than they will have spent in classrooms (Phillips, 1991, p. vii). In a two-volume 1982 National Institute of Mental Health report, summarizing twenty years of research and more than 3,000 scientific studies, a major finding was that televised violence is linked to later aggressive behavior in children (Rubenstein, 1983). Liebert and Sprafkin (1988) also reviewed twenty years of research and support these findings. "The accumulated data provide strong and unambiguous support for the hypothesis that TV violence viewing can cultivate antisocial attitudes and shape viewers into acceptance of aggressive behavior as an appropriate and acceptable way of dealing with others. . . . The value-shaping effects of TV violence appear to hold for children of both sexes and to the full age range from preschool through late adolescence and adulthood" (p. 158).

Phillips (1991) suggests that parents take a direct approach in controlling the amount of violence children see on TV. His five-point plan is as follows:

1. Count the number of different weapons. . . . If more than three are used, or one is used more than three times, turn it off.
2. Count the number of people killed. If anyone is killed, turn it off.
3. Count the number of unprovoked attacks (whether the character is good or bad). If there are any, turn it off.
4. How do the good characters resolve conflict? Do they use the same methods as the bad guys? If so, turn it off.
5. Do the good guys break laws? If so, turn it off. (p. 71)

Other Effects of Television
Lisa Kuhmerker (1976), editor of the *Moral Education Forum,* wrote:

We have become very much aware of the potential harmful effects of violence on television, of the fragmentation of children's attention, of the lack of demand that the medium makes on children's attention span. But there are other potential effects of television whose influence have hardly begun to be explored. . . . I think we should look long and hard to see what the effect on children may be when they repeatedly hear canned laughter in situations where sympathy might be the appropriate reaction. . . . In real life children get many non-verbal cues from adults which correct the initial impression that another person's misfortune is funny. The stereotypes of situation comedies and the simplistics of cartoons carry no such corrective message. (p. 263)

> **The learning theory stress on the importance of the environment and the way in which the environment relates directly to overt behavior is one we all share.**

Parents Need to Recognize the Value of Learning Psychology
The learning theory stress on the importance of the environment and the way in which the environment relates directly to overt behavior is one we all share. It *does* make a difference what type of home the child grows has, and the moral environment of the home is as important as any other aspect of the environment. A moral environment is present when parents are good models of moral behavior and when they condition their children to act in socially desirable ways.

GUIDELINES FOR PASTORS

The word *pastor* means shepherd. Jesus called Himself "the Good Shepherd" and exemplified all the characteristics and duties of a shepherd. Being a pastor is a high calling from God and one to be taken seriously.

THE PASTOR'S USE OF CLASSICAL CONDITIONING
What is the child's reaction when the words *church, God,* or *Bible* are heard? Is the response favorable? The answer lies in the experiences (unconditioned stimuli) the child associates with these words (conditioned stimuli). These associations, in turn, are either directly or indirectly the result of policies and arrangements made by the pastor in conjunction with other leaders of the congregation.[4]

For the very young child, eating graham crackers, knowing that mother is near, and not being restricted in moving around is pleasant;

being hungry, lacking contact comfort,[5] and being made to sit still is unpleasant. As the child grows older the specific conditions that bring pleasure will change, and these too will be linked with events within the church. In time hundreds of other incidents are added to the list, favorable or unfavorable unconditioned stimuli, that cause the person to either look forward to attending the place of worship or dread the prospect of being there. Knowing this, church leaders have Sunday School classes and activities within the church that meet the needs of the different age groups.

What is the young person's reaction to other words (conditioned stimuli) associated with the church; words like *prayer* or *Bible study* or *evangelism* or *pastor* or *God?* According to the November 30, 1992 issue of *National & International Religion Report,* the word *clergy* does not rate high in many people's minds. The Princeton Religious Research Center found that "public confidence in the clergy has reached an all-time low. . . . Just 54 percent of respondents gave clergy 'high' or 'very high' marks for honesty and ethics" (Wike, 1992, p. 1). Pharmacists received a 66 percent vote of confidence with car sales personnel being the lowest at 5 percent. Also near the bottom were members of Congress (11 percent) and lawyers (18 percent). It would seem that clergy are not living up to their high calling of being moral and spiritual persons. The recent televangelist scandals have no doubt lowered pastors' ratings, as their financial and sexual misdeeds have been generalized to all clergy.

Learning about God relates both to the everyday activities in the home (Deut. 6:7) and to those special times when the people of God gather together to worship and praise their Redeemer. In the Old Testament we read that these special occasions meant a break from the regular duties of the week (Lev. 23:3-4) and provided an opportunity for feasting (Ex. 12:14) and for storytelling (Josh. 4:21-24) — events all children enjoy. In the New Testament we learn that Jesus Himself at the age of twelve journeyed to Jerusalem to observe the Passover (Luke 2:42).

But twentieth-century America is different. Times have changed and going to the place of worship may not be the high point of a person's week or traveling to another town to observe a religious holiday the principal reason for taking a vacation. How can the church of today compete with all the stimuli in a child's life — the TV, the movie theater, and the ever-present video game? How can the Sunday School capture the interest of those who have no religious background and little encouragement from their families? Is there an answer?

Some church leaders say that there is. Interestingly, the answer lies in a full-scale implementation of instrumental techniques which we will take up next. The results are impressive and show that operant procedures are as effective when used in the church as when used anywhere else. If success can be measured by numbers of people, and many feel that it can, there are few success stories that rival those of churches that have gone all out for a program based on contingency management.

THE PASTOR'S USE OF INSTRUMENTAL CONDITIONING

The First Baptist Church of Hammond, Indiana, boasted of an average weekly Sunday School attendance of 13,500, most of whom were children bused from the Chicago area. How did the church do it? Edgerton (1975) explains:

> There is fierce competition between the bus workers to increase attendance at the Sunday school. The children are offered everything from on-board entertainment (such as the man in the gorilla outfit) to food and gifts (rubber spiders and "flowers for mom"). Recently, children who brought in new members were told to dip into a bucket of "pennies from heaven," and next week they will be taken to McDonald's for "Egg McMuffin Sunday." (p. 1)

From candy to Kung Fu exhibitions to a trip to Jamaica as a prize for "soul-winning," the reinforcers were given, and all with the purpose of reaching boys and girls with the message of Jesus Christ.

Those who find the method intriguing will enjoy Bill Wilson's *Buses, Bibles, and Banana Splits: Promotional Ideas for Bus Ministry and Children's Church* (1977). Activities follow the yearly calendar, and pages in the book are perforated so that individual sheets may be removed and copied or used for advertising purposes. Events include breakfast on the bus, hot dog day, pumpkin Sunday, and haunted house, with a free boat ride or helicopter ride for the boy or girl bringing the most visitors. Children on the bus with the most passengers are treated to a giant banana split. The ideas in the book are said to be passed on to the reader "as a manual for evangelism, to be used in your Jerusalem, Judea and to the uttermost parts of the world" (Wilson, 1977, inside back cover).

Some people object to the use of tangible reinforcers to increase church school attendance, and yet the method probably is used to some extent in all churches.[6] Gold stars are placed after children's names each time they come or pictures of Bible story characters are colored and proudly taken home. When children attend enough Sundays consecutively they are given pins to wear or certificates to keep, and their names are printed in the church bulletin. In one study (Captain, 1975) the tangible reinforcer of money was found to be effective in getting high school students to read the Bible and to have a positive attitude toward themselves in relationship to Bible reading.

Instrumental conditioning is used to enhance the work of the church in other ways as well, and several writers have explained how it is done. Collins (1969) describes the use of teaching machines and programmed booklets to teach Bible stories, and Ratcliff (1978) explains how laypersons may be shaped into effective soul-winners by gradually reinforcing closer and closer approximations to the desired behavior seen in actual witnessing. Bufford (1981) shows how memorizing Scripture verses, learning religious concepts, and planning the Sunday School curriculum are enhanced by the use of operant procedures, and George and Dustin (1970) write that the pastor of the church should function as a behavioral counselor pinpointing for the parishioner-client the actions that produced the problem and being "a potent source of reinforcement" (p. 18) when those actions change to more acceptable forms of behavior. It appears that a number of Christian authors would agree with Steckel (1979) when he says that "religious institutions will be enriched by behavior modification in their tasks of . . . social action, pastoral care and counseling, and religious education. . . . And church education programs may become far more successful in specifying the kinds of persons and institutions we want ourselves to be as religious people, by using behavioral analysis and behavior modification methods" (p. 166).

Despite numerous criticisms, the behavioral approach will continue to be used in the church. It will be used by both the critic who is seemingly unaware of the ways in which he or she uses it and the supporter who may need to exercise greater caution and restraint. As additional research is conducted and more attention is given to methodology, our understanding of how to apply the principles of behavioral psychology to the ongoing work of the church will be increased.

THE PASTOR'S USE OF SOCIAL LEARNING

One Sunday morning one of our parishioners brought her three-year-old granddaughter to church. As my husband entered the pulpit, the child whispered, "There goes God."

We find such comments amusing, but they also make us stop to think. Do children really get their ideas about God and His attributes by watching and listening to those of us who are His representatives on earth? If this is so, it is indeed sobering. What image does a child have of God when told that God is a Heavenly Father? Some have even quit using the term "Heavenly Father" in Sunday School classes with children who had been abused or abandoned by their fathers.

One of the ways in which the pastor and other church leaders encourage moral behavior is to live a moral life and to help others to do the same. Stott (1992) puts this under the pastoral duty of *leading* the sheep. As the rector of All Souls Church in London, he writes:

> It is our solemn responsibility to lead people in such a way that it is safe for them to follow us. That is, we have to set them a consistent and reliable example. We need to remember that Jesus introduced into the world a new style of leadership, namely leadership by service and example, not by force. . . . It is frightening to think how undiscerning many sheep are. That is why it is essential to lead well, to set a good example, with no dichotomy between our preaching and our practice. (p. 285)

As was mentioned in the last chapter, behavior imitated must always be reinforced in some way for it to continue. The reinforcer for imitating the behavior of another may come from the attention one receives when imitating, or it may come from the consequence of the behavior itself, or in some cases, it is vicarious in that the one imitating sees himself or herself as having the experiences and characteristics of the one imitated. Coming to the place of worship, bowing one's head in prayer, and singing hymns of praise are learned by seeing others do these things, and if copying these behaviors meets with approval or if people feel better for having done them they will engage in these behaviors again and again. The young person who thrills to the stories told by missionaries and who pictures himself or herself as a missionary with all the adventure and risk involved is more apt someday to become a missionary than the young person who has never been exposed to such a model.

The work of the church is served by those who are aware of their influence and are careful to live exemplary lives. The Apostle Paul understood this when he said to the Corinthians, "Follow my example, as I follow the example of Christ" (1 Cor. 11:1). But exemplary models are not always sufficient to assure similar behaviors in others. Paul wrote to Titus that an elder in the church must not only be "blameless" (Titus 1:6), but "must hold firmly to the trustworthy message as it has been taught, so that he can encourage others by sound doctrine" (v. 9). Training programs or discipling arrangements will help future leaders understand the truths of God's Word both with regard to Christian doctrine and with regard to appropriate conduct. As Paul exhorted Timothy, "What you heard from me, keep as the pattern of sound teaching. . . . Flee the evil desires of youth, and pursue righteousness . . . so that the man of God may be thoroughly equipped for every good work" (2 Tim. 1:13; 2:22; 3:17).

NOTES

1. The attitudes, actions, and experiences mentioned are not necessarily those of the author.

2. For helpful guidance in finding quality children's books see G. Hunt (1989), *Honey for a child's heart: The imaginative use of books in family life.* Grand Rapids: Zondervan; E. Wilson (1987), *Books children love: A guide to the best in children's literature.* Wheaton, IL: Crossway Books; D.P. Donaviri, ed. (1992) *Best of the best for children.* New York: American Library Association/Random House.

3. One of the more effective applications of classical conditioning has been in the treatment of enuresis or chronic bedwetting. The child sleeps on a moisture-sensitive pad and any moisture on the pad activates an alarm (unconditioned stimulus) that awakens the child (unconditioned response). The association of the alarm with bladder

tension (conditioned stimulus) means that in time the bladder tension will cause the child to awaken (conditioned response) before urination begins. When this occurs, the child has been classically conditioned not to wet the bed.

4. My earliest recollections of church were indeed favorable and occurred when I was two and three years of age. Our family went to the Church of the Open Door which was then in downtown Los Angeles and was affiliated with the Bible Institute of Los Angeles (Biola). Two- and three-year-olds were placed in a room next to the nursery. While munching on graham crackers I would slip into the nursery to look at the babies. What could be more fun than munching on graham crackers and looking at babies? I loved going to church.

When I turned four I was promoted from the "graham cracker and milk class" to the "coloring book class" that was located further from the nursery. In fact, I couldn't even find the nursery even though I tried. No longer were there crackers to munch on; no longer could I slip in to see the babies when no one was looking. Now in Sunday School, Bible stories were told and after a story we were given crayons to color a picture that related to the story. My disappointment was great. I didn't want to color pictures; I wanted to see the babies. No longer did I like going to church.

5. Contact comfort refers to the satisfaction an organism feels when in close physical contact with another being. A toddler cradled and rocked in her father's arms experiences contact comfort. Child psychologists believe that contact comfort is as important to psychological development as good food is to bodily growth.

6. My husband and I became aware that church people differ in their ideas of what constitutes an acceptable prize (reinforcer) when we purchased a thoroughbred cocker spaniel puppy to be given to the child who brought the most visitors to Sunday School. Placing the pup in a box on top of the piano during the Sunday School hour for all to witness her cute antics did far more to inspire the children to bring their friends than it did to win the approval of some of the older and more staid members of the congregation. Since that time more Bibles have been purchased than puppies.

REFERENCES

Amory, C. (1971, February 27). Trade winds. *Saturday Review,* p. 10.

Biehler, R.F., & Snowman, J. (1993). *Psychology applied to teaching.* (7th ed.). Boston: Houghton Mifflin.

Bufford, R.K. (1981). *The human reflex: Behavioral psychology in biblical perspective.* San Francisco: Harper & Row.

Captain, P.A. (1975). The effect of positive reinforcement on comprehension, attitudes, and rate of Bible reading in adolescents. *Journal of Psychology and Theology, 3,* 49–55.

Collins, G.R. (1969). *Search for reality: Psychology and the Christian*. Wheaton, IL: Key Publishers.

Edgerton, M. (1975, November 3). Sunday school uses bus fleet and candy to win kids' souls. *The Wall Street Journal*, pp. 1, 24.

George, R.L., & Dustin, E.R. (1970, December). The minister as a behavioral counselor. *Pastoral Psychology, 21,* 15–20.

Glueck, S., & Glueck, E. (1974). *Of delinquency and crime: A panorama of years of search and research*. Springfield, IL: C.C. Thomas.

Graney, M. (1977). Role models in children's readers. *School Review, 85,* 247–263.

Gursky, D. (1992, October). Personal best. *Teacher Magazine, 4*(2), 30–35.

Hotaling, G.T., Straus, M.A., & Lincoln, A.J. (1990). Intrafamily violence and crime and violence outside the family. In M.A. Straus & R.J. Gelles (Eds.), *Physical violence in American families: Risk factors and adaptations to violence in 8,145 families* (pp. 431–470). New Brunswick, NJ: Transaction Publishers.

Howard, D.R. (1979). *Facts about Accelerated Christian Education*. Lewisville, TX: Accelerated Christian Education.

————. (1993, February 8). Personal communication with Pastor Robert Clouse, First Brethren Church, Clay City, IN.

Keane, B.M. (1984, May). Are you modeling honesty in your high school classroom? *Momentum, 15,* 36–38.

Kelly, D. (1992, December 22). Incentives grab teens' attention. *USA Today*, pp. 1D, 2D.

Krumboltz, J.D., & Krumboltz, H.B. (1972). *Changing children's behavior*. Englewood Cliffs, NJ: Prentice-Hall.

Kuhmerker, L. (1976). Social interaction and the development of a sense of right and wrong in young children. *Journal of Moral Education, 5,* 257–264.

Liebert, R.M., & Sprafkin, J. (1988). *The early window: Effects of television on children and youth* (3rd ed.). New York: Pergamon Press.

Meacham, M.L., & Wiesen, A.E. (1970). *Changing classroom behavior: A manual for precision teaching*. Scranton, PA: International Textbook Company.

Parsons, P.F. (1987). *Inside America's Christian schools*. Macon, GA: Mercer University Press.

Patterson, G.R. (1976). *Living with children: New methods for parents and teachers*. Champaign, IL: Research Press.

Phillips, P. (1991). *Saturday morning mind control*. Nashville: Oliver-Nelson Books.

Ratcliff, D.E. (1978). Using behavioral psychology to encourage personal evangelism. *Journal of Psychology and Theology, 6,* 219–224.

Rowe, H.E. (1990). *True education: What every parent needs to know.* Lewisville, TX: Accelerated Christian Education.

Rubenstein, E.A. (1983). Television and behavior. *American Psychologist, 38,* 820–825.

Sears, R.R., Maccoby, E.E., & Levin, H. (1957). *Patterns of child rearing.* Evanston, IL: Row, Peterson.

Sichel, B.A. (1988). *Moral education: Character, community, and ideals.* Philadelphia: Temple University Press.

Staats, A.W. (1988). Skinner's theory and the emotion-behavior relationship: Incipient change with major implications. *American Psychologist, 43,* 747–748.

Steckel, C.J. (1979). *Theology and ethics of behavior modification.* Washington, DC: University of America Press.

Stott, J. (1992). *The contemporary Christian: Applying God's word to today's world.* Downers Grove, IL: InterVarsity Press.

Sulzer, B., & Mayer, G.R. (1972). *Behavior modification procedures for school personnel.* Hinsdale, IL: Dryden Press.

Wiggin, E.E. (1981, August). Should your grade schooler receive Accelerated Christian Education? *Christian Life,* pp. 40–44.

Wike, S.M. (1992, November 30). *National and International Religion Report, 6*(25), 1–8.

Wilson, B. (1977). *Buses, Bibles, and banana splits: Promotional ideas for bus ministry and children's church.* Grand Rapids: Baker Book House.

EIGHT

Moral Growth by Moral Reasoning: A Cognitive View

You are a member of a Board of Review at a general hospital that is meeting tonight to decide which of seven applicants will be provided with the use of a home dialysis machine. Each of the seven has been evaluated by the medical staff and determination has been made that each will probably die in one to two months without the kidney machine. The board must rank order the seven candidates. Only four machines are available.

You are given a brief description of each of the applicants: Larry is thirty-one, married, with one small child, works as a teller in a bank, and his wife is employed as an elementary school teacher. Maria is thirty-nine, unmarried, and a physical therapist at a VA hospital. Pamela is twenty-three, married, no children, and teaches social studies at the local junior high school. John is seventy, retired, has a wife, three grown children and several grandchildren. He is still active in the community. Jennifer is thirty-four, divorced, has three dependent children, and works as a secretary. Willow is about fifty, has several children by three wives, lives by himself, and is unemployed. Robert is eleven and one of six children.

You are now faced with a moral dilemma. How will you decide which four should be given the highest rankings? It is a serious decision, for you are, quite literally, deciding who will live and who will die. What criteria do you use to make your decision? Does age matter? Should one's contribution to society make a difference? Does the love of family and friends give one an advantage over someone who lives alone or has few friends? Will you say that all seven have equal worth and the only way to decide is to "draw straws"?

Because you are a conscientious person you will give this careful thought. You will review the characteristics of each candidate and think through the criteria you are using to decide which four should be given a life-saving machine. You are using your mind to come to a decision. You are doing what cognitive psychologists say must be done if moral behavior is to take place, namely, you are thinking first—and acting second.

WHAT IS COGNITIVE PSYCHOLOGY?

The term cognitive comes from the Latin word *cognito,* which means "knowledge" and includes the higher mental processes of memory, attention, information-processing, decision-making, and understanding. Early work in cognitive psychology came from a group of German scholars known as Gestalt psychologists who were interested primarily in the nature of perception. The term Gestalt may be loosely translated to mean "form" or "pattern," and studies were conducted as to the way patterns are seen by the individual.

Gestalt psychologists noted that although the parts of a pattern may be analyzed, it is not the parts themselves but rather the relationship of the parts to each other that produces a particular Gestalt. For example, a whirlpool is made up of drops of water, but it is a whirlpool only because the drops are in a specific relationship to each other. Place a stopper in the sink and the whirlpool no longer is present even though drops of water remain. A melody is heard as the same tune regardless of the key in which it is played because the parts retain the same relationship or pattern even though the actual notes differ. Studies in Gestalt psychology showed that people come to understand their world not so much by the effect of the actual environment upon them as by their own inborn capacity to organize life into understandable patterns or wholes.

Today's cognitive theorists, borrowing from Gestalt psychology, focus on the person as a conscious, perceiving organism capable of acquiring meaning from the world. Each person plays a constructive role in his or her own learning and development. Rather than being an emotional creature with irrational passions and instincts, or a pawn of environmental contingencies, each of us is endowed with the ability to interact with the world in such a way as to make sense out of what goes on around us, to construct our own experiences, to understand ourselves and others. This does not mean that the realm of emotions is negated or that the nature of the environment is unimportant, but it does mean that the focus of attention is on the person rather than on external stimuli. The world has no meaning apart from the image of that world on the consciousness of the person.

Thus, the most important topic in psychology, according to the cognitive theorist, is the study of individuals as persons capable of understanding the world around them, of putting it together in meaningful ways, and interacting with it so that future growth is ensured. Each of us generates our own development as we are shaped, in turn, by previously acquired cognitions.

> **The bulk of the literature on moral growth today, both in terms of theoretical statements and in terms of research, is within the framework of cognitive psychology and emphasizes stages of moral reasoning as given by Jean Piaget (1932) and Lawrence Kohlberg (1984).**

COGNITIVE PSYCHOLOGY AND MORAL GROWTH

The bulk of the literature on moral growth today, both in terms of theoretical statements and in terms of research, is within the framework of cognitive psychology and emphasizes stages of moral reasoning as given by Jean Piaget (1932) and Lawrence Kohlberg (1984).

THE EARLY WORK OF PIAGET

The outstanding pioneer in the field of moral reasoning was Jean Piaget, a Swiss-born, French-speaking biologist and philosopher who watched children at play and told them stories involving a moral dilemma to see what their responses would be. Piaget did not adhere to separate and discrete stages of moral development, but by observing children between the ages of four and twelve, he noted that older children gave more mature responses to questions than did younger children. Piaget saw moral development as proceeding from *heteronomy,* or the constraint of an external authority, to *autonomy,* or self-rule. Heteronomy occurs in early childhood between the ages of three and seven when the child is under the domination of the parent. Rules are thought by the child to be timeless and to emanate from God. Goodness lies in respecting those in authority, in obeying their commands, and in accepting whatever rewards and punishments are given. Justice is what the parent says is right. "Right is to obey the will of the adult. Wrong is to have a will of one's own" (Piaget, 1932, p. 193). This unequal relationship between children and parents, or "unilateral respect" as Piaget calls it, is accepted by children because they are *moral realists.* This means that young children structure their thinking to their own experi-

JEAN PIAGET (1896–1980)

Jean Piaget was born in Neuchâtel, Switzerland, the first of three children and the only son of Arthur and Rachel Piaget. As a young child he was interested in mechanics, birds, sea shells, and fossils. At the age of ten he went to Latin School, and after school hours he helped the director of the Natural History Museum put labels on the collections. He enjoyed writing, and at age seven penciled a story about an "autovap" — an automobile provided with a steam engine. His first published article, a short essay on an albino sparrow, came when he was ten. By age fifteen he was writing a series of articles in the *Swiss Review of Zoology* and was receiving letters from scientists all over the world who wanted to talk with him about his findings.

It was during his midteens that Piaget developed an interest in philosophy. His godfather, a philosopher, feeling that Piaget's education needed to be broadened, invited him to spend time with him. While Piaget looked for mollusks along a lake, his godfather talked with him about the teachings of Bergson. It was through this experience that Piaget decided to devote his life to a biological explanation of knowledge. Even though he received the doctor's degree in his early twenties in the natural sciences with a thesis on mollusks, Piaget was more interested in the relationship of biology and philosophy. He thought that if he obtained work in a psychological laboratory he could better relate to this epistemological problem.

His first experience in a laboratory was in Zurich in 1918 where he was introduced to psychoanalysis. The next year in Paris he adapted the clinical technique to questioning school children at the Alfred Binet Institute, probing their understanding of space, time, numbers, physical causality, and moral judgment. Piaget came to believe that logic is not inborn but develops little by little with time and experience. It was in the area of developmental psychology that Piaget found what he had been looking for — a link between the biological adaptation of organisms to the environment and the philosophical quest for the source of knowledge.

In 1921 Piaget was named director of the Jean-Jacques Rousseau Institute in Geneva, a post he held until his death. His greatest desire was to study the origins of intellectual development. This meant he would have to study infants. His desire was realized when he became the father of three children, two girls and a boy. He and his wife, a young woman he met at the Institute, spent considerable time observing the behaviors of their babies and three books were published on their observations. Because of this interest, Piaget is known as a genetic epistemologist.

Piaget also held academic rank at the University of Neuchâtel and the University of Geneva and was president of the Swiss Commission of UNESCO. He was awarded honorary degrees from Harvard University in 1936, the Sorbonne in 1946, and the University of Brussels in 1949. In 1969 he became the first European to receive the Distinguished Scientific Award from the American Psychological Association. By the fifties and into the sixties and seventies, he was surrounded by men and women from around the world who represented many disciplines of study and who wished to learn from him. Knowing French was a prerequisite as that was the language Piaget spoke.

Piaget loved the outdoors. After a morning of interacting with colleagues, he would take long walks, collect his thoughts, and then write for the remainder of the afternoon. Summertime found him in the mountains of Switzerland, hiking, and writing. He remained physically and mentally active into his eighties.

ences, and the consequences of behavior determine what is good and what is bad.

Heteronomy is a vital process in moral development, necessary for the training and safety of the child, and a part of the legal system. But the child needs to move on from a morality that is imposed from without to one that is guided from within, from one that is determined by objective consequences to one that is judged by motives, from one based on authority to one based on equality and fairness.

Autonomy begins around seven or eight years of age and should be well formed by the age of eleven or twelve. Intellectual growth and opportunities for peer interaction are basic to the development of autonomy, which includes cooperation, reciprocity, and mutual consent. For a time, heteronomy and autonomy will "coexist at the same age and even in the same child. . . . Objective responsibility diminishes on the average as the child grows older, and subjective responsibility gains correlatively in importance. We have therefore two processes partially overlapping, but of which the second gradually succeeds in dominating the first" (Piaget, 1932, p. 129). Rules are still respected but are based on consensus rather than on authority. Rules may be altered "on the condition of enlisting general opinion on your side" (p. 18). Concern for the rights and welfare of others develops naturally through interaction with one's age-mates and leads the child to non-egocentric, reciprocal thought. "Autonomy therefore appears only with reciprocity, when mutual respect is strong enough to make the individual feel from within the desire to treat others as he himself would wish to be treated" (p. 194).

Beginning at age eleven or twelve, the child progresses to an even higher concept of justice called *equity,* which includes benevolence and an understanding of universal love and forgiveness. The older child has become a *moral relativist,* which means that he or she now is aware of differing viewpoints regarding rules. Piaget mentions this final process only briefly, the bulk of his writing on moral judgment being a description of heteronomy and autonomy with examples of statements made by school-age children representative of the "two moralities of the child" (p. 326).

THE LATER WORK OF LAWRENCE KOHLBERG
It was not until the early 1960s that Piaget's ideas gained in popularity. Part of the increased recognition was due to the writings of American

psychologist Lawrence Kohlberg of Harvard University, who is considered by many to be the foremost authority on the development of moral judgment. The intrigue with Kohlberg's theory is seen in the numerous articles and books that have been written linking stage of moral judgment to values, opinions, socio-political orientations, educational practices, religious beliefs, emotions, and demographic characteristics of populations. It has been estimated that 5,000 studies have been conducted using Kohlberg's theory, thus "representing the largest substantive effort in any single area of personality theory" (Sprinthall & McVay, 1987, pp. 126-127).

Like Piaget, Kohlberg developed a distinction between moral realism and moral relativism, maintained that a person passes through earlier or lower stages of development before going on to later or higher stages, and emphasized the form of moral thought rather than the expression of moral behavior. Kohlberg's research, however, focused on the adolescent and young adult in contrast to Piaget's studies, which were conducted with children between the ages of four and twelve. By observing young people who are at a higher level of cognition, Kohlberg was able to expand Piaget's original two-process system to a six-stage sequence that extends from early childhood through adulthood.

> **Each of Kohlberg's six stages occurs in an invariant sequence, is qualitatively different from the one preceding it, and represents a more comprehensive system of intellectual organization.**

Each of Kohlberg's six stages occurs in an invariant sequence, is qualitatively different from the one preceding it, and represents a more comprehensive system of intellectual organization. A key term used by Kohlberg is *conventional*, which means that right and wrong is determined on the basis of convention or what society expects of its members. The conventional level is at the midpoint of moral development and includes the two middle stages (stages 3 and 4) in the hierarchy of moral reasoning. A child at the earlier *preconventional* level (stages 1 and 2) interprets a situation in terms of physical consequences rather than in terms of what society says is right or wrong. An adult at the *postconventional* level (stages 5 and 6), having progressed through the previous four stages, is able to see beyond social norms and regulations and make decisions based on principles upon which any good society is established (Kohlberg, 1984). It is not unusual for a person to make statements at more than one stage and sometimes at more than one level. If we say that a person is "at" a given stage we mean that most of the person's reasoning is at this stage. Progression is made from one stage to the next by listening to and understanding the reasoning of someone at the next higher stage. Let us look first at a brief outline of the three levels and their respective stages and then give closer attention to each of the six stages.

Preconventional Level
At this level the child is responsive to cultural rules of good and bad, right and wrong, but interprets these labels in terms of either the physical consequences of the action — punishment, reward, exchange of favors — or in terms of the physical powers of those who make the rules and labels. The level is divided into two stages:

Stage 1 — The Morality of Obedience: *"You do what you're told."*[1]
The physical consequences of action determine its goodness or badness. Avoidance of punishment and unquestioning deference to power are valued in their own right.

Stage 2 — The Morality of Instrumental Egoism and Simple Exchange: *"Let's make a deal."*
Right action consists of that which instrumentally satisfies one's own needs. Human relations are viewed in terms like those of the marketplace. Elements of fairness, reciprocity, and equal sharing are present, but they are always interpreted in a physical, pragmatic way. Reciprocity is a matter of "you scratch my back and I'll scratch yours."

Conventional level
At this level, maintaining the expectations of the individual's family, group, or nation is perceived as valuable in its own right regardless of the consequences. The attitude is not only one of conforming to the social order, but of being loyal to it and actively maintaining, supporting, and justifying the order. The following two stages comprise this level:

Stage 3 — The Morality of Personal Concordance: *"Be considerate, nice and kind, and you'll get along with others."*

Good behavior is equated with whatever pleases or helps others and with what others approve of. Stage 3 people conform to stereotypical ideas of how the majority of people in their group behave. Being a "good boy" or a "nice girl" or a "good neighbor" comes at this stage.

Stage 4 — The Morality of Law and Duty to the Social Order: *"Everyone in society is obligated to and protected by the law."*

Right behavior consists of doing one's duty, showing respect for authority, and maintaining the given social order for its own sake.

Postconventional (Principled) Level

At this level people reason according to moral principles that have validity apart from the authority of groups to which the individuals belong. This level has the following two stages:

Stage 5 — The Morality of Societal Consensus: *"You are obligated by whatever arrangements are agreed to by due process procedures."*

Right action tends to be defined in terms of general individual rights and standards that have been examined critically and agreed upon by the entire society. Stage 5 provides a rationale for choosing among alternative social systems and supplies guidelines for the creation of new laws and arrangements.

Stage 6 — The Morality of Universal Ethical Principles: *"How rational and impartial people would organize cooperation is moral."*

Decisions result from an obligation to self-chosen ethical principles that apply to all humankind regardless of age, sex, race, nationality, socioeconomic status, ability, or contribution to society. Stage 6 people emphasize human rights and the respect for the dignity of each human being as an individual person.

THE PROGRESSION OF KOHLBERG'S STAGES

A closer look at each of the stages will reveal the progression that occurs in understanding as one advances from lower to higher expressions of moral reasoning.

Small children have no say in what the rules will be, nor do they understand that restrictions imposed by parents reflect the norms of society. Unable to see the purpose or plan behind the rules, they focus attention on the consequences of behavior and judge rightness and wrongness on the basis of the end result. What is rewarded must be good; what is punished must be bad. The *stage 1* child obeys parents out of fear of a spanking or the withdrawal of affection. Focusing on the physical consequences of the act means that the value of punishment becomes greatly exaggerated, and the young child will advocate painful discipline even for minor infractions. If "might makes right," it follows that the value of human life is dependent on the social and physical attributes of the possessor. A person who is strong and has the power to command others has greater worth than a person who is weak or in a subservient position.

Stage 2 children have advanced to an understanding that other people have interests and needs that may or may not be the same as their own. Although the basic motive is to satisfy one's own desires, there are times when this can be done best by entering into an agreement with someone else. Social interaction becomes possible and is a step up from the first stage in which the child is not involved in the decision-making process. Human relations, however, are viewed in terms of the marketplace, and bargaining is expressed in instrumental and physical terms. One is obligated only to those who are in a position to return the favor, and obeying the law or following regulations becomes important if doing so is personally profitable. This attitude, that an act is right only if it enhances one's own pleasure or meets one's own needs, obviously leaves much to be desired. Sometimes called the *selfish-need* stage, there is no genuine concern for the welfare of others apart from a kind of temporary mutual satisfaction. The value of human life is seen as it relates to the needs of the possessor.

At *stage 3* the person is aware that certain commitments and social norms must be maintained in order for group living to be orderly. "Right" is no longer a matter of meeting one's own interest, but rather of living up to the expectations of others, of helping and supporting family and friends, and of maintaining the social system for its own sake. The shift from "let's make a deal" at stage 2 to "let's have an understanding" at stage 3 begins for most people during preadolescence and is prominent throughout the adolescent period. Studies show that stage 3, along with stage 4, remains the dominant stage for most people during adulthood. Being able to understand and care for others requires a higher level of cognition than that established previously, for it demands that people step outside themselves, so to speak, and be concerned with what others *think* of them, not just what they might *do* to them. The stage 3 person understands that "no man is an island" and that loyalty to the groups to which one belongs is necessary for positive and stable relationships. Selfishness is wrong because it does not include a mutual commitment to others. The value of human life is based on the affection of family and friends toward the possessor rather than on one's social standing in the community (stage 1) or on the ability of the person to satisfy the needs of another (stage 2).

Part of one's obligation to society is to respect and obey the laws of the land, as this assures that all citizens meet the same standards of conduct and receive equal treatment. This *stage 4* attitude is more advanced than that of stage 3, for it takes into consideration not only one's immediate or primary relationships such as family, neighbors, and friends, but also provides a way of living with strangers or those one may not like or wish to associate with. Laws are binding on everyone and are necessary for the maintenance of life and property. A pluralistic society necessitates that rules and regulations take precedence over personal wishes or the enhancement of any particular group. It is only in this way that we can coexist. Those delegated to enforce the laws also deserve our support and loyalty for without them the system could not hold together. The value of human life is seen as it relates to the rights and duties of the individuals in the larger society.

But sometimes laws conflict or are unclear, and sometimes laws that are agreed upon by the larger society place an undue burden on some of its citizens. The question then asked is whether there are principles that will determine what is right in such instances. The answer is found at the next two stages of moral judgment.

Stage 5 reasoning recognizes that there are a variety of ways to arrange the social order and that guidelines must be created for choosing among alternative systems so that everyone within the society will want to cooperate. The stage 5 person is like an impartial spectator judging the social system in terms of community welfare, making sure that the laws reflect the will of the people and that safeguards are built into the operation so that all, minority as well as majority, are guaranteed certain inalienable rights. The United States Constitution is a stage 5 document, for it makes provision for changing legislation that is not fair to everyone and for interpreting the intent of the law so that justice is maintained. The essence of morality is not so much in unquestioning obedience to the law (stage 4) but in changing those laws which do an injustice to a portion of the citizenry. Man was not made for the law, but the law was made for man.

Stage 5 provides a more democratic view of individuals and their respective roles than is possible at stage 4. James Rest (1975) explains the difference.

> One aspect of principled thinking is that people in leadership roles are not seen as a different breed of humankind, nor as infallible, but are seen as individuals having certain prerogatives in order to perform certain functions in society's division of labor. Accordingly, one can criticize or question the job performance of an "authority" . . . without being disloyal to the whole group. Moreover, the prerogatives of authority are limited to the necessities of the role. This less exalted view of authority contrasts with the more exalted concept of authority of conventional thinking, which regards loyalty and support of authority as a sign of loyalty and support for the whole social system. (p. 89)

Stage 5 persons having progressed through the previous stages are aware of the importance of social norms and of why a society needs people in leadership roles. They also understand that those who disobey the law will have to face the consequences. But they know that there is a higher law than that devised by humankind, and if a choice must be made one's allegiance should be to the principle of human justice rather than to what is legislated by the courts. Martin Luther King, Jr., faced this dilemma when he conducted the civil rights marches in the South. In a letter written from a Birmingham jail in April of 1963, he said:

> You express a great deal of anxiety over our willingness to break laws. This is certainly a legitimate concern. . . . One may well ask: "How can you advocate breaking some laws and obeying others?" The answer lies in the fact that there are two types of laws, just and unjust. . . . One has not only a legal but a moral responsibility to obey just laws. Conversely,

one has a moral responsibility to disobey unjust laws. . . . Any law that uplifts human personality is just. Any law that degrades human personality is unjust. (King, 1964, pp. 84-85)

Some confuse stage 5 and stage 2 because reasoning at either of these may lead to a rejection of the law. The difference is considerable, however. Persons at stage 2 take the attitude that the law interferes with their freedom, keeping them from doing as they please. They do not understand why anyone would experience anxiety over breaking the law, nor do they ponder the difference between just and unjust laws. They would not say that one has "a moral responsibility to obey just laws."

Moral reasoning at *stage 6,* the highest stage possible, considers that human life is sacred and that individuals are ends in themselves rather than means for some other good. The moral test is one's willingness to apply the same principles to oneself as to others. This means people at stage 6 must have the intellectual ability to imagine themselves in someone else's place, to consider the claims that person would make, and then be willing to act toward that individual as they would feel it appropriate were they in the same situation. This application of the Golden Rule is not just to family and friends (stage 3) but to all people everywhere, regardless of their circumstances. It includes a concern for both the culprit and the victim, for the pregnant woman as well as her unborn child, for the rich and the poor, young and old, male and female, foreigner and American. Stage 6 provides no easy answers or quick responses to the question of what is just. Justice for one group must not be at the expense of justice for another. Nor is legislation that serves to close discussion on these matters the answer. Ethical principles indicative of stage 6 are different than rules or commandments. A commandment (stage 4) says, "Thou shalt not kill" (Ex. 20:13, KJV). A principle says, "Thou shalt love thy neighbor as thyself" (Matt. 19:19, KJV).

Few individuals in any society reach stage 6 reasoning and those who do find themselves greatly misunderstood. If they make a significant impact on others as did Socrates, Mahatma Gandhi, and Martin Luther King, Jr., they may suffer martyrdom. Society does not like people who are too good or too bad. Jesus was crucified and so were two thieves.

One was too good, the others too bad. Although Kohlberg believes only a handful of people have reached stage 6, research studies indicate that from 2 to 10 percent of the adult population make statements indicative of this stage.

The postconventional level, as we have seen, allows for judging right and wrong, good and bad, not in terms of one's own interests (level 1) or in terms of what is best for one's group (level 2), but rather by what is best for all humankind (level 3). Justice, equality, and the dignity of human life are higher than one's own needs or any given law. The individual at the highest level has progressed in moral reasoning from one who is directed by the consequences of behavior (stages 1 and 2), to what society says is right (stages 3 and 4), and finally to a self-directed, socially responsive and responsible person who has an integrated set of values that apply to the whole human race (stages 5 and 6).

LAWRENCE KOHLBERG (1927–1987)

Kohlberg was born into an affluent family in Bronxville, New York, the youngest of four children. His father was Jewish, his mother Christian. Kohlberg's affinity appeared to be with his father, not so much in terms of religion as with a sense of belonging to the Jewish people.

Kohlberg always had a sense of fair play. The only time he got into a fight in grade school was when a new kid was picked on by a bully for being different. "Laurie tore into the bully, got knocked down himself several times, but we and the bully could see Laurie was never going to give up, and a group of us stopped the fight. And we all learned something about fighting for principle that day" (Alvin

Kracht at a memorial service for Lawrence Kohlberg held May 20, 1987).

When Kohlberg returned to speak at his high school many years after graduating, he noted that a number of his old teachers in the audience looked at him with disbelief. "They remembered me as a high school boy who was always on probation for smoking, drinking, and visiting the girls in a nearby school" (Lawrence Kohlberg, "My personal search for universal morality" in Moral Education Forum 11(1), 1986). Summers were spent hitchhiking across Canada (he did magic tricks along the road to get motorists' attention), sleeping in flophouses and on park benches, fishing in mountain streams, and working on farms and in an airplane factory. He was voted wittiest in his class.

In 1945 while still in his teens, he joined the Merchant Marines, then volunteered as an unpaid engineer to bring a ship of Jewish refugees illegally through the British blockade and land them in Palestine. The ship with its 2,000 occupants was rammed by the British navy, tear gas was used, and several children died. The others, including Kohlberg, were taken to a British internment camp in Cyprus. He escaped from Cyprus to Palestine with false papers, staying on a kibbutz until it was safe to leave the country. It was this experience that caused him to wonder when it is permissible to follow "rules of justice or concern for the rights and welfare of other persons" even if doing so violates the "rules of arbitrary convention."

Kohlberg enrolled at the University of Chicago, receiving both the B.A. and the Ph.D. At that time a student could get credit for a course by passing the final exam, and he passed so many tests that he got the B.A. in just one year. In graduate school he studied psychoanalysis under Bruno Bettelheim, humanism with Carl Rogers, and behaviorism with Jacob Gewirtz. He felt that none of these psychologies dealt adequately with the moral problems people face. It was during this time that Kohlberg began reading Piaget's work in which moral development was viewed not as the consequences of socialization but as inherent within the person as reasoning processes mature. He also studied the writings of such philosophers as John Locke, John Stuart Mill, and John Dewey. Gradually, Kohlberg came to see that the basic principle of morality is to treat every person as an end in himself or herself, not as a means to some other end. Respect for every human being is the essence of justice.

Kohlberg held appointments at Yale University, the University of Chicago where he instituted the Child Psychology Training Program, and Harvard University's Graduate School of Education where he established the Center for Moral Development and Education. In 1972, while doing cross-cultural studies in Central America, he contracted a rare parasitic disease that left him continuously nauseated. There would be days on end when he was too dizzy to get out of bed. Unable to find a cure, he quickly went from a young man with vibrant energy to a man racked with pain and depression. By the time this tragedy had befallen him, his fame had spread and he was surrounded with eager scholars who were flattered to collaborate with him in research and writing. His courage and production continued to be phenomenal given his severe disability. On January 17, 1987, he disappeared. On April 6, his body washed ashore in Boston Harbor. He had died at age fifty-nine by drowning.

Hundreds of friends, family, colleagues, and former students met on

May 20 to hear recollections about him. Hundreds more penned their remembrances, their remarks being entered into several publications. Kohlberg's sister remembered him as a tow-headed, winsome, amiable, and funny child who loved adventure. James Fowler spoke of Kohlberg's influence on thousands of people who have used his ideas in their work in moral education. Thomas Lickona remembered him as an exacting teacher: "Larry assigned about 2,000 pages of reading, required a term paper and a research project, and a midterm exam and a final. The course was great but it just about killed everybody who took it." (Cited by Lisa Kuhmerker, 1991, "The Kohlberg legacy to friends," in W.M. Kurtines & J.L. Gewirtz, Handbook of moral behavior and development, Vol. 1. Hills-

dale, NJ: Lawrence Erlbaum.) Liam Grimley used four words to describe his former colleague: lovable, courageous, exciting, and dedicated (Kuhmerker, 1991). And Clark Power of the University of Notre Dame wrote that for Lawrence Kohlberg, "moral psychology and moral education were not interests to be pursued simply because they were self-fulfilling, they were the means he chose to give his life to the cause of justice" (Clark Power, 1991, "Lawrence Kohlberg: The vocation of the moral psychologist and educator. Part I." In W.M. Kurtines & J.L. Gewirtz, Handbook of moral behavior and development, Vol. 1. Hillsdale, NJ: Lawrence Erlbaum.)

All who knew him had come "under his influence" in some way. The world had lost a great and gentle person.

Is There a Seventh Stage?
Kohlberg (1973b) in *The Gerontologist* has written of a possible seventh stage based on a sense of oneness with the cosmos. This union of the mind with nature, the feeling of being an integral part of all creation, is more apt to occur during life's later years and is the successful resolution of the despair we all feel at one time or another when we picture ourselves as an insignificant speck in a vast universe. Kohlberg referred to this cosmic perspective, or feeling of oneness with infinity, as a reversal of figure and ground. Rather than seeing ourselves as finite beings, alienated and alone, we come to view ourselves as a part of all that exists, as a portion of the totality of life.

Many people have experienced this rush of mystic awareness, perhaps when watching the ocean or listening to beautiful music, but moments like this are fleeting. Although not a true moral stage, for it has no definable structure nor is it logically or cognitively more adequate than the previous stage, this seventh stage is nevertheless a phenomenon of psychological or religious significance that brings a sense of meaning to those who have experienced it. It has been known to enable the elderly to face death confidently and without fear.

THE USE OF STORIES

The method used to determine a person's stage of moral judgment is to present a story with a moral dilemma and to listen to the person's reasoning as related to the dilemma. The story may be one used by Piaget a half century ago, one developed by Kohlberg, or one taken from a local newspaper. There are also booklets and films that present a variety of moral dilemmas.

A typical story is one in which a conflict occurs between the needs of the actor in the story, obedience to the law or to an authority, and the welfare and interests of others also portrayed in the story. One such story is of a man named Heinz who lived in Europe. His wife was near death from a special kind of cancer, but there was one drug, a form of radium that the doctors thought might save her. The druggist in the town was charging ten times what it cost to make and told Heinz he could not have any of it unless he paid $2,000 in advance. Heinz said that even if he borrowed all that he could, it would only amount to $1,000. He asked the druggist to either sell it for less or let him pay the rest later, but the druggist said no. So, Heinz, being desperate, broke into the store and stole the drug for his wife.

The question is asked, "Did Heinz do right or did Heinz do wrong?" It is the reasoning behind the answer rather than the answer itself that determines the stage of moral reasoning. A child at the first stage who interprets an action as good or bad according to its physical consequences may say, "He shouldn't have done that because then he'd be a thief if they caught him and put him in jail." The stage 2 child, believing that right action consists of that which instrumentally satisfies one's own needs, may say that Heinz did right to save his wife's life because "if she dies there will be no one to cook his dinner." Kohlberg has done considerable cross-cultural research and finds that a typical stage 2 response in some countries is that Heinz did right because "if she dies it will cost him too much for the funeral." However, if Heinz does not love his wife or if she would not do the same for him under similar circumstances, then the stage 2 child will say he should not have done it.

The stage 3 person, who is oriented to social conformity, may say that Heinz did wrong because a person should not steal or that Heinz did right because he should take care of his wife. In either case the judgment is made on the basis of what society expects of its members. The person at stage 4 being oriented to show respect for the law and to maintain the social order will probably say that Heinz did wrong. As one stage 4 child put it, "It was wrong because he was breaking the law no matter how you look at it, and although I can see why he would have done it, I don't think he was justified in doing it."

Those who progress to stage 5, believing that the purpose of the law is to preserve human rights, may say that even though it was wrong for Heinz to steal, it would be more wrong to let his wife die. For those who reason at stage 6 and believe that morality is grounded, not in legality or specific rules, but in abstract principles of justice and respect for the individual, the answer will probably be that "Heinz was wrong legally but right morally."

Although presenting a moral dilemma is the usual technique employed in determining the level of moral judgment, it is not the only way. People face decisions every day and make comments as to desirable solutions on a variety of issues. Given sufficient familiarity with the stages, one may listen to what is said and assess the level of moral reasoning. Is one's desire to enhance self (stages 1 and 2), conform to social expectations (stages 3 and 4), or be concerned with the rights and humanity of others (stages 5 and 6)? Listening to one's own speech may prove an interesting exercise.

BASIC ASSUMPTIONS

Cognitive psychologists, as we have seen, emphasize the reasoning or intellectual functions that occur in moral development and measure the stage or level of morality by what the person says. The cognitive answer to the question of how moral growth takes place is that *the child becomes capable of morality as he or she advances in thinking processes "from an egocentric, but externally directed being, to a self-directed but socially responsive and responsible person"* (Simon, 1976, p. 173). The egocentric, externally directed child is the one who is able to assume only her own view and judges good and evil on the basis of what will happen to her as a consequence of behavior. This is Piaget's heteronomous child and Kohlberg's stage 1 individual. By contrast, the self-directed but socially responsive and responsible person has a morality that comes from within and judges right and wrong, not so much by how one is affected personally, but on the basis of consequences to society and to the people that make up that society. At early stages this is Piaget's autonomous child and Kohlberg's stage 2 individual interested in concrete forms of reciprocity. At later stages the child exchanges reciprocity for altruism and becomes concerned with the rights and privileges of an ever-increasing segment of humanity, feeling personally responsible for developing a just society for all. A look at the basic assumptions of the cognitive approach to morality will serve to clarify in our minds what we have learned.

First, cognitive psychologists view morality as developmental in nature and are interested in changes that occur as a person progresses from lower to higher levels of moral maturity. A concept basic to the cognitive position is that *moral development occurs within the individual.* Morality cannot be produced or generated by an outside source. By its very definition, morality must be rooted within the personality. People are not moral simply because they engage in moral acts; they are moral as they understand moral concepts and their subsequent behavior reflects a more mature level of cognitive organization. Although the environment may encourage morality or may produce conditions that impede it, the dynamic remains within the organism.

Second, cognitive theorists also hold that *moral development parallels intellectual development.* As children increase in mental ability, they also increase in the ability to reason at higher levels of moral judgment. There is obviously not a one-to-one correspondence between morality and intelligence. We all know capable people who do not show high levels of moral reasoning. But studies using groups of children or adults show positive correlations between these two factors. Although one may be intelligent but not moral, one cannot be moral in the cognitive sense of the term and not have reached a certain level of intellectual attainment.

Third, *moral development occurs in a series of stages that are invariant, hierarchical, and universal.* Each person passes through the same progression of stages, sequenced in a certain order because earlier stages are less differentiated and are attainable before later stages. Just as children sit before they walk and babble before they talk, they also exhibit less mature forms of moral thinking before going on to more comprehensive patterns of moral thought. Although any particular individual's development may cease at any given stage, there is no skipping those stages that precede the final attainment. For this reason, the sequence of stages of moral development is said to be invariant. The stages also constitute a hierarchy because each stage is the product of learning that occurred during the previous stage and becomes a preparation for the stage that follows. Although each stage or level is qualitatively different from the one preceding it, lower levels are prerequisite to higher ones, and the attainment of any particular level must include understandings from earlier ones. As each gradation in the hierarchy constitutes a greater integration of the individual's thinking and enables the individual to do a better job of analyzing problems and relating to the world, higher stages are preferable to lower ones. The hierarchy thus becomes not only an integrative model but also one that provides a framework for evaluating the merit or worth of any particular stage. Considerable cross-cultural research has shown that children in countries around the world go through the stages in the same order. The rate of progression may differ from one culture to another and the percentage of adults who attain to the higher levels of moral reasoning may also vary but the sequence remains universal.

Fourth, *moral development comes by cognitive conflict.* When cognitive conflict occurs, that is when individuals become aware of discrepancies between their experiences and their perceptions, a kind of disequilibrium is created which motivates them to restructure their views and thus accommodate themselves to the world around them. "A fundamental reason why an individual moves from one stage to the next is because the later stages solve problems and inconsistencies unsolvable at the prior stage of development" (Kohlberg, 1973a, p. 13). Cognitive conflict does not necessarily imply turmoil or distress, though these may be included, but rather it refers to conceptual contradictions that continuously occur as a person forms and reforms ideas about the world. Conflict speaks to the whole process of learning and understanding, a process which is for the most part an exciting and rewarding adventure.

Fifth, cognitive psychologists believe that *moral development is philosophically sound and is not contrary to any major religion.* Because conflict occurs by questioning, social dialogue, raising doubt, or being introduced to new ideas, it follows that cognitive theorists would claim their position "had its origins in Socrates' Athens . . . a universal conception of justice which was rational or cognitive" (Kohlberg, 1976b, p. 213). Plato wrote of a society where men would be educated for justice, and he envisioned a republic where just men or philosopher kings would rule. Descartes, Leibnitz, and Kant are considered to be forerunners of the cognitive position in that they were interested in the genesis of self-consciousness in the individual. John Dewey, with his "democratic reformulation of Plato's Republic," is historically important in moral development theory (Kohlberg, 1976a, p. 14). Dewey believed that the "greatest of all construction" is "the building of a free and powerful character," and this is accomplished by education "supplying the conditions" so that individuals can "mature and pass into higher functions" (Dewey, 1895, pp. 207-208).

Each of the stages in the moral developmental process deals with one or more of the issues with which philosophers of ethics have

> **Each of the stages in the moral developmental process deals with one or more of the issues with which philosophers of ethics have traditionally been concerned — issues of authority, property, cooperation, social adjustment, conscience, equity, and the value of life.**

traditionally been concerned — issues of authority, property, cooperation, social adjustment, conscience, equity, and the value of life. These are matters of concern to the major religions of the world as well, for they speak to basic human aspirations in this life and the next. Studies have shown that religious values seem to go through the same stages of development as do other values, and members of a variety of religious groups (e.g., Catholics, Protestants, Jews, and Muslims) proceed through the stages of moral reasoning in the same invariant order (Kohlberg, 1981).

Sixth, cognitive psychologists accept the premise that *moral development is a fully scientific claim about human nature and can be measured.* Science cannot say what morality is or what it should be, but it can test whether a philosopher's conception of morality fits the psychological facts. The cognitive position that morality proceeds in invariant universal stages with justice (concern for the equality of others) being the cornerstone, makes possible the construction of measuring instruments that will determine one's position in the hierarchy of moral stages. Differences in moral judgment that exist between individuals or between cultures are explained, not by ethical relativity, but by differences in the stage or level of moral development of the individuals and cultures being considered.

An internal dynamic lying within all healthy people is to accept higher levels of moral reasoning when the next higher level is understood. As such, morality is transcultural, nonrelative, and rooted in reality. Assessment instruments based on this fixed standard may be open-ended, providing opportunity for an extended response to a story involving a moral dilemma; or the tests may offer a number of statements representative of different stages of moral judgment, and the person chooses those statements that are thought to be most relevant to the moral problem in question. Either way, determination of the level of moral judgment is made, not by what one does, but rather by what one says. Although one's behavior is recognized as being important, the cognitive theorist listens to one's verbal reasoning as the basis for the measurement of moral judgment. The cognitive approach measures, then, not so much the content of morality, but the process by which a moral position is formed.

PROBLEMS

The work of Jean Piaget and of Lawrence Kohlberg has been evaluated by both advocates and opponents of cognitive psychology. Advocates, having accepted the basic assumptions of cognitivism, opt for methodological changes or call for a more careful analysis of how a person moves from one stage of moral judgment to the next. Opponents, questioning the very foundation of a morality based on reasoning, prefer a behavioral or affective approach to a study of morality, or they object to the nonrelative stance of the cognitive theorist that says that higher stages are preferable to lower stages. Occasionally an aspiring scholar will conduct research that does not support the developmental findings of Piaget or Kohlberg and will assume that, as in the story of David of old, a giant Goliath has been felled with one blow. Such, of course, is not the case. But whether any particular criticism points to a genuine problem will depend in large measure on the orientation of the evaluator. We will now examine several pertinent questions, seeking to determine which of the following concerns merit serious consideration.

DOES MORAL GROWTH PARALLEL INTELLECTUAL GROWTH?

The assumption that the course of moral development is the same as the course of development in other areas of cognition has been challenged. Although people who are more intelligent also tend to be higher in moral judgment, there are many exceptions. An individual may be a brilliant scientist and yet not make moral judgments at the postconventional level. Given the nature of the task of responding verbally to moral dilemmas, no one would refute a relationship between moral judgment and general cognitive ability, but it remains difficult to show just what this relationship is.

Both Piaget and Kohlberg would concur that although there are similarities between the cognitions involved, they are not the same. Piaget, the genetic epistemologist, speaks of a parallelism between morality and intellectual thought but defines intelligence in terms of his own epistemological theory rather than on the basis of standardized ability tests. Kohlberg (1963) states that "these relations between cognitive development of morality and its internalization are not matters of simple cognitive learning of cultural norms. Such simple cognitive learning fails to take account of the sequential qualitative transformation through which moral thinking proceeds" (p. 322). Kohlberg goes on to say that the cognition involved in moral thinking is not "a simple matter of mental age" and that the level of moral development is only moderately correlated with IQ. Thus it would seem that there is little discrepancy between what the critics are saying and what the cognitive theorists report. Needed are definitive studies which would give a clearer understanding of just what cognitions are necessary for moral reasoning and development.

Is Moral Reasoning Related to Moral Behavior?

A second concern often cited in the literature has to do with the relationship between moral judgment and moral behavior. What a person does affects others more directly than what a person thinks or says; so the charge is made that unless higher stages of moral judgment are accompanied by moral acts not seen at lower stages, an understanding of the reasoning processes has little value. A person may make sophisticated judgments without ever acting upon them, and conversely, a person who is lacking in intelligence but is well trained may act in socially respectable ways. Some critics say that for a theory of moral development to be relevant, it should predict distinctive patterns of behavior for each of the stages or levels of moral judgment. The assertion also is made that people act according to acquired behavior patterns that are relatively fixed and that being asked to respond to hypothetical moral dilemmas has little correspondence to a world of reality.

> Cognitive theorists are aware that to know the good is not necessarily to do the good and that thinking about moral issues is not a substitute for moral living.

Cognitive theorists are aware that to know the good is not necessarily to do the good and that thinking about moral issues is not a substitute for moral living. They agree that moral reasoning is only one part of a much larger picture and that a connection needs to be established between judgmental processes and moral behavior. "The sheer capacity to make genuinely moral judgments is only one portion of moral character. . . . One must also apply this judgmental capacity to the actual guidance and criticism of action" (Kohlberg, 1967, p. 179). But cognitive theorists would not agree that "the claims . . . regarding the relationship between moral judgment and action are greatly overstated" (Scharf, 1978, p. 76) or that "there appears to be a wide gap between moral judgment and moral actions" (Wynn, 1977, p. 67).

Numerous studies on this matter have been conducted, and although specific behaviors do not relate exclusively to specific stages, there are positive correlations between the two. Sprinthall and Sprinthall (1981) in their text on educational psychology reported that 75 percent of thirteen-year-olds at the preconventional and conventional levels cheated, whereas only 11 percent of the postconventional students cheated. Ziv (1976) found a significant correlation between resistance to temptation and level of moral judgment, supporting Kohlberg's (1964) statement that the same variables that favor advance in moral judgment also favor resistance to temptation. Richards, Bear, Steward, and Norman (1992) looked at classroom conduct of 143 boys and girls in the fourth and eighth grades, and noted that "conduct deteriorates as youngsters advance from stage 1 to stage 2, then improves again as they consolidate their thinking at the conventional level" (pp. 185-186). Their explanation for this curvilinear relationship was that stage 1 children behaved in order to avoid punishment; stage 2 children were more interested in "peer-oriented reciprocity"; and stage 3 children were beginning to internalize standards of conduct that included an increased respect for the rights of others and a desire to please the teacher.

Golda Rothman (1980), Rest (1986a), and Kutnick (1986) have summarized the research on the relationship between moral reasoning and moral behavior, and their conclusions provide an excellent source for anyone who wishes to pursue this topic in depth. Rothman believes the relationship to be complex and sees moral reasoning as influencing moral behavior, "but in interaction with other situational and personal dimensions" (p. 123). Rest states that a review of over fifty studies using the DIT (an objectively scored test based on Kohlberg's stages) shows moral reasoning to be "significantly correlated to a wide variety of behavioral and attitude measures" (p. 178). Kutnick writes that "the original statement that higher stages would become more prescriptive and, hence, more likely to dictate action has remained and been supported in the literature. . . . Moral cognition both causes moral actions and arises out of moral action" (p. 142). In reviewing the research on delinquent behavior and moral reasoning, Berkowitz, Guerra, and Nucci (1991) conclude that "despite the strong body of research supporting the relation of moral reasoning to behavior, it is clear that the relation is not direct" (p. 41).

Is Moral Judgment Dependent on the Immediate Environment?

A third criticism is that what one says may depend as much on the particular situation one is in at the time as it does on an enduring disposition or attitude. If situations are similar, responses also will be similar; if situations vary, responses likewise will vary. Piaget saw constancy as being related to age. A child understands morality first on a practical level and later on a theoretical or hypothetical level. When small, the child will often imitate the speech and actions of an adult. But unless there is an accompanying change in conviction, which is not apt to occur in one so young, the desirable speech and performance may not continue when the adult is absent. As age increases and moral understanding is on a higher level of cognitive organization, greater stability results. Whereas disequilibrium with its accompanying changes is essential for the child to advance to higher stages, stability is increasingly desirable as higher levels of moral reasoning are attained.

Kohlberg has found that most people are about half in one stage of moral judgment and half in the two surrounding stages. This would indicate that the particular situation does make a difference in what the person says. Even so, the person also has a part in the process and brings some consistency based on attitudes or beliefs. Given the range of situational contingencies and the variety of belief systems, it is impossible to reach a definitive conclusion on the relative effects of a changing environment and an enduring disposition. But as research continues, closer approximations to an answer will be forthcoming, although one must keep in mind that both variation and constancy will always be present.

How Important Are Emotions?

A fourth criticism of the cognitive approach is that the affective components of morality are not given sufficient consideration. Opponents say that emotions are essential to moral development, and one cannot be certain that a moral concept is grasped unless there is an emotional accompaniment. "When someone, for instance, fails to have remorse for voluntarily harming an innocent person, it would be reasonable to say that the individual has not fully grasped the concept of harm. Or if an individual commits premeditated murder and experiences no guilt for his act, then he is likely not to have a well-developed concept of murder" (Rich, 1980, p. 82). An inappropriate emotion, such as showing glee over someone's misfortune, also indicates a lack of moral understanding. Emotions play a vital part in the judgmental process, and whether they influence the person in desirable or undesirable ways, they cannot be ignored. It is true that cognitive psychologists have not stressed the emotional aspects of moral development, but this does not mean the affective has been ignored. An emphasis on cognition does not exclude other elements of the moral process. Both Piaget and Kohlberg have acknowledged the importance of emotions in moral reasoning. Piaget (1932) writes that "the relations between parents and children are certainly not only those of constraint. There is a spontaneous mutual affection, which from the first prompts the child to acts of generosity and even of self-sacrifice, to very touching demonstrations which are in no way prescribed. And here no doubt is the starting point for that morality of good which we shall see developing alongside of the morality of right or duty" (pp. 192-194).

Kohlberg, likewise, recognizes the significance of emotions on moral development. Aware that his theory has been criticized for ignoring affect, he has closely linked the cognitive and the affective. The following statement reflects his views:

> Discussions of cognition and affect usually are based on the assumption that cognitions and affects are different mental states, leading to the question, "Which is quantitatively more influential in moral judgment, states of cognition or states of affect?" In contrast, the cognitive-developmental view holds that "cognition" and "affect" are different aspects of, or perspectives on, the same mental events, that all mental events have both cognitive and affective aspects, and that the development of mental dispositions reflects structural changes recognizable in both cognitive and affective perspectives. It is evident that moral judgments often involve strong emotional components. (Kohlberg, 1980, pp. 39-40)

Kohlberg (1981) also writes that each stage has its own motive. Stage 1 action is motivated by a fear of punishment, stage 2 by a desire for reward or benefit, stage 3 by an anticipation of disapproval of others, and stage 4 by anticipation of dishonor. The emotion of fear is more prevalent at the preconventional level, whereas the emotion of guilt is more apt to be seen at the conventional level. Anxiety may be included in both fear and guilt. Kohlberg's observation has been supported by a number of researchers, including Ruma and Mosher (1967) and Ziv

(1976) who have found highly significant correlations between guilt and moral reasoning.

Regardless of the relationship between thinking and feeling, Kohlberg (1981) maintains that the cognitive takes precedence over the affective:

> Two adolescents, thinking of stealing, may have the same feeling in the pit of their stomachs. One adolescent (Stage 2) interprets the feeling as "being chicken" and ignores it. The other (stage 4) interprets the feeling as "the warning of my conscience" and decides accordingly. The differences in reaction is one in cognitive-structural aspects of moral judgment, not in emotional "dynamics" as such. (pp. 140-141)

DOES WOMEN'S MORAL REASONING DIFFER FROM MEN'S?

Carol Gilligan (1982), Professor of Human Development and Psychology at Harvard Graduate School of Education, claims that the moral development of girls and women differs from that of boys and men. In her book, *In a Different Voice,* she says that females are more responsive to social relationships, the feelings of others, and real-life moral problems. Concern for the needs of others takes precedence over the rights of others, and harmony and compassion come before reciprocity and respect. Females are more inductive; males are more deductive. Females are attached; males are separated or detached. Females accept caring as the basis for morality; males believe justice to be the foundation of the moral quest.

Gilligan faults Kohlberg for using only males in his studies, thereby relegating the moral characteristics of females to a lower position (stage 3) than those of males of the same age (stage 4). She believes that individual rights and justice should not take priority over human relationships and caring. This is not to say that men are not capable of caring or that women do not believe in justice, but rather that there are gender differences in moral progression that must be recognized in order to adequately understand the human condition. Ideally, both the ethic of responsibility and the ethic of justice should combine in moral decision-making.

Kohlberg's response to Gilligan's charge of sex-bias is that the psychological study of the moral domain may be enlarged to include the affective ideas of caring, love, loyalty, and responsibility, but these should not be construed as a separate morality quite apart from the rational reconstruction of justice reasoning. Rather, these special relationships and obligations complement and are included within a basic understanding of moral development as a growing differentiation of the prescriptive and the universal. For example, personal decisions as to the way aging parents will be cared for supplement and deepen the generalized or universal obligation of justice for the well-being of the elderly. The moral issue is adequate care, not the method employed. By including affective responses to real-life moral dilemmas the scope of the psychological assessment of the moral domain is broadened, but this in no way changes the fundamental position that the basis of moral development is an understanding of justice for all people (Kohlberg, Levine, & Hewer, 1983).

Research that supports or refutes Gilligan's claim of gender differences has, for the most part, been done with adults rather than with children or young people. Gilligan interviewed twenty-nine women who were considering having an abortion, a real-life moral dilemma involving care and responsibility both for the self and for the unborn child. It would be difficult to find a comparable dilemma for men.

Some studies support Gilligan's thesis that males score higher than females (e.g., Haan, Smith, & Block, 1968; Holstein, 1976; Lockwood, 1975); other studies have found just the opposite to be the case with females scoring higher than males (e.g., Bull, 1969; Funk, 1987; Plueddemann, 1989; Porteus & Johnson, 1965). But the majority of studies show no significant differences. In response to Gilligan's "different voice," a literature review on sex differences has been conducted by Bebeau and Brabeck (1987), Rest (1986a), Thoma (1984), and Walker (1984). In each survey, gender differences were found to be negligible. Whatever differences were found could be accounted for by age, education, type of moral dilemma story, or the situation in which the moral dilemma was framed. Rest (1986a) states that across all studies less than one-half of one percent of the variance is attributable to gender (p. 113).

As more studies are conducted and gender differences appear to fade, the topic is now shifting to how a morality of justice and a morality of care can be combined to produce optimal results. Sichel (1988) speaks of "two voices"; one based on neo-Kantian principles and the other on altruistic emotions. Sichel opts for both voices to be heard, both to be included in the "jigsaw puzzle" of the moral domain.[2] Humphrey and Oordt (1991) place the ethic of justice in the public domain, the ethic of care in the private domain. The ethic of justice is based on logic and reason; the ethic of care on sympathy, empathy, and compassion. Care in the form of empathy "must be added to justice for full morality to occur" (p. 300).

After reviewing the research on moral orientation, reason or affect, Brabeck (1986) concludes that to resolve the conflict by assigning one orientation to males and the other to females is to do an injustice to the capacities of both sexes. Rather, when Kohlberg's and Gilligan's theories are taken together "the moral person is seen as one whose moral choices reflect reasoned and deliberate judgments which ensure that justice be accorded each person while maintaining a passionate concern for the well-being and care of each individual. Justice and care are then joined; the demands of universal principles and specific moral choices are bridged and the need for autonomy and for interconnection are united in an enlarged and more adequate conception of morality" (p. 85).

ARE THERE OTHER PROBLEMS?
These criticisms of a morality based on reasoning are but samples of those found in the literature. Some writers disagree with one or more of the basic assumptions and cite insufficient or conflicting evidence to support the view that stages of moral judgment are invariant, hierarchical, and universal; or that morality is a fully scientific claim about human nature or that conflict is necessary for moral development to occur. Others dissent from a position in which character traits such as honesty, courage, and determination compare unfavorably with principles such as justice (Peters, 1971), or "justice" is narrowly interpreted to mean "social morality" (Wilson, 1980). Some accuse cognitive theorists of creating a moral aristocracy composed of individuals with superior verbal skills and excluding those who may have an intuitive grasp of ethical components but are not able to articulate them. The aristocracy would favor the middle class over the lower class and girls over boys, thus creating unfavorable and unnecessary class and gender comparisons. Fraenkel (1976) questions the fundamental premise that higher

stages are always preferable to lower stages and argues that children may take rules too lightly if adults discuss with them the conditions in which rules should be obeyed and in which rules should not be obeyed. He indicates that getting a child to the conventional level may be as much as we can hope for and that discussions at the postconventional level serve to confuse the child and may result in socially unacceptable behavior.

Still others have reported problems with administration and scoring. It takes a relatively long time to give Kohlberg's Moral Judgment Instrument, and analyzing open-ended verbal statements and placing them at appropriate stages requires special training. But the effort is worth it for some like Edmund Sullivan (1975) of the Ontario Institute for Studies in Education who comments, "We have found Kohlberg's instrument for the psychological assessment of moral judgment the most sophisticated and reliable instrument that psychological assessment devices have to offer. The instrument can be reliably scored and its validity is argued within the perspective of cognitive developmental theory" (p. 95). A new scoring system for Kohlberg's stages is now in place (Rest, 1986b). Objectively scored tests are also available, which will be helpful to researchers and educators,[3] and pedagogical and curricular materials are being made easier to utilize.

No theoretical position is without its critics, and cognitive psychology has acquired its share. Yet no theory has had greater impact on our understanding of how moral growth takes place than the cognitive approach of Jean Piaget and Lawrence Kohlberg. This is due in part to the interdisciplinary nature of their findings. Piaget was a biologist, logician, sociologist, and psychologist. Unlike Sigmund Freud who emphasized emotions and instincts, or B.F. Skinner who focused on environmental influences, Piaget selected for his topic the rational, perceiving child who

No theoretical position is without its critics, and cognitive psychology has acquired its share. Yet no theory has had greater impact on our understanding of how moral growth takes place than the cognitive approach of Jean Piaget and Lawrence Kohlberg.

has the capacity to make sense of the world. Moral knowledge is a process, not a product; it is dynamic, never static; self-regulatory rather than imposed from without.

In "My Personal Search for Universal Morality," Kohlberg (1986) writes that he was influenced by the writings of such philosophers as Immanuel Kant, Jean Piaget, and John Dewey. "Central to my own sense of how to approach the study of moral development was the assumption that the study must be guided by moral philosophy. What was to count as moral or as developmental advance must start with some philosophic definitions, assumptions and arguments. These assumptions would be open to question in light of empirical findings, but one could not start with the effort to be value free" (p. 7).

It is to an application of the cognitive approach to moral growth that we now turn.

NOTES

1. The statements within quotation marks following each stage are taken from *Development in judging moral issues* by James Rest (1979). Minneapolis: University of Minnesota Press.

2. For an in-depth discussion of the moralities of justice and care, see chapter 6, "Two Voices Are There: . . . Each a Mighty Voice" in Betty Sichel (1988), *Moral education: Character, community, and ideals.* Philadelphia: Temple University Press.

3. The Defining Issues Test (DIT) by James Rest is an objectively scored instrument patterned after Kohlberg's stages. It has been used in hundreds of studies. Six stories with a moral dilemma are presented and after each story the subject is asked to rate the importance of each of twelve statements on a five-point scale. The statements are representative of thinking at the various stages. The four statements ranked highest for each story are then marked in order of preference and given weights of 4, 3, 2, and 1, respectively. Weights are summed to give scores for each subject at each stage. Stages 5 and 6 are put together for scoring purposes and are called the principled (P) level. Rest recommends the use of the P level as having greater validity than lower stages, although stages 3 and 4 also may be used.

REFERENCES

Bebeau, M.J., & Brabeck, M.M. (1987). Integrating care and justice issues in professional moral education: A gender perspective. *The Journal of Moral Education, 16,* 189–203.

Berkowitz, M.W., Guerra, N., & Nucci, L. (1991). Sociomoral development and drug and alcohol abuse. In W.M. Kurtines & J.L. Gewirtz (Eds.), *Handbook of moral behavior and development: Application* (Vol. 3, pp. 35–53). Hillsdale, NJ: Lawrence Erlbaum.

Brabeck, M. (1986). Moral orientation: Alternative perspectives of men and women. In R.T. Knowles & G.F. McLean (Eds.), *Psychological foundations of moral education and character development: An integrated theory of moral development* (pp. 65–89). Washington, DC: University Press of America.

Bull, N.J. (1969). *Moral judgment from childhood to adolescence.* Beverly Hills, CA: Sage Publications.

Dewey, J. (1895). What psychology can do for the teacher. In R.D. Archambault (Ed.), (1963). *Dewey on education.* New York: Modern Library. Cited in Kohlberg, L. (1973). Implications of developmental psychology for education: Examples from moral development. *Educational Psychologist, 10,* 2–14.

Fraenkel, J.R. (1976). The Kohlberg bandwagon: Some reservations. *Social Education, 40,* 216–222.

Funk, J.L. (1987). Gender differences in the moral reasoning of conventional and post-conventional adults. (Doctoral dissertation, The University of Texas at Austin, 1986). *Dissertation Abstracts International, 47,* 4326A.

Gilligan, C. (1982). *In a different voice: Psychological theory and women's development.* Cambridge, MA: Harvard University Press.

Haan, N., Smith, M.B., & Block, J. (1968). Moral reasoning in young adults: Political-social behavior, family background, and personality correlates. *Journal of Personality and Social Psychology, 10,* 183–201.

Holstein, C.B. (1976). Irreversible, stepwise sequence in the development of moral judgment: A longitudinal study of males and females. *Child Development, 47,* 51–61.

Humphrey, L.A., & Oordt, R.M. (1991). Ethic of justice and ethic of care as compared to biblical concepts of justice and mercy. *Journal of Psychology and Theology, 10,* 300–305.

King, M.L., Jr. (1964). *Why we can't wait.* New York: Harper & Row.

Kohlberg, L. (1963). Moral development and identification. In H.W. Stevenson (Ed.), *Child psychology: 62nd yearbook of the National Society for the Study of Education* (pp. 277–332). Chicago: University of Chicago Press.

———. (1964). Development of moral character and moral ideology. In M.L. Hoffman & L.W. Hoffman (Eds.), *Review of child development research* (Vol. 1, pp. 383–431). New York: Russell Sage Foundation.

_____. (1967). Moral and religious education and the public schools: A developmental view. In T.R. Sizer (Ed.), *Religion and public education* (pp. 164–183). Boston: Houghton Mifflin.

_____. (1973a). The contribution of developmental psychology to education — Examples from moral education. *Educational Psychologist, 10,* 2–14.

_____. (1973b). Stages and aging in moral development — Some speculations. *The Gerontologist, 13,* 497–502.

_____. (1976a). The quest for justice in 200 years of American history and in contemporary American education. *Contemporary Education, 48,* 5–16.

_____. (1976b). This special section in perspective. *Social Education, 40,* 213–215.

_____. (1980). Stages of moral development as a basis for moral education. In B. Munsey (Ed.), *Moral development, moral education, and Kohlberg: Basic issues in philosophy, psychology, religion, and education* (pp. 15–98). Birmingham, AL: Religious Education.

_____. (1981). *Essays on moral development: The philosophy of moral development* (Vol. 1). New York: Harper & Row.

_____. (1984). *Essays on moral development: The psychology of moral development* (Vol. 2). New York: Harper & Row.

_____. (1986). My personal search for universal morality. *Moral Education Forum, 11*(1), 4–10.

Kohlberg, L., Levine, C., & Hewer, A. (1983). *Moral stages: A current formulation and a response to critics.* New York: Karger.

Kutnick, P. (1986). The relationship of moral judgment and moral action: Kohlberg's theory, criticism and revision. In S. Modgil & C. Modgil (Eds.), *Lawrence Kohlberg: Consensus and controversy* (pp. 125–148). Philadelphia: The Falmer Press.

Lockwood, A. (1975). Stage of moral development and students' reasoning on public policy issues. *Journal of Moral Education, 5,* 51–61.

Peters, R.S. (1971) Moral development: A plea for pluralism. In T. Mischel (Ed.), *Cognitive development and epistemology* (pp. 237–267). New York: Academic.

Piaget, J. (1932). *The moral judgment of the child* (M. Gabain, Trans.). London: K. Paul, Trench, Trubner, & Co.

Plueddemann, J.E. (1989). The relationship between moral reasoning and pedagogical preference in Kenyan and American college students. *Religious Education, 84,* 506–520.

Porteus, B.C., & Johnson, R.C. (1965). Children's responses to two measures of conscience development and their relation to sociometric nomination. *Child Development, 36,* 703–711.

Rest, J.R. (1975). Recent research on an objective test of moral judgment: How the important issues of a moral dilemma are defined. In D.J. DePalma & J.M. Foley (Eds.), *Moral development: Current theory and research* (pp. 75–93). Hillsdale, NJ: Lawrence Erlbaum.

————. (1986a). *Moral development: Advances in research and theory.* New York: Praeger.

————. (1986b). Moral research methodology. In S. Modgil & C. Modgil (Eds.), *Lawrence Kohlberg: Consensus and controversy* (pp. 455–469). Philadelphia: The Falmer Press.

Rich, J.M. (1980). Moral education and the emotions. *Journal of Moral Education, 9,* 81–87.

Richards, H.C., Bear, G.G., Stewart, A.L., & Norman, A.D. (1992). Moral reasoning and classroom conduct: Evidence of a curvilinear relationship. *Merrill-Palmer Quarterly, 38,* 176–190.

Rothman, G.R. (1980). The relationship between moral judgment and moral behavior. In M. Windmiller, N. Lambert, & E. Turiel (Eds.), *Moral development and socialization* (pp. 107–127). Boston: Allyn and Bacon.

Ruma, E., & Mosher, P. (1967). Relationship between moral judgment and guilt in delinquent boys. *Journal of Abnormal Psychology, 72,* 122–127.

Scharf, P. (1978). *Moral education.* Davis, CA: Responsible Action.

Sichel, B.A. (1988). *Moral education: Character, community, and ideals.* Philadelphia: Temple University Press.

Simon, F. (1976). Moral development: Some suggested implications for teaching. *Journal of Moral Education, 5,* 173–178.

Sprinthall, N.A., & McVay, J.G. (1987). Value development during the college years: A cause for concern and an opportunity for growth. *Counseling and Values, 31,* 126–138.

Sprinthall, R.C., & Sprinthall, N.A. (1981). *Educational psychology: A developmental approach* (3rd ed.). Reading, MA: Addison-Wesley.

Sullivan, E.V. (1975). *Moral learning: Some findings, issues and questions.* New York: Paulist Press.

Thoma, S.J. (1984). *Estimating gender differences in the comprehension and preference of moral issues.* Unpublished manuscript, University of Minnesota, Minneapolis.

Walker, L.J. (1984). Sex differences in the development of moral reasoning: A critical review. *Child Development, 55,* 677–691.

Wilson, J. (1980). Philosophical difficulties and "moral development." In B. Munsey (Ed.), *Moral development, moral education, and Kohlberg: Basic issues in philosophy, psychol-*

ogy, religion, and education (pp. 214–231). Birmingham, AL: Religious Education.

Wynn, J.C. (1977). *Christian education for liberation and other upsetting ideas.* Nashville, TN: Abingdon.

Ziv, A. (1976). Measuring aspects of morality. *Journal of Moral Education, 5,* 189–201.

NINE

Guidelines from Cognitive Psychology for Teachers, Parents, and Pastors

There are many things we want for our children. We want them to be healthy and happy, capable and strong, emotionally stable and spiritually aware. As they grow to adulthood, our "wish-list" for them is extended to include gainful employment, meaningful relationships, continued good health, and a walk with God. But these favorable qualities are less apt to be present if our children are not also morally mature. Being a good and decent person is basic to almost any other desirable characteristic we would want in our children.

Cognitive psychologists believe their methods come closer to bringing about this desired state than those used by their peers who represent other psychological theories. Let us hear what cognitive psychologists have to say.

A cognitive theory of morality is founded on the premise that some values are to be preferred to others. Kohlberg as the principal exponent of this theory has provided a philosophical-developmental basis for the hierarchy of moral thought. Teachers, parents, and pastors need not be caught in the bind of a relativity of ethics, for according to the moral reasoning approach, what is at higher stages is what ought to be.

Cognitive psychologists hold that true morality, by definition, must come from within the individual rather than being imposed from without. However, the environment may impede or facilitate this development. It is to a consideration of the environment in the school, the home, and the church that we now turn.

GUIDELINES FOR TEACHERS

Curricular programs based on moral reasoning are increasing in popularity. The classroom method used is to present a story with a moral dilemma and to ask each child within the group to state a position regarding the dilemma and tell why that position is taken. When this is done, the teacher fits each child's response into one of Kohlberg's six stages. But the teacher will not indicate that one response is right and another response is wrong, nor will the students know the teacher is analyzing what they say. In this way indoctrination is not used, but children are drawn to the reasoning of someone at the next higher stage. For those children who are more mature in moral judgment, the teacher may act as the plus-one model, thereby encouraging further progression.

Higher stages are preferred to lower stages, and anyone who makes a statement at the next higher stage is a plus-one model to the child whose reasoning is just below that represented by the statement. The teacher is aware that just because people do have different moral values does not mean that they ought to have different moral values. Ethical relativity and value neutrality so prominent in some approaches are not accepted in moral judgment. Nevertheless, one does not expect children to reason at stages higher than their cognitive development would allow, nor does one expect moral development to take place by telling children what their values should be.

ENCOURAGING MORAL GROWTH IN THE ELEMENTARY SCHOOL

The story presented at the elementary school level should be one the children can understand and to which they will relate. All children are able to respond to the following story adapted from Ziv (1976): "Let's pretend there is a boy (girl) just your age who is walking down the street and suddenly discovers a wallet on the sidewalk with $5.00 in it.

He (she) looks around. Do you think the boy (girl) will keep the money?" After the child has answered yes or no, the question that follows is *why*. The answer to this question determines the stage of reasoning, not whether the child says the one in the story will keep or not keep the money.[1]

Children's Responses to a Moral Dilemma Story

A stage 1 child may say the girl in the story will keep the money, "because she noticed nobody was around and thinks she can get away with it," or she will not keep the money, "because if her mommy finds out she'll really get it." A child at stage 2 will usually say that the child in the story will keep the money, "so he could spend it—maybe buy a baseball bat or mitt," or "so she can save it and someday buy a new car." One fifth-grade student, also responding at stage 2, said the child would not keep the money, "because if you return it you may get more."[2]

At stage 3 the child is concerned with being a good person in the eyes of others and will probably say that the boy or girl in the story will not keep the money. As one third-grader put it: "Because she's not supposed to. That's what we're told not to do is take someone else's things." Another third-grader, however, replied that the child would keep the money, "because my mom doesn't care if I find something." There are not many responses at stage 4 at the elementary level. A number of children talk about taking the wallet to the police station, but it is not always possible to tell whether the reason for doing so is a concern for the consequences if one does not tell an authority (stages 1 and 2), a way of pleasing others by doing what others would want one to do (stage 3), or a respect for the law and for police officers who are the enforcers of the law (stage 4). An occasional statement may reflect postconventional thinking with its concern for the welfare of another human being. "It may be an old man's money" was one child's response. "It might be someone else's lunch money," said another.

The same child may make statements at more than one stage, so it is important to remember that no one should be labeled as being "at" a particular stage unless the majority of responses are reflective of that stage. Several stories are usually given to which the child responds, and in this way an overall assessment may be made. It is also important that we not judge a child at a lower stage of moral reasoning as being less moral than a classmate who is at a higher stage. Emphasis is given to what a person may become rather than to one's present state. There is also a recognition among cognitive psychologists that being moral includes what a person does as well as what a person says.

As children discuss a story in the classroom, the stage 1 child will be attracted to the reasoning of the child at stage 2. Keeping or not keeping the money is viewed as related to concerns other than whether someone has seen what has happened. The stage 2 child, in turn, will listen to the judgment of the child at stage 3. He or she begins to understand that "finders keepers, losers weepers" is not quite right. What others think of our actions is also important. We live in a world with parents, neighbors, peers. How do they feel about what we have done? Getting along with them is essential for a good life.

Sources of Moral Dilemma Stories
Moral dilemma stories may be taken from booklets especially designed for this purpose, from the local newspaper, or from the experiences of the children themselves. For several years each issue of the *NEA Journal*, published by the National Education Association, featured an unfinished story designed especially for students in grades four through seven. School corporations with adequate resources may elect to purchase videos or filmstrips. The moral-reasoning approach has generated so much interest among educators that a number of companies have produced stories on film. For older children, news magazines and television broadcasts are excellent sources from which to draw. Dilemmas stemming from problems of labor and management, industry and environment, nationalism and internationalism have moral implications. Students may wish to bring before the class problems they have encountered with the hope that a discussion with peers will produce new ways to cope.

Increasingly, students are encouraged to do just this — to relate their own moral dilemma stories. "The beginning point of moral education lies in the stories of those who are taught. . . . Rehearsals of lessons already learned by educators, whether taught in narrative or other forms, are no substitute for the moral experiences that students bring with them from their daily lives" (Day, 1991, p. 167). Self-narrative deals with real problems in real situations and gives more meaning to the phrase "know thyself."

Tappan and Brown (1989) suggest that students tell or write their stories first to the teacher. This may be done in response to the question: "All people have had the experience of being in a situation where they had to make a decision, but weren't sure what they should do. Would you describe a situation when you faced a moral conflict and you had to make a decision, but weren't sure what you should do?" (p. 195) The teacher becomes the audience and responds in a sensitive, sympathetic way. Student and teacher then decide together if the story is to be shared with other members of the class. Any interpretation given by the teacher must be done carefully. Dramatization of the story through a skit or play is also a possibility, giving children practice in putting themselves in the place of another and trying to assist in the decision-making process.

Educating for Good Citizenship
An interesting way of encouraging children to reason at the conventional level was done by Myrna Spurgeon in her third-grade class at Deming Elementary School in Vigo County, Indiana ("3rd-graders find," 1990). The children first discussed what it means to be a good citizen and then each child wrote what he or she could do to be a good citizen. Their responses are unique combinations of reasoning at stages 3 and 4, with stage 4 usually preceding stage 3. Examples include Christina who writes, "Being a good citizen means doing things you are supposed to do, like paying bills and doing homework. It means even being good at school and home. If you help someone, you are a good citizen"; John who says, "You can be a good citizen if you don't break the laws in your city or town. If you don't rob a bank, you can be a good citizen. Now that you are a good citizen, everyone likes you a lot"; and Danielle who writes, "I can be a good citizen. I can obey the law that says don't drink and drive. I can help others by helping them and not get paid. People need laws. They need places to have fun. They need ways to get good ideas from their community" (p. E2). This exercise can be done easily in any elementary classroom and is an excellent way to promote conventional thought among children whose thinking is usually at the preconventional level.

"Educating for Citizenship" is the title of a program developed jointly by the Constitutional Rights Foundation, the Law-Related Education Program for the Schools of Maryland, and the National Institute for Citizen Education in the Law. It has been field-tested in more than fifty Maryland schools with revisions based on teachers' evaluations. At the elementary school level, animal characters are used; at the intermediate grades, students learn how representatives are chosen in a democratic society.

In choosing representatives, the class must decide the criteria to use for selecting five to ten of its members to represent them on such issues as "funding for day care, minimum wages for young people, rights of children in a divorce, and garbage recycling bills" (Pepeira, 1991, p. 224). Those who are not chosen meet in groups of five or six to study the issue being discussed and to decide if they want the bill to pass. Each group presents information to the representatives in an effort to get the representatives to vote their way. The class may role-play a legislative session. Should representatives always vote the way their constituency wants? If not, why not? By engaging in the democratic process the students begin to see how the legal system works and what their part in a democracy should be.

Building a Moral Community and Self-Esteem
Thomas Lickona (1991) believes that each child needs to have a sense of competence and worth, and then to extend that sense of worth to other children in the school. This should begin the very first day of class by pairing children who do not know each other into two-person teams called "partners." Each team is given a sheet divided into two columns: "Ways We Are Different" and "Ways We Are Alike." Included are activities they enjoy and what they do well. Each team then tells the rest of the class what they discovered about each other.

Another day can be "appreciation time" in which children respond to the teacher's request to "tell something that someone else did that you appreciate." Or the teacher may ask, "Who has a problem they would like others to help them solve?" Activities such as these make for a strong sense of group identity and a feeling of responsibility for the well-being of other members of the class. Developing the classroom "as a moral community means to develop a group in which children come

262

to: (a) know each other, (b) respect and care about each other; and (c) feel membership in, and accountability to, the group" (Lickona, 1991, p. 147).[3]

ENCOURAGING MORAL GROWTH IN THE SECONDARY SCHOOL

High school students may be found at all stages of moral understanding, although some stages are more prominent than others during the teen years. A student whose reasoning is at stage 1 may say it is all right to copy test answers as long as the teacher is not looking, or to drive fast as long as parents do not find out, or to cheat on one's boyfriend or girlfriend as long as he or she does not know you are doing it. It is only wrong if one is caught and the consequences are not to one's liking.

The teenager at stage 2 goes a step further in that reward and punishment come as the consequences of behavior, rather than being the determiners of whether the behavior is good or bad. Copying test answers may result in a failing grade, driving fast may mean car privileges are suspended, cheating on a friend may give rise to a broken relationship. One doesn't want these things to occur. However, one is obligated only to those who are in a position to return the favor. The teacher must reward one for being honest, parents must hand over car keys if driving is acceptable, and a boyfriend or girlfriend must remain true. If others do not do their part, one is no longer responsible to do his or her part. Turnabout is fair play.

Stage 3 thinking is a big step up from stages 1 and 2, for now the student equates good behavior with loyalty to the groups to which he or she belongs. What others think takes precedence over what they may do to an individual. Being moral implies concern for the approval of others. "Let's have an understanding" becomes more important than stage 2's "Let's make a deal." Most adolescents view themselves as members of several groups or subgroups and this may cause confusion if allegiance is given to those with differing definitions of how a person should act. If the teenager wants to get along with teachers and also with classmates, and if teachers frown on copying answers while classmates say it is all right, then a decision must be made as to what direction to take. Parents and peers may not agree as to what constitutes "good" driving; and although both parents and peers would applaud relationships that would involve mutual commitments, whom those relationships should be with may not be the same. Stage 3 usually begins in preadolescence and is a dominant stage during the adolescent period (Hersch, Paolitto, & Reimer, 1979).[4]

The inadequacy of stage 3 becomes apparent when the young person must deal with problems on a societal level. Now the larger society takes precedence over the particular groups to which one belongs. The adolescent comes to understand that there are rules that are binding on everyone and that respect for delegated authority is essential to keep society in one piece. The law should be followed not only when it benefits the self and one's friends, but also when it benefits people we do not know and have never met. We do not have rights that strangers do not have.

High school students, on occasion, may make statements at the postconventional level, stages 5 and 6, although this is not common. Adopting self-chosen ethical principles that are at variance with the attitudes of others or seeking alternative social arrangements that meet the needs of a larger portion of the citizenry usually comes later than the teen years if it comes at all. Adolescents may say that certain laws or rules are unfair and may demonstrate against institutions such as a nuclear plant or an abortion clinic even though these institutions are operating within the law.

But one must look at the reasoning behind the statements or behind the demonstrations to determine the stage of moral growth. If a young man refuses to register for the draft, is he doing it to preserve his own life and health (preconventional), because his family or his church says it is wrong to engage in combat (conventional), or because he feels within himself that war is a moral evil and does an injustice to people everywhere (postconventional)? Only when right is determined by conscience in accordance with the dignity and worth of human beings as ends in themselves rather than as means for some other good can it be said that a person is reasoning at the postconventional or principled level.

A Moral Dilemma Story for High School Students
Students at the high school level also engage in discussions of moral problems. A typical heterogeneous group of teenagers should provide a

plus-one model for almost everyone in the class. Historical incidents such as Watergate or My Lai are especially interesting to students at this age for they bring up the question of when loyalty to a political party (stage 3) or duty to a commanding officer (stage 4) disregards human rights and violates the higher principles of justice and mercy (stages 5 and 6).

In discussing any social issue it is important to know the facts. Peter Scharf (1978) presents statements made by military personnel involved in the My Lai massacre. High school students need to know what happened at My Lai and to become familiar with the reasons given by those involved. Some students will agree with the preconventional statements of Meadlow, a soldier who admitted killing Vietnamese civilians in order not to be punished for disobedience (stage 1) and as revenge for his friends who were killed (stage 2). As he put it, "During basic training if you disobeyed an order, if you were slow in obeying orders, they'd slap you on the head, drop-kick you in the chest and rinky-dink stuff like that. If an officer tells you to stand on your head in the middle of the highway, you do it," and "I was getting relieved from what I had seen over there . . . my buddies getting killed or wounded" (p. 59).

Other students will take the position of Lieutenant Calley, the officer charged with ordering Meadlow to shoot and whose reasoning appeared to be at the conventional level. To Calley a "good" officer was one who tried to please his superiors (stage 3) and who did what he considered to be his duty (stage 4). "I was a run-of-the-mill average guy. I still am. I always said people in Washington are smarter than me. If intelligent people say Communism is bad, it's going to engulf us. I was only a Second Lieutenant" (p. 60). And, "I was ordered to go in there and destroy the enemy. That was my job on that day. That was the mission I was given" (p. 62).

Still other students will argue the position of Bernhardt, a soldier who refused to obey Calley's orders and who made the following postconventional statements: "The law is only the law, and many times it's wrong. . . . It's not necessarily just, just because it's the law" (stage 5); and, "Nothing needs an excuse to live. The same thing goes for bombing a village. If there are people in the village, don't bomb it" (stage 6) (p. 64).[5]

Is the Moral Reasoning Approach Effective?
James Leming (1981) reviewed fifty-nine moral education programs, twenty-six of which used a cognitive development approach. Of these twenty-six programs, fifteen were conducted at the secondary level with eleven of the fifteen reporting statistically significant differences between adolescents enrolled in the programs and a control group of adolescents not enrolled in the program. Leming concluded that "the moral development research indicates that with adolescents there is a reasonable expectation that one will find mean class growth of between 1/7 and 2/3 of a stage in cases where the intervention lasts from 16 to 32 weeks" (p. 160). Methods used in the programs were those described by Kohlberg (1978) as being necessary for stage growth development: exposure to the next higher stage of reasoning, exposure to situations posing problems that the person's current level of reasoning does not solve, and an atmosphere of interchange and dialogue where conflicting moral views are compared in an open manner.

Does Postconventional Reasoning Lead to Lawless Behavior?
Some adults oriented to the conventional level express the concern that discussions of this nature will lead to anarchy—to the absence of order and control. Parents and teachers find it highly desirable for children to attain to stages 3 and 4. Getting along with others and obeying the law of the land is far better than determining right and wrong on the basis of reward and punishment (stage 1) or on what will enhance one's own pleasure and satisfy one's own needs (stage 2). Conventional adults fear a society in which people feel they have the right to make their own judgments. Faced with an increasingly lawless society and being the victims of that lawlessness, it is understandable that responsible citizens would oppose any ideology that might contribute to this sorry state of affairs.

Such concern by conventional adults is unwarranted, for studies reveal that people who reason at the highest level are less apt to cheat and hurt others, and more apt to help someone in trouble than either preconventional or conventional individuals. They have a greater resistance to temptation and are less likely to conform to group pressure. Although these principled individuals may demonstrate against an industrial polluter, march on Washington to demand equal rights for minorities, refuse to shoot civilians in Vietnam, or demonstrate against an abortion clinic, nevertheless, they understand the importance of getting along with other people and in conforming to societal regulations. Laws are not challenged unless they are seen as working toward the detriment of others.

But societies have never liked people who were too good or too bad. They crucified Jesus, and they crucified two thieves on either side. One was too good, the others too bad. Rather than condemning the postconventional members of the society, we would do well to listen to what they have to say, note the personal sacrifice some have borne in acting on their convictions, weigh the consequences of their ideas, and then judge the merit of their specific cause. Being a good citizen and a moral person involves a determination of what changes need to be made in this world of ours and then setting about by word and deed to institute those changes.

> **But societies have never liked people who were too good or too bad. They crucified Jesus, and they crucified two thieves on either side. One was too good, the others too bad. Rather than condemning the postconventional members of the society, we would do well to listen to what they have to say. . . .**

The Just Community School
Another approach at the high school level is the creation of the "just community school." Devised by Kohlberg, there are prepared guides for organizing and administering the program which calls for sixty to ninety students and five to six teachers. According to Graham (1975), the program has two objectives: to make the school a happier place to be and to help students come closer to principled thinking. Membership in a just community is voluntary, leadership is democratic, and the group must have a sense of shared goals. Students, teachers, and administrators together decide on issues of fairness and morality — issues such as stealing, cutting classes, disruptive behavior, grading procedures, and the use of drugs. The opportunity for participatory democracy is in contrast to the structure of traditional programs in which

students have little say as to the policy of the school and in which they are expected to conform or be punished. To insist that young people adhere to established rules regardless of perceived fairness makes for administrative ease but does not encourage moral development. By contrast, the implementation of a just community is time-consuming, necessitates careful planning, and involves the expertise to resolve problems as they occur. But it gives students the opportunity to think through value-related issues.[6]

Kohlberg, Levine, and Hewer (1983) write that changing the moral atmosphere of the schools from one in which rules are given to the students to one in which the students engage in participatory decision-making, relates to actual differences in behavior. "For instance, in the first year of the Cambridge Cluster School, stealing was endemic. In the second year, collective norms of trust and norms of collective responsibility had developed to the point that each member of the community pledged to contribute 25 cents to restitute 10 dollars stolen from one student's purse. There were no further episodes of stealing in the school for the next three years" (p. 56). The use of drugs, however, was not eliminated at the Cluster School. Drugs were eliminated, though, at the Scarsdale Alternative School, another school using the just community approach.[7]

Where Schools Are Today
Kohlberg (1980) says that a student should emerge from high school at stage 4. "Unless a person leaves high school already at the fourth stage and with corresponding interests and motivations, he or she is unlikely to be in a position to have the capacities and motivation to enter positions of participation and public responsibility later" (p. 466). It would be preferable, of course, for students to be at the post-conventional level, but it does not appear that this is a realistic expectation. During the 1970s it was thought that educating students for principled thinking would be possible. Implementation of the just community and the development of social studies programs integrating Kohlberg's techniques into the classroom (Fenton, 1976) were expected to move students in this direction.

But the 1980s and 1990s have found us no further along. Perhaps too few schools have used the programs. Perhaps other forces are at work that undermine the development of principled thinking. In any event, there are indications that progress — or what appeared to be progress — has not taken us far, making the mood of some proponents of the moral-reasoning approach more guarded and less optimistic. "My 1976 lecture on education for justice stressed a retrenchment from my 1968 Platonic stage 6 to a stage 5 goal and conception of justice. The present paper reports a further retrenchment to stage 4 goals as the ends of civic education" (Kohlberg, 1980, p. 459).[8]

Even more serious are signs that our young people may be regressing to the level of the preconventional. Patricia McCormack (1981), United Press International education editor, has written of the changing values in our high schools. An investigation ordered by the federal government's National Center for Education Statistics and carried out by the National Opinion Research Center of Chicago surveyed 58,000 high school seniors across the nation and compared their values with those of the high school graduating class of 1972. "Working to correct social and economic inequalities" was cited as "very important" by only 13 percent in 1980 compared to 27 percent in 1972. "Having lots of money" was rated "very important" by 31 percent in 1980, up from 19 percent in 1972. In another more recent survey of high school and college students, this one by the Joseph & Edna Josephson Institute of Ethics, "78 percent of all students counted as 'essential' getting a job they enjoy, while only 54 percent of high schoolers and 63 percent of college students considered 'being honest and trustworthy' as essential" (Wike, 1992).

Young people appear to be interested primarily in what will serve their own interests. The parents of these teenagers also applaud these goals. They too want their children to acquire this world's goods. This is why they want their children to graduate from high school and are willing to send them on to college. If they want more for their children than the power to make a good living, it is seldom expressed. During the Vietnam era, many young people decided to go into one of the helping professions. Now, by comparison, fewer appear to be interested in areas such as social work and more gravitate toward business professions.

As important as it is to earn a living, the goal of having enough money falls far short of principled morality. "If schooling is only oriented toward preparing students for assuming preestablished occupational slots, then the educational system will have failed one of its most crucial functions in a democracy" (Rest, 1979, Sec. 1, p. 24). Yet schools are a part of the communities they serve and reflect the will of the people. A society at the conventional level will demand schools at the conventional level. Some preconventional attitudes are considered to be in accord with reality and some postconventional beliefs are recognized as important, but moral reasoning that is either lower or higher than that of the populace must be limited or it will be perceived as a threat.

CAN WE PREDICT THE FUTURE?
What does the future hold for educational programs based on the cognitive approach of moral reasoning? The answer depends on who is being asked. Those who play down the importance of the judgmental in contrast to the behavioral or the affective, or who say that moral training should be the province of the home or the church and not of the school, or who feel that time spent in a discussion of moral issues leaves too little time for teaching the basics will answer that moral reasoning programs should not be encouraged. They are just a passing fad and probably not worth the effort. Conversely, those who are intrigued by the insights of Piaget and Kohlberg and who grasp the import of what it would mean to a society for more individuals to be at higher stages of moral judgment will insist that the present trend of including moral discussions in all types of subject matter must continue. If moral reasoning is not a part of the curriculum, there will be less opportunity for children to profit from a plus-one model, and development in the hierarchy of moral thought will be less apt to take place.

GUIDELINES FOR PARENTS
As parents we want to know what to do to help our children progress to more mature levels of moral understanding. Let us consider first the implications of the findings of Jean Piaget (1932).

PIAGET'S MORAL REASONING APPLIED TO THE HOME
In *The Moral Judgment of the Child*, Piaget is critical of the way parents relate to the child. For example, he notes that the average housewife

"in the very poor districts where we conducted our work" showed more anger over several cups being broken than over one broken cup regardless of the circumstances in which the damage occurred. By fixing attention on the consequences of an act and ignoring whether the act was accidental or intentional, the adult "leads the child to the notion of objective responsibility and consolidates in consequence a tendency that is already natural to the spontaneous mentality of little children." Piaget says that unless a child has more mature models to emulate in other adults or older peers, he may grow to be "as stupid with his own children as his parents were with him" (Piaget, 1932, pp. 37, 189, 191).

Intentionality

Such a statement is anything but complimentary, but that does not mean we should turn Piaget off without hearing what he has to say. We have all seen parents like this who punish their child for accidents that cannot be helped and decide the severity of punishment based on the cost of the object broken and whether it can be replaced.

Such criticism may not be deserved in our own homes, but it does point to the fact that as parents we need to exemplify in behavior and speech mature patterns of moral judgment. Accidents should not be dealt with in the same manner as deliberate acts even though the amount of damage may be the same. If we punish or reward on the basis of consequences rather than taking into consideration the circumstances, it will be more difficult for the child to progress in moral reasoning. Piaget refers to this as intentionality, and it is one of several ways in which Piaget saw younger and older children differing in moral reasoning. Older children, being more mature, can take into consideration the intent of the culprit. As parents we should be as mature as the older children Piaget observed.

Relativism

Younger and older children also differ in the ability to engage in what Piaget calls relativism. Relativism does not mean that one view is as good as another or that truth is relative. Rather, it means that a person is able to put himself or herself in the place of others, to see events from perspectives quite different than one's own, and to be empathic with the thoughts and feelings of other people. As parents we need to be capable of relativism, to understand how a child feels when scolded, sent to bed without supper, or told there will be no TV for three days. Whether the punishment is appropriate will depend on the misdeed, the age of the child, and whether a person should be dealt with in this way. Parents who consider children's feelings and who recognize that they should be treated as people provide a just environment in which children can grow.

But being a good model and providing a just environment are not sufficient in themselves. We have all seen good parents who love and care for their children, bestowing upon them kindness and consideration, but they do not insist on the same kind of treatment from their offspring. The results are unfortunate indeed! Even as we need to be considerate of our children, children need to learn consideration for us and for siblings and peers. Asking the child questions such as, "How would you feel if everyone in this family yelled 'shut up' at you like you just did to your brother?" or "Did everyone have a good time at the party?" will probably do more to encourage relativity than asking, "Do you want to get spanked for fighting all the time with your brother?" or "Did you have a good time at the party?" Children enjoy playing house or school and often imitate community helpers such as police officers and fire fighters. Or they may pretend to be one of the cartoon characters seen on Saturday morning television. Such role-playing is important in the development of relativity. Relativity also may be encouraged by reading stories to children and discussing with them the feelings and thoughts of the characters. On occasion, certain TV shows may also lend themselves to discussions of this nature.

Independence of Sanctions

Independence of sanctions means that an act or attitude is not determined to be good or bad solely on the basis of whether it is sanctioned by someone in authority. There are times when children are told to do something they should not do. They need some way of sorting out when they should obey an adult and when they should not. We caution our children not to accept a ride with a stranger even though the stranger may tell them to do so. A teacher may insist that members of the class reveal who caused the commotion and upset one of the desks.

Must the children tell the teacher because they are ordered to do so? Some would say yes; the teacher is in charge and children should obey. But what happens to the mutual trust among peers if they comply with the demand? How can children proceed from heteronomy to autonomy under these circumstances? The very young child is unable to understand any criterion other than obedience; but as children grow older, parents need to help them determine whom they should obey and under what circumstances. In homes where obedience is the only measure of right and wrong; where "I told you so" is the only reason given, children will be hindered in the development of moral reasoning.

Mature Forms of Reciprocity

As parents we encourage our child to go from immature to mature forms of reciprocity. To the small child, justice is an eye for an eye and a tooth for a tooth. To tell young children that two wrongs don't make a right makes no sense in their world. Hitting someone who has just hit you *does* make it right in their eyes for it evens the score. What could be more fair? Little by little parents need to show the child that sometimes it is best to overlook a wrong, give a soft answer, or turn the other cheek. As difficult a principle as this is for any of us to learn, we know that meaningful and lasting relationships with others necessitates taking into consideration past favors and friendships, not just the most recent action on their part. Nor can we reply in kind when to do so would escalate ill will.

Just Punishment

Punishment must be in keeping with the misdeed. To punish with the intent to hurt rather than with the intent to change unacceptable behavior or to bring restitution to one who has been wronged serves to lengthen the time the child is at the stage of heteronomy. "The little ones prefer the most severe [punishments] so as to emphasize the necessity of the punishment itself; the other children are more in favour of the measures of reciprocity which simply serve to make the transgressor feel that the bond of solidarity has been broken and that things must be put right again" (Piaget, 1932, p. 225). Some parents favor the attitudes of "the little ones" and advocate a back-to-the-woodshed approach to keep the child in line. It is as though the only way to correct the child is by inflicting pain, by coercion imposed from without. But both observation and research tell us that "in homes where heavy punishment predominates and rules are stringent, the children continue to believe in the effectiveness of punishment, or retributive justice, much longer than children who move toward more advanced stages of distributive justice" (Windmiller, 1980, p. 17). Parents need to exemplify mature rather than immature forms of punishment, to

PIAGET AND RELIGION

Piaget's interest in religion appeared to be greatest during his late teens, and his personal search for the highest good led him to the concept of the Idea. The Idea, though never defined, was linked to God, justice, personal suffering, selflessness, and faith. "In the beginning was the Idea," Piaget wrote, and "Jesus is the Idea made flesh" (Piaget, 1916/1977, p. 27). Piaget condemned organized religion as restrictive of individual and societal attainment. Jesus was admired for He lashed out at an establishment considered to be respectable and legitimate yet one that treated people without compassion and justice.

At age nineteen, Piaget penned the following vignette. Note the emotional turmoil and the resulting calm when the Idea makes its presence known. "The winter traveler sees the cold, still world around him, the snowflakes falling crazily. By turns he senses the emptiness and sadness of the world, feels himself filled with the painful bitterness of his solitude, is united in an immense sympathy with the snow around him, finds the calm of the idea that brings him closer to God. We fear that our efforts may be all in vain, we do not see the ideal, but we construct it nevertheless. Such is life for the idea, painful, and fecund, for to suffer is truly to live" (p. 28).

Piaget believed that the ultimate in ethical and spiritual understanding is a concern for others. "Life is good but the individual pursuing his self-interest renders it bad. . . . Self-interest may lead the individual to keep for himself some of the vital energy which he might bring to others" (p. 29).

Piaget, J. (1977). The mission of the Idea. In H.E. Gruber & J.J. Vonèche (Eds.), *The essential Piaget* (pp. 26-37). New York: Basic Books. (Originally published from J. Piaget, *La mission de l'idee*. Lausanne, Edition la Concorde, 1916.)

secure "the bond of solidarity" between themselves and their children, to see that things are "put right again."

Causes of Misfortune

Children also need the help of parents in understanding that there are many causes of misfortune. We know that trouble may come because of negligence or disobedience or because of judgmental errors. Sometimes problems occur through no fault of our own. We are simply in the wrong place at the wrong time. Or disaster may strike naturally as in the case of fire or flood. Children need direction in sorting out the circumstances so they can differentiate between "immanent justice" and natural causes. If they have had a bad day at school, having been scolded by the teacher, it may be that they were unruly and deserved the punishment, or it may be that the teacher is emotionally unstable and should be replaced. When the child's grandmother dies the child needs to know that her death is in no way related to the fact that he sometimes forgot to pray for her at night before going to bed. Although God may speak to us through misfortune, and the child should be sensitive to this possibility, to believe that all trouble is willed by God because of wrongdoing only serves to keep the child at an immature level of moral reasoning.

Many would not agree with Piaget's view that peers are more influential than parents in the growth of moral judgment, but most people would admit that a child's friends do play an essential role. It becomes important for parents to give attention to a child's choice of companions. It is easier to help children in their choice of friends during the early years than when they are in adolescence and spend more time away from home. The key is to guide rather than to tell. The direct approach of telling children with whom they may or may not spend time will hamper the kind of development that comes from being involved in the decision-making process. Discussion of possible consequences of friendships with certain types of people sets the stage for cognitive decisions that enable moral development to take place.

A mature sense of justice seldom comes before the adult years. But we cannot wait until our children are grown to express mature views. We continue to state principles our children may not understand with the hope that in later years they will remember what we have said and will adopt similar values. By far the most effective way to encourage moral development in the home is by the creation of a just environment — one in which intentions are considered, relativism is practiced, mutual trust is stressed, and mature forms of reciprocity are practiced. Punishment should fit the misdeed, and misfortune should not be linked automatically with wrongdoing. Treating children with respect and expecting no less from them in return will facilitate development from heteronomy to autonomy and finally to the mature process of equity.

KOHLBERG'S STAGES APPLIED TO THE HOME

Kohlberg said less about the influence of the parent than did Piaget. This may be due in part to Kohlberg's having studied older children and in part to evidence in some studies that stage of moral reasoning in parents is not highly correlated with stage of moral reasoning in their children.

The Parent as a Plus-One Model

Kohlberg stressed, however, the importance of the parent as a role model. Children pattern their ideas and behaviors after the people they know — parents being among this group. How much influence the parent has relative to the peer group or other adults will depend on the significance of each person to the child. However, parents provide the child's first encounter with an environment that is either just or unjust and the first example of speech and behavior that is either morally mature or morally immature.

Other writers have expanded on Kohlberg's view of parents as role models (Lande & Slade, 1979; Lickona, 1983; Woodward, 1976). Parents who are familiar with Kohlberg's stages can determine where the child is in the hierarchy of moral thought and verbalize ideas at the next stage. Does the child do what is right to avoid punishment (stage 1), because it brings pleasure (stage 2), so family or friends will be pleased (stage 3), because it is a rule (stage 4)? The parent should appeal to the next stage. A stage 1 child may be told, "When you finish picking up your toys, I'll read you your favorite story," rather than being told, "If you don't get your toys picked up, you'll wish you had!" A stage 2 child who takes the attitude, "Make it worth my while," when asked to help around the house needs to understand that being a member of a household includes mutual consideration and responsibility. A home is no longer a home if everyone goes his or her own way. Belongingness mandates caring about what others think of us and caring for them in return. Once the child is strongly entrenched at stage 3, the next step is to realize that the maintenance of order goes beyond the seeking of approval. Rules for behavior are established in the home, the school, and the society for the smooth functioning of the group. Laws are to be obeyed not to avoid punishment, but to create a world in which we can live together in harmony.

Although helping our children attain stages 3 and 4 is difficult, especially with others telling them to "look out for number one," "do your own thing," and "you only go around once, so you owe it to yourself," the conventional is not sufficient. We breathe a sigh of relief when our children come to care for family and friends and willingly obey the laws of the land. But so much more is needed. Do we encourage our children to weigh alternatives before deciding on a course of action and to look forward to the time when they can participate directly in democratic decision-making (stage 5)? Do we communicate to them on a regular basis that all people have rights and should be treated with respect regardless of gender, age, race, lifestyle, or contribution to society (stage 6)?

The Home as a Just Community

Two publications (Krebs, 1980; Ward, 1989), both written from a Christian perspective and in a style that all parents can understand, apply Kohlberg's three levels of moral reasoning to child-rearing techniques. Ted Ward (1989) in *Values Begin at Home* emphasizes the importance of the family as a "just and moral community" (p. 96) in which children are treated fairly, experiences for social interaction are provided, discussions of moral concerns are open, and opportunities for role-playing are given. Ward advocates rewards and punishments for the child at level 1, models and rules for the child at level 2, and dialogue and interpersonal transactions for the young person at level 3 (p. 94).

How to Bring Up a Good Child by Richard Krebs (1980) is similar in emphasis but more detailed in that the entire book is an application of Kohlberg's theory to child-rearing procedures. By using anecdotes and nontechnical terms, Krebs effectively explains to the reader how to relate to children at each of the three levels. The child at the preconventional level should not be called bad for the young child is premoral, not immoral. "With a premoral child, we are not teaching morality; rather, we are laying the groundwork for later moral development. By consistently rewarding honesty, truthfulness, helping, or whatever moral traits we would like our children to display, we are establishing patterns of behavior that can develop at the next level, the conventional level, into true morality" (p. 45). The premoral child needs care, consistency, fairness, and both reward and punishment.

Children at the conventional level, which encompasses the school years, begin to understand societal standards of right and wrong. Krebs suggested that it is especially important for children at this period to have adequate models of morality. Parents and other legitimate authorities, such as teachers and police officers, should supply this need. Interaction with age-mates also matters as the child must learn that interpersonal relationships with equals are affected by violating a trust. At the postconventional level the adolescent or young adult will come to understand the principles behind the rules and regulations imposed on a society. Young adults also come to realize that some actions are immoral even though the actions remain within the law, whereas other actions are immoral if a law is obeyed without regard to the underlying principle. If there is a discrepancy between the law and the principle, the principle should take precedence. Krebs gives the example of breaking down a neighbor's door to warn of fire. It is the spirit of the law, not the letter, that makes for moral action. "While principled children obey specific laws and obey them more consistently than children at either of the earlier moral levels, principled children are also capable of standing against an illegitimate authority of law and bringing about social change and justice" (p. 119).

Moral Stages of Parents and Their Children
The results of research conducted by Walker (1990) question the evidence of previous studies that stage of moral reasoning in parents has little relationship to stage of moral reasoning in their children. Sixty-three family triads (both parents and a child) with the child from four different grade levels (1, 4, 7, and 10) were interviewed and tested.

When hypothetical moral dilemmas were used, there was little difference. But when real-life moral problems were the topic of discussion (areas such as friendships, theft, fighting, or honesty) the moral reasoning of parents related directly to the moral reasoning of the child.

Two years later, Walker repeated the interviews and family sessions, and the children were retested for stage of moral understanding. The greatest growth occurred in those children whose parents were supportive, elicited the child's opinion, listened carefully to what the child said, and provided comments that were one stage higher than those of the child. "Although these parents were apparently accommodating to the child's level, they were also providing the stimulation of higher-stage moral reasoning" (Walker, 1990, p. 18). The least growth in moral reasoning occurred in children whose parents were critical of the child's reasoning, who tended to "lecture" the child on what was right, and who engaged in other behaviors that brought on defensive reactions.

In another study, Dirks (1989) obtained postconventional scores for 118 college students (93 of them from a Christian liberal arts university) and conducted interviews with both the students and their parents to assess the "socialization practices" of the parents when the students were children. Students scoring highest in moral reasoning came from homes in which parents described God as loving rather than someone to be feared, had frequent and spontaneous discussions about religious beliefs, related conduct to faith, communicated the biblical basis for expected behaviors, and provided a warm and relaxed atmosphere when talking about life events and faith.

Dirks states that "such an approach to parenting contrasts with dogmatic statements like, 'This is the way good Christians act! And this is the way you will behave in this house,'" or "guilt-inducing statements such as, 'The Bible says you are bad when you do that'" (pp. 85-86). Parents should place less emphasis on outward conformity to biblical teaching and more emphasis on "guiding children to think through dilemmas prompted by application of biblical principles to life situations" (p. 89).

Distinguishing Between Good Manners and Substantive Moral Issues
Lickona (1983) and Duska and Whelan (1975) give a number of practical rules for parents who would encourage the development of moral

reasoning in the child. Lickona writes that parents should respect their children and require respect in return. Parents teach by example and can help children take on responsibilities and acquire positive self-concepts. Duska and Whelan include making a distinction between rules for good manners and issues of moral substance, being attentive to the child's reasons for moral judgment, not reacting with more aggravation to the child's carelessness than one would to the same action committed by an adult, and respecting the child's right to an apology when parents have been unjust. Older children should be able to discuss what they consider to be fair or unfair in family relationships and should feel free to talk with parents about contemporary issues that involve moral decisions without fear of censure. As parents we need to remember that although we may encourage moral development by creating a just environment, we cannot imprint our values on our children. Our children must construct their own system of beliefs, rethinking the views given by us and others, and then decide to accept or reject those views in accordance with their own pattern of moral reasoning.

GUIDELINES FOR PASTORS

That great body of believers called the church is composed of people at all stages of moral reasoning. Yet, whatever the stage, the Christian message is meaningful. Some come to Christ to escape the fires of hell and obtain the blessings of heaven (stage 1). Others see the Christian life as a good bargain. They will acknowledge Christ now, and Christ will acknowledge them later (stage 2). Still others think of Jesus as their friend, and the fellowship of the saints takes on great importance (stage 3). Those at stage 4 look to Christ as the Lord of their lives and to the Scripture as their guide to faith and practice. Stage 5 Christians emphasize Christ as the Redeemer of the world and endeavor to follow His example of putting people before the law. They are usually more creative and more flexible than those at stage 4. Believers at stage 6 see God as the one who holds together the universe, and they believe that every individual is created in the image of God and has personal worth. They emphasize that true religion is loving others even as Christ loved us.

Most Christian ministers have sufficient familiarity with Scripture that they are able to bring messages that meet the needs of parishioners at all stages of moral reasoning. Fortunate is the church that has a pastor who is sufficiently mature in his own cognitive thinking that he or she is able to understand not only the reasoning of the members of the congregation but can provide a "plus-one" model for those who already reason at higher stages.

PROBLEMS WITHIN THE CHURCH AND KOHLBERG'S STAGES

Understanding where the congregation is in moral reasoning will help to answer the question of why church members often disagree with one another. Problems within the church may occur because Christians at one stage or level are unable to understand Christians at a different stage or level. Let us pursue this thought in more detail.

> That great body of believers called the church is composed of people at all stages of moral reasoning. Yet, whatever the stage, the Christian message is meaningful.

The Preconventional Level

Believers at the preconventional level focus on what God has done for them and on how much better off they are now than before they accepted Christ. Their favorite hymns are songs of personal testimony, " 'Twas a Glad Day When Jesus Found Me," "He Lifted Me," and "The Lord Is My Shepherd."

The Conventional Level

Those at the conventional level not only see themselves in an advantageous position because of what Christ has done for them, but they also have an appreciation of the family of God and of the fellowship of the saints. Joining hearts and hands with brothers and sisters in the Lord, receiving encouragement, and sharing joys and sorrows gives meaning to their lives. "Blest Be the Tie That Binds" and "Come, We That Love the Lord" are enjoyed.

Being at the conventional level also means taking seriously the ceremonies and traditions of the church. Conformity to a particular mode of baptism, a way of taking communion, or the manner in which the worship service is conducted is important. For some believers these forms take on such significance that they become part of church doctrine, and such traditions, in turn, become all important. Some stage 4 Christians believe that losing the tradition or the form is tantamount to losing everything. They say that if one domino falls, they all will fall. Such believers are often the pillars of the church and display a loyalty that is most impressive. They are true to what they believe, and they believe fervently. "A Charge to Keep I Have" and "Come, Thou Almighty King" have special meaning. However, they seldom understand a morality other than their own, and for this reason they do not move to higher stages of moral thought.

The Postconventional Level

Postconventional Christians, having traversed through the previous stages of moral reasoning, appreciate what Christ has done for them personally. They value the fellowship of the saints, and they understand the importance of tradition. But they appreciate, value, and understand far more. If they follow convention — and they usually do — it is done out of conviction, not because they are told they must. They weigh alternatives and judge what is best in a given situation. They will implement innovative methods of witnessing or of teaching a Sunday School class if past methods are shown to be ineffective. If a minister brings new ways of doing things to the church, postconventional Christians will not be perturbed, providing the new ways do not become "gospel." When the young people of the church adopt unconventional dress and hairstyles, it is overlooked. Worshiping God in spirit and in truth takes precedence over form and custom. Favorite songs are "This Is My Father's World" and "Love Divine, All Loves Excelling."

Stage 5 Christians are a blessing to some and a cross to others. They are often more caring and accepting and loving than those at stage 4. They are concerned not only for fellow church members but also for a world that needs Christ. They understand that evil comes not only in the form of personal sins like drunkenness, deceitfulness, and infidelity but also in the form of social sins like racism, poverty, and sexism. An enigma to fellow parishioners and a thorn in the side of church leaders at stage 4, the stage 5 Christian may be accused of hindering the Spirit of Christ, of not having a proper respect for authority.

From the perspective of the postconventional member, authority is respected and church policy is understood. But this does not mean that the minister or the church board has a special line to God that others cannot tap. All believers may go directly to God in prayer and to the Scripture to determine God's will and to know what is right and what is wrong in God's sight. Some churches have been known to penalize believers for behaviors based on principled morality when these conflicted with the church's conventions or convenience. When this occurs, postconventional Christians do not feel compelled to stand before a tribunal to be judged for their "liberal" ways. To one's own Master one stands or falls.

Believers at stage 6 will not discriminate against the poor, the less educated, or the less socially aware. All who are true Christians are welcomed into the church. "Sixes" do not take the attitude that families are more important than singles, that the Men's Bible study class has more favor with God than the Women's Bible study class, or that representatives of one's own race are preferable for church membership to those of a different complexion. Nor do stage 6 believers consider that they are better Christians than those who reason at other stages of moral development. All people have equal worth in God's sight, and God uses Christians at all stages. Emphasis is on what one can become rather than on one's present state.

Christians Are at All Levels of Moral Reasoning
Jack Pressau (1977) in his carefully reasoned *I'm Saved, You're Saved— Maybe* makes a case for the ideal Christian being one who functions, not at the conventional level and not at the postconventional level, but *"at all moral levels at once."*

> Ideal Christians . . . are persons who consciously affirm that there are valid moral reasons at many moral stages. . . . They try to do what they do at the highest Level possible, but they are more concerned about responsible behavior than perfect motivation. . . . I believe the condescension and suspicion between the different moral Levels of salvation understanding is a scandal to the church. By keeping in touch with all those reasons-for-believing positively we improve our chances of hearing and being heard by others who need our ministry. (p. 111)[9]

One is not a better Christian for reasoning at a higher level. Rather, the advantages come in being able to function at more levels at a time, in achieving greater equilibrium when problems occur, and in finding more effective ways to cope.

Why the Conventional Level Is Good — And Not So Good

Duska and Whelan (1975) write of difficulties faced by older Catholics who, having spent all their adult lives at the conventional level, were faced with recent changes in the church. Loyalty to them meant an unswerving attachment to the practices of worship. "The good thing to do is that which the Church approves . . . bowed heads after communion, somberness and seriousness in church, not eating meat on Friday, fasting during Lent, etc., etc." But then these people were told that the church did not really care about these forms of worship. Confused after a lifetime of fidelity, they asked what practices they should engage in now and were told that they would have to decide for themselves. At their age, this was impossible. "Their road map for doing good was taken away and nothing was put in its place" (p. 87).

Younger people find independence attractive but may suffer from a similar type of problem, a problem that DiGiacomo (1979), an educator in a Catholic high school, calls "a Stage Four cop-out." Rather than trying to understand the principles behind the moral life, such as why premarital sex, stealing, and lying are wrong, they just say that their religion is against it. "For this mentality, religion becomes the arbiter of morals, and church membership is a short-cut to enlightenment by way of the unexamined life. Dogmatism in any form is unacceptable to the post-conventional mind and should be" (p. 69).

Such a mentality is not unique to the Roman Catholic Church. It is found in Protestant groups as well. Progression to the level of the post-conventional comes slowly, and many never attain it. For those in churches where the list of do's and don'ts is exceedingly long and strongly enforced, the letter of the law may take precedence over an understanding of the law. "If God says it I believe it, and that settles it" is a favorite expression. But those who search the Scriptures do not always agree on what God has said, and so divisions come with each group insisting that it knows the mind of the Lord.

Other problems also may occur. Some churches have been forced to close their doors due to mergers at the national level, leaving members of the local congregations confused and angry. Or the minister may be found to have dipped into the offering plate or to have engaged in sexual immorality. The believer at the conventional level whose loyalty is with the local congregation and who looked to the pastor as one sent from God is often at a loss to know how to cope.

Postconventional members of a congregation are less disturbed by such events. If the district church folds, they recognize that the cause of Jesus Christ is far greater than the local congregation. If the minister is run out of town, their less exalted view of authority serves to help them pick up the pieces, put them together into a new design, and continue to serve a God who is perfect and who will never leave them or forsake them.

ARE WOMEN CONFUSED AS TO THEIR ROLE IN THE CHURCH?

The place of women in the church has been a topic of interest since the days of the apostles. Women, as well as men, were prominent figures in the early church, so it was important to know what their respective positions and responsibilities should be. Paul addressed this question even as he had so many other problems facing first-century Christians.

Nineteen hundred years have passed since this time and changes have occurred that have affected the society and subsequently the church. As Christians we are called upon to sort out which of these changes are desirable and which may be detrimental to the cause of Christ. Because we are Christians, we take as our guide the Holy Scriptures. We may quote Paul's words to Timothy that "a woman should learn in quietness and full submission . . . she must be silent" (1 Tim. 2:11-12), or we may quote Paul's words to the Galatian church that "there is neither . . . male or female . . . in Christ" (Gal. 3:28). As these verses appear to give very different messages, it is understandable that women today find it difficult to know what roles they should have within the local congregation. Some churches emphasize the subjection of women, other churches emphasize their equality.

As all Scripture is given by inspiration of God, we find ourselves called upon to decide which passages of Scripture we should emphasize and which passages we should give lesser consideration. Alvera Mickelsen (1989) writes that a distinction must be made between the highest ideals or standards emphasized by Jesus Christ and the Apostle Paul and "regulations for people where they were" (p. 179). Walter

Liefeld (1989) refers to making such a decision as "theological scaffolding," in which a crucial passage tends to be cited as governing the interpretation of other relevant texts. Like Mickelsen, Liefeld distinguishes those teachings that are universally true for all time from those teachings that applied to a particular church. He says, for example, that Paul's principle of being "all things to all men, that I might by all means save some" (1 Cor. 9:22, NKJV) meant that in the pagan world of the first century, women were to wear veils and be silent. "Today it is just the reverse. A society that accepts women as corporation executives and university presidents will find it difficult to listen to a church that silences them" (p. 143).

Catherine Stonehouse (1992) grapples with the question of the role of women in the church, using Gilligan's theory of women's moral growth as the basis for her remarks. Young girls may not know how to describe themselves or be able to articulate who they are or how they should relate to others. As they mature, they become aware that females find their identity in caring for others and in being dependent upon the wishes of family and friends. With this perspective, women are quite content to look to the interests of others and defer to the decisions of those around them. As time goes on, however, "women become increasingly aware of an inner voice, the voice of a self with unmet needs — needs that differ from those she serves" (Stonehouse, 1992, p. 35). At this point, women resent being told what to do. They are weary with self-sacrifice and being expected to do what others want. Resentment builds, sometimes accompanied by guilt and anger; and women begin to look to their inner selves to learn who they are and to determine how to make decisions on their own. At the final mature stage, women take responsibility for their own actions. They know who they are, and caring is not so much a matter of pleasing others as it is a commitment to help those in need. "The responsibility is no longer an ought laid on her by society but a self-chosen ethic of care" (p. 36).

Stonehouse believes the implications of women's moral growth have

> **Women's voices must be heard, and as women are listened to, the role of men as well as the role of women will be clarified.**

importance for Christian education and the community of the church. Women's voices must be heard, and as women are listened to, the role of men as well as the role of women will be clarified. Gilligan asks for an orchestration of the themes of care and justice. According to Stonehouse, this orchestration is best achieved in the church, not when women are concerned with care and men are concerned with justice, but rather when both women and men are all God wants them to be; namely, caring persons who seek justice for everyone.

THE CHURCH SCHOOL AND MORAL REASONING

The cognitive view of morality may be applied as well to the teaching of children in the church school or Sunday School. As was mentioned in chapter 1, Bible stories are an excellent source of moral dilemmas. The teacher finds it important not only to present the lesson, but to listen to what each child has to say, recognizing that children are not passive organisms shaped only by the environment but active human beings involved in their own development and understanding. Concepts taught must be at the child's level of cognition, or the result will be unrelated bits and pieces of information. As children respond to the lesson, the teacher should respect what is said as being appropriate to their level of cognition. A child's words should not be reinterpreted so they make sense to the adult mind, for to do so is to misunderstand what the child knows. Nor should a child's ideas be laughed at as being cute or criticized as being wrong. An atmosphere of acceptance and affirmation does not imply value neutrality however. Quite the contrary, the teacher will endeavor to help pupils understand the truths of Scripture and relate these to a more mature relationship with God. Creating conditions whereby ideas at the next stage of moral reasoning can be presented will foster both cognitive and spiritual development.

Teaching for Moral Growth: The Preconventional Child

The stage 1 child is afraid of God's anger and sees him as the great punisher. An appeal to stage 2 or "selfish need" is in order where God's love and care are taught. Each of us needs to be loved. As a shepherd cares for the sheep, God cares for us. As He clothes the flowers of the field and feeds the birds of the air, so He will clothe and feed us. He loves us and wants us to be happy. Favorite stories are how

God rescued Moses from Pharaoh, David from Goliath, and Daniel from the lions. "Jesus Loves Me" may be sung again and again and not lose its message.

In an effort to move the child toward the conventional level, the child can play the part of one of the characters in a Bible story. This appeals to the active nature of children and will help them learn that others have thoughts and feelings similar to their own. Role-playing helps the child "decenter," that is, to see things from the perspective of another. This, in turn, enables the child to move from a morality of constraint at the preconventional level to a morality of cooperation at the conventional level.

Teaching for Moral Growth: The Conventional Adolescent
Older children, at the junior high level, are ready for conventional thought. At this age belonging to a group one can identify with and be loyal to takes on special significance. Unless the church has such a group, the young person may give allegiance to friends outside the church community and thus be lost to the influence of the Gospel message. Young people also need adult models after whom they can pattern their lives. The personality and lifestyle of the teacher or class leader becomes as important as what is said. A church library with good Christian fiction or biographies of missionaries also provides role models for pupils.

The Sunday School class or junior church not only supplies a home base for its members but also defines the rules and duties by which the members of the community must abide. The student learns that God has laws, and these laws must not be broken. If the law is broken then someone must pay. This is what sent Jesus to the cross — to pay for our sins. The Scriptures become the rule book for how one is to live, and the community provides the social pressure to conform. The commandments of God are true and righteous and must be followed. Role-taking may continue through skits and plays but is more apt to occur by dialogue as ideas and beliefs are shared. Moral dilemmas in the Bible take on a larger dimension than was possible at the preconventional level. Moses' escape from Pharaoh and David's encounter with Goliath, of special interest to the preconventional child, are superseded at the conventional level with Moses as the leader of a great nation giving out the commandments of God and David as a representative of the people of God, of right against might. Daniel's experience with the lions now becomes one of a series of incidents in the lives of a group of young men who encouraged each other to be true to God in the face of incredible odds.

Teaching for Moral Growth: The Postconventional Adult

Teachers of senior high students and of adults should endeavor to develop postconventional thinking in their classes. This precludes that the teacher is capable of such thinking and is allowed by church officials to conduct a class in this way. Discussion of why the Scriptures condemn certain behaviors and attitudes will enable members of the class to develop more advanced understanding than was possible at stage 4. Emphasis at the postconventional level is also on internal control and self-chosen principles. Moses stood alone even when his own people were against him. David, likewise, knew what he had to do in spite of the ridicule of his brothers. Daniel prayed before God in full view of the enemy, even though disobedience to the king's law could cost him his life. Worship takes on a deeper meaning than is possible at previous levels of cognition for one now serves a God who is interested not only in the worshiper and his or her friends and family but also in all people everywhere. Jesus told His disciples to go to the ends of the world and witness to every person, bringing to all the good news of salvation.

THE PASTOR AND THE YOUNG ADULT AT STAGE 4½

Most adults in our society, including pastors of churches and their congregations, tend to reason at the conventional level, stages 3 and 4. Consequently, they find it difficult to deal with young people who may be in a transition period between the conventional and postconventional levels. The reasoning of someone at this period, sometimes referred to as stage 4½, takes on a subjectivism and relativism that manifests itself in the attitude that right and wrong should not be prescribed for anyone including oneself. No one should have to do what others say but rather each person decides for himself or herself. At the beginning of stage 4½, the young person may confuse relativism with an egocentric perspective but as he or she advances in moral understanding, a self-centered view of individual natural rights gives way to a recognition that social demands are sometimes necessary to preserve the rights of all persons.

Thomas Lickona (1983) writes that stage 4½ is more apt to come in the late teens as the result of "diversity shock." When young people go to college, for example, they meet all sorts of people who believe all sorts of things about sex, God, politics, and morality.

> **Most adults in our society, including pastors of churches and their congregations, tend to reason at the conventional level, stages 3 and 4.**

For kids who have been exposed to only one "system" of morality or truth, that's a bucket of cold water in the face. They go from thinking, "There's only one right system — mine," to thinking, "If so many people believe so many things, it must be just a matter of opinion. There's no right or wrong." (pp. 242-243)

Such an attitude is understandably disconcerting to parents and pastors, especially when accompanied by a change in behavior. If the young person stops going to church, argues from a political position quite different from that of the family, or has a live-in boyfriend or girlfriend, the thinking may be stage 4½ but the behavior cannot be differentiated from stage 2 egocentrism.

Richard Young (1981) calls this a period of hedonistic experimentation in which the introjected values of childhood are rejected. It is a confusing time for many adolescents who feel fear, anger, and alienation while at the same time experiencing the emotions of freedom, anticipation, and excitement. The young person is sorting out which values to retain and which values to reject. Both affective and cognitive conflict are present. Young takes the position that after the period of experimentation "the individual will be faced with the need to reestablish order and coherence in his or her system of values in order to provide for stability and predictability" (p. 169). A return to the church and to the values taught in the home is not atypical in adulthood.

But this is less apt to occur if leaders within the church, many of whom reason at the conventional level, take the attitude that the rebelliousness of youth is the direct result of satanic influence rather than being a normal process of growing up. Sunday School teachers, pastors, and other adults cannot condone attitudes and behaviors that are contrary to their religious faith, but they should understand the importance of each person adopting self-chosen ethical principles rather than merely obeying rules laid down by those in authority. Morality by definition must come from within.

In an article entitled, "A Developmental Perspective on Adolescent 'Rebellion' in the Church," Cathryn Hill (1986) elaborates further on the importance of a period of doubt on the part of the adolescent. Hill believes that a time of questioning is necessary in order to achieve steadfastness in one's faith. Even as youth from unchurched homes may rebel against their parents' godlessness and join a church, youth from religious homes may react against their parents' lives and values and reject for a time what they have been taught. To accept the former as right and the latter as wrong may be in accordance with our theology but it does not reckon with a basic principle of adolescent development. Hill writes that "if adolescents do not return to their original values, perhaps this may be a result of the church's inability to grow beyond a conventional level of development and meet the developmental challenge of adolescent faith" (Hill, 1986, pp. 316-317).

IN CONCLUSION

The cognitive view of morality has caught the attention of educators and pastors in a way no other psychology has done. Moral reasoning describes our attitudes toward ourselves and how we feel about others. It is a statement of society's obligation to us and what we, in turn, should contribute to the society.

It is necessary that all institutions that affect the child — the school, home, and church — be involved in the development of moral reasoning. "The task is to 'give the psychology of moral development and education away' to as many teachers, administrators, parents and interested others as possible. That will begin to make morality a common cause. . . . It is time to 'mainstream' moral education as one means to enhance overall human capability" (Mosher, 1980, p. 221).

Unless this is done, those at the preconventional level who seek no good other than their own, and those at the conventional level who do not understand that morality may exceed getting along with neighbors and obeying the law, will never realize their potential. The enterprise is of such magnitude that assistance is needed from as many sources as possible.

NOTES

1. Money isn't worth what it was in 1976 when Ziv first related this story. Consequently, my undergraduate students when telling the story to children at the elementary school level have raised the amount to $20.00. In the last two years, a number of children at the elementary level were saying that the child in the story would keep the money "because $5.00 doesn't matter."

2. The statements in quotes are verbatim responses of elementary school children in Vigo County, Indiana.

3. For more ideas, see T. Lickona (1991), *Educating for character: How our schools can teach respect and responsibility*. New York: Bantam Books.

4. Kohlberg (1984) in *Essays on moral development: The psychology of moral development* (Vol. 2), New York: Harper & Row, presented data for stage responses of middle class urban boys in the United States, ages ten, thirteen, and sixteen. Approximately 40 percent of ten-year-olds were at stage 1, 30 percent at stage 2, 20 percent at stage 3, and 10 percent at stage 4. By contrast, the dominant stage for thirteen-year-olds was stage 3 (approximately 30 percent) with about equal numbers responding at stages 2 and 4 (approximately 20 percent each). Not until one tests sixteen-year-olds are statements seen at the postconventional level. Stage 5 accounted for about a fourth of the responses of sixteen-year-olds with stages 4 and 3 following close behind. Stages 1 and 2 were less frequent and stage 6 was the least frequent of all.

5. For additional stories, see P. Scharf, W. McCoy, & D. Ross (1979), *Growing up moral: Dilemmas for the intermediate grades*. Minneapolis, MN: Winston Press.

6. The theme of the Winter 1981 issue of *Moral Education Forum*, Vol. 6, is the "just community school." Details are given as to the implementation of the just community approach in schools in the Cambridge and Boston areas. Both the victories and the defeats are detailed.

7. The "just community approach" has also been tried in the elementary grades. See Dennis Murphy (1988, February), The Just Community: At Birch Meadow Elementary School, in *Phi Delta Kappan, 69,* 427–428.

8. All six stages were presented by Lawrence Kohlberg in a lecture delivered at Indiana State University on January 26, 1983. Professor Kohlberg spent two days on campus at the invitation of his personal friend and my colleague, Liam Grimley. Because Kohlberg had requested that he not spend all his time with large groups, and because my husband and I were on the committee that made the arrangements for his visit, it was decided that the two of us would have breakfast the next morning with him and a friend who came with him. One of the questions I asked Dr. Kohlberg at that time was about his statement of a retrenchment to stage 4. His response was that he must have been discouraged when he wrote it.

9. For a more detailed examination of Kohlberg's stages and Christian belief, J. Pressau (1977), *I'm saved, you're saved — Maybe* is recommended. Atlanta: John Knox.

REFERENCES

Day, J.M. (1991). Narrative, psychology, and moral education. *American Psychologist, 46,* 167–168.

DiGiacomo, J.J. (1979). Ten years as moral educator in a Catholic high school. In T.C. Hennessy (Ed.), *Value/moral education: Schools and teachers* (pp. 51–71). New York: Paulist Press.

Dirks, D.H. (1989). Moral maturity and Christian parenting. *Christian Education Journal, 9*(2), 83–93.

Duska, R., & Whelan, M. (1975). *Moral development: A guide to Piaget and Kohlberg.* New York: Paulist Press.

Fenton, E. (1976). The cognitive-developmental approach to moral education. *Social Education, 40,* 187.

Graham, R. (1975). Moral education: A child's right to a just community. *Elementary School Guidance and Counseling, 9,* 299–308.

Hersch, R.H., Paolitto, D.P., & Reimer, J. (1979). *Promoting moral growth: From Piaget to Kohlberg.* New York: Longman.

Hill, C.I. (1986). A developmental perspective on adolescent "rebellion" in the church. *Journal of Psychology and Theology, 14,* 306–318.

Kohlberg, L. (1978). The cognitive-developmental approach to moral education. In P. Scharf (Ed.), *Readings in moral education* (pp. 36–51). Minneapolis: Winston Press.

————. (1980). Educating for a just society: An updated and revised statement. In B. Munsey (Ed.), *Moral development, moral education, and Kohlberg: Basic issues in philosophy, psychology, religion, and education* (pp. 455–470). Birmingham, AL: Religious Education Press.

Kohlberg, L., Levine, C., & Hewer, A. (1983). *Moral stages: A current formulation and a response to critics.* New York: Karger.

Krebs, R. (1980). *How to bring up a good child.* Minneapolis: Augsburg.

Lande, N., & Slade, A. (1979). *Stages: Understanding how you make moral decisions.* New York: Harper & Row.

Leming, J.S. (1981). Curricular effectiveness in moral/values education: A review of research. *Journal of Moral Education, 10,* 147–164.

Lickona, T. (1983). *Raising good children: Helping your child through the stages of moral development.* New York: Bantam Books.

_____. (1991). *Educating for character: How our schools can teach respect and responsibility.* New York: Bantam Books.

Liefeld, W.L. (1989). A plural ministry view: Your sons and your daughters shall prophesy. In B. Clouse & R.G. Clouse (Eds.), *Women in ministry: Four views* (pp. 127–153). Downers Grove, IL: InterVarsity Press.

McCormack, P. (1981, April 23). Values change in high schools. *The Terre Haute Tribune,* p. B16. UPI press release.

Mickelsen, A. (1989). An egalitarian view: There is neither male nor female in Christ. In B. Clouse & R.G. Clouse (Eds.), *Women in ministry: Four views* (pp. 173–206). Downers Grove, IL: InterVarsity Press.

Mosher, R.L. (1980). Moral education: Let's open the lens. In L. Kuhmerker, M. Mentkowski, & V.L. Erickson (Eds.), *Evaluating moral development: And evaluating educational programs that have a value dimension* (pp. 213–221). Schenectady, NY: Character Research.

Pepeira, C. (1991). Educating for citizenship in the early grades. In J.S. Benninga (Ed.), *Moral, character, and civic education in the elementary school* (pp. 212–226). New York: Teachers College Press.

Piaget, J. (1932). *The moral judgment of the child* (M. Gabain, Trans.). London: K. Paul, Trench, Trubner, & Co.

Pressau, J.R. (1977). *I'm saved, you're saved — Maybe.* Atlanta, GA: John Knox.

Rest, J.R. (1979). *The impact of higher education on moral judgment development* (Technical Report #5). Minneapolis: Minnesota Moral Research Projects.

Scharf, P. (1978). *Moral education.* Davis, CA: Responsible Action.

Stonehouse, C. (1992). The church: A place where all God's children grow? *Christian Education Journal, 13*(1), 33–48.

Tappan, M.B., & Brown, L.M. (1989). Stories told and lessons learned: Toward a narrative approach to moral development and moral education. *Harvard Educational*

Review, 59, 182–205.

3rd-graders find many ways to be good citizens. (1990, March 25). *The Tribune-Star,* E2, p. 37.

Walker, L.J. (1990). The family: A viable context for moral development? *Moral Education Forum, 15*(4), 13–20, 37.

Ward, T. (1989). *Values begin at home* (2nd ed.). Wheaton, IL: Victor Books.

Wike, S.M. (1992, November 30). *National & International Religion Report, 6*(25), pp. 1–4.

Windmiller, M. (1980). Introduction. In M. Windmiller, N. Lambert & E. Turiel (Eds.), *Moral development and socialization* (pp. 1–33). Boston: Allyn & Bacon.

Woodward, K.L. (1976, March). Who should teach your children right from wrong? *McCall's,* pp. 97, 154, 168, 170.

Young, R.G. (1981). Values differentiation as stage transition: An expansion of Kohlbergian moral stages. *Journal of Psychology and Theology, 9,* 164–174.

Ziv, A. (1976). Measuring aspects of morality. *Journal of Moral Education, 5,* 189–201.

Ten

Moral Growth by Moral Potential:
A Humanist View

øren Kierkegaard, the Danish philosopher, once told a story about a flock of barnyard geese in Denmark. Every Sunday the geese would gather in the barnyard near the feeding trough. One of their number, a 'preaching goose,' would struggle up on the top rail of the fence and exhort the geese about the glories of goosedom. He would tell them how wonderful it was to be a goose, rather than a chicken or a turkey. He would remind them of their great heritage and tell them of the marvelous possibilities in the future.

"Occasionally while he was preaching, a flock of wild geese, winging south from Sweden, across the Baltic Sea on their way to sunny France, would fly overhead in a marvelous V-formation — thousands of feet in the air. When that happened, all the geese would excitedly look and say to one another, 'That's who we really are. We are not destined to spend our lives in this stinking barnyard. Our destiny is to fly.'

"But then the wild geese would disappear from sight, their honkings echoing across the horizon. The barnyard geese would look around at their comfortable surroundings, sigh, and return to the mud and filth of the barn.

"They never did fly.

"Sadly, there are a number of people in the Kingdom of God who remain in the barnyard, rather than spread their wings and learn to fly" (Buckingham, 1983, pp. 71-72).[1]

Learning "to fly" involves a struggle. It does not come easily but it is worth the effort. It has been said that the greatest desire of a child is to "grow up." According to humanistic psychologists, this desire relates not only to the realm of the physical in which the infant constantly exercises each muscle as it matures so that sitting, creeping, and walking will occur; or to the realm of the mental in which babbling is the foundation for talking, reading, thinking, and planning; or to the realm of the social in which interaction with family members provides a basis for interpersonal relationships with those outside the family unit; but this desire relates to the realm of the moral, as well, in which each child has a natural propensity to become a better person, to learn what is right and what is wrong, and to go in the right direction.

But always there is a struggle. If the baby remained in the crib and never moved, she would never learn to walk. If the toddler did not utter sounds, coming closer and closer to adult speech, verbal communication would not be possible. If the young person is so comfortable at home with food, clothes, and shelter provided, but no demands are made upon him by the parents, he will not learn to live on his own, taking responsibility for himself and for the next generation. In the same way, each child grows morally as he or she is encouraged to choose, affirm, and act upon those values that make him or her a fully functioning individual. Within each of us is the potential to become morally mature.

What It Means to Be Human

Humanism, as the term implies, reflects the idea that the greatest of all attributes are those that make people distinctly human. Awareness of self, sensitivity to others, appreciation of the potential within humankind, and the ability to express and analyze feelings are traits stressed by humanists. Being human sets us apart from all other forms of life and provides a sharp contrast to any other creature.

People may be similar to animals in some ways, but they are, nonetheless, quite superior in other ways. Animals cannot fall in love, express themselves verbally, or plan for the future. Nor are people like the objects they create. A machine or computer may do some things better and faster than a person, but a machine is not an emotional being having self-awareness, and a computer is not an intelligent creature with a mind of its own. Only people possess those qualities that are of greatest worth.

> Humanism, as the term implies, reflects the idea that the greatest of all attributes are those that make people distinctly human. Awareness of self, sensitivity to others, appreciation of the potential within humankind, and the ability to express and analyze feelings are traits stressed by humanists. Being human sets us apart from all other forms of life and provides a sharp contrast to any other creature.

THE RISE OF HUMANISM AS A MOVEMENT

Although humanism as a philosophy goes back to the time of classical Greece, humanism as a psychology began to emerge in the 1940s as a reaction against the two leading psychologies of the day, namely, behaviorism (learning theory) and psychoanalysis.[2] Accepting neither the behaviorist position that a person is the product of the environment nor the psychoanalytic view that a person is born depraved and in need of cultural alteration, humanists affirm that each of us becomes what we make ourselves by our own perceptions and by our own actions. Inner qualities are stressed, but these are seen as positive rather than negative.

This reaction earned humanism the title of *third-force* psychology. Although a cousin to cognitive theory in that both humanism and cognitivism stress the potential of humankind, humanism places greater emphasis on the emotional, motivational, and social aspects of human existence, whereas cognitivism stresses the intellectual or reasoning processes.

HUMANISM HAS DIFFERENT MEANINGS

There are several varieties of humanism, each taking a different form and each having a different emphasis. Humanism may be linked with a type of psychotherapy, educational reform, or the study of humanity's struggle throughout history. Humanism is a vital part of many religions, including Christianity, and yet it is claimed by avowed agnostics and atheists. To place all humanists under the same framework would therefore do a great disservice to an understanding of the differences that exist between them.

After studying the literature, Wertheimer (1978) found at least three distinguishable meanings of the term. First, humanism is a curricula within the liberal arts that focuses on an understanding of the human race and includes such subjects as anthropology, sociology, history, economics, and biology. Second, the term *humanism* is used to refer to the human potential movement with its psychotherapies and with the theories of humanistic psychologists such as Arthur Combs, Abraham Maslow, and Carl Rogers. Third, the term *humanism* focuses on the person as an integrated whole. People are greater than the sum of their parts and are actively involved in an integration of the parts. This antimechanical view of human beings is adopted by many who do not espouse humanistic psychology (even as many professors within the liberal arts do not accept humanism as a philosophy).

Despite the differences, there are commonalities as well, and a lack of agreement as to the meaning of the term does not preclude the fact that all humanists are concerned with the development and welfare of that being called "man." Part of man's welfare includes the realm of the ethical or moral, and a number of basic ideas of what constitutes morality would be accepted by the majority of humanists even though they come to the position from a variety of backgrounds.[3]

VALUES CLARIFICATION

Moral choices are made when we clarify our values. The word *values* is used often by humanists, and it is recognized that each person's values come from a number of sources — some old and well-known and others new and waiting to be tried. The old includes organismic needs each of us possesses as a member of the human race and interpersonal relationships shared with family and acquaintances. The new incorporates a variety of lifestyles portrayed for us through the mass media and the trend to accept all people everywhere regardless of background or culture or religious preference. The old and the new combine to provide a greater number of options for valuing than was known a generation ago. As Carl Rogers (1964) expressed it: "It is no longer possible, as it was in the not too distant historical past, to settle comfortably into the value system of one's forebears or one's community and live out one's life without ever examining the nature and the assumptions of that system" (p. 160).

CARL ROGERS (1902–1987)

Carl Rogers was born in Oak Brook, Illinois, the fourth of six children, five of whom were boys. He died suddenly following hip surgery in La Jolla, California, and was survived by his son David, his daughter Natalie, and several grandchildren and great-grandchildren. His wife Helen died eight years earlier after fifty-two years of marriage.

In his autobiography written in 1966, Rogers described himself as "fundamentally positive in my approach to life, somewhat of a lone wolf in my professional activities, socially rather shy but enjoying close relationships; capable of a deep sensitivity in human interaction though not always achieving this; often a poor judge of people, tending to overestimate them; possessed of a capacity for setting other people free, in a psychological sense; capable of a dogged determination in getting work done . . . eager to have an influence on others but with very little desire to exercise power or authority over them" (p. 343). He never felt a sense of belonging to any social or professional group, a fact that would have bothered him more had he not always had the security of a family to come home to—his parents and siblings as a child, and his wife and children as an adult.

Helen was the gregarious one, arranging trips and social events that Rogers was not eager to engage in but which he later admitted he enjoyed. Without her influence, he probably would have spent any spare time on one of his many projects which included color photography, gardening, making mobiles, painting, and carpentry. Both Carl and Helen enjoyed snorkeling in the Caribbean.

Rogers' father was a contractor and civil engineer. His mother, a deeply religious woman, devoted her time to rearing the children and quoting Bible verses to keep them on the right path. Family prayers, church attendance, hard work, and a life that centered around the family was what young Carl knew. It was understood that dancing, playing cards, attending movies, smoking, drinking, or showing any sexual interest was strictly taboo. When Carl was twelve the parents moved the family to a large farm thirty miles west of Chicago in an effort to keep their six children from the temptations and evils of suburban and city life.

Carl learned to read before he started to school and spent so much of his time reading that he was made to feel guilty about always having his nose in a book. When he exhausted all the books he could find he read the encyclopedia and then the dictionary. In high school he attended three different schools, but was expected to be home immediately after school to do his chores. He got up every morning at 5:00 to milk a dozen cows. Consequently, there was no time to form friendships with anyone. He attributed his inability to feel close to people outside the family to his parents' desire to isolate him and his sister and brothers in an effort to keep them on the straight-and-narrow.

In 1919 he went to the University of Wisconsin to major in scientific agriculture, but after attending a conference on evangelism during his sophomore year he decided to change his life goal and go into Christian work. A series of events caused him to question the fundamentalism of his parents and after obtaining a degree in history rather than agriculture he chose Union Theological Seminary to prepare for the ministry precisely because it was more liberal in theology. He and his bride arrived there in 1924 in a second-hand Model-T coupe which he had purchased for $425. By the end of his second year at Union, he decided that he could no longer espouse religious faith and began taking courses in clinical and educational psychology at Teachers College, Columbia University. He received the doctorate in 1931 with a dissertation on personality adjustment in children nine to thirteen.

Rogers' professional career was spent at the University of Rochester, Ohio State University, the University of Chicago, and the University of Wisconsin, with summers at Harvard, UCLA, Occidental College, and Brandeis University. In 1968, he and several colleagues founded the Center for Studies of the Person in LaJolla where he remained until his death. As one of the founders of the Association for Humanistic Psychology, he served on the board of directors of the *Journal of Humanistic Psychology* since its beginning in 1961. Carl Rogers is best known for his theory of person-centered therapy, a non-directive approach in which the client takes charge of the therapeutic process, discovering within the self ways of dealing with behavior and attitudes.

Rogers, C.R. (1966). In E.G. Boring (Ed.), *A History of Psychology in Autobiography, Vol. 5,* (pp. 343–84). Worcester, MA: Clark University Press.

Values are inferred from the choices we make. We choose how to use our time and how to spend our money. We choose what to wear, whom to be with, and where to go. We choose what book to read, what cassette to listen to, what television program to watch. Our desires, motives, needs, attitudes, and beliefs all affect in some way the kinds of choices that we make. Whenever we choose we are expressing a value. We are saying that a particular object, person, or behavior is more acceptable, desirable, or right for us than another object, person, or behavior. Some values may be means to an end and are called instrumental because they help us to accomplish those ends. Other values may be ends in themselves and are called terminal because they are culminating experiences or states. Being ambitious, capable, courageous, and helpful are examples of instrumental values whereas happiness, equality, self-respect, and wisdom are terminal values (Rokeach, 1973).

THE PERSONAL NATURE OF VALUES

Values are personal. By definition they must come from within the individual. Although a person may possess many of the same values that others possess, this in no way detracts from the private nature of these internalized guides. Because of the intimate nature of values, they cannot be imposed by an outside source. The direct approach of telling someone what values he or she should have or the indirect approach of modeling those values that are of greatest worth will be effective only if the person decides to adopt those values as his or her own. No one can make another person accept certain values — a fact most parents, ministers, and educators find difficult to keep in mind.

THE MORAL NATURE OF VALUES

Although humanists would not separate moral values from other values, care must be taken not to make a moral issue of all the choices we make. Indeed, valuing encompasses so many aspects of a person's life that values that are assuredly moral in nature comprise only a small portion of the total valuing process. Whether we buy a Ford or a Toyota, study to become an accountant or a teacher, prefer white or yellow curtains in the kitchen, pride ourselves on being financially independent or on being a careful manager of our spouse's paycheck is not within the realm of the moral. Judgments of right and wrong should not be applied to matters of personal taste.

Yet, the moral part of the valuing process is of great importance for it prepares the way for those cognitions, motives, and behaviors that are directly related to issues of good and bad, to matters of right and wrong. Do we yield to temptation or "just say no"? Do we criticize others who are not like ourselves, or do we give them the respect all people deserve? Do we engage in whatever behavior we wish to do at the moment, or do we take the time to act responsibly toward others? Each day we are faced with choosing values that are essentially immoral or moral.

THE PROGRESSIVE NATURE OF VALUES

Humanistic psychologists place emphasis on the process of valuing, thus following in the progressive tradition of John Dewey. Although not discounting either the content or product of values, the focus of attention is on the procedures whereby one becomes aware of values already held as well as values in the process of emerging. The stress is on process rather than product, on becoming rather than being, on potential rather than current state. We are told that life can be more productive, more satisfying, more enjoyable, and more meaningful. But in order for this to take place, we must be aware — of our feelings, thoughts, beliefs, and above all of what we can become.

SELF-ACTUALIZATION: THE HIGHEST VALUE

The ultimate of this potential is called self-actualization, a favorite term among humanistic psychologists. The word *self* designates that the process comes about through changes that occur within the person, or self, rather than by changes imposed from without. *Actualization* has the meaning of arriving at a desired state, of making realistic possibilities one has by virtue of being human. "Perhaps the core assertion of this personality theory is that there is but one motivational force for all humanity: the tendency toward *self-actualization*. All persons have an inherent tendency to develop their capacities to the fullest, in ways that will either maintain or enhance their own well-being" (Jones & Butman, 1991, p. 257). By fastening on the goodly aspects of human nature and by holding up as models those individuals within the society who are psychologically well-adjusted, humanists have produced a list of characteristics of people who are self-actualized.

MASLOW'S HIERARCHY OF NEEDS

The principal source of this information comes from the writings of Abraham Maslow, who was interested in the needs people have and in the way they go about meeting them. Maslow (1970) noted that there appears to be a universal order in which needs are satisfied with earlier and more basic needs having to be met, at least in part, before later or higher order needs will emerge. First in the hierarchy are *physiological needs* such as the need for food or drink or shelter. Life cannot be sustained without the physiological needs being met. Next in order are the *safety needs* of security, protection, and stability. When the safety needs are met, we are then in a position to move on to a satisfying of the *love needs,* which include a feeling of belonging, being accepted, and receiving affection. The *esteem needs* of gaining prestige and recognition, of feeling competent, and of having social status are next in line, followed by the *aesthetic* and *cognitive needs* of appreciating beauty and order and of desiring knowledge and understanding. Meeting the need for *self-actualization* is contingent upon our having met to a certain degree those needs that have preceded.

> According to Maslow (1973), self-actualized people tend to accept themselves, others, and the natural world for what they are. They are realistically oriented and yet spontaneous and creative in their thinking and behavior.

CHARACTERISTICS OF THE SELF-ACTUALIZING PERSON

According to Maslow (1973), self-actualized people tend to accept themselves, others, and the natural world for what they are. They are realistically oriented and yet spontaneous and creative in their thinking and behavior. Although they enjoy close relationships with other people and are democratic in their attitude toward others, they tend to be loners in the sense that they have a need for privacy, autonomy, and resisting conformity to the culture around them. They have a continuous appreciation of the world, a sense of awe for much of nature that most people seldom notice, and a feeling of one-ness with all humankind. They will devote themselves to a task or mission, centering their attention on their work rather than on them-selves. Humor is enjoyed, but never at the expense of another, nor is it expressed in a hostile or vulgar manner. People who are self-actualized have a highly developed sense of ethics that is apparent in both speech and action, are more aware of their values than are other individuals, and have a better understanding of why they think, act, and feel as they do. They have clarified what is important to them and have determined what pattern of life will make for a rich, happy, and fulfilling existence.[4]

SELF-ACTUALIZATION BEGINS WITH AWARENESS

All of us have values, but not all of us are aware of them. We are left less knowledgeable and alert than we should be. We may be confused, apathetic, withdrawn, or overly conforming. Or we may be flighty, aggressive, and overbearing. We may want to relate to others in a serious and meaningful way, but we do not know how to go about establishing such relationships. In today's complex world, we need more than ever to clarify what we really believe, to bring to the surface those values that will give our lives greater significance and direction. We need more consistency and more confidence. We need to discover the discrepancies that make for confusion and dismay, and we need to establish guidelines as to what to do when values are found to be conflicting. In short, we need to clarify our values.

SEVEN STEPS TO VALUES CLARIFICATION

The expression of values has always been pervasive within a society, but only in the last three decades have there been organized programs to guide in the process of valuing. The approach best known was designed by Louis E. Raths who, with his students Merrill Harmin and Sidney Simon, developed a number of creative ways to implement what is now known as values clarification. Their book *Values and Teaching* (Raths, Harmin, & Simon, 1966) brought attention to how the approach may be used in an educational setting. Since that time numerous books, journal articles, and workshop manuals have been published that give careful directions for conducting values clarification sessions in any context.

Seven criteria must be met for a person to clarify a value. One must:

1. Be able to choose freely without restriction;
2. Consider viable alternatives;
3. Choose only after thoughtfully considering the consequence of each alternative;
4. Be happy with one's choice;
5. Affirm the choice publicly;
6. Act on one's choice; and
7. Incorporate the choice into one's life pattern.

The first three criteria involve the act of actually *choosing* a value; the next two signify a *prizing* or celebrating of the value chosen; and the last two mean *acting* upon the value chosen, making it a regular part of one's everyday life.

> **The clarification of moral values will go through the same steps as the clarification of all other values. One must choose freely with no hint of coercion, alternatives must be considered, and possible consequences of each alternative must be weighed.**

Suppose, for example, that you are concerned with the problem of pollution in the environment. First, this concern must come from your own beliefs rather than from external pressures. Second, you will consider a number of ways in which you can help improve the environment. (Do you wish to stop burning trash? Walk rather than drive your car? No longer buy beverages in nonreturnable bottles? Recycle newspapers and cans? Put on a sweater and turn down the thermostat?) Third, you will weigh the consequences of each of the ways considered before choosing which of these you will pursue. Fourth, you will feel good about the choice you have made. Fifth, you will tell others about your choice. Sixth, you will put the choice into practice. And seventh, you will incorporate the antipollution behavior or behaviors into your life on a regular basis (Knapp, 1973).

The clarification of moral values will go through the same steps as the clarification of all other values. One must choose freely with no hint of coercion, alternatives must be considered, and possible consequences of each alternative must be weighed. Once the choice has been made, the value must be prized and cherished along with a desire to let others know the decision that has been made. The person then must be willing to act on that decision, to change his or her behavior, not just on occasion, but on a regular basis.

OTHER TECHNIQUES EMPLOYED

Values clarification as a seven-step process is only one of many techniques used by humanistic psychologists. Much of the popularity of the humanist movement came from a variety of programs and therapies designed to help individuals deal with emotional problems. As people learned to strip away the facades that masked their true natures and revealed their innermost thoughts, feelings, and aspirations, they began to understand who they really were. Hypocrisy, unresolved hostility, crippling guilt, and unexpressed love were exchanged for a nonjudgmental acceptance of themselves and of others.

Humanists say that we all need to see ourselves as human beings, to understand the importance of being a part of the human race, to approve of those characteristics that make us a representative of that species called "man." We must learn to accept ourselves — even to like ourselves. And, as we accept and like ourselves, we learn to accept and like other people. Liking others follows directly from liking oneself.

The purpose of the techniques, then, is to unlock the potential that lies within each person and to make the person aware of what she is and who she is. Encounter groups, transactional analysis, primal scream therapy, Gestalt therapy, and psychodrama, to name a few, enable the individual to become more in touch with the self; to become, in essence, more human.

THE ENCOUNTER GROUP

In the 1950s, 1960s, and 1970s encounter groups sprung up in homes, community centers, churches, and motels. The term "encounter" refers to an interaction or confrontation with others for the purpose of exploring the affective component of life. The appeal of these groups appeared to be great. Although it is true that most of us encounter others on a daily basis, joining a special group composed of ten to fifteen people and a trained leader with the intent of finding out more about ourselves is quite different. The encounter group is a way of filling a void created by an emphasis in our society on social adjustment rather than on personal adjustment, on duty rather than pleasure, on the intellect rather than the emotions. We have been taught since childhood to be polite and pleasant, to say we are fine even when we are not, to compliment even when we do not mean what we say. We are told not to wear our feelings on our sleeves and not to reveal too readily our likes and dislikes. We are trained to keep under wraps the kind of persons we really are. The result is a deficit in our lives, a lack of authenticity. We scarcely know who we are.

Encounter groups were designed to meet the needs of normal people. They were not intended for individuals suffering from deep-seated emotional deficits. The group might include a housewife who felt confined to a clean house and an uncommunicative husband, an executive who was contemplating a new business but feared he might lose his life's savings, a couple who were uncertain about patching an unrewarding relationship, a career woman who was tired of one-night stands and had the need to be treated as a person. Almost all were lonely or frustrated in some way, and they came together to share their concerns. It was important to know that someone cares, that someone understood and wanted to help. The catharsis of revealing hidden fears, forbidden desires, and secret hopes kept some individuals going back again and again to these groups. Sessions lasted for hours, continued all night, or were set up for a three-day weekend. The more elaborate sessions were sometimes held at luxurious resorts complete with beautiful accommodations, elaborate meals, and possibilities for yoga, dancing, and nude swimming.

TRANSACTIONAL ANALYSIS

Another popular technique is that of transactional analysis. Often referred to as TA, transactional analysis was developed by Eric Berne in the book *Transactional Analysis in Psychotherapy* (1961) and popularized in his *Games People Play* (1974). Berne holds that the personality is composed of three ego states which he calls Child, Adult, and Parent. The Child within each of us reflects the desires and feelings we developed while young and includes such emotions as joy, sadness, love, anger, fear, and elation. Each of us has a somewhat different Child because each of us had a somewhat different childhood. In the process of growing up children are pressured to mask or suppress the Child.

The Adult ego state represents the rational component of the personality and functions as an independent agent making decisions that are in the best interest of the person. In analytic sessions one is helped to recognize and understand the Child within the self and then is trained to put the Adult in charge. The Parent, or third ego stage, resembles a boss that commands others and judges the behavior and attitude of others. The Parent may or may not be effective, depending on the manner in which it operates (James, 1976).

Each person has all three ego states and will be Child, Adult, or Parent, depending on the circumstances. Any interaction with another person can be diagrammed as an interaction of ego states: Child to Child, Adult to Adult, Parent to Parent, Child to Adult, Child to Parent, and on and on. The purpose of TA is to help people recognize both their own state and the state of another during any particular interaction.

In TA, participants are educated to train the Adult and diminish Child and Parent. "Therapy . . . starts with helping clients understand their ego states, make choices about which to experience at a given time and enable them to experience more of those states that have been blocked. Transactions are then analyzed . . . basic life position is examined and the client challenged to make a deliberate and Adult decision about life position" (Jones & Butman, 1991, p. 331).

In *I'm OK, You're OK,* Thomas Harris (1969) further popularized transactional analysis by constructing four attitudes toward any interaction. These are: (1) "I'm not OK, you're OK," a position often taken by young children in relationship to their parents and by adults who have poor self-concepts and feel they are at the mercy of others; (2) "I'm OK, you're not OK," the view held by bullies and tyrants who get status by negating the rights of others; (3) "I'm not OK, you're not OK," in which the person is depressed and does not enjoy self or others; and (4) "I'm OK, you're OK," the ideal position in which a person is confident and accepting of both self and others. By analyzing what people say and do, a person can begin to feel OK and can learn to help others feel OK too. All three ego states—Child, Adult, and Parent—may be OK or not OK, depending on the mode of functioning, although the combination of Adult to Adult and I'm OK, you're OK produces the most optimal results.

Transactional analysis is widely used in schools and as a trouble-shooter in the world of business. Thousands more use it as a parlor game, analyzing themselves and others at home or at work or at a party. The fascination shown in transactional analysis by people from a large variety of backgrounds may be as interesting a phenomenon as the technique itself.

The Primal Scream

Another humanistic procedure is primal scream therapy. Developed by Arthur Janov (1970), this therapy is a way to relive the primal pain that occurs in early life when physical or psychological needs are not met. As a baby, one may not have been held enough or rocked enough or fed when hungry. As a toddler one may not have been comforted when frightened or talked to when lonely. As the child grows older, and pressures to conform increase, the pain becomes intolerable. Finding no relief, the pain is masked and neurotic defenses develop. What the therapist must do is to take the person back to the troubled time, help the person relive the unfortunate events (even birth trauma may be experienced), enabling him or her to feel in full force the primal pain. Relief is gained by an outpouring of moans, screams, utterances, and cries. Therapy may take weeks, months, or years.

Gestalt Therapy

Pioneered by Fritz Perls (1969), Gestalt therapy places emphasis on helping the client live fully in the here-and-now and encourages an avoidance of excessively dwelling on the past or anxiously waiting for the future. Self-awareness is the key to therapy. As clients grow in self-awareness, they find they can take the support given during therapy and translate it into self-support. They realize that they alone are responsible for the life they live and that they must accept the challenge to experience it fully. Personal wholeness is aided by throwing off (acting out) internal restrictions such as anger, pain, and guilt and by being aware of social restrictions that have robbed them of an adequate self-concept. Perls saw therapy as a way of plugging up the holes of the personality put there by a repressive environment. Psychoanalysis, Gestalt psychology, and existentialism are all part of Gestalt therapy. In method it is decidedly humanistic and, as in other humanistic therapies, people are seen as basically good, and society is viewed as essentially oppressive.

PSYCHODRAMA

Psychodrama is yet another technique used. Designed by Jacob Moreno (1944), psychodrama is a means for acting out the private world in which we live. The logic of psychodrama is that by actually simulating an experience we will be able to cope more adequately with that experience. By bringing an event into the open, we can get a closer look at it and find release from the anxiety or guilt or dread that accompanied it. If psychodrama is done by a group with a trained leader, strangers may help one another find relief from painful and traumatic events and provide encouragement to try new endeavors.

By taking the part of someone in an event and acting out the sequence of events, new perceptions are possible and new solutions may be acquired. By putting ourselves in the place of another and endeavoring to work through the thoughts and emotions of another, we learn to understand others in a way we did not before. We become for the moment someone else. The parent "becomes" a child, thus seeing himself or herself through the eyes of the child. A couple during a quarrel engages in role reversal, the husband "becoming" the wife and the wife "becoming" her husband. Each is acting the part of the other, thus learning to see things from the perspective of the other. The parent who can "be" a child will be a better parent, and the couple who can "be" each other will not quarrel long.

WHO CAN BENEFIT FROM HUMANISTIC TECHNIQUES?

As with all psychological theories, a person may or may not accept the philosophy of humanistic psychology to profit from the techniques. Encounter groups, transactional analysis, and psychodrama, for example, have been used in a variety of settings by those not in sympathy with humanistic thought as well as by those who are. Jones and Butman (1991) found that Christian publications regarding TA seldom criticized the method. Instead, the publications "reinterpret Christian experience and truth in TA terms and/or enthusiastically apply TA as the panacea that will allow true ministry to flourish" (p. 332). Van Rooy (1986), a therapist at the Primal Institute in Houston, writes that he has witnessed thousands of hours of "subconscious decontamination through primaling" and is convinced that "it is a profound healing tool for psychological pain . . . it destroys the cause for . . . sinful behavior" and "it effects the peaceable fruit of righteousness" (p. 35). Van Rooy believes that whether used in the church or in secular institutions, "primal therapy is a powerful tool for moral reformation" (p. 36).

A strong disagreement, however, with the basic assumptions of any psychological theory may place an individual in a position whereby some methods cannot be used, some areas of life cannot be enacted, and some conclusions must be reinterpreted. The code of ethics of the leader or therapist is important in deciding how a session will be conducted and in determining what inferences will be drawn.

As was mentioned, humanistic psychologists do not see morality as separate from other concerns. Whatever is a part of being human is basically good. Whatever detracts from living life fully must be exorcised. Humanistic therapies are designed to repair the damage of a restrictive environment and bring about an awareness of the true potential within humankind.

HUMANISM AND MORAL GROWTH

The topic of this book is how we as teachers, parents, and pastors can teach for moral growth. It is an inquiry into the process whereby the young child learns what is right and what is wrong, has the desire to do the right, and translates that desire into action. Humanistic psychologists would not agree with Freudian psychoanalysts that children are born depraved and have a bent toward satisfying sexual and aggressive urges rather than doing those things of which the society approves. Nor would humanists accept the learning position that young children come into life neutral, becoming either good or bad depending on their environment. Nor would they agree with cognitive psychologists that newborns have an innate desire to make sense of their world and achieve moral maturity through the use of thinking processes. Rather, humanistic psychologists believe that children are born as beautiful creatures with the potential to appreciate the best in themselves and in others and with a natural inclination to go in the right direction.

Humanistic theory has its roots in the philosophy of Jean-Jacques

Rousseau who saw the child as a noble savage. Children are noble in that they are goodly or godlike. They are savage in that they do not adhere to social custom but seek to go their own ways and make their own decisions. Society is not willing to accept either the nobility of the child or the child's savagery. Instead, from infancy on, the child is pressured to conform to stereotypic ways of behaving and to adopt societal standards of acceptable conduct.

Mothers are especially culpable because they are the first to begin the civilizing process. Later, other adults continue to thwart the child's normal propensity toward self-actualization. The consequence is a stifling of the creative potential and an increase in confusion, frustration, and neurotic behaviors. This unfortunate state may be somewhat ameliorated by the use of humanistic therapies, although a better way would be for parents, educators, and other adults to show a proper respect for the developing child and to affirm the child's natural tendency to do what is best.

Humanistic psychologists would say, then, that *people develop morally as they are allowed to choose, affirm, and act upon those values that make them fully functioning individuals. Each child is born with the potential for good citizenship, responsibility, creativity, and intelligent behavior, and these characteristics will develop naturally if adults provide an atmosphere of encouragement and opportunity.*

BASIC ASSUMPTIONS

As we have noted, humanists place emphasis on the positive aspects of the human condition. Infants are born goodly creatures and are equipped with self-generative abilities that enable them to perceive the environment, interact with it, and put it together in meaningful ways. The striving for creativity, identity, meaning, and psychological health is all part of the potential present at birth. This capacity to grow, develop, and mature encompasses every area of life, including the realm of the ethical. *Human beings are born with the potential for moral development.* They will strive for goodness, truth, wholeness, perfection, and for norms to guide their lives. They have the capacity to be self-critical and self-correcting. "They can recognize their mistakes, aberrations, and transgressions. . . . It is a part of our ethical nature to keep watch over our egotistic, selfish, or criminal impulses" (Kolenda, 1980, p. 4). The inherent dignity of people makes this force-for-moral-growth a part of the intrinsic nature of humankind.

Changes occur when a person perceives the world in a new way. *Moral development comes from within the individual and is dependent on the perceptions available at the time of development.* The real world is each person's phenomenal world — the world as each one sees it. One's awareness of self, one's concept of his or her own values and the values of others, one's conscious beliefs, are part of the perceptions acquired in the progress toward moral maturity. Morality, by definition, must come from within the person rather than being imposed by an outside source. As the child grows, the perceptive field increases to include, not only one's own needs, but the needs of others as well. But the basis of all development is personal, subjective, and introspective. Overt manifestations of morality, although visible, are not the principal concern. "Humanism . . . regards behavior only as symptom, the external manifestation of what is going on inside a human being. The humanist believes that effective understanding of persons requires understanding, not only of behavior, but also the nature of an individual's internal life" (Combs, 1978, p. 301). As important as moral behavior is, emphasis remains on the source of the development — on people themselves as conscious, perceiving organisms.

> Human beings are integrated wholes, not a number of compartments. For this reason, morality cannot be separated from other areas of the person's life. All development is interrelated, each individual having an internal locus of control that integrates every portion of the personality. To develop morally is to develop cognitively, affectively, and behaviorally.

Although moral development must come from within, *the environment may facilitate or impede one's strivings for morality.* A warm, accepting, positive, nondirective environment provides the occasion for moral growth to take place. By contrast, an oppressive, authoritarian, punitive environment will hinder moral maturity. What a person needs is encouragement, not judgment;

assistance, not opposition; facilitation, not threat; friendship, not hostility. Fewer restrictions or controls will enable individuals to develop their own potential. Those who provide an accepting milieu are themselves moral for they are giving support to the growth of others. Affirmation frees the perceptual system of distortions and lays the foundation for healthy adaptation.

Human beings are integrated wholes, not a number of compartments. For this reason, *morality cannot be separated from other areas of the person's life.* All development is interrelated, each individual having an internal locus of control that integrates every portion of the personality. To develop morally is to develop cognitively, affectively, and behaviorally. Whatever one experiences or perceives has an effect upon the whole organism. What one learns translates to values and a sense of direction. What one feels becomes the basis for future learning and activity. What one does is integrally related to attitudes and beliefs. The realm of morality cannot be considered apart from the totality of all that makes us human.

Morality has many forms of expression. Moral expression may take the form of joyful and creative emotions such as openness, spontaneity, exhilaration, prizing, and love. Or it may come in the form of increased awareness of self and the quality of our existence. As we reflect on our experiences, analyze and integrate our thoughts, find meaning from the past and hope for the future, we become aware of the value of many things previously not recognized. Life becomes more than a day-by-day existence that goes on and on as it has always gone on before. Rather, each day brings wonders and surprises if we but tune in to the possibilities. Morality finds expression as we share with others in a multitude of ways, communicating our attitudes, motives, and expectations to them and listening in turn to their hopes, feelings, and beliefs.

The importance of friendship — of letting others know of our interest in them, of wanting to be a part of their world, of helping them whenever they have a felt need — becomes the basis for the assertion that *morality finds its greatest meaning in relationships between people.* "The fully functioning, self-actualized person, whom the humanists hold up as an ideal, experiences a deep feeling of identification with others, has strong feelings of sympathy with and affection for them, and a genuine desire to help them. He perceives his interest as being not in conflict but in harmony with those of his fellow man" (Kolesnik, 1975, p. 45).

Tom Malone (1989, February) stated this desire to help others in the form of a personal testimony: "I trace my own commitment to the service of humanity back to my early admiration for the work of Dr. Martin Luther King, Jr. It may be odd for a secular humanist to have such a devout Christian as his philosophical mentor, but King's messages of love, tolerance, and the duty to heed the call of one's conscience are as applicable to humanism as they are to any other religion or philosophy" (p. 49). Self-interest must not take precedence over interests in others.

Moral maturity, then, means an inclination toward being generous, altruistic, and cooperative. Democracy is highly prized and freedom is cherished. But freedom is not a license for selfish, self-centered behavior. "The watchword of Humanism is service to humanity" (Lamont, 1957, p. 189). The humanist condemns any ideology that would make people less than human, that would strip them of their dignity and worth. Developing morally sometimes will result in a greater adjustment to society, but sometimes it will mean opposing or challenging the existing structure. Any discrimination on the basis of race or religion or national origin is contrary to the tenets of humanism. The ideal society is one "that would free humans to be themselves while retaining love for and attachment to others" (Elkind, 1981, p. 521). Humanists say that these two, self and others, must not nor need not be separated.

PROBLEMS

Perhaps no psychological theory has come under greater attack than humanism. There have always been those who would not accept the view that people are basically good and are able to decide for themselves what is right and wrong. But the number of opponents appeared to increase in the 1980s, or at least they became more visible.

Antihumanists and humanists both say that their ideas are best — for the individual and for society. Both feel they have the truth and speak of mystic religious experiences. Both are asking people to join with them, to spread the word, and to resist the opposing view. Among the most vocal in the 1980s was a subgroup of nonhumanists who called themselves the Moral Majority and a subgroup of humanists who called themselves secular humanists. Both the Moral Majority and the secular humanists were minorities within the opposing ideologies, but they commanded considerable attention.

Falwell, founder of the Moral Majority, claimed a television audience of more than one in ten Americans, although independent sources put the viewing audience at considerably less than this with Majoritarians being only a fraction of this number (Moody, 1981). Not only was the Moral Majority not a majority of nonhumanists, but secular humanism was not a majority among humanists. Smith (1991), wrote, "In the humanistic psychology movement, the quadrant in which I feel at home — theoretically oriented secular humanism — is sparsely populated. . . . The mainstream of the humanistic movement has been considerably more likely to find affinity with mysticism and Eastern religion — or with ESP as watered-down mysticism — than with secular humanism" (p. 98).

The Moral Majority no longer exists as an organization, although many conservative Christians agree with Falwell's criticisms of the humanist movement. Secular humanists continue their work but do not feel they are given the attention they deserve by other humanists. Even less recognition is given by psychologists in other fields.[5] Let us look at some reasons for this phenomenon.

How Should Humanism Be Defined?

The first problem is that definitions of humanism are vague and numerous. Based on nebulous propositions, humanism means many things to many people. If one is critical of humanism, the question may be asked what the person has in mind when the term is used. Is the person opposed to a liberal arts curriculum, to the human potential movement, to the holistic and antimechanical nature of human beings? All three meanings of humanism have been challenged, although the bulk of criticism has been leveled at the second of these, namely, a psychology that emphasizes people as being sufficient within themselves to achieve self-actualization.

Even as the term *humanism* has a variety of meanings, words used by humanists also are vague and may be used in a number of ways. An example of this is the word *values*. Values are never precisely defined, nor are we told their origin. Are they from without? From within? Humanists emphasize the internal nature of values, but one may ask how this is possible. Can any of us generate values independent of our circumstances? To what are our values tied? To our own best interests?

To the best interests of friends? To society as a whole?

And, what are the ground rules for accepting some values and reject-ing others? Do we not need a value system rooted in a source other than ourselves? "If two people were to disagree as to what we ought to do, there is no transcendent ground of value to which we may appeal in order to arbitrate between them. We are thrown into the relativity of conflicting values at a time when absolute decisions about the one future of humankind need to be made" (Peters, 1978, p. 146). Kohlberg states that "values covers everything under the sun" (Kohlberg and Simon, 1972, p. 19); and in *Morality and Mental Health,* Mowrer (1967) says:

> "Values" is . . . an essentially useless term, which has recently come into vogue because it serves as a sort of lowest common denominator for all who recognize, however vaguely, the reality of some sort of axiological dimension in human existence but who don't want to be pinned down to anything too specific. Everyone, I suppose, values something, regard-less of how perverse or self-defeating it may be. So the term, unless extensively qualified, verges on meaninglessness, and certainly lacks power and precision. (p. viii)

ON WHAT FOUNDATION DOES HUMANISM STAND?

A second problem is that humanism lacks a well-defined theory to support its assumptions. How do we know that being human is better than being something else? On what basis can it be said that people have worth and that personal growth and development are of utmost importance? Why does it matter what a person thinks or how a person feels or what a person does? "Psychologists . . . have not offered a theory of man that explains the dignity of his being or justifies the concern society professes to have for his development and protection" (Silber, 1975, p. 197). Humanists have not faced squarely the issues. This becomes apparent in their unwillingness to differentiate between what is moral and what is not and in their lack of interest in "ought" as well as in "is."

Without a well-defined theory, humanists are hindered in an under-standing of other relationships as well. What is the place of reason in relation to the emotions? By stressing affective states it would appear that humanists relegate cognitive processes to a lesser position. Goals and objectives also lack specificity. On what basis can it be said that one goal is better than another, one purpose should be pursued rather than another, or one state of being is optimal rather than another? How can objectives be stated in behavioral terms if feelings have priority over what one does? Without a carefully reasoned theory we are left without satisfactory answers to these questions.

IS HUMANISM SCIENTIFIC?

A third problem, closely tied to the second, is that humanistic claims are based on testimonials rather than on empirical data and hard evidence. The nature of a testimonial is such that it can be neither verified nor falsified. Publicly agreed upon norms cannot be applied to individual preferences and feelings, nor can the scientific method be used to show the position of the testifier to others also expressing preferences and feelings. Furthermore, it is against the spirit of humanism to conduct a study in such a way that people are placed in one experimental group or another and then manipulated in some arbitrary fashion. Independence, autonomy, and self-determination are not to be violated. This ethical stance on the use of human subjects translates to fewer external controls and a greater reliance on introspective reports.

Given this orientation it might be expected that humanists would not emphasize the role of science or give credence to the scientific method. Such is not the case. Paul Kurtz (1976) expressed the humanist position in this way: "Humanism has supported and encouraged the development of the scientific method as a way of understanding nature and applying the findings of the sciences to the betterment of humankind, and the scientific world view has had immeasurable success in the contemporary world" (p. 4).

One might ask at this point how humanists can allow for validating some facts through personal testimony yet praise the use of science, which for more than half a century has spoken out against introspection as a valid technique. Is this not a contradiction? Opponents of humanism would say that it is. Supporters of humanism would say it is not. Let us look at these opposing views.

Paul Vitz (1977), an opponent, states that "humanistic selfism is not a science but a popular secular substitute religion, which has nourished and spread today's widespread cult of self-worship." Vitz continues:

> In spite of the non-scientific character of humanistic selfism, it has frequently claimed to be or allowed itself to be taken as a science and, as a result of this misrepresentation, it has gained greatly in money, power, and prestige. . . . The selfist response to . . . attacks is to attempt to redefine science so as to include their position. This ends up making the concept of science vague beyond any usefulness. (pp. 103-104)

That science has been redefined would not be contested by supporters of humanism. That it is "vague beyond any usefulness" would, of course, be rejected. Humanists claim that their way of understanding science is far superior to that of the behaviorist (learning theorist). According to the humanists, true scientists are "men of courage who are willing to study the difficult, not men who are terribly proficient in techniques but have no vision and who study less and less important things with more and more skill" (Welch & Rodwick, 1978, p. 341). Carl Rogers (1969) is critical of graduate schools that "attach enormous importance to turning out 'hardheaded' scientists, and strongly punish any of the sensitive, speculative, sportive openness which is the essence of the real scientist" (p. 181). And, in writing about the history of the humanist movement, Smith (1990) states that "the founders of humanistic psychology were not antiscientific. They sought rather to correct the biases of behaviorism and psychoanalysis so as to produce a psychology truer to human life and more useful for its improvement" (p. 11). Humanists argue that the greatest scientists of all time — men like Aristotle, Einstein, and Leonardo da Vinci — were men of vision and courage who refused to be restricted to the logic and techniques of their day but rather used their genius and individuality to work toward new insights and new methods.

The arguments of both the antihumanists and the humanists can be quite convincing. Is there a place for both views of science? The reader is invited to decide.

DOES HUMANISM CONTRIBUTE TO NARCISSISM?

A fourth problem, according to some critics, is that an adoption of humanistic views will make a person egocentric and selfish. The argument is: If I'm OK, what right has anyone to be critical of what I say or what I do? And, on what basis need I be critical of myself or seek to change my ways? If you're OK, the same thing holds. You should receive praise and adulation and not be questioned as to motive or performance.

Humanistic ideas are attractive because they appeal to our vanity. We all like to be flattered and told that we are intrinsically wise and good and master of our own lives. But what kind of people will we be if we accept this as truth? Humanism implies that we must do what is best for ourselves before we can do what is best for others, that we cannot love and appreciate and respect others until we love and appreciate and respect ourselves, that we cannot bring happiness to those around us until we know true happiness ourselves.

But is this really so? Are these the only options — myself and others or neither myself nor others? What about the man who feels he would be happier with another woman but leaving his wife would create loneliness and financial difficulty for her? What about the woman who may not wish to remain in an unrewarding job but quitting would mean her children would not have nourishing food? The results of some decisions do not appear to profit both the decision-maker and others. To choose the best for oneself may mean that someone else is left with less than the best. The high divorce rate and a lack of proper care of dependents are examples of the consequences of selfism. Opponents say that humanism has contributed to the "me generation" of the 1970s and has encouraged an age of narcissism. In *The Culture of Narcissism*, Christopher Lasch (1979) portrayed the dire effects of an egocentric mind-set that pervaded every aspect of American life. Thomas Lickona (1991) writes that the "personalism" of the 1960s and 1970s "spawned a new selfishness" (p. 9), and William Kilpatrick (1992) believes that "the decision-making model . . . has created a generation of moral illiterates: students who know their own feelings but don't know their culture" (pp. 16-17).

Humanists feel that to be charged with contributing to selfish behavior is unfair. They say that one is not to harm others for the benefit of the self, that "the emphasis on the self . . . carries with it no implications of selfishness as that term is ordinarily used, or of any unhealthy, unsocial kind of self-centeredness" (Kolesnik, 1975, p. 45). But one may well ask how far past egoism and self-gratification humanism and humanistic techniques really take us. If one perceives that self-denial and self-sacrifice result in a blocking of self-actualization, what direction should that person take? In the practical everyday world in which we live, it would seem that an emphasis on the rightness and beauty of the self would encourage an attitude popularized by such expressions as "looking out for number one," "doing your own thing," and "creative selfishness."

The concern with "me-ism" applies to the rearing of children as well. What kind of children will we have if they are brought up in accordance with humanistic views? If children are basically good, as humanists say, and if they know intuitively the right direction to go, and if what they need is affirmation and encouragement rather than judgment and control, the logical inference is that adults should be careful not to place many restrictions on them. Parents are to take good physical care of the child, be friends and companions, and serve as models of good behavior, but they are not to make demands upon the child or insist on orderly behavior. Parents who follow these ideas are said to be permissive because they permit the child to do almost anything he or she wishes. They are seldom punitive and may even succeed in hiding their annoyance and impatience with the child. If children were like flowers in the garden, growing and blooming when fed and watered, it would be worth the effort for parents to use permissive techniques. Studies in child psychology (Ausubel & Sullivan, 1970; Baumrind, 1977), however, show that rather than being lovely creatures for all to see, children reared in permissive homes are often uncooperative with adults, overbearing with peers, and lacking in purpose and motivation. It appears that nonjudgmental behavior on the part of parents does not provide a basis for children to develop their own self-critical abilities. Consequently they consider whatever they do is all right. If not corrected at home, they feel unjustly treated when corrected elsewhere. Although some children reared permissively are a joy to their parents and an asset to society, this does not appear to be the norm.[6]

Do Humanists Claim Too Much?

A fifth criticism or problem is that humanists claim too much. They promise more than they can deliver. For example, it would appear by reading the literature that everyone can become self-actualized. Is this so? Is it possible that given the right circumstances each of us can be realistic yet spontaneous and creative, enjoy close relationships yet be able to resist conforming to those about us, tell jokes that don't put down any person or group, know ourselves and our values so well that we can live rich, happy, and fulfilling lives?

This criticism of promising more than can be delivered appears in the literature especially as it relates to humanistic techniques and therapies. Is the group leader or therapist qualified? Are sessions conducted discretely? Are participants really helped by attending the sessions?

Some leaders and therapists are experienced mental health professionals, well trained, and eminently qualified. They know what questions to ask, when to probe, and when to withdraw. They are able to recognize the one in the group who is too disturbed to profit from the encounter and should be removed. They are able to use the personalities of group members to work for the good of all. Other leaders, however, are self-appointed, have little or no training, and may know nothing about the technique other than what they have witnessed as a member of a group. They are unable to function effectively as leaders and would not know how to handle an emergency should one occur. Some of these amateurs are well-meaning individuals who wish to help others. Others are charlatans and hucksters out to make a fast buck. They con the public into believing that a session will leave them glowing and happy. Judging from the numbers who flock to these sessions, deceiving the public appears to be relatively easy. Everyone warms to a promise of love and brotherhood and caring. We all like to be told that we are truly beautiful and that we owe it to ourselves to discover our true selves. We all want to hear that we are capable and can do anything we wish to do.

The session may or may not proceed in accordance with humanistic principles. Humanists hold that every individual must be treated with respect. But some therapists who give lip service to humanism act in inhumane ways in conducting their sessions. If it is good for people to talk about how they feel, the argument is made that people should be made to talk about how they feel. Pressure is put upon group members to participate, to talk about their feelings, to "let it all hang out." But such pressure, whether flagrant or subtle, is in violation of the tenets of humanism for it does not respect the person as an autonomous individual who should choose freely and without coercion. No leader or therapist should insist that group members reveal their innermost thoughts, show emotion, or become intimate with others by physical contact. It is an intrusion into one's privacy to expect the person to tell what he or she ordinarily would not tell or to engage in a "touchy-feely" if the propriety of doing so is questioned.

What occurs during an encounter or therapy session should not be confused with what happens in real life. A short-term intense emotional experience cannot become a long-term affective state. To maintain such a "high" indefinitely would consume the individual. The body and the psyche are not made for continuous elation and endless passion. A bride with stars in her eyes and a young man who receives a promotion soon learn that the excitement of the moment all too quickly gives way to a world of reality with its unceasing demands. In the same way, a client who expects the closeness of the encounter to last will find that after the session is over or the weekend is past, one must return to the world from which one came. The low that follows the high may put the person in a worse state than before.

Therapists would say that if a session enables a person to have a better self-concept and to live more fully, that is fine. If it does not, it cannot be helped. A temporary high to those who live boring and unfulfilled lives is better than no high at all, and a little happiness and caring, though shortlived, is better than no happiness and no caring. Besides, does not all of life have risks? Why should participation in therapy sessions be different? But some participants may not understand this. They have been given a taste of what they thought was possible on a regular basis, and by raising their expectations they have found a new level of discontent.

Do humanists really claim too much? Both humanists and nonhumanists agree that some people are helped by humanistic techniques, others remain as they were, and still others may be harmed. The disagreement comes with the numbers given to each of these categories, humanists being more generous than nonhumanists in the number of people they say are helped.[7] More studies need to be conducted before it can be determined to what extent therapists and group leaders are qualified, whether sessions are conducted properly, and what percentage of participants are benefited.

Criticisms of humanism are not confined to those that have been mentioned. Nevertheless, the problems discussed serve to show valid reasons for the concerns many have about this movement. To decide which or how many of these problems apply to any particular humanistic theory would be an interesting exercise and much preferred to a blanket condemnation of all humanistic psychology.

THE DECLINE OF HUMANISM AS A MOVEMENT

Humanism continued to develop in the 1950s, spread rapidly in the 1960s and 1970s, and peaked in the 1980s. Morain (1980) said that time was on the side of humanism as more and more people were joining the movement (p. 10); and Carl Rogers, one of the pioneers of today's humanistic movement, said that humanistic psychology would never go down in history for what it is *against* but rather what it is *for* (Rogers, 1978, p. 45). Those who joined the movements in the 1960s and 1970s may have joined because "humanistic psychology tied in nicely with various other protest movements" (Kolesnik, 1975, p. 47). But in retrospect, time did not appear to be on the side of humanism, at least not in humanism as a movement within psychology. Let us look at some of the reasons the popularity of humanism as a movement has lessened within the past decade.

One explanation is that humanistic psychology is associated in many people's minds with the drug culture of the 1960s and 1970s. M. Brewster Smith (1991), who calls himself a secular humanist, said it this way: "By fateful historical coincidence, humanistic psychology was being founded just as the counterculture of the flower children and drug-oriented hippies emerged as a phenomenon of the 1960s. Especially as typified by Esalen and encounter groups, the humanist movement was essentially captured by the counterculture with its irrationalism, its hedonism and emphasis on the here and now with minimal baggage of moral commitments, its extreme individualism" (p. 99). Smith (1990) comments elsewhere that some humanists dropped out in dismay over these "counter-cultural excesses" while others stayed but were ambivalent about the movement being associated with groups that disparaged rational problem solving, relied on intuition rather than evidence, and were "in uncritical affinity with the occult, and in the celebration of drug-induced 'highs' " (p. 11).

A second reason for the decline of humanism as a movement is that one of its archenemies, namely, groups of conservative Christians labeled by the media as the Christian Right, have less to say now about the evils of humanism than they did ten or fifteen years ago. Nothing strengthens an organization like being given public attention. Humanists were put in the spotlight by the Moral Majority and given notoriety in newspapers, magazines, and on television. Millions of Americans who otherwise would not have known anything about humanism learned there was such an organization and that it was evil, "secular," and "godless."

Some Christians saw humanism as so dangerous they felt compelled to write and speak in constant condemnation of the movement. Tim LaHaye's *The Battle for the Mind* is a case in point.

> Most of the evils in the world today can be traced to humanism, which has taken over our government, the UN, education, TV, and most of the other influential things in life. (Introduction)
> Today's wave of crime and violence in our streets, promiscuity, divorce, shattered dreams, and broken hearts can be laid right at the door of secular humanism. (LaHaye, 1980, p. 26)

In response to an outpouring of anathemas, humanists doubled their efforts to explain their position, defend their views, alert others to the errors of their opposition, and make their own appeal for converts. Paul Kurtz (1976), former editor of *The Humanist,* in a special issue on "The Evangelical Right: The Attack on Secular Humanism" had this to say:

> This form of religious intolerance and bigotry threatens the very basis of our pluralistic democratic society: it could be the beginning of a new tyranny over the mind of man and of a new inquisition. . . . The fact is that humanism – in the broad sense – is the deepest current in Western civilization. . . . It . . . was influential during the founding of the American republic (where humanistic giants emerged, such as Jefferson and Paine). . . . Humanists have sought to cultivate a large number of . . . key moral values: a compassionate concern for others, freedom, equality, justice, creativity, dignity, and tolerance. These values are fundamental to our national democratic tradition and are widely shared. . . . Humanism is the movement to achieve democracy in all phases of our social life. (pp. 4-5)

The Christian Right has now gone on to new targets: prochoice advocates, pornographic art, and those oriented to a homosexual lifestyle, to name a few. "The fundamentalist attack on humanistic values has taken new form. Humanists are no longer singled out as the enemy; now fundamentalists attempt to rally their forces behind the banner of 'traditional values' or 'family values' " (Larue, 1991, p. 17).

Many humanists advocate a woman's right to choose. Furthermore, they do not believe that forms of art should be restricted, or that one's sexual orientation should be considered a moral issue. "Our agenda discourages censorship of literature, art, and other forms of human expression and encourages the right of individuals to make choices based upon reason, ethical values, and concern for human well-being. It champions the freedom of individuals to make decisions concerning their own bodies, their own futures, and their own modes of dying" (Larue, 1991, p. 38). But humanists are no longer specifically named by the Christian Right as they were before. They are no longer given the attention they formerly had.

A third reason why humanism as an organization does not have the prominence it had a decade or two ago is that cognitive psychology has increased in popularity, overshadowing the humanistic agenda. "Scientific psychology has changed since the founding of the humanistic movement as a 'Third Force.' The cognitive revolution swept through psychology, legitimizing concern with experience of consciousness" (Smith, 1990, pp. 17-18). This is no more apparent than in the area of moral growth. Values clarification and other humanistic techniques remain in place in many schools, but Kohlberg's stages of moral reasoning increasingly take center stage. A perusal of the spring issues of *Moral Education Forum* with its listing of books, special issues, periodical articles, and ERIC entries for the preceding year, attest to the fact that most of the theoretical statements and research articles in the late 1980s and 1990s are written with a cognitive-developmental framework in mind.

HUMANISTIC IDEAS ARE MORE POPULAR TODAY THAN EVER BEFORE

This does not mean that humanism is not alive and well or that its influence has not permeated every aspect of our culture. Quite the opposite! Humanism may have declined as a movement, but humanistic ideas are now commonly accepted by the population as a whole. We learn that we should feel good about ourselves, that we cannot like others until we learn to like ourselves, that shame and guilt are debilitating emotions we must rid ourselves of as quickly as possible. Teachers are instructed that every child asks three questions at school: Am I safe? Can I cope? Will I be successful? It is the teacher's responsibility to be sure all three questions are answered in the affirmative.

Parents read in popular journals that they must express unconditional love regardless of their child's behavior. "I may not like what you do, but I'll always love you" has become standard fare, to be taken in by the child every morning with her Wheaties. "Shaming children, calling them bad, is considered a primary form of abuse" (Kaminer, 1992, p. 18). Wendy Kaminer,[8] however, does not believe that shame is necessarily bad, for she continues, "There's a name for people who lack guilt and shame: sociopaths. We ought to be grateful if guilt makes things like murder and moral corruption 'harder' " (p. 18).

Therapists, including Christian practitioners, often show a preference for humanistic ideas and methods. They find it important in their practice to ease the guilt and anger expressed by their patients. Eric Johnson (1989) expresses concern that "a number of Christian psychologists and pastors have defined self-esteem with reference to a system of values that seems all too similar to the context of a Carl Rogers or Leo Buscaglia rather than a Paul or a Jeremiah" (p. 231). Dodgen and McMinn (1986) take a more accepting view when they write that "at the same time as Christians have protested surrounding scholarship, such as the secular humanisms, they have developed theologies that are conformed to the very basis of the humanisms of the moment. . . . For example, our current Christian emphasis on self-esteem and worth as a result of having God's image is almost certainly a consequence of the human potential movement that spawned humanistic psychology" (p. 200).

Those who accept humanistic ideas come from all walks of life and are attracted to the positive message humanism brings. An emphasis on becoming, fulfillment, realization, purposefulness, peak experiences, joy, and transcendence has universal appeal. Surely God has given us all things to enjoy.

On the other hand, some of us who are committed to the teachings of Scripture find ourselves not only appreciating the positive message of humanism, but we also find ourselves asking the question posed by Karl Menninger (1973): *Whatever became of sin?* If I'm OK and you're OK, we have no need of a Savior. As Jesus told the disciples, "It is not the healthy who need a doctor, but the sick. I have not come to call the righteous, but sinners" (Mark 2:17).[9]

In the next chapter we will see ways that humanistic ideas and techniques provide guidelines for teachers, parents, and pastors. These techniques need not go against the sensibilities of those committed to the Gospel of Christ. Rather, they can be used in ways that enhance the moral growth of children and adolescents, preparing these young people, in turn, for their role as teachers in the schools, homes, and churches of the twenty-first century.

NOTES

1. Printed by permission from *Power for living* by Jamie Buckingham. Copyright, Arthur S. DeMoss Foundation.

2. M. Brewster Smith (1990) places the founding of humanistic psychology as a social movement within psychology in 1964 at a conference in Old Saybrook, Connecticut with such notables as Gordon Allport, Henry Murray, Gardner Murphy, Carl Rogers, Abraham Maslow, and Rollo May being present; but acknowledges that Carl Rogers' (1942) *Counseling and psychotherapy* and Maslow's (1954) *Motivation and personality* introduced many of the basic tenets of humanistic psychology. As Smith (1990) put it: "So both Rogers and Maslow embraced self-actualization as an empirical principle and as an ethical ideal. They aligned themselves with Jean-Jacques Rousseau's romantic view of human nature as intrinsically good but corrupted by society, as distinguished from Freud's Hobbesian view of human nature as problematic, tinged with intrinsic evil, and from the behaviorists' Lockean assumption of human plasticity under environmental programming" (p. 9 of "Humanistic Psychology" in *Journal of Humanistic Psychology, 30*[4], 6–21).

3. The American Humanist Association and its publication, *The Humanist*, celebrated its fiftieth anniversary in 1991.

4. For a more detailed description of the self-actualized person see J.A. Oakland (1974), Self-actualization and sanctification, *Journal of Psychology and Theology, 2*, 202–209.

5. A colleague of mine who belongs to Division 32, Humanistic Psychology, of the American Psychological Association (APA) told me that it is easy to see how much humanistic psychology is valued by counting the number of articles on humanism accepted for publication within the past ten or fifteen years by the *American Psychologist*, the official publication of the APA which is sent to all its members. My own scanning of the journal already had told me there were very few.

6. Ausubel and Sullivan (1970) in *Theory and problems of child development*, New York: Grune & Stratton, used the term "overvalued non-satellizer" to describe the child who has been reared permissively. "The child is installed in the home as an absolute monarch and is surrounded by adulation and obeisance. . . . These eventualities first threaten when the protection offered by his unreal home environment is removed and his hypertrophied ego aspirations are confronted by peers and adults unbiased in his favor" (p. 268). The authors described the overvalued non-satellizer as unable to curb "hedonistic impulses" or acquire "executive independence" and thus not apt to become "invested with moral obligation" (p. 269).

Baumrind (1977), whose research on authority patterns in parents and instrumental competence in children has gained widespread recognition, wrote that an "assumption that advocates of permissiveness have made is that unconditional love is beneficial to the child, and that love which is conditional upon the behavior of the child is harmful to the child. I think that the notion of unconditional love has deterred many parents from fulfilling certain important parental functions. They fail to train their children for future life and make them afraid to move towards independence. . . . The parent who expresses love unconditionally is encouraging the child to be selfish and demanding while she herself is not. Thus she reinforces exactly the behavior which she does not approve of—greedy, demanding, inconsiderate behavior" (pp. 254–255). (Some thoughts about child rearing, in S. Cohen & T.J. Comiskey [Eds.], *Child development: Contemporary perspectives*, Itasca, IL: Peacock.)

7. Richard James in *The Wall Street Journal*, April 16, 1979, 59, pp. 1, 18, reported that nearly 60 percent of encounter-group members and 90 percent of encounter-group leaders say the sessions are beneficial. This is in contrast to a study conducted by Lieberman and Yalom (reported by James) in which 200 encounter group participants were given a number of psychological tests, and only about one-third appeared to receive any longlasting benefits. As the figure of one-third is close to the number that improves even without therapy, it would seem that "many, if not most, of the methods may hardly be better than doing nothing at all" (James, 1979, p. 1). Michael Wertheimer (1978) in *American Psychologist, 33*, 739–745 comes to the same conclusion for he states that therapy has only "a slight positive effect" (p. 744) and that the difference between clients and control groups may be due to a self-fulfilling prophecy; that is, clients expect to be helped and so report they feel better after a session much as one would report less tension or less pain after taking a placebo. In another study (M.L. Smith & G.V. Glass, 1977, *American Psychologist, 32*, 752–760), the results of almost 400 evaluations of psychotherapy and counseling cited in the literature were surveyed.

Smith and Glass found that humanistic techniques had approximately the same success rate as psychodynamic and behavioristic approaches. Regardless of type of therapy, clients were better off than about 75 percent of untreated individuals.

8. Wendy Kaminer (1992) describes herself in *I'm dysfunctional, you're dysfunctional: The recovery movement and other self-help functions* as "a skeptical, secular humanist, Jewish, feminist, intellectual lawyer, currently residing in the Ivy League" (p. 121). Her criticisms of the Recovery Movement and other self-help groups are witty and informative.

9. While visiting a friend in the hospital, my husband noticed two books on the stand beside the bed. One was Harris' *I'm OK, you're OK*, the other was the Bible. "That's interesting," my husband said. "You've got two books you're reading. One book says you're OK; the other book says you're not OK. Which one are you going to believe?"

REFERENCES

Ausubel, D.P., & Sullivan, E.V. (1970). *Theory and problems of child development* (2nd ed.). New York: Grune & Stratton.

Baumrind, D. (1977). Some thoughts about child rearing. In S. Cohen & T.J. Comiskey (Eds.), *Child development: Contemporary perspectives* (pp. 248–258). Itasca, IL: Peacock.

Berne, E. (1961). *Transactional analysis in psychotherapy: A systematic individual and social psychiatry.* New York: Grove Press.

————. (1974). *Games people play: The psychology of human relationships.* New York: Grove Press.

Buckingham, J. (1983). *Power for living.* USA: Arthur S. DeMoss Foundation.

Combs, A.W. (1978). Humanism, education, and the future. *Educational Leadership, 35,* 300–303.

Dodgen, D.J., & McMinn, M.R. (1986). Humanistic psychology and Christian thought: A comparative analysis. *Journal of Psychology and Theology, 14,* 194–202.

Elkind, D. (1981). Erich Fromm (1900–1980). *American Psychologist, 36,* 521–522.

Harris, T. (1969). *I'm OK, you're OK: A practical guide to transactional analysis.* New York: Harper & Row.

James, M. (February, 1976). The OK boss in all of us. *Psychology Today,* pp. 31–36, 80.

Janov, A. (1970). *The primal scream.* New York: G.P. Putnam's Sons.

Johnson, E.L. (1989). Self-esteem in the presence of God. *Journal of Psychology and Theology, 17,* 226–235.

Jones, S.L., & Butman, R.E. (1991). *Modern psychotherapies: A comprehensive Christian appraisal.* Downers Grove, IL: InterVarsity.

Kaminer, W. (1992). *I'm dysfunctional, you're dysfunctional: The recovery movement and other self-help fashions.* Reading, MA: Addison-Wesley.

Kilpatrick, W.K. (1992). *Why Johnny can't tell right from wrong.* New York: Simon & Schuster.

Knapp, C.E. (1973). Teaching environmental education with a focus on values. In H. Kirschenbaum & S.B. Simon (Eds.), *Readings in values clarification* (pp. 161–174). Minneapolis: Winston.

Kohlberg & Simon: An exchange of opinion. (1972). *Learning, 1*(2), 19.

Kolenda, K. (1980). Humanism and Christianity. *The Humanist, 40*(4), 4–8.

Kolesnik, W.B. (1975). *Humanism and/or behaviorism in education.* Boston: Allyn & Bacon.

Kurtz, P. (1976). The attack on secular humanism. *The Humanist, 36*(5), 4–5.

LaHaye, T. (1980). *The battle for the mind.* Old Tappan, NJ: Fleming H. Revell.

Lamont, C. (1957). *The philosophy of humanism.* New York: Philosophical Library.

Larue, G.A. (1991). The humanist agenda. *The Humanist, 51*(1), 16–18, 38.

Lasch, C. (1979). *The culture of narcissism: American life in an age of diminishing expectations.* New York: W.W. Norton.

Lickona, T. (1991). *Educating for character: How our schools can teach respect and responsibility.* New York: Bantam.

Malone, T. (1989). Self-fulfillment through service to others. *The Humanist, 49*(1), 24, 49.

Maslow, A.H. (1970). *Motivation and personality* (2nd ed.). New York: Harper & Row.

_____. (1973). Self-actualizing people: A study of psychological health. In R.J. Lowry (Ed.), *Dominance, self-esteem, self-actualization: Germinal papers of A.H. Maslow* (pp. 177–201). Monterey, CA: Brooks/Cole.

Menninger, K. (1973). *Whatever became of sin?* New York: Hawthorn Books.

Moody, S. (1981, October 27). The Moral Majority. *The Tribune,* Terre Haute, IN, p. 13.

Morain, L.L. (1980). Humanist manifesto II: A time for reconsideration? *The Humanist, 40*(5), 4–10.

Moreno, J.L. (1944). *Sociodrama: A method for the analysis of social conflicts.* New York: Beacon House.

Mowrer, O.H. (1967). Preface. In O.H. Mowrer (Ed.), *Morality and mental health* (pp. vii–x). Chicago: Rand McNally.

Perls, F.S. (1969). *Gestalt therapy verbatim.* Lafayette, CA: Real People.

Peters, T. (1978). *Futures — Human and divine.* Atlanta: John Knox.

Raths, L.E., Harmin, M., & Simon, S.B. (1966). *Values and teaching: Working with values in the classroom.* Columbus, OH: Charles E. Merrill.

Rogers, C.R. (1964). Toward a modern approach to value: The valuing process in the mature person. *Journal of Abnormal and Social Psychology, 68,* 160–167.

———. (1969). *Freedom to learn.* Columbus, OH: Charles E. Merrill.

———. (1978). Some questions and challenges facing a humanistic psychology. In I.D. Welch, G.A. Tate, & F. Richards (Eds.), *Humanistic psychology: A source book* (pp. 41–45). Buffalo, NY: Prometheus.

Rokeach, M. (1973). *The nature of human values.* New York: The Free Press.

Silber, J.R. (1975). Encountering what? In D.A. Read & S.B. Simon (Eds.), *Humanistic education sourcebook* (pp. 196–200). Englewood Cliffs, NJ: Prentice-Hall.

Smith, M.B. (1990). Humanistic psychology. *Journal of Humanistic Psychology, 30*(4), 6–21.

———. (1991). *Values, self, and society: Toward a humanist social psychology.* New Brunswick: Transaction.

Van Rooy, G. (1986). Treating infected sin through primal therapy. *Journal of Psychology and Christianity, 5*(3), 32–36.

Vitz, P.C. (1977). *Psychology as religion: The cult of self worship.* Grand Rapids: Eerdmans.

Welch, I.D., & Rodwick, J.R. (1978). Communicating the sciences: A humanistic viewpoint. In I.D. Welch, G.A. Tate, & F. Richards (Eds.), *Humanistic psychology: A source book* (pp. 335–342). Buffalo, NY: Prometheus.

Wertheimer, M. (1978). Humanistic psychology and the humane but tough-minded psychologist. *American Psychologist, 33,* 739–745.

ELEVEN

Guidelines from Humanistic Psychology for Teachers, Parents, and Pastors

humanistic theory of morality is founded on the premise that morality is not a separate component of the personality but rather an integral part of every aspect of life, interwoven with the physical, the cognitive, and the social, as well as being related to the affective, creative, and spiritual. Humanism emphasizes those characteristics that make us distinctly human, thereby giving us a better understanding of ourselves and of others. The humanist emphasis on each person's taking responsibility for his or her own life and the assumption that morality comes from within the individual rather than being imposed by an outside source are views adopted by many individuals whether or not they consider themselves in the humanist camp. Teachers, parents, and pastors who are effective in their respective positions often adopt humanistic concerns and employ a number of techniques commonly linked with third-force psychology.

GUIDELINES FOR TEACHERS

To the humanist educator, the child is a whole person, a totality composed of many parts — the physical, social, cognitive, affective, and moral. All parts are interrelated and an understanding of this relationship must be considered when planning curricula. To fasten attention on only one kind of learning while ignoring others is to do the child a grave injustice. The three Rs are important, but they must not be taught to the exclusion of the fourth R of human relations. Only as children develop an understanding and a caring for others will they endeavor to discipline themselves. They learn that misbehavior makes other people unhappy; and even as they do not want others to make them unhappy, they do not wish to make others unhappy. They learn to behave in ways that are socially acceptable. In essence, they learn to be moral. And importantly, the desire comes from within rather than being imposed by a teacher or an administrator.

The teacher is concerned not only with the child as a whole person and with the child's interactions with others, but the teacher is willing to bring himself or herself to the classroom as a complete person with emotions and feelings that can be shared with the children. Both the child's and the teacher's needs are to be considered in matters such as the amount of freedom each person has and the curricula that will be pursued. The development of positive human relationships and honest interpersonal communication are as important as the acquisition of information. An open classroom that follows the interests of the students is to be preferred to one in which subject matter is determined by age or grade level.

MAGIC CIRCLE

The scene is a first-grade class, and at the front of the room are ten chairs arranged in a circle and occupied by the children and their teacher. This is not just any circle. It is a Magic Circle. It is called magic because as the boys and girls share their ideas, express their feelings, and listen to one another, something magic seems to happen. Each child discovers that he or she is not somehow different or inferior to the other children. Rather, the child learns that all people have times when they are happy and times when they are sad. Everyone experiences love and hate, pride and shame, warmth and loneliness. Even big people have times when they feel the way little people do. The teacher may tell of a time when she felt "left out" or frightened or embarrassed or "empty inside."

Each Magic Circle session (formerly known as the Human Development Program founded by Bessell and Palomares, 1973) begins with a topic that centers on one of three themes: (1) an awareness of one's own thoughts, feelings, and actions; (2) a demonstration of mastery of some skill; or (3) the development of competence in social interaction. The subject for the day may be "something that gives me a good feeling," "something that gives me a bad feeling," or "I had a nice thought when. . . ." Or the topic may be, "I did something nice for someone else," or "somebody got me into trouble." The leader of the group (teacher or student) begins by reviewing the rules. "Raise your hand when you wish to participate. Everyone gets a turn. Listen to the one who is speaking." The atmosphere must be positive with no laughing or smirking allowed. At the end of the twenty-minute session when all who wish have responded, the leader reviews what each child has said, calling the child by name. The teacher then will ask, "What do you think we learned here today?"

What is learned, according to the humanist educator, is an increased respect for self and others, greater responsibility for one's own behavior, better interpersonal relationships, and improved speaking and listening skills. The child's self-concept is greatly enhanced by the use of Magic Circle. Every child upon entering school wants to be successful. It is as though the child asks three questions: "Am I safe?" "Can I cope?" "Will I be successful?" Magic Circle helps the child answer in the affirmative. The child comes to see himself or herself as secure, capable, and lovable — an important member of the class and the community.

Every Wednesday in Gayle Reiter's class at the Community Nursery School, sponsored by the First Lutheran Church in Alexandria, Minnesota, you will find seven four- and five-year-olds sitting on carpet squares in a circle around their teacher. Each child has his or her own square and waits eagerly to see where the square will be placed. After twenty minutes of Magic Circle, another seven children take their places to share with each other their feelings and thoughts. In order to accommodate all the children, Mrs. Reiter has three sessions in the morning and three in the afternoon when another group of nursery school children are present. Wednesday is a very special day to these children and is marked on their take-home calendar as Magic Circle Day.[1]

Magic Circle is only one of several such programs available for children at the nursery and primary levels. Others include the Most Important Person (MIP) Series, Developing an Understanding of Self and Others (DUSO), and values clarification (VC), described in the last chapter. Both MIP and DUSO are multimedia approaches and have special appeal to younger children. Values clarification may or may not use props but is applicable to students at all grade levels. Like Magic Circle, these programs deal with the humanistic themes of accepting self and others, understanding one's own feelings and the feelings of others, achieving mastery and competence, setting purposeful goals, and dealing with choice and the consequences of choice.

VALUES CLARIFICATION

Values clarification remains the approach most frequently used. It can be learned quickly, materials are readily available, it is applicable to a large number of classroom and subject areas, and it arouses student interest (Chazan, 1985). "Forty books on values clarification were published during the Seventies. One of them, *Values Clarification: A Handbook of Practical Strategies for Teachers and Students,* sold more than 600,000 copies" (Kirschenbaum, 1992, p. 772). Values clarification has been applied to every school subject and has been used for health education, career education, and drug education.

A Three-Step Process

The clarification of a value is really the culmination of a three-step process that begins with a knowledge of the facts, details, events, and actualities of the matter and then proceeds to an understanding of the concepts or principles underlying the facts. It is only after the students have gained familiarity with the facts and have integrated the facts into relevant concepts that they are in a position to choose their values based on their feelings, opinions, and interests.

Suppose, for example, a fourth-grade class is studying the Pilgrims (Harmin, Kirschenbaum, & Simon, 1973). The students must learn when the Pilgrims came to America, how they got here, what experiences they had the first year in a new land, and why they decided to celebrate the first Thanksgiving. After learning the facts, the teacher and students discuss the concepts or principles behind the facts. The concepts may include those of prejudice, cultural assimilation, emigration,

337

helping, and ceremony. Unless the unit also includes the values level, it will make little difference in the lives of the students. It is only at this third level that they become personally involved in choosing a value, in prizing the value chosen, and in acting consistently on the value chosen. Each child, for instance, needs to come to terms with the meaning of prejudice, for others and for the self. The child must determine his or her own attitudes and feelings and decide how to respond to those who are culturally different.

> **The clarification of a value is really the culmination of a three-step process that begins with a knowledge of the facts, details, events, and actualities of the matter and then proceeds to an understanding of the concepts or principles underlying the facts.**

Many schools teach only the facts. Some teach concepts as well. By comparison, only a few endeavor to help students cope with a changing world by teaching the process of valuing. The method gained popularity during the 1970s and was mandated for teacher training in some public schools. At that time, Robert Hall (1978) wrote that "the values-clarification movement . . . boasts a network of about one hundred trainers, who have conducted workshops in the method for more than two hundred thousand teachers, counselors, and other helping professionals" (p. 7).

Values and Character

Articles and books on values clarification are ubiquitous and contain exercises that are easy to follow and fun to implement. In William Hendricks' (1984) book *Values*, suggested values at the elementary school level include patience, self-identity, self-confidence, stability, self-control, responsibility, wise judgment, optimism, honesty, limiting TV viewing time, cheerfulness, good manners, and kindness — to name a few. The list appears to differ little from lists given by those who advocate character education.

In the exercise on self-identity, the teacher at the early elementary grades will print the words "ALL ABOUT ME" on the chalkboard and introduce the lesson by calling to mind ways in which we are all different. Students are asked to answer such questions as: What are some of your favorite foods? What are some of your favorite sports or games? What do you hope to be when you grow up? What is your favorite subject in school? Added questions include items such as favorite color or item of clothing.

Poster paper is given to each child, who prints ALL ABOUT ME at the top. Using old magazines and scissors, pupils cut out pictures of items they listed in response to the questions about themselves. Pictures are pasted on the poster paper and each child can display and explain his or her poster (pp. 10-11).

In the exercise on honesty, the teacher of students from grades four through eight takes up the matter of cheating on a test. The purpose of clarifying this value is "to help pupils understand that cheating on a test is both dishonest and harmful to ourselves" (p. 159). Before a test is handed out, the teacher explains that cheating is a form of stealing, and stealing is contrary to all religions and is also against the law. Furthermore, cheating does not give an honest assessment of a student's ability and achievement, and it is an affront to other members of the class. The class then discusses how a test can be taken so that cheating does not occur. The exercise ALL ABOUT ME gives the child complete freedom for it deals with personal tastes; the exercise on honesty is directed by the teacher for it deals with a moral issue that affects others as well as the self.

ARE MAGIC CIRCLE AND VALUES CLARIFICATION A WASTE OF TIME?

In response to those who say there is not enough time in the classroom for such frills as Magic Circle or values clarification, supporters respond that there is no better way to spend twenty minutes a day. A close relationship of the child with the teacher, as well as with peers, will motivate the child to learn in every way, including mastering the three Rs. The teacher sees the child, not as an empty vessel into which information is to be poured or as an inadequate and sinful creature whose will must be bent into conformity, but as a member of the human race having tremendous potential. Furthermore, the teacher understands the task of the educator to be that of facilitator of the child's potential. Learning in all its ramifications is best accomplished in an atmosphere of cooperation and mutual regard. This is a transforming educational insight.

VALUES EDUCATION

Values education takes on many forms but often differs from values clarification in that the young person is taught some values and given the opportunity to choose others. Differentiation is made between those values generally agreed upon by the larger society and those values that are highly individualistic. D.L. Barr (1974) uses the terms "consensus values" and "contended values" to distinguish between the two. Consensus values, such as not stealing or not murdering, are inculcated into the lives of students. If young people refuse to adopt consensus values, at least they have been told what these values are and that deviation is accompanied by judicial punishment. Contended values — and most values fall into this category — are chosen by the individual in terms of one's own needs and one's own preferences. "The school's responsibility in regard to these values is not to inculcate, but to clarify . . . to devise techniques and strategies that will help the student in his choice" (Barr, 1974, p. 19).

Other writers also differentiate between the two kinds of values: terms like "basic," "universal," "societal," "traditional," and "fixed" being used to indicate a value that is not subject to personal whim or choice; whereas "contended," "personal," "individual," and "private" are used to indicate those values that the person has a right to choose for oneself. As was mentioned, the contrast in Hendrick's (1984) approach to honesty, a consensus value; and his approach to self-identity, a personal or contended value, would appear to come under values education although he prefers the term "values clarification" for both.

There are those who oppose values education programs on the same grounds that they oppose values clarification. They fear that school values may conflict with values taught in the home, or they say that the church is the only place to formally present values. Some critics make the charge that values education, like values clarification, deals only marginally with moral values and so should not be referred to as moral education. Some have cited research showing that school children do not profit from valuing programs (Lockwood, 1978; Perlmutter, 1980).

MACOS

In addition to values clarification, other humanistic approaches have been implemented at higher grade levels. One of these is "Man: A

Course of Study" (MACOS), designed for teaching social studies to upper elementary and junior high pupils. Developed by Jerome Bruner (1966), the course integrates both cognitive and affective learning and has the central theme of understanding the nature of that being called "man." Students think through what is human about humans, how humans got the way they are, and how humans can become more human. There is an emphasis on the discovery method, and students are encouraged to engage in informed guessing, to use problem-solving techniques, and to contrast humans with other forms of life.

Like other humanistic programs, MACOS has been criticized by those who say that children are not in a position to decide what is good and true or to form independently a sound value system. Rather than discovering what it means to be human, children must be *taught* who they are and how they relate to the rest of God's creation. Some parents feel that a classroom discussion of how humans and baboons are alike in personality traits and in social behaviors undermines the teaching in the home of the person being made in the image of God. Several members of Congress, seeking ways to cut costs, have objected in the past to using federal funds to support the MACOS program. Other groups have criticized MACOS on the grounds that the personal rights of children are violated, claiming that in some cases psychological trauma has occurred.

THE HUMANIST REBUTTAL

Humanist educators refuse to accept any blame for failures within the public schools. To their way of thinking very few schools have actually implemented humanistic techniques or established a curriculum based on humanistic principles. Arthur Combs (1981) writes that "the majority of today's teachers and administrators were schooled in some form of behavioristic psychology as the theoretical base for their professional thinking. Such views concentrate attention primarily upon behavior and the external conditions that produce it" (p. 447).

In response to those who report that valuing programs do not help students, humanists are quick to cite studies that show that the programs have indeed produced optimal results (e.g., Goldbecker, 1976; Simon & deSherbinin, 1975). Kirschenbaum (1976) states that "there is a growing body of data, over thirty-five studies, which indicate that value clarification can lessen apathy, enhance self-esteem, reduce drug abuse, and contribute to other laudable goals, while simultaneously maintaining just as much or greater learnings in cognitive skills and subject matter as curricula that omit the valuing process" (p. 4). Prakash (1988) also defends values clarification by noting that "the VC process is designed to help individuals prioritize their desires so that in the quest for integration, higher priorities are not mistakenly sacrificed for lower priorities. It is crucial for learners to realize that those goals higher up in their priority lists will invariably entail duties and obligations. . . . Duties and obligations have an important place even in an ethic which defines moral ideals in terms of desire-satisfaction" (p. 123).

Humanists emphasize the changes that are taking place in our society and say we must be ready to meet the challenges brought by these changes. They feel the best that educators can do is to prepare the next generation for the world in which they will live, to prize them as persons, to care for them without possessing them, and to assist them in learning methods of valuing that will enable them to live genuine, meaningful, and productive lives.

WHERE WE ARE TODAY IN VALUES EDUCATION
The trend in the 1990s is to avoid the extremes of both the permissive approach of moral relativity and the traditional approach of moral indoctrination, while at the same time taking the best of both. Increasingly, there appears to be a shift from the idea that "good feelings about the self are always healthy, whereas bad self-feelings are to be avoided" (Curry & Johnson, 1990, p. 4). In fact, "good feelings can be self-deceptive and narcissistic (excessive pride) just as bad feelings can be constructive and energizing (healthy guilt)" (p. 4). In the long run, children will feel good about themselves if they see themselves as productive members of the society, and this will come when children are capable of constructive self-criticism as well as taking pride in their accomplishments.

But indoctrination will not produce a generation of morally educated persons either. "Sooner or later, our young people are going to confront situations that require them to make decisions on their own. . . . Unless we are completely cloistered from the pluralistic and changing world

342

around us, the most successful inculcation does not free us from many difficult life decisions that we, and we alone, must resolve" (Kirschenbaum, 1992, p. 775).

Indoctrination may work when the child is young and impressionable. But even if it works, the question that arises is whether indoctrination shows respect for the child as a conscious, perceiving organism, endowed by God with capabilities of maturing morally as well as physically and mentally. Furthermore, indoctrination does not allow for a consideration of why one value or belief is better than another value or belief. A better method for the development of moral attitudes and behavior may be to present views that are not in keeping with universal and religious standards of morality in a context in which the child is given the opportunity to use his or her cognitions and feelings to combat these views. Sometimes referred to as "inoculation," this method will help the student build up a resistance to future views that may be harmful both to the self and to the society. A discussion of why cheating or stealing or premarital sex is wrong is much to be preferred to issuing injunctions against these behaviors. The importance of personal thought and decision-making is not to be underestimated.

GUIDELINES FOR PARENTS

It is a well-established fact that showing delight in the growing child and affirming his or her strivings for competence enhances development and becomes what is often referred to as a self-fulfilling prophecy. The more the child is encouraged, the better the child does. The better the child

> It is a well-established fact that showing delight in the growing child and affirming his or her strivings for competence enhances development and becomes what is often referred to as a self-fulfilling prophecy. The more the child is encouraged, the better the child does. The better the child does, the more confident the child becomes. The result is increased motivation and a healthy self-concept.

does, the more confident the child becomes. The result is increased motivation and a healthy self-concept. Children also tend to be like their parents. If we are warm and cordial, excited about life, and respectful of others, our children are more apt to be pleasant, interested in learning, and considerate in their relationships with others. Humanists want their children to live purposeful, satisfying lives; to be open to new experiences; and to have close, rewarding friendships with others. Surely there can be no quarrel with these goals for children everywhere.

Thoughtful people also adopt the humanistic view that to be fair with others and to understand them, we should try to see things from their perspective. As parents we will endeavor to put ourselves in the place of our child, to see the world as the child sees it. We will wonder what perceptions and emotions the child is experiencing. We know that providing for our child's physical well-being is not enough. The child is a unified whole, a complex organism with many needs. As parents we will also be aware that each child is different and should be respected for his or her own individuality. To decide what kind of child we want and then to pressure the child each moment to conform is not to reckon with the child's uniqueness as a person or to show respect for the child's dignity as a member of the human race. Individual temperaments, abilities, and interests must be taken into account if we are to deal with our children in humane ways.

A Humanist Definition of Family

The Board of Directors of the American Humanist Association (AHA) has taken the following position relative to the family (AHA's Statement on the Family, 1980).

> Families . . . are the well-spring of human interaction, compassion, love, productivity, and creativity that the individual bequeaths to the larger society. The family provides the security and germinates and fosters the altruism that makes civilization possible. . . . A safe, healthful environment, balanced nutrition, adequate housing, medical care, and quality education are minimum family requirements. . . . The family is a creative, vital force that can meet the challenges of the future as it has met the demands of the past. (p. 40)

Few of us would disagree with this position.

Other portions of the statement are less palatable — especially to those of a more conservative persuasion, although those holding liberal views would agree with many of them.

Any two people or group of people wishing to make a commitment to one another over time and to share resources, responsibilities, goals and values should be considered a family. . . . Child-care programs, encouraged by government, for the children of working parents have been too long postponed. . . . And no law or regulation should require women to bear unwanted children. Children have a right to be wanted and a right to be born into the bosom of the family, not into an unnatural, unloving atmosphere. . . . Equality for women and human rights for children should be the law of the land. (p. 40)

Today's families are described as "pluralistic, intergenerational, multi-racial, and multi-cultural" (p. 40), a condition endorsed by the American Humanist Association.

WHAT KIND OF DISCIPLINE IS BEST?

Control and guidance of the child are major parental tasks. Humanists take the view that the only discipline that is truly effective is self-discipline, not a discipline imposed by others. As one might expect, humanists differ in the degree of permissiveness considered optimal but generally agree that adults should try to solve the problems of parenting in less authority-centered, power-based ways. Friendship with one's children is encouraged. Children should be self-confident, curious, and independent — traits developed best in an atmosphere of openness and mutual concern.

Humanists readily admit that there are risks involved in rearing children permissively, as some children will adopt values in contradistinction to the values of the parents. But these are risks parents must be willing to take. Unless children are allowed to develop their own moral sensitivities and choose their own ways, they will never be free, self-directed persons, cognizant of the reasons for believing as they do and capable of developing responsibility for their behaviors. Robert Hall (1976), writing for *The Humanist,* links the opposing position of stricter controls with deficits in moral understanding. "It is because morality has been promulgated as rules rather than as reasons that so many people today seem to have so little sense of right and wrong. . . .

Parents who want their children to be taught 'the only one right way' in contrast to liberty and toleration want in effect, to live in a closed society; this is not, however, what America is, nor, it is hoped, what it shall become" (p. 45).

Parents who agree with Hall will have little difficulty using humanistic methods. Parents, however, who believe there is truly one right way and therefore reject a relativity of truth and ethics will be obligated to sort through humanistic suggestions and strategies and adopt only those that enhance rather than conflict with their own beliefs. Furthermore, humanistic values have been held for centuries by those who do not espouse humanism as a philosophy. Humanists do not have a monopoly on humanistic qualities. Many parents and other adults show love and respect for the children entrusted to their care. They provide an atmosphere of encouragement and sensitivity to others and are aware of qualities both within themselves and in others that make people distinctly human.

ARE THE "THREE M's" REALLY MISLEADING?

Sidney Simon and Sally Olds (1976) in *Helping Your Child Learn Right from Wrong: A Guide to Values Clarification* have presented in interesting and understandable fashion exercises parents may use in the home. Written from a humanist perspective, the authors believe that all of us need guidance in learning how to analyze ideas and situations and that we learn best in an atmosphere of openness and freedom. Although moralizing (invoking guilt, religion, and patriotism), manipulating (limiting the child's options by rewards and punishers), and modeling (expecting the child to act as we do) are all appropriate at times, these methods are the "Three Misleading M's" (p. 18) because they do not help children work out their own values and develop their own understanding of what is right and what is wrong. Values cannot be taught directly but the process for arriving at values can be.

The parent may start by saying at the dinner table something like, "Let's talk about everyone's high point of the day," or while riding in the car, "Let's play a game. Each one will tell which season of the year is his or her favorite and why." (This could just as well be a favorite food or color or flower, and the like.) Each member of the family then responds appropriately. The idea is that by answering such questions, children learn to understand themselves and others. There are ground rules to be followed, and these may be explained to family members either before the game begins or applied as the need arises. The rules are: (1) No one jumps on anyone else (the ideas of another are to be respected); (2) there are no right or wrong answers, attitudes, or responses; (3) only one person talks at a time and nobody interrupts; (4) everyone has the option of passing at any time (this safeguards one's privacy); (5) no "killer-statements" that put down other people; (6) no self put-downs (self-denigrating statements are not allowed); and (7) changing one's mind is a sign of growth (pp. 43-45). It is through this sharing of feelings and opinions that children learn to examine life rationally, consider possible options, make choices based on those options, and consider the consequences of their decisions.

The exercises suggested in *Helping Your Child Learn Right from Wrong* are delightful, may be enjoyed by all members of the family, and serve to bring the family closer together. The rub may come if the discussion turns to ethics and religious belief, for these are areas that many feel are not subject to relative judgment and subjective preference. Some of us may not care to discuss with our children the question, "Are there times when it is right to cheat?" (p. 196) or, "If you were going to convert to another religion, which one would you choose and why?" (p. 198). But eliminating some questions need not preclude the use of clarification strategies for those values not related to morality or to religious commitment. Nor do we need to rule out all questions suggested by Simon and Olds directed to one's faith, such as, "When have you been close to a miracle?" (p. 198) or, "What more could you do to live a holier life?" (p. 199).

Values and Christian Faith

Applying the valuing process to the Christian faith is what Roland and Doris Larson (1976) do in *Values & Faith: Activities for Family and Church Groups.* The authors give credit to Simon and others who helped to shape their understanding and use of methodologies in the area of values education and seek to show how the methodologies apply to an examination of "opinions, attitudes, beliefs, and values in a Christian context" (p. 3). In introducing the book, the Larsons express their faith in God as "the absolute, the beginning point of ourselves and of our world" and declare that His revelation comes to us "through the Bible, the Church, the life of Christ, and the activity of the Holy Spirit among us" (p. 5).

In this context, values clarification becomes more than the blind leading the blind. It becomes a method for internalizing and clarifying one's faith. We learn to value and prize our relationship with God as we consider what that relationship means to each of us personally. Values clarification was used by Jesus when He told a parable and then asked His disciples to interpret what He had said. As parents we may also use it to help our children develop a greater appreciation of the Christian heritage and of a faith that gives meaning to life. Respect for each member of the family is enhanced by the sharing of ideas, and the resulting cohesiveness allows us as parents more influence in the lives of our children.

> Another contribution of humanistic thought is the holistic health movement. The focus of *third-force* psychology is on prevention rather than treatment, wellness rather than sickness, doing for oneself rather than relying on a physician.

The Larsons caution parents not to yield to the temptation of imposing their views on their children. Telling children they must believe as you do is not as effective in the long run as sharing with them the reasons for your faith. They know that after a consideration of other belief systems, you have chosen Christianity as having the greatest value. Prizing the choice made and showing delight in the faith, along with living a life consistent with that choice, will have its influence on the child. But in the end, each person must decide individually. We cannot choose for our children, nor are we responsible for the choices they make. We only hurt ourselves by feeling accountable for their decisions.

Some parents cannot use values clarification procedures. The approach is inimical to their personalities and too far removed from their idea of how children should be reared. Nor are values clarification techniques adaptable to all situations or all topics. But parents who use the technique find it rewarding. These parents liberate as well as control, listen as well as expound, let their children go as well as hold them close. They are willing to risk letting children make their own judgments as to those values having the greatest meaning, and by doing this they encourage their children to take responsibility for their own moral development.

VALUES AND HEALTH

Another contribution of humanistic thought is the holistic health movement. The focus of *third-force* psychology is on prevention rather than treatment, wellness rather than sickness, doing for oneself rather than relying on a physician. Although it is recognized that at times medical assistance is needed, it is also recognized that doctors cannot always do what we can do for ourselves. Adequate nutrition, weight control, proper exercise, and sufficient rest is each one's responsibility. Wellness is also enhanced by meaningful and productive work and by rewarding relationships with others. Good health is an ongoing process, seldom attained by a pill, powder, or surgeon's knife. As parents we guard the health of our children, but as they grow older they must take responsibility for themselves. Encouraging them to say more about how they feel when they are happy and things are going well and less about their aches and pains or psychological hurts will help them focus on the positive aspects of life and bring about a kind of self-fulfilling prophecy. To the humanist a healthy mind and a healthy body are expressions of morality.

VALUES AND FAMILY THERAPY

Other humanistic ideas that apply to the home include the use of family therapy (Charny, 1974) and the application of transactional analysis to adults who have had unfortunate home backgrounds (Yablonsky, 1976). In family therapy the whole family is included in the sessions even though only one member appears to be having difficulty. In this way family members come to see themselves and each other in ways not previously understood.

With transactional analysis, the counselor or therapist may set up role-playing sessions in which other adults play the part of family members, and events in the person's life are reenacted so that childhood trauma can be dealt with openly and in a rational manner. The participant recognizes the Child, the Adult, and the Parent in the self and in others and comes to understand why he feels as he does about the self. By the use of TA the unwholesome attitude of I'm not OK may be changed to the optimal I'm OK position, and the client learns to relate to others in an Adult to Adult fashion. Through encounter sessions participants can learn not to make the same mistakes in rearing children that their parents made with them. The therapist and group members provide the incentive, while the discussions and role-playing activities equip participants with the information needed to become good parents.

GUIDELINES FOR PASTORS

What does the church have to offer to the child in the Sunday School, to the young person in the youth group, to the adult in the Bible study class? How will it meet the needs of the seeker after truth? Is it a loving, caring community of believers interested in each person as a total individual? Is it a joyful community rejoicing in the Lord, prizing the life they have in Christ, and celebrating the excitement of a commitment to Jesus Christ? Is it a church that sees in each person all the potential that person has as a member or future member of the family of God? The ' answers to these questions rests with the pastor and with other leaders of the congregation.

Michael Anthony (1991) writes that humanistic principles are based on a sound understanding of how learning takes place and that "many churches would do well to incorporate these principles into their learning environment" (p. 86). He lists these as establishing a warm, accepting atmosphere; allowing students to share in a choice as to instructional activities; helping students develop positive feelings about themselves; engaging in role-playing and simulation games; making use of object lessons; and setting a good example. "Don't be afraid to teach absolutes and demonstrate the importance of moral standards" (p. 86), he adds to the list, although this, unlike the others, is not a humanistic principle. Many of us in the work of the church would agree that humanistic techniques are often appropriate, and we would also agree that at times absolutes should be taught.

VALUES CLARIFICATION

The ease with which values clarification may be used with any age group and in any setting has caught the interest of Sunday School teachers and pastors as well as teachers and administrators in the public schools. In a book by Hall and Smith (1973), dedicated to "the Franciscans at Alverna," a number of arguments are given to justify and support the use of values clarification in religious education. "It can be justified because it works, or because it allows us to apply valid group dynamic techniques to essentially religious issues of meaning and value. It can be justified because . . . it follows the action and revelation of God, personified in his Son, experienced historically and currently in that communion of his people, called the Church" (p. 242).

Simon and deSherbinin (1975) would also say that values clarification is useful in the work of the church. "Values clarification already has a solid place in Sunday and church schools, where thousands of teachers are using it. These teachers are face to face with the question of whether moralizing is a suitable way to deal with religious education" (p. 683). Leaders within the church are aware that true spirituality, like true morality, must come from within the person rather than being imposed by a minister or teacher; and although spiritual values may be taught by those in authority or acquired by association with Christian parents and teachers, unless these values are incorporated by choice within the life of the individual, attitudes and behaviors may not remain secure. Those advocating values clarification feel that more choice and less unquestioning acceptance of what is taught will make for greater cognitive and affective stability when one is in a situation varying from that in which the instruction was received.

Three Levels

The suggestion has been made (Simon, 1973) that the Sunday School teacher or church group leader should use all three levels of teaching when presenting a lesson: facts, concepts, and values. Bible stories are excellent sources with which to begin. When telling of God's dealings with the Children of Israel, for example, the teacher or pastor will start with the facts. He or she will explain how God brought the Israelites out of Egypt, supplying them with food and water and protecting them from the enemy.

Next will come a discussion of relevant concepts. What does this story tell us about God? What are the attributes of someone who loves and cares for others? Does God love everyone equally? In what ways does God love us? What does deliverance mean? Has God delivered us? If so, from what? The third level of values is then considered, based on a knowledge of the facts and an understanding of the concepts. Values relate personally to each member of the class. What choices will each child or young person make as a consequence of knowing God's love? How will it change each life? Is God's love prized? Will it make a difference in behavior? If so, how?

Choice Valued in the Old Testament
We read in the Old Testament that Joshua used this approach. He recounted for the people the facts of their escape from Pharaoh, their survival in the wilderness, and their entrance into the promised land of Canaan (Josh. 24). Joshua then reminded them of the concepts of who God is, of His holy and jealous nature, and of the allegiance He requires if blessings are to continue. Finally, Joshua asked the people to make a value judgment—a choice of whom they would serve. They could value and serve the Lord who had done great things for them, or they could value the gods of their heathen neighbors, turning their backs on Jehovah. Which would it be? "Choose for yourselves this day whom you will serve," Joshua told the people, and then added, "As for me and my household we will serve the Lord" (v. 15). As the people listened, they considered the consequences of choosing the Lord versus those of serving idols and decided to join Joshua in serving God.

The Book of Proverbs mentions numerous values with graphic illustrations of what may occur if a person (usually a young man) does not act in accordance with these values. Some of these values are: "trust in the Lord and not in oneself; violence and sexual immorality (specifically, associating with an adulteress) are to be avoided . . . gossiping is a source of trouble; and control of the tongue to be admired; the parent should instruct the child; and discipline is necessary for his well-being . . . diligence and hard work are praiseworthy . . . those who are kind to the needy are blessed; the proud and arrogant are damned" (Kilby, 1993, p. 169). There are many other values as well, and young people growing up in the Jewish community would be taught that adhering to these values would make them "blessed" and ignoring these values would make them fools, bringing about their own destruction.

Choice Valued in the New Testament
In the Gospels, we read that Jesus encouraged people to make choices. He did not force His value system on others but let them know what would happen if they decided one way as opposed to the consequences of deciding another way. The rich young ruler came to Jesus to ask what he could do to inherit eternal life and was told that he could either give up his possessions and achieve eternal life, or he could keep his wealth and not see the kingdom (Luke 18:18-23). The young man knew the alternatives and that the choice was his; and even though he made the wrong choice, Jesus did not call him back or try to get him to change his mind. Jesus invites but does not pressure; He knocks but does not pound; He offers but does not force. Each of us must do our own choosing and our own valuing. Whether we read Joshua, the Proverbs, the Gospels, or other books in the Bible, it is clear that values in Scripture have a moral dimension; that is, some values are good and lead to a happy life whereas other values are evil and will lead to destruction. Values may be personal in that each person must choose, but values are not relative in the sense that one value is as good as another. Obviously, some values are better than others.

Three Levels Used in the Church
In *Values and Faith,* Roland and Doris Larson (1976) provide a number of ways values clarification may be used in the church. They feel it is important for believers to "take actions to make their behaviors more consistent with their beliefs and values" (p. 3). Using Hebrews 11 as the basis for discussion, a class can look first at the *facts* about faith—how faith is defined, which people showed faith, what they did to show their faith, what their goal was, and why they did not receive all that was promised to them. Next, the class will explore *concepts* related to faith. What kind of relationship did those recorded in the Hebrews passage have with God? What characteristics did they possess that enabled them to act upon their faith? What were the results of their faith? After a discussion of the facts and the concepts, the matter of *values* comes into play. Values are personal, and although one may share what faith means personally or consider how one's faith is like or unlike the faith of another or think of ways that faith may be strengthened, values remain an individual matter. Faith must come from the heart.

Few churches go beyond the facts level. If the lesson for the day is the triumphal entry of Jesus into Jerusalem, most Sunday School pupils will learn only the facts surrounding the event, such as the directions Jesus gave to His disciples or the reaction of the large crowd singing Hosanna or what the Pharisees said about the demonstration (Simon, 1973). But there is more to be learned than just a recounting of what happened. The lesson will take on greater interest if the class considers the concepts of what it meant for Jesus to ride into the city on a colt, what the people who threw palm branches before Him expected to have happen, and the ways in which the Pharisees and the disciples differed.

Even more exciting and meaningful is the valuing process in which each child thinks through what this event means to him or to her. Does the child wish to praise the Lord? If so, in what ways can the child do this? Should a person engage in a demonstration as did the people in Jesus' time? Does it matter if a demonstration makes those in authority angry as it did the Pharisees? Why or why not? Should one demonstrate even if the law says one should not? The possibilities of valuing are great, and each member of the class must decide individually. The questions asked will depend in large measure on the position of the teacher or pastor with regard to religious, social, and political issues. Most churches would welcome a discussion of how each of us can praise the Lord. Fewer would approve of asking children to decide when it is appropriate to demonstrate if those in authority condemn the action.

Religious Values and Personal Values

Teachers and ministers within the church must be able to distinguish between values all must accept and those that children and young people have the right to choose for themselves. Brownfield (1973) offers a helpful delineation and calls this distinguishing "core values from secondary and even superficial values, which may not be values at all" (p. 234). The teacher's "relationship with Jesus Christ" takes precedence over a concern for whether the class recites the correct prayer or folds hands in a certain way. Brownfield continues: "Somehow, value teaching needs to conform to the value structure of Scripture. If God cherishes human worth, then so must the religious educator. If God values free choice, so must the religion teacher. . . . The message is to strip away the crust of nonsense, to return freshly to the clear invitation of God to life" (p. 235).[2]

ROLE-PLAYING

Children may enjoy role-playing the characters in a Bible story and discussing the values of those whose lives they reenact. They may consider what would have happened if the person in the story had made a different choice or what choice they would have made had they been the one in the story. Reading biographies of Christian missionaries and other men and women of God will set before them values they may decide to adopt as their own; and having a teacher who is open, personable, confident, and fully functioning will produce satisfying results.

WHAT VALUES SHOULD THE CHURCH ACCEPT?

At one end of the religious continuum are churches that take the position that it does not matter what values one has or what beliefs one cherishes as long as the person has some values and as long as the person lives by those beliefs. At the other end of the continuum are churches that consider any idea even remotely associated with humanistic thought corrupt by virtue of that association. Both positions are extreme, and neither can be supported from Scripture. Some values *are* basic to the Christian faith and cannot be compromised. In matters of the divinity of Jesus Christ and the inspiration of Scripture no concession can be made. One is not a Christian in the historic sense of the term unless one is a follower of Jesus Christ, and one who follows incorporates within the self the values and beliefs of the one being followed.

But did Jesus not turn toward humanistic concerns? Did He not help those in need, regardless of their position in life? Did He not see the potential in the disciples long before that potential was realized through their association with Him? Did He not say even to the Pharisees, "The kingdom of God is within you"? (Luke 17:21) And did He not come to redeem a people confused by sin though originally created in His own image? Jesus, by His own words and deeds, showed Himself to be a great humanist.

TRANSACTIONAL ANALYSIS

Applying transactional analysis (TA) to the church is the theme of Muriel James' *Born to Love* (1973). Each person may be analyzed in terms of Parent, Adult, and Child ego states, and relationships between individuals or groups may be diagnosed as an interaction between ego states. Why one Sunday School class or church group is successful and another is not is more readily understood if verbal interactions of group members are diagrammed to indicate whether a person is speaking as one in authority (Parent), as one who views events objectively (Adult), or as one coming from a dependent position (Child). Crossed-transactions occur when a message sent from the ego state of one person elicits an unexpected response from the ego state of another. Crossed-transactions lead to misunderstandings and confusion.

Suppose, for instance, that a member of an adult class speaks from the Adult ego state and suggests that lesson material for the next quarter include information on humanism and the technique of transactional analysis. If the teacher responds from the Parent ego state with a diatribe on the evils of humanism, saying that as the teacher of the class he is responsible for keeping heresy out of the church, the result will probably be anger or dismay. The class member making the suggestion may react by thinking, "The teacher knows best and is only trying to help me be a better Christian" (Child), or, "The teacher is speaking from a perspective different than my own because his background and training are different" (Adult), or "The teacher is stupid and I'll show him and the rest of the class that I know more than he does" (Parent). If a church group is to thrive and meet the needs of its members, verbal behavior must change so that tensions and divisions are less apt to occur. Understanding TA is one method for bringing about this change.

I'M OK, YOU'RE OK?

The four psychological positions of I'm OK, you're OK; I'm OK, you're not OK; I'm not OK, you're OK; and I'm not OK, you're not OK may be expressed in the plural in order to examine the attitude of one church or denomination to another. According to Muriel James, churches that are accepting of both themselves and other groups, the We're OK, you're OK position, are healthy and vibrant. They appreciate and respect both their own views and the views of others. The second position of We're OK, you're not OK is adopted by many churches that consider their congregation or denomination to be the one true church, and by comparison other churches and denominations propagate falsehood. This position is one of arrogance, and even though these groups say they love all people, hating only their sin, one cannot tell by their actions that this is so. The third position of We're not OK, you're OK is taken by churches that aspire to greatness by copying the methods of other religious groups. Lacking in confidence, they seem willing to try almost any technique in order to grow and be recognized. "We're not OK, you're not OK" churches soon disintegrate, being of little value to themselves or to others (James, 1973, pp. 92-93).

Members of the church represent different states depending on activities and interests. "TA proposes that we are almost always in one ego state or another. . . . The preacher proclaiming universal sinfulness is in the Critical Parent; the charismatic believer dancing before the Lord in ecstasy is in the Natural Child; the student in a Bible study on major doctrines of the church is in the Adult" (Jones & Butman, 1991, p. 326). Healthy individuals are able to go from one ego state to another, although the adult state is optimal. Unhealthy individuals "play games," that is, they act in such a way that their "not OK" self-concept is confirmed by others.

An analysis of ego states (Parent, Adult, Child) and a working knowledge of the four psychological positions relative to one's worth (e.g., "I'm OK, you're OK") is met with enthusiasm by some ministers and group leaders and strongly opposed by others. Those fascinated by "the games people play" enjoy analyzing their own and other people's speech and find that using a paradigm such as transactional analysis makes for an engaging interpretation of interpersonal relationships. Pastors and seminary students sometimes take courses in counseling and many of these classes are based on humanistic assumptions, thus introducing humanist ideology and humanistic methods into the church.

By contrast, church leaders who oppose humanistic psychology consider transactional analysis to be silly or outright dangerous. They do not wish to have their motives and statements diagnosed, especially if this is done by someone they consider less knowledgeable and less spiritual than themselves. They believe that parishioners should understand the God-ordained hierarchy within the church and should come to the house of worship expecting to be instructed. In TA terminology, this means that the preacher sees the minister's role as Parent and the parishioner's role as Child. There is little room for the Adult, for the one who exhibits a free spirit and independence of thought. Creative ideas and rational analysis are not welcome in many churches if they are perceived as interfering with church polity in any way.

Some congregations assume that to take a position other than "We're OK, you're not OK" will undermine the reason for the existence of their particular group or denomination. Their church is the one true church, stemming directly from apostolic times and blessed in a special way by God. That so many churches make the same claim does not bother those who "know" they have the truth. It does, however, result in considerable confusion for the seeker after truth, for the one who has not yet found the way.

Although it may be said that the "I'm OK, you're OK" attitude has invaded some churches to such an extent that there is no longer any basis for judging right and wrong, and this is not in keeping with the Word of God, it also can be said that the church cannot become the healing community it is supposed to be until all individuals are afforded the respect and dignity befitting one made in the image of God.

So, the church family will pray together and worship together and celebrate in song, waiting for the day when our potential will be fully realized, for "we shall be like Him, for we shall see Him as He is" (1 John 3:2).

NOTES

1. I am indebted to my graduate assistant, Nancy Kiger, for this information. Mrs. Kiger's three children all enjoyed Magic Circle when in Gayle Reiter's class.

2. Other sources providing suggestions and exercises for using the valuing process within the church are as follows: *Instructor's resource book for redesigning man: Science and human value* (1974), San Francisco: Harper & Row. McEniry, R. (1982), Values clarification: An aid to adolescent religious education, *Counseling and Values, 27*, 40–51. Savary, L.M. (1974), *Integrating values: Theory and exercises for clarifying religious values*, Dayton, OH: Pflaum. Simon, S.B., Daitch, P., & Hartwell, M. (1973), Value clarification: New mission for religious education, in S.B. Simon & H. Kirschenbaum (Eds.), *Readings in values clarification* (pp. 241–246), Minneapolis: Winston.

REFERENCES

AHA's statement on the family. (1980). *The Humanist, 40*(5), 40.

Anthony, M.J. (1991). Humanism in American Christian education. *Christian Education Journal, 12*(1), 79–88.

Barr, D.L. (1974, September). Is "moral education" possible? *Eternity,* pp. 17, 19–20, 26.

Bessell, H., & Palomares, U. (1973). *Methods in human development theory manual.* San Diego: Human Development Training Institute.

Brownfield, R. (1973). Those old-time values. In H. Kirschenbaum & S.B. Simon (Eds.), *Readings in values clarification* (pp. 231–236). Minneapolis: Winston Press.

Bruner, J.S. (1966). *Toward a theory of instruction.* Cambridge, MA: Harvard University Press.

Charny, I.W. (1974). The new psychotherapies and encounters of the seventies: Progress or fads? *The Humanist. 34*(3), 4–9.

Chazan, B. (1985). *Contemporary approaches to moral education: Analyzing alternative theories.* New York: Teachers College Press.

Combs, A.W. (1981). Humanistic education: Too tender for a tough world? *Phi Delta Kappan, 62,* 446–449.

Curry, N.E., & Johnson, C.N. (1990). *Beyond self-esteem: Developing a genuine sense of human value.* Washington, DC: National Association for the Education of Young Children.

Goldbecker, S.S. (1976). *Values teaching.* Washington, DC: National Education Association.

Hall, B.P., & Smith, M. (1973). *Value education as learning process: A handbook for religious educators.* New York: Paulist Press.

Hall, R.T. (1976). Moral education: A bicentennial defense. *The Humanist, 36*(2), 44–45.

———. (1978). Moral education and secular humanism. *The Humanist, 38*(6), 7.

Harmin, M., Kirschenbaum, H., & Simon, S.B. (1973). *Clarifying values through subject matter: Applications for the classroom.* Minneapolis: Winston.

Hendricks, W. (1984). *Values: Suggested activities to motivate the teaching of values clarification.* Stevensville, MI: Educational Service.

James, M.M. (1973). *Born to love: Transactional analysis in the church.* Reading, MA: Addison-Wesley.

Jones, S.L., & Butman, R.E. (1991). *Modern psychotherapies: A comprehensive approach.* Downers Grove, IL: InterVarsity.

Kilby, R.W. (1993). *The study of human values.* Lanham, MD: University Press of America.

Kirschenbaum, H. (1976). Dialog: Howard Kirschenbaum talks with Lisa Kuhmerker. *Moral Education Forum, 1*(5), 1, 4–6.

―――――. (1992). A comprehensive model for values education and moral education. *Phi Delta Kappan, 73,* 771–776.

Larson, R.S., & Larson, D.E. (1976). *Values and faith: Activities for family and church groups.* Minneapolis: Winston.

Lockwood, A.L. (1978). The effects of values clarification and moral development curricula on school-age subjects: A critical review of recent research. *Review of Educational Research, 48,* 325–364.

Perlmutter, R. (1980). *The effects of the values clarification process on the moral and ego development of high school students.* Unpublished doctoral dissertation, Boston University.

Prakash, M.S. (1988). "Desires" clarified, much of "value": A plea for values clarification. *Journal of Moral Education, 17,* 114–126.

Simon, S.B. (1973). Three ways to teach church school. In S.B. Simon & H. Kirschenbaum (Eds.), *Readings in values clarification* (pp. 237–240). Minneapolis: Winston.

Simon, S.B., & deSherbinin, P. (1975). Values clarification: It can start gently and grow deep. *Phi Delta Kappan, 56,* 679–683.

Simon, S.B., & Olds, S.W. (1976). *Helping your child learn right from wrong: A guide to values clarification.* New York: Simon & Schuster.

Yablonsky, L. (1976). *Psychodrama: Resolving emotional conflicts through role-playing.* New York: Basic Books.

PART III

PSYCHOLOGY AND
CHRISTIANITY

TWELVE

The Psychology of Moral Growth and Christian Belief

Historically, orthodox Christianity has been a religion of faith, faith in Jesus Christ as Lord and in the Holy Scriptures as the inspired Word of God, the only unerring guide of faith and morals. Psychology, as a science, is not prepared to deal with "faith" but has shown, however, an increasing interest in the area of morality and in the methods for assessing moral development.

In this book, we have looked at traditional methods for enhancing moral growth — methods that have stood the test of time: storytelling, the authority of Scripture, and character education. We also studied four major psychologies: psychoanalysis, learning psychology, cognitive psychology, and humanistic psychology. We noted that each psychology emphasizes a different expression of morality, begins with different assumptions as to the nature of humankind, and employs different techniques for enhancing moral growth.

In this chapter we will delve more deeply into ways each of these four psychologies relate to Christian belief. We will see that each theory finds support from Scripture and each theory has elements that are not in agreement with what the Bible teaches. At the end of this chapter we

361

will summarize briefly what we have learned, endeavoring to answer the question: How shall we then teach?

PSYCHOANALYSIS AND CHRISTIAN BELIEF

DEPRAVITY AND SIN

Freudian psychology and Christian theology both begin with the premise that the condition of the human race is one of depravity. Each person comes into the world imperfect and in need of salvation. Freud saw the newborn as having irrational passions and instincts and being oriented to pleasure; but as children grow older they learn to adjust to the world, adopting the mores and restrictions of the society, and in this way they become better persons. Older children are easier to live with because they have learned to consider the wants and needs of others as well as their own, and their behavior is in line with what will benefit the social order.

> The concept of sin in Christian theology resembles the psychoanalytic view of irrational passions and instincts insofar as sin is wanting one's way and caring for self more than for others. But the Christian understanding of sin goes beyond the psychoanalytic understanding of depravity.

Freud believed, though, that underneath the surface of propriety the depraved portion of the personality remains, and throughout one's life it waits like a volcano ready to erupt whenever the opportunity is given. Anxiety is one's lot when sexual and aggressive urges are denied expression, and punishment becomes one's lot when these urges are released in socially unacceptable ways, so that whether people repress their desires or allow them demonstration they are anxious and fearful. Violence and war occur when the molten lava of instinctive desires finds a crack in the surface of the unconscious and breaks through to gratification, spewing out hatred and vengeance and destroying everything in its path. Freud recognized that it is not only the will to transgress that gets us into trouble but also the failure of the will to control the universal impulse to transgress.

The concept of sin in Christian theology resembles the psychoanalytic view of irrational passions and instincts insofar as sin is wanting one's way and caring for self more than for others. But the Christian understanding of sin goes beyond the psychoanalytic understanding of depravity. Sin is alienation from God as well as alienation from others. Sin is missing God's standard of perfection as well as failing to meet society's expectation of good conduct. "In the Old and New Testaments . . . sin is missing the mark, badness, rebellion, iniquity, going astray, wickedness, wandering, ungodliness, crime, lawlessness, transgression, ignorance, and a falling away" (Ryrie, 1986, p. 212).

The Christian knows that the purpose of life is more than coping with a real world, for one can gain the whole world and lose his own soul (Matt. 16:26). The purpose of life is to have a meaningful relationship with the Creator and Redeemer, and this is possible only by salvation in Christ Jesus. Nevertheless, the sinful portion of the personality remains even though we want to please God. "If we claim to be without sin, we deceive ourselves and the truth is not in us" (1 John 1:8). The inclination to transgress the law of God persists so that we must depend on Him who is "faithful and just and will forgive us our sins" (v. 9).

Defensive Reactions to the Concept of Depravity

The psychoanalytic concept of depravity and the Christian doctrine of sin is offensive to those who adopt the philosophy of learning psychology that people start out neither good nor bad but become whatever they are made to be by the environment. It also is offensive to those who adhere to the philosophy of humanistic psychology that people are naturally good and have within themselves the ability to become self-actualized. To both the behaviorist and the humanist it is an affront to the influence of the society (as in the case of the learning theorist) or to the dignity and worth of humankind (as in the case of the humanist) to say that the environment cannot make people what they should be or that people cannot make themselves what they should be. If this is true, what hope is there, then, for the human race? Is it not pessimistic and even morose to see people in need of alteration when neither the world around them nor the world within them can bring about the needed changes?

Depravity Ameliorated as the Child Matures

Freud's response would be that even though people start out with little to commend them to others, a combination of social mandates and their own adjustment to these enables them to become better persons. It is not one but both forces at work—a force without and a force within. The society demands compliance, and the person demands satisfaction of individual needs. Together they struggle while the ego makes compromises between them. At first the compromises take the form of defense mechanisms, but later, as the person matures, the ego will shed its defenses and will find ways to cope that are more rational and less apt to produce neurotic consequences. In this way, even though children are born depraved, they become more goodly persons.

But the balance between id, ego, and superego remains a delicate one. If the scales are tipped too far in the direction of the id, the result is sociopathy; if the scales are tipped too far in the direction of the superego, the result is neuroses. In Freudian psychology the ego must remain strong, keeping both id and superego in their proper places. And, because the balance is delicate and because the ego often falters in its mission or may never be strong in the first place, Freud did not hold much hope for the human race. The charge that psychoanalysis is pessimistic is probably warranted.

Sin Forgiven by a Holy God

The Christian message, in contradistinction, is one of hope and promise. We learn from the Bible that an all-powerful, all-loving God has chosen to free us from the bondage of sin. We cannot save ourselves, for we have neither the ability nor the inclination to do so, so that without Him we can do nothing (John 15:5). Nor can the society save us for it too is evil (1 John 5:19). Only in Christ, a force greater than ourselves and greater than the social order, can salvation be found.

THE CASE OF SANDRA

The case study approach is the one used by psychoanalysts to communicate with each other as to how therapy sessions proceed and to discuss what analytic methods appear to be most effective with certain types of neuroses. In a book entitled, *Great Cases in Psychoanalysis,* we read about Sandra (Slavson, 1973).

Sandra is described as an intelligent and attractive sixteen-year-old referred for treatment through the New York City police department who apprehended her after a runaway escapade with another girl, Helen. Often truant from school, Sandra stayed away from home overnight on a number of occasions and picked up sailors on the street. In therapy, Sandra told the analyst that she had a harmonious family life, but this was far from the truth. Her parents quarreled constantly, the father being authoritarian and abusive and the mother accepting her "inferior" position as wife while openly having sexual relations with other men. Both parents considered Sandra to be a "troublemaker" and favored her older sisters. On the positive side, Sandra showed unusual talent in music and art and hoped some day to be an accomplished musician.

One night Sandra had a dream. She was at the piano practicing when a small ape stood near her and distracted her. Thoroughly irritated, she ran to her mother's room for help but the ape followed her. Finally, she struck the ape and it sank its teeth into her arm. The ape then became Helen who told her not to practice the piano anymore.

Sandra interpreted the dream herself. She said that practicing the piano showed she wanted to make something of herself and be a good person. The ape, Helen, was holding her back. (Helen, of low mentality, had induced Sandra to go on blind dates, pick up sailors, run away from home, and participate in other delinquent acts.) The psychoanalyst, faithful to his training, asked Sandra if the ape might not be her father with whom she experienced a love-hate relationship. Sandra then remembered that when she was quite small her father had made monkey faces at her.

The psychiatrist also analyzed that Helen was a "displacement" for Sandra's father, Helen being both loved (interpreted as latent homosexuality) and hated (because she typified evil). Sandra was diagnosed as having a "behavior disorder, pre-Oedipal group, conduct type." The recommendation was for Sandra to remain in therapy in order to strengthen her "weak ego" so she would be able to face her difficulties rather than run from them.

Although each case is different, Sandra's experience is typical of what occurs during the therapy session. The focus of psychoanalysis is on the sexual nature of one's being, especially as it relates to the parent of the opposite sex. This, in turn, is said to affect one's relationship with others. By bringing into awareness unconscious processes, analyst and patient together can deal with the problem. In Sandra's case the id was too strong and the ego and superego were too weak. This brought her into conflict with a society that demands certain behaviors.

The purpose of analysis is to resolve the conflicts — conflicts between evil and good, between an id that demands gratification of sensual and aggressive desires and a superego that wants to please the society in which one lives. The ego needs to be strengthened to make the necessary decisions. A mature ego is able to understand the nature of instinctual demands and the coercion of outside constraints and achieve an optimal balance between them. The person can then go about his or her daily life as a productive and satisfied individual.

This brings us to the question of how psychoanalysis compares with Christian conversion. Was Sandra's experience in therapy in any way similar to what happens when someone comes to Jesus Christ for salvation?

Those of us who have experienced the redeeming love of God know what it means to be converted even though we express it in different ways. We say we have been "born again," passed from darkness into light, or become a new creation in Christ Jesus. Our life is changed and everything is seen in a new light. Whether our conversion was sudden and dramatic like that of the Apostle Paul, slow and deliberate like that of Nicodemus, inquisitive and spontaneous like that of the woman at the well, we know that a remarkable event has taken place. Or, perhaps, like Timothy, we were fortunate in having been raised in a Christian home and cannot remember a time we did not believe, but we do remember when we responded to that special call to serve God and to commit our lives to Him.

Had we engaged the services of a psychoanalyst would it have been the same? Would we have completed therapy with the same emotions, the same cognitions, the same purpose that we now have as children of God? The answer is obvious but let us look more closely at the distinctions.

THERAPY AND CONVERSION

Both analytic therapy and Christian conversion would redeem from evil, and both would help the anxious person enter into a state of well-being. But the procedures differ, evil is not defined in the same way, and what constitutes well-being also is at variance. Psychoanalysis brings unconscious processes into consciousness where they can be dealt with by the ego. Christian conversion brings both the unconscious and the conscious into the light of God's Word where they can be dealt with by an omniscient God. Psychoanalysis uses the method of free-association; Christian conversion uses the method of confession. One deals with guilt feelings, the other with guilt. One provides a release from emotional tension enabling the person to come to terms with himself or herself and with the society; the other provides a release from the power of sin enabling the person to come to terms with a holy and righteous God. One brings a cathartic release; the other brings atonement. One puts the ego in charge; the other puts Christ in charge.

A person may benefit from psychoanalytic therapy, but the limitations of psychoanalysis should be recognized, and one should not confuse its methods or results with Christian salvation. Psychoanalysis saves people from the evil of neuroses; Christianity saves people from the evil of enmity against God. Well-being in psychoanalysis is a state of normalcy in which id, ego, and superego are all in the right relationship to each other. Well-being in Christianity is more than a regrouping of forces already present within the personality. It is being made a new creation in Christ (2 Cor. 5:17). "God is not satisfied with 'the given' in man. He demands something new and creates the new. The creative spiritual aptitudes which are released are not a given quantum of energy doled out to everyone and reserved in the subconscious. There are inexhaustible resources in the love of the living God, and his encounter with man is not a matter of bringing antithetical drives into harmony, but the recreating of a new life" (Runestam, 1958, p. 123).

In psychoanalysis the person comes to know the self better, and through the process of transference with the analyst is aided in the search for better mental health. In Christian conversion the person also comes to know the self better and through the process of transference with Christ comes to see the self as God would see it and is aided in the quest for spiritual well-being.

Conflict in Therapy and Conversion

Both mental and spiritual health are preceded by anguish of the soul. Conflict occurs when people see what they are really like in comparison with what they should and would like to be. Just as it is conflict that brings one to the psychoanalytic couch, it is conflict that brings one to Christ. Conflict is at the core of all changed behavior. But in psychoanalysis the conflict is between the natural desires one is heir to and the cultural restrictions needed to assure the survival of the society. In Christian theology, however, the conflict is between the old nature that is sinful and the new nature that is righteous. Both neuroses and sin produce inner turmoil, and both neuroses and sin render the person an unfinished product crying out for completion. But in psychoanalytic therapy the benefits extend only to this earthly life, whereas in redemption through Jesus Christ the benefits extend throughout eternity. An important ingredient and distinctive of the Christian hope is knowing that our salvation will last forever (1 Cor. 15:19).

> Conflict occurs when people see what they are really like in comparison with what they should and would like to be. Just as it is conflict that brings one to the psychoanalytic couch, it is conflict that brings one to Christ.

Law and Grace

Freudian psychoanalysis condemns more than it forgives; it restricts more than it liberates. Catholic theologian Albert Ple (1976) speaks to this point. "Morality according to Freud appears . . . to be a morality of law, composed of prohibitions, restraints of the instincts, and source of obsessive guilt. . . . The morality of the Gospel . . . requires that one should be animated by love . . . that liberates from sin" (p. 103). Psychoanalyst Erich Fromm (1980) puts it succinctly when he says, "Freud's therapeutic aim was control of instinctual drives through the strengthening of the ego . . . *there is no place for grace*" (emphasis mine) (p. 7).

Without grace, where would we be? Without grace the Apostle Paul could not have said after his moral and spiritual struggle recorded in Romans 7, "There is now no condemnation for those who are in Christ Jesus, because through Christ Jesus the law of the Spirit of life set me free from the law of sin and death" (Rom. 8:1-2). The Christian message is one of grace — "For it is by grace you have been saved through faith — and this not from yourselves, it is the gift of God" (Eph. 2:8).

COMPONENTS OF THE PERSONALITY IN PSYCHOANALYSIS AND IN SCRIPTURE

In comparing psychoanalysis with Christian doctrine, one is inclined initially to equate the id with the baser desires of the flesh, the ego with the will or mind of humans, and the superego with the nobler virtues of the spirit. But the analogies do not hold.[1] There are commonalities, to be sure — the id being self-serving and impulsive, the ego making decisions and coping with the challenges of the day, and the superego feeling guilt and the need to confess — but there are differences as well. Within the id is love as well as hate, self-preservation and procreation of the species (which are not condemned in Scripture) as well as selfishness and aggression. And, some of the desires of the flesh could be better relegated to the ego than to the id.

Id and Flesh?

Clinical psychologist Paul Meehl (1958) speaks to this point.

> Some pastoral counselors, overeager to make the Freudian lion lie down with the Christian lamb, have made an incautious identification of the two. . . . An example would be Freud's concept of the id and the Christian concept of original sin. . . . Now insofar as the imperious demand for impulse gratification is a property of the id, the id is like "the flesh" in New Testament language . . . but a complete identification of the concepts can certainly not be defended. For one thing . . . avarice, pride, and envy are works of the flesh, theologically speaking. From the Freudian point of view none of these could possibly be found in the id. Pride, for example, is a manifestation of the "ego's narcissism" in Freud's system and is therefore relegated to the ego, which is contrasted with the id. (p. 168)

Ego and Will?

By the same token, the Freudian ego cannot be equated with "the will of man" (John 1:13, KJV) as given in Scripture. Both ego and will involve decision-making, but in analytic theory a strong ego that weighs the demands of the id and the restrictions of the superego and makes a decision as to the best course of action is the mark of the psychologically healthy person; whereas in Christian theology a strong will is not the mark of a person committed to Christ. Rather, spiritually healthy people know they are not capable alone of making the right decisions and that they must turn to God for direction (James 1:5). Although there need be no quarrel with the Freudian concept of the ego when taken on the human level, the ego being recognized as important by psychoanalysts who are Christians as well as by psychoanalysts who are not Christians; nevertheless, the ego will not bring one into the kingdom. The ego is restricted to the social order, whereas the will or volition given to people by God taps the very source of wisdom that is from above.

Superego and Conscience?

Likewise, the superego is not the same as the fruit of the Spirit nor should the superego be confused with the conscience of the Bible. The superego is heir of the Oedipus complex and remains a part of the personality throughout life, yet it becomes less important as the person matures and the ego is substituted in its place. The conscience, however, is not a product of human development but is given by God as a natural property and becomes more sensitive as the person matures in the Christian life (Acts 24:16). The believer does not outgrow the need for a conscience but rather uses it as a basis for decision-making.

> According to the NT, man has in the depths of his personality a moral monitor which sin has affected but not destroyed, placing him in touch with the objective moral order of the universe. That order is translated into human awareness by means of the conscience. That it does not arise from the cultural mores can be seen when men press for moral reforms that directly challenge the existing social patterns. (Pinnock, 1973, p. 127)

Another way of comparing the superego with the conscience is to see the effect each has on the personality. Gregory Zilboorg (1962), a student of Freud and psychoanalyst, wrote:

> The origin of the superego lies in the child's ambivalence and fear. And conscience is not made up of fear, but of regret for having done something wrong. The superego is by its nature unforgiving; it is the epitome of aggression and hatred. The superego cannot be quieted; it can only be pacified. . . . Conscience *regrets,* where the superego is *angry.* Conscience glows with hope when its owner repents and makes amends. (p. 187)

William May (1975) compared the superego and the conscience by describing the superego as "past-oriented: primarily concerned with cleaning up the record with regard to past acts" and the conscience as "future oriented: creative; sees the past as having a future." The superego "commands that an act be performed for approval, in order to make oneself loveable"; the conscience "invites to action, to love." The superego has the "urge to be punished"; the conscience "sees the need to repair" (pp. 56-57).

The superego, then, is blind, dictatorial, internalized during the first few years of the child's life, and yet essential for the continuance of a civilized world. But once internalized it produces anxiety and feelings of guilt that in some people become chronic.[2] The superego is sensitive to the social order but insensitive to the psychological health of the person. Needed is what the Apostle Paul calls "a pure heart, a good conscience, and a sincere faith" (1 Tim. 1:5). This combination of virtues makes for good relationships with others (Rom. 14:1-23) and contributes to both psychological and spiritual well-being.

THE CERTAINTY OF CONFLICT

Sigmund Freud dealt with the great issues of all time, issues of life and death, of good and evil, and of the human struggle to satisfy personal desires while living in a world replete with restrictions and taboos. Conflict is inevitable and although essential for social and moral development, nevertheless brings misery and neuroses. Conflict begins in the cradle and continues to the grave when life is no more.

The Christian also knows conflict and struggles with the issues of life and death, good and evil, self and others. But the Christian believer has the Spirit of God within that enables him or her to emerge victorious. We learn that it is only as we lose our life for Christ's sake that we will find it (Mark 8:35), that the battle is not against flesh and blood but against the spiritual forces of evil (Eph. 6:12), and that life does not end with the grave but lasts forever (John 3:15). And so we count it as joy when the inevitable conflict comes, knowing that the "present sufferings are not worth comparing with the glory that will be revealed" (Rom. 8:18). The whole creation waits in eager anticipation for the time when it will be liberated and brought into "the glorious freedom of the children of God" (v. 21).

LEARNING PSYCHOLOGY AND CHRISTIAN BELIEF

Whereas psychoanalytic theory would look at the child as depraved and in need of changes that occur by relating to a world of reality (ego) and to the internalization of the mores of the society (superego); another theory, referred to as stimulus-response (S-R) or learning psychology, takes quite a different perspective. Learning psychologists believe that rather than being depraved, children start out neutral. Basically no one is either good or bad to begin with; rather, we become good or bad depending on the kind of environment in which we are raised.

THE ENVIRONMENT IS ALL-IMPORTANT

If we grow up in a good environment, we learn to be good; if we grow up in a bad environment, we learn to be bad. In other words, we *learn* to be what we are made to be by the environmental conditions in which we find ourselves.

> **If we grow up in a good environment, we learn to be good; if we grow up in a bad environment, we learn to be bad. In other words, we *learn* to be what we are made to be by the environmental conditions in which we find ourselves.**

In chapter 6 we noted Watson's claim that if he were given a dozen healthy infants, he could take any one of them at random and make him any kind of person he desired. He said he could do this because there is no inherent difference in babies. They all have at birth the same capacity, talent, temperament, and mental constitution. What he was saying, in essence, was that if he were allowed to control the stimuli or environmental events the child grew up in, he could guarantee certain responses or behavior patterns in adulthood.

Although Watson's statement would be considered extreme by many learning psychologists today, it nevertheless expresses much of the emphasis of current S-R theorists—an emphasis not on individual differences as they relate to behavior or on ages and stages which come about by the maturing of the biological organism, but rather on the effect of the environment as it relates to the growing and developing child. If we are not pleased with the behavior of the child, we can rearrange the events of the child's life in such a way as to obtain the behavior we desire.

SOCIETY DECIDES WHAT IS GOOD AND WHAT IS BAD

B.F. Skinner held that it is society that determines what is moral and immoral, and this determination is based on what benefits the society and what harms it. Actions such as telling the truth, helping those in need, and acting responsibly benefit the social order, enabling it to grow strong. Actions such as robbery, rape, and murder are harmful to the society and result in its destruction.

But the question we may ask is whether societies are sufficiently perceptive and virtuous that they are in a position to make a judgment of this magnitude. Are not societies, like individuals, warped by sin and unable to see the many injustices that are part of the social order? Poverty, racism, and sexism are condemned in much of our Western society (although they are not considered evils in some places in the world); yet, greed and aggression are so woven into the social fabric of our own Western civilization that these evils appear to be accepted without question by most citizens. Does not our society measure success by wealth and power, happiness by full acceptance of self and others, and psychological adjustment by freedom from guilt and being responsible only for ourselves? Are these values best for the society? Are they in keeping with what the Bible teaches? And is the preservation of the society, in and of itself, the greatest good? Could there be a cause that is higher than this present world?

LEARNING PSYCHOLOGY AND SCRIPTURE

The terminology used in learning psychology, as in most of the field, would not be found in Scripture. However, examples or illustrations of the principles of learning psychology may be readily seen in the Bible and are of interest to those of us who see a link between psychology and what the Scriptures teach.

Classical Conditioning and Scripture

In the Old Testament, signs were used to remind the people of God of the times when Jehovah had intervened on their behalf in some miraculous way. By pairing the sign (conditioned stimulus) with the event (unconditioned stimulus), the Children of Israel were made aware of God's blessing long after the miracle had taken place. The sign also served as an object lesson by which the next generation would learn the story of deliverance. "When your descendants ask . . . 'What do these stones mean?' tell them. . . . The Lord your God did to the Jordan just what he had done to the Red Sea. . . . He did this so that all the people of the earth might know that the hand of the Lord is powerful and so that you might always fear the Lord your God" (Josh. 4:21-24).

In the New Testament, as well, signs and ordinances were instituted to remind believers of important events. The star seen by the wise men was a sign that the Messiah had come. And long after the Messiah had fulfilled His purpose on earth and had returned to the Father, Christians were admonished to come together to remind one another of Christ's death and coming again, even as Christ had met with His disciples on the day of the Passover. "The Lord Jesus, on the night he was betrayed, took bread, and when he had given thanks, he broke it and said, 'This is my body, which is for you: do this in remembrance of me.' . . . For whenever you eat this bread and drink this cup, you proclaim the Lord's death until he comes" (1 Cor. 11:23-24, 26).

In classical conditioning, the conditioned stimulus is not to be equated with the unconditioned stimulus but rather serves as a reminder of the unconditioned or original event. In the same way, the sign or ordinance in Scripture is not the event itself but is given to the people of God to refresh their memories of past deliverance and future blessing. Readily visible conditioned stimuli are needed to help us retain an image of God's workings in our lives and to keep before us the more remote, but nevertheless important, hallmarks of Christian experience. Without tangible reminders we soon forget, and without behavioral opportunities to respond to the reminders we often become neglectful.

Instrumental Conditioning and Scripture
Reinforcers also are needed so that we "never tire of doing what is right" (2 Thes. 3:13). God made us and knows what we are like. He knows that we will continue those behaviors for which we are rewarded and discontinue those behaviors for which we are punished; so, in His Word He offers blessings (reinforcers) dependent upon acts of obedi-

ence and curses (punishers) contingent upon acts of disobedience. In the Christian life, as with all of life, the reinforcers and punishers do not always occur at the moment of behavior, making it difficult for us to stay on course. We may look around and feel as did the psalmist that it is the wicked who prospers and the righteous who in vain keeps his heart pure (Ps. 73:13). To offset this confusion of the temporal with the eternal, David went to the sanctuary of God and after contemplation came to an understanding of one's final destiny (v. 17).

We too are asked to go to the house of the Lord, to meet with other believers, and to look forward to the time when God's final blessing will be revealed — a time when we will receive "the crown of righteousness" (2 Tim. 4:8).

> We are told to pair the social reinforcement of praise, encouragement, and comfort with the rewards that await us in heaven to motivate us toward good deeds. . . . The social reinforcement of speaking confidently, associated with the hope of eternal life, provides an incentive for desirable behavior. . . . These reinforcers may also serve as discriminative stimuli for the primary reinforcement of Christ's return. (Bolin & Goldberg, 1979, pp. 171-172)

SOCIAL LEARNING AND SCRIPTURE

It is well known that children learn to act in accordance with what they observe. The homes they are born into in large measure determine whether they are honest or dishonest, cooperative or competitive, mild or aggressive. If children are given affection, they learn to love. If parents enjoy their children, the children, in turn, will learn to appreciate their parents. If parents are patient, children learn to be tolerant. And, if parents follow the biblical command to diligently teach their children "the commands, decrees and laws" (Deut. 6:1) of the Lord, the children will inquire as to the meaning of the decrees and laws (v. 20). Obedience to the law in terms of overt behavior is the ultimate of what God asks of His people, promising them that obedience will be their righteousness (v. 25).

One of the ways in which we encourage one another to good works is to live a life that is pleasing to God. The Scriptures provide examples of such a life. We learn "patience" from the prophets (James 5:10), "endurance" from Job (v. 11), "sound speech" from the minister (Titus 2:8), and the importance of hard work from the Apostle Paul (2 Thes. 3:7-9). A whole roster of men and women who lived by faith is given for us in Hebrews 11. But it is only when we look to Jesus that we see the perfect model, for it is only in Jesus that we see a perfect life. In Him alone we find forgiveness and healing, holiness and the promise of eternal life. And in Him we find love — love that covers a multitude of sins. Paul told the believers at Ephesus to "live a life of love, just as Christ loved us" (Eph. 5:2).

In *The Jesus Model,* David McKenna (1977) explains why Jesus as our model is of prime importance.

> Christian Faith pivots on a person — Jesus of Nazareth. . . . As the Son of God, he claimed to be our Lord; as the Son of Man, he claimed to be our Model; and as fully God and fully man, he claimed to be our Redeemer. When the case of Christianity is presented in the secular world, the authority of Jesus as Lord and Redeemer carries the weight of the argument. . . . In response, we cannot forget that Jesus' claim to be the Son of Man holds equal authority in the Christian portfolio. If Jesus was a real and complete man who participated fully in the human experience, then he must be our model and our hope. Anything less and the case for Christianity is dismissed. (pp. 13-14)

The Christian hope is that someday "we shall be like him, for we shall see him as he is" (1 John 3:2), and even though we presently fall short of exemplifying Christ in our lives, we can look forward to that wonderful day when we will indeed be like Him.

LEARNING PSYCHOLOGY BELIEVED AND PRACTICED — CAN WE SEPARATE THE TWO?

Psychologists and theologians interested in relating learning psychology and Christian belief have taken sides on the issue of whether the philosophy underlying behaviorism and the technology practiced by behaviorists are so inextricably linked that an acceptance (or rejection) of one mandates an acceptance (or rejection) of the other. McKeown (1981) states that theory and methodology cannot be divorced, for "to embrace 'methodological behaviorism' implicitly means accepting theoretical behaviorism because one incorporates its language and its metaphysics" (pp. 18-19). Vos (1978) likewise writes that "an application of behavioral psychology cannot disown its commitment to the thesis that the environment alone is a cause in human affairs. This thesis contradicts what is both implied in and asserted by biblical principles, namely, that man is an agent, free and responsible" (p. 210).

The majority opinion (Bolin & Goldberg, 1979; Bufford, 1978; Collins, 1977; Cosgrove, 1982; Hammes, 1973; Llewellyn, 1973; MacKay, 1979; Steckel, 1979), however, is that philosophical behaviorism and technological behaviorism differ, and that when each is compared with Christian belief the philosophy of behaviorism is incompatible with Christianity, whereas the technology of behaviorism is consistent with Scripture and reflects the way in which God created us. This view is expressed in a variety of ways. Donald MacKay (1979) uses the terms *negative behaviourism* and *positive behaviourism,* negative behaviorism being "behaviouristic *philosophy* as distinct from science" and "characterized by what it *denies.* . . . Religious values are downgraded to mere 'reinforcers.' . . . Freedom of choice is held to be an illusion." Positive behaviorism, by contrast, "is theologically neutral and not of itself at all inimical to human dignity" (p. 47). Gary Collins (1977) writes, "The scientist and the theologian might disagree over behaviorism, mechanistic determinism, or the irrelevance of religion, but this is a conflict not so much over empirical facts as over the presuppositions that guide one's data-gathering and interpretation of facts" (p. 109). Russell Llewellyn (1973) puts it succinctly when he says, "Skinner as science is great. Skinner as religion is terrible" (p. 7).[3]

LEARNING PSYCHOLOGY AND CHRISTIAN BELIEF CONTRASTED

That behavioral philosophy and Christian belief differ is readily apparent. One holds that children are born neither good nor bad but learn to be what they are made to be by the environment; the other holds that children come into the world with a natural propensity for wrongdoing, and even the best of environments will not bring an about-face. One says that morality is moral behavior; the other says it is an inward condition, and overt behaviors are a manifestation of that inward state (Matt. 23:25-26). One believes that people are moral if they advance the cause of the social order; the other believes that people are moral if they advance the cause of the kingdom of God (6:33). For one, goodness is submitting self-interests to the well-being of the group; for the other, goodness is submitting self-interests to the plan and will of God (Rom. 12:1-2). One has dispossessed autonomous man (Skinner, 1971); the other has witnessed the Fall of man because humans were given autonomy by God and made the wrong choice. Yet, it is the freedom of choice that offers hope, as once again through Christ's sacrificial death, we are offered "the gift of righteousness" (Rom. 5:17).

LEARNING PSYCHOLOGY AND CHRISTIAN BELIEF COMPARED
Ideological differences, as great as they may be, do not negate the fact that God created us as beings who respond to reinforcers and punishers in our environment and who have a natural inclination to imitate the behaviors of the people around us. The learning approach, although deficient in terms of *a priori* principles, is, nevertheless, an informative source to help us understand ourselves and others. By being knowledgeable of the techniques used and applying them appropriately as the occasion demands, we can enhance God's plan in the lives of those entrusted to our care and demonstrate by our actions that we belong to Him (James 2:18). Morality as moral behavior is an important ingredient of the Christian life.

COGNITIVE PSYCHOLOGY AND CHRISTIAN BELIEF
Cognitive psychologists would say that both psychoanalysts and learning psychologists place too much emphasis on the environment and not enough emphasis on people as perceptive, creative, and active organisms able to organize their world in meaningful and constructive ways. "Psychodynamic theory places that dominant weight on early environment and family. . . . Behaviourism places dominant weight on the environment as the shaper of the person." By contrast, "to the extent that Kohlberg is rooted in Piaget, he brings forward the observation that the person is not trapped in the environment as a victim. . . . The result is a high view of the freedom of persons to respond to external events and environments in ways that enhance self-worth and predict diversity" (Joy, 1986, p. 404).

When God created the world, He said, "Let us make man in our image, in our likeness" (Gen. 1:26). Rationality is part of the divine image and has an ethical component. We read that we are not to be like other created beings who have no understanding (Ps. 32:9) or as children who lack knowledge (1 Cor. 14:20). Rather, we are to be as adults in our thinking processes. As Christians we are admonished to set our minds on things above, to be renewed in knowledge in the image of the Creator, and to let the Word of Christ dwell in us richly in all wisdom (Col. 3:16).

COGNITIVE PSYCHOLOGY AND SPIRITUAL GROWTH

The Scriptures present numerous comparisons between cognitive development and spiritual growth. For example, as children become adept in the use of language, they develop the capacity for verbal exchange, words become internalized, and thought processes emerge. Likewise, Christian development thrives in an atmosphere of thinking upon the Scriptures and on that which pertains to Christ. New believers may accept without question the doctrines of the church, even as children in Piaget's stage of heteronomy may accept without question a morality taught them by their parents. However, if spiritual growth is to take place, Christians must study God's Word for themselves and decide which doctrinal beliefs to keep and which to reject, even as children who proceed from heteronomy to autonomy must come to their own conclusions as to what is right and what is wrong. The processes of heteronomy and autonomy "might mingle and overlap more or less" (Piaget, 1932, p. 171) as the believer accepts some external constraints while internal controls are developing.

Morality by definition is never imposed, and belief in Jesus Christ is never mandated. God wants us to choose freely — to decide for ourselves. He gave us minds — minds that can accept or reject, believe or disbelieve, love or hate. He knew full well that by giving Adam and Eve the freedom to choose, there would be unleashed infinite possibilities for evil. But that is the risk God was willing to take for He wanted those who follow Him to do so freely, not as robots who obey their masters without giving thought to the matter.

THE TEACHINGS OF JESUS AND PIAGET'S CONCEPT OF MORAL MATURITY[4]

There are marked similarities between our Lord's teachings and Piaget's concept of moral maturity (Clouse, 1981). Jesus taught the importance of *intentionality* by saying that we should look at the thoughts and intents of the heart rather than at outward forms and ceremonies (Matt.

23:27). He practiced *relativism* in judgment for He knew everyone's thoughts and was aware of all possible views (12:25). He showed that right and wrong may be *independent of sanctions* by teaching that the weightier matters of justice, mercy, and honesty are more important than the Pharisees' interpretations of the law (23:23). In the Sermon on the Mount He taught a *reciprocity* that called for a turning of the other cheek, going the extra mile, and loving the enemy (5:39-44), thus surpassing Piaget's view of autonomy and even of equity.

> **Jesus knew all things and represented the most advanced thinking possible in the area of moral judgment. Those of us who hold to the historic Christian position would do well to look to the life of Jesus as the supreme example of moral conduct and to His words as the ultimate in moral discernment.**

Punishment as restitution or reform is preferable to punishment that would not make for a changed life; so when the teachers of the law brought to Jesus a woman caught in the act of adultery, rather than saying she should be stoned to death, which the law required, He said to her, "I do not condemn you . . . but do not sin again" (John 8:11, GNB). Jesus also taught that a belief in immanent justice (which Piaget held to be immature) is sometimes in error and should be replaced by a concept of *naturalistic causes of misfortune* (the mature view). He gave as examples the time when Pilate killed the Galileans and the time when the Tower of Siloam fell on eighteen people, not because they were more wicked than others (Luke 13:1-5), but because they happened to be in the wrong place when the misfortune occurred.

Jesus knew all things and represented the most advanced thinking possible in the area of moral judgment. Those of us who hold to the historic Christian position would do well to look to the life of Jesus as the supreme example of moral conduct and to His words as the ultimate in moral discernment.

GOD'S PROGRESSIVE REVELATION AND KOHLBERG'S STAGES OF MORALITY

Kohlberg's stages of moral reasoning have been used by writers to show God's progressive dealings with His people. Jack Pressau (1977)[5] wrote that when the Israelites left Egypt, God dealt with them at stage 2, promising blessing if they followed Him and judgment if they turned away. After being established in the Promised Land, the morality of stages 3 and 4 was instituted with laws governing transactions of land and services. In time, the rich found ways to circumvent the law and oppress the poor, making it necessary for God to raise up prophets like Amos and Hosea, who spoke at the postconventional level. During the captivity, the people reverted to a stage 2 morality, the stage which becomes dominant whenever survival is threatened.

A similar approach has been taken by Dan Motet (1978) who pictures Kohlberg's developmental theory as "analogous to what we find in Scripture, where we can follow God's work to raise human moral judgment through the six stages" (p. 18). After seeing Pharaoh's army annihilated, the Israelites "feared the Lord," a stage 1 response. During the wilderness wanderings they were most concerned with their own needs, desiring the food they had in Egypt (stage 2). Stage 3 is illustrated by Aaron's making a gold calf for the people, seemingly wanting their approval. The law and order of stage 4 comes with the giving of the Ten Commandments. "It is at this fourth stage that later the Pharisees remained fixated, and many of the conflicts between them and Jesus arose because He tried to bring them to the superior level of moral judgment" (p. 19).

The Conventional Christian

In recent years evangelical Christians have become increasingly familiar with the cognitive approach to morality. One question which has arisen is how to interpret research studies showing that those adhering to basic Christian truths are more apt to score at the conventional level and less apt to score at the postconventional level than those who are agnostic or liberal in their religious views (Clouse, 1985; Ernsberger & Manaster, 1981; Haan, Smith, & Block, 1968; Lawrence, 1978; Moore, 1979; Sanderson, 1973; Sapp, 1986).[6] Other studies show that conservatives have an overall preference for conventional level, stage 4 (Clouse, 1991; Getz, 1984; Holley, 1991; Rest, 1986; Richards, 1991). Rest (1986) wrote that fundamentalist seminarians have the highest stage 4 scores found, and Sapp and Jones (1986) concluded that "while religion may stimulate earlier movement toward conventional moral reasoning, adoption of a restrictive set of religious beliefs may preclude the possibility of moving to postconventional levels" (p. 209).

A rationale given (Clouse, 1985) is that the conservative nature is to conventionalize or to conserve. The conservation or preservation of the society is based on getting along with others (stage 3) and doing one's duty including obeying the law (stage 4). Without large numbers of citizens at stages 3 and 4, the society as we know it could not survive. Those who are conservative are more apt to accept without question the teachings of their religion, whereas those who are liberal place more value on change and look for ways to modify the existing system (stage 5). Dirks (1988) suggested that in order for young adults in Christian higher education to advance beyond the conventional level of moral development, Christian schools must encourage reflection on the content of one's faith, promote questioning of what is taught, provide opportunities for caring for others, stimulate discussions, and foster role-taking opportunities that make for greater understanding of persons in other cultures.

Conventional and Postconventional Christians:
Can Both Survive within the Church?
The line of skirmish between the benefits of the conventional as opposed to the postconventional appears to be drawn between stage 4 and stages 5 and 6. Stage 4 Christians emphasize conformity to the church and to church doctrine. They have the true faith and rightly divide the Word. "With inerrant Bible in hand [they] busily dot the i's and cross the t's of fixed systematic theology which places the legal view of salvation at its center" (Pressau, 1977, p. 55). They believe that a good Christian will accept without question the teachings of the elders of the congregation for they are the ministers of God.

The Fours are often suspicious of Christians at stages 5 and 6 because postconventional believers are less dogmatic, less structured, and sometimes deviate from the rules. They accuse the Fives of leaning toward socialism and the Sixes of flirting with humanism, ideologies the Fours feel to be in opposition to the Word of God. They point to Jesus and Paul as being concerned, not about the issues of poverty and slavery, but about bringing into the kingdom those who would be saved.

Believers at the postconventional level place love above law, choice above conformity, social concerns above institutional profit. Having already traversed through stage 4, they are cognizant of conventional attitudes and may look with nostalgia to a time when they had more answers than questions, and life fit into a neat doctrinal pattern. But given the choice, they would not return to a cognition that demanded submission without examination and an obedience to the letter of the law apart from the spirit of the law. "To bind Christians by rules and regulations is unworthy of our tradition. It was from such legalism Christ came to set us free. . . . Morality is not so much rules as it is a calling from God" (Wynn, 1977, pp. 72-73).

Postconventionals criticize the Fours for having too narrow an understanding of the cause of Christ. They say that the Fours will ostracize a true believer who does not meet their specifications or remove from the denomination any church that does not agree on every point of doctrine. By contending for the faith the conventionals become contentious, forgetting that the Bible says love is greater than faith (1 Cor. 13:13) and concern for the individual more important than conformity to the law (John 8:3-11).

Both conventional Christians and postconventional Christians love God and want to further His cause. Both have a grasp of truth and can support their respective positions with Scripture. What may not be realized is that each needs the cognitions of the other. The believer at the conventional level needs to understand principled level thinking so he or she may relate to a larger number of people in love and enjoy the freedom that is in Christ. The believer at the postconventional level needs to be reminded that love alone is not enough. Generous thoughts and liberal attitudes will not bring one into the kingdom, and an acceptance of universalism (should one go so far) is not in keeping with the words of Jesus, "I am the way and the truth and the life. No one comes to the Father except through me" (John 14:6).

When the young lawyer asked what he could do to inherit eternal life, he was told that the law was not enough (stage 4). He must love his neighbor as himself (stage 6) (Luke 10:25-37). Conversely, the disciples were told that obedience is the confirmation of love. "If you love me, you will obey what I command" (John 14:15). "Love needs law to guide it. It is rather naive to claim that love has no need of any

direction outside itself. . . . Love is not infallible. Indeed, it is sometimes blind. So God has given us commandments to chart the pathways
of love" (Stott, 1970, p. 151).

Conventional and Postconventional Combined
within the Person of Our Lord Jesus Christ

Thus, we see that the two moralities of law and love are inextricably
combined. In the Old Testament we read, "Thou *shalt* love the Lord
thy God" (Deut. 6:5, KJV) and in the New, "The entire law is summed
up in a single command: 'Love your neighbor as yourself' " (Gal. 5:14).
Jesus explained in the Sermon on the Mount that He did not come to
destroy the law but to fulfill it (Matt. 5:17). He then proceeded to add
a principled statement to the mandates of the law. "Do not murder" is
a law; "do not be angry" is a principle. "Do not commit adultery" is a
law; "do not look on a woman to lust after her" is a principle. "An eye
for an eye" is a law; "resist evil" is a principle. The washing of hands is
a law; the cleansing of the heart is a principle. The law regulates
behavior; a principle monitors the attitudes and cognitions that precede
behavior and on which the behavior is based.

The Pharisees had an obsession with keeping the law so they could
be seen of people (Matt. 23:5). They took it upon themselves to watch
not only their own behavior but everyone else's. They often asked the
question, "Is it lawful?" "Is it lawful for a man to divorce his wife?"
(19:3) Is it lawful to pick grain on the Sabbath? (12:2) Is it lawful to
pay taxes to the Roman emperor? (22:17) But Jesus confronted them
face to face. He chided them for attending to the lesser elements of the
law (conventional) and neglecting the more important matters of the
law — matters of justice, mercy, and faithfulness (postconventional)
(23:23). When asked if it was lawful to heal on the Sabbath, Jesus
responded that it was lawful to do well on the Sabbath (12:10-12).

Jesus was the culmination of the Mosaic Law (Rom. 10:4) and the
personification of Divine Love (John 15:12-13). He was law in its most
complete form and love at its highest level. He taught both obedience
and commitment, duty and compassion, conformity and autonomy.
The letter of the law was the schoolmaster to lead us to Christ, and the
spirit of the law was the means by which the letter of the law was to be
interpreted.

The realization of the law of love takes place when those of us who know Christ willingly obey His command. Law in its initial form is from without, an external force to assure compliance. Love is from within, a desire to respond, inspired by gratitude to God and a sense of relationship to Him. The law of love is seen when we freely respond to God's will. It is loving obedience and obedient love.[7] "We must not forget that fulfillment is not just a development or elaboration of rules. Fulfillment is a metamorphosis. Its goal is in a person, Jesus Christ. . . . Our ideal is a Christlike character and nature" (Barclay, 1978, p. 148).

JUSTICE AND RIGHTEOUSNESS

The more important matter of justice is central to Christian belief even as it is the focal point of the cognitive approach to morality. Justice originates in the righteousness of God and is revealed in both the Old and the New Testaments, having been taught by Amos and Hosea and by our Lord Himself. Liam Grimley (1991) relates how Scripture brings "a theological foundation on which to base respect for the dignity of human beings which is central to Kohlberg's highest stage of moral development, the Universal Ethical Principles orientation" (p. 293). And Donald Joy (1983) writes:

> When one reads both Kohlberg and the prophets, therefore, it is striking that ancient men were in possession of a conception of justice as the Divine character in times when there was no substantial sample of Level III reasoning in the human population from which to infer those attributes. Yet the Piaget-Kohlberg descriptions of "justice" are virtual carbon copies of the Divine character as described. (p. 57)

The Christian should have little difficulty in making common cause with cognitive psychology on the subject of justice.

As believers we should be able to function at all levels at the same time. At the preconventional level we appreciate a personal relationship with a God who will bless and keep—with one who has our best interests in mind (stage 2) (Jer. 29:11). At the conventional level we enjoy the fellowship of the saints (stage 3) and delight "in the law of the Lord" (stage 4) (Ps. 1:2). At the postconventional level we care for a world that needs Christ and are willing to reach people where they are rather than expecting them to fit into a prescribed pattern (stage 5). Finally, we respect each person as one for whom Christ died. Discrimination is condemned, for in God's sight all are equal and should be treated as such (stage 6) (James 2:1). Having competencies at all levels places the Christian in a better position to "understand what is right and just and fair" (Prov. 2:9). Thus, it is apparent that the cognitive approach to morality and the revelation of God to His people have many similarities.

HUMANISTIC PSYCHOLOGY AND CHRISTIAN BELIEF

Humanists, like cognitive psychologists, reject the psychoanalytic and learning positions that environment shapes the person, preferring to believe that persons become whatever they make themselves by their own actions and perceptions. But unlike cognitive psychologists who stress the higher mental processes, humanists are more apt to see the total personality — emotions and interests as well as cognitions. People are basically good, and if allowed to make their own decisions they will choose what is best for them and for others.

In the minds of many Christians, humanism is a worldview that glorifies "man" but leaves out God. If people are good, as the humanist claims, and if they have within themselves the potential for self-actualization, there can be no reason for the message of the Gospel. We are masters of our fates and captains of our souls. The darker side of the human condition — our greed and selfishness — appears not to be recognized apart from an unfortunate environment, thus negating any need for a Redeemer who lifts us from a fallen state.

It is understandable that a number of Christian authors have written in condemnation of the humanist movement. J.I. Packer (1978) asked, "How long will a sense of human dignity survive after man's creation in God's image has been forgotten? . . . How long before Christian toleration, which was based on respect for God's image in man, will turn, as in some quarters it is already doing, into a total permissiveness based simply on hedonism — 'living for kicks' " (p. 89). And David Benner (1989) observed, "Self-fulfillment quickly deteriorates into mere ego-enhancement unless we discover the paradoxical truth of Christ's words that to find our life we must first lose it. To live, we must first die. To discover our true self, we must first die to our old self, that is to our

386

ego. Dying to this idolatrous self-as-God, we are then able to discover our true self, our self-in-God" (p. 21).

Is Humanism a Religion?

Well-known author Ernest Gordon (1980), a practicing humanist before he became a Christian during his incarceration in a World War II Japanese prisoner-of-war camp, wrote of two faiths: humanism and Christianity. He concluded that humanism leads to despair and Christianity leads to hope. Humanism is the faith that fails; Christianity is the faith that prevails. "As Christians we have the confidence that God has interpreted our humanness for us. . . . The activity of the living Word gives us our identity. . . . Without the identity given to us by our Father's love, we would lack the ability to think creatively and personally. We would be processed computers" (p. 224). James Beck (1992) expressed concern that courses in psychology are more numerous in Christian seminaries today than are courses in theology. "The human person was not designed merely to be aware of self. The human must also be aware of God. . . . Helping people look inward, as valuable as that might be, is incomplete if we fail to help them to look upward" (p. 104).

All Humanists Are Not Alike

All humanists do not agree, however, that as members of the human race we have no need for God. Nor would all humanists say that a belief in a personal deity debilitates rather than enhances moral development. But historically there have been humanists who have taken this position, and their number continues today.

Secular Humanists

Most visible among them is a group who call themselves, quite appropriately, secular humanists and who disseminate their views through publications, workshops, and debates. The notoriety of the secular humanist movement came in part, as we have seen, because those holding this position became more organized and sought ways to add to their constituency, and in part because secular humanism was the target of a scathing attack by a number of politically conservative preachers who felt called upon to alert "pro-moral, pro-American, and

Christian citizens" to an organization that is "leading our country down the road to a socialist Sodom and Gomorrah" (LaHaye, 1980, pp. 100, 143-144).

Although not enjoying the notoriety they once had, humanists can appreciate the fact that their ideas have pervaded every aspect of our society. This is true not only in the school and in the home but also in the church. In a chapter entitled "The Lie That We're OK," Rebecca Pippert (1989) senses that the humanist message of suppressing all that is unpleasant has invaded Christian circles to such an extent that rather than being honest and forthright with each other, we feel "we must smile, be upbeat, and always victorious" (p. 21). She tells of a Bible study group she attended in which the participants seemingly had no problems but rather talked "a lot about God's answers and promises." Are we afraid that if we share our feelings we might be seen as not being mature in the faith, she asks. Do we "disguise our deepest fears and problems even from ourselves?" (p. 21)

The Humanist Manifesto — The Secular Humanist Creed
The most succinct statement of the secular humanist position is found in "Humanist Manifesto II," published in 1973 and designed as an update to the first *Humanist Manifesto,* written forty years earlier. In keeping with the humanist emphasis on change, those wishing to offer suggestions for the revision of Humanist Manifesto II or to have input into a possible third manifesto are invited to do so. "These affirmations are not a final credo or dogma but an expression of a living and growing faith" (Humanist Manifesto II, 1980, p. 10).

Some of the ideas in Humanist Manifesto II may be shared by Christians. Especially in those areas dealing with social concern, the follower of Christ will have little difficulty. The Christian sees the need to "fuse reason with compassion in order to build constructive social and moral values," and wishes to "provide humankind with unparalleled opportunity for achieving an abundant and meaningful life" (Humanist Manifesto II, 1980, p. 5). The Christian, as well as the humanist, believes in "the preciousness and dignity of the individual person" and desires to "cultivate the development of a responsible attitude toward sexuality, in which humans are not exploited as sexual objects, and in which intimacy, sensitivity, respect, and honesty in interpersonal relations are encouraged"

(p. 7). Christians share in a recognition of the "common humanity of all people" (p. 10) and work toward a "world community in which all sectors of the human family can participate" (p. 9). Christians agree with the wise use of technology, so that "we can control our environment, conquer poverty, markedly reduce disease, extend our lifespan" (p. 5).

Other statements in the manifesto, however, are in direct opposition to the Christian faith, and it is with these statements that the believer must part company with the secular humanist. The sections that are most offensive are those dealing with religion and ethics, for it is here that secular humanism rejects the foundation of Christianity and makes light of a morality based on an understanding of who God is. The following excerpt will serve as an example.

> We find insufficient evidence for belief in the existence of a supernatural; it is either meaningless or irrelevant to the questions of the survival and fulfillment of the human race. As nontheists, we begin with humans not God, nature not deity. . . . We can discover no divine purpose or providence for the human species. . . . No deity will save us; we must save ourselves. . . . Promises of immortal salvation or fear of eternal damnation are both illusory and harmful. . . . The human species is an emergence from natural evolutionary forces. . . . There is no credible evidence that life survives the death of the body. (Humanist Manifesto II, 1980, p. 6)

This denial of basic Christian truths means the secular humanist will look at morality in a different light than the believer in Christ. To the humanist there is no sin, and guilt is something laid on one by others. We create our own values, are saved by our own efforts, and the final court of appeal is our own conscience. "Moral values derive their source from human experience. Ethics is *autonomous* and *situational,* needing no theological or ideological sanction. . . . We strive for the good life, here and now" (Humanist Manifesto II, 1980, p. 7). Humanism places faith in oneself not in God, and guiding principles are drawn from human experience rather than from the revealed Word of God. Needless to say, such statements are antithetical to Christian belief.

SECULAR HUMANISM AND CHRISTIAN BELIEF

To the secular humanist there are many alternative paths; to the Christian there is only one (John 14:6). To the humanist this life is all and enough; to the Christian "if in this life only we have hope . . . we are of all men most miserable" (1 Cor. 15:19, KJV). To the humanist "the chief end of thought and action is to further this—earthly human interests on behalf of the greater happiness and glory of man" (Lamont, 1957, p. 189); to the Christian "man's purpose is to know and to love God in this life, and to be forever happy with Him in the next" (Hammes, 1971, p. 184). The secular humanist wants no denial of self, but rather an enhancement and affirmation of one's identity; the Christian knows that only by denial, by losing one's life for Christ's sake, will one find true identity (Matt. 10:39). The goal of the humanist is to be self-actualized; the goal of the Christian is to be restored to God's likeness. The humanist says, "I can do all things"; the Christian says, "I can do all things through Christ" (Phil. 4:13, NKJV). Herein lies the difference. Feeling no need for God, the humanist declares the self to be god and gives to the self those attributes befitting deity. The Christian knows he or she is nothing without God. One's existence is dependent on the creative will of God, and any virtue one possesses cannot be separated from the redemptive power of Christ.

Morality to the secular humanist is on a horizontal plane—the relationship of one person to another. Morality to the Christian is on a vertical plane as well—the relationship of man to God. It is only as we touch God that we can fully understand the enormous worth of every living soul. For the Christian, guilt feelings are relieved not by a denial of guilt, but by a recognition of the sin producing that guilt and by confessing the sin to the one who has promised to cast our sins "into the depths of the sea" (Micah 7:19). "I'm OK, you're OK" comes not by self-acclamation but by a pronouncement from God.

CHRISTIAN HUMANISM
Secular humanism is but one of many humanistic groups. Some humanists accept deity, some do not. Some believe in the Bible, some do not. There now appears to be a trend for Christians once again to claim the term "humanism" as their own. J.I. Packer (1978) stated: "I am a humanist. In truth, I believe it is only a thoroughgoing Christian who can ever have a right to that name. . . . It is part of the glory of the gospel to be the one genuine humanism that the world has seen" (p. 11). Donald MacKay (1979) echoed this sentiment by saying: "Chris-

tian humanism affirms that the only true fulfillment is to be found in working out our destiny in line with the will of our Creator through whom alone we can hope to learn what true compassion and healthy self-reliance mean" (pp. 109-110). Dale Brown (1970) puts it this way, "Christianity at its best does not oppose humanism: rather, Christianity is humanism-plus" (p. 54).

These writers are saying that the word *humanism* rightfully belongs to the Christian, that humanism has its greatest meaning in the context of the Christian faith. They have a good case. To relinquish a word simply because it is used by nonbelievers or is narrowly defined by some Christians is not the best approach. We do not cease to use the word *God* because it has been used to refer to deities other than the true God. Nor do we stop using terms like "morality" or "ethics" because these words also are used by those "who call evil good and good evil" (Isa. 5:20). Love, joy, peace, kindness, and goodness—fruit of the Spirit (Gal. 5:22)—are words used by those who do not know the Spirit and therefore have only a shallow understanding of their meaning, yet we continue to speak of them when describing the working of the Spirit in the life of the believer. In the same way, "humanism" which is basic to the Christian position of our being made in the image of God should be a part of the Christian's vocabulary. There is no humanism more beautiful, more inspiring, more in keeping with the true nature of people than the humanism of the Bible.

> **There is no humanism more beautiful, more inspiring, more in keeping with the true nature of people than the humanism of the Bible.**

A Christian Humanist Manifesto

A number of Christian leaders including Donald Bloesch, George Brushaber, Richard Bube, Arthur Holmes, Bruce Lockerbie, J.I. Packer, Bernard Ramm, and James Sire worked with the editors of *Eternity* magazine to prepare a statement entitled "A Christian Humanist Manifesto" (1982). The purpose of the manifesto was to declare "the place of the human species in the universe" and to "seek to recover the term 'humanism' to its traditional lofty meaning and to articulate the Christian world- and life-view against the secular one" (Secular vs. Christian humanism, *Eternity,* 1982, p. 15). An invitation was given for those who wished, to amend or revise the statement "to make it a more perfect expression of the Christian world-view" (p. 15). Even as all secular humanists do not accept every statement in Humanist Manifesto II, all Christians will not accept every statement in "A Christian Humanist Manifesto," but the effort to reclaim a term that finds its highest expression within the Christian tradition is to be commended.

WHEN GOD SAYS YOU'RE OK

The purpose of God as revealed in Scripture is that people would have fellowship with Him. Made in the image of God (Gen. 1:27), the first human beings were given that opportunity. However, sin entered when they tried to be like God through their own initiative and in their own way. But God in His infinite love devised a plan so that the potential within the human species would not be lost. God sent His Son to become incarnate, to dignify the human race by becoming a person, making it possible once again for human beings to have fellowship with their Creator. "God made Him who had no sin to be sin for us, so that in Him we might become the righteousness of God" (2 Cor. 5:21).

This is the message of salvation. It is a message of hope and joy. It is a message that says we have value because God has given us value. It is a message that says we are moral, not by our own efforts, but by His gift of righteousness. Finally, it is a message we can choose for ourselves, prizing it as we tell others of our choice and acting upon it repeatedly in our daily lives.

HOW SHALL WE THEN TEACH?

TRADITIONAL METHODS OF TEACHING FOR MORAL GROWTH

This book has offered a number of suggestions to teachers, parents, and pastors seeking to teach for moral growth. We looked first at traditional methods that have stood the test of time, methods that continue to be used today.

We began with storytelling, probably the most effective way ever known for getting across a moral lesson. Storytelling is effective because stories catch our attention, entertain while they instruct, and continue to intrigue us as the plot unfolds. It doesn't matter if the story is fact or fiction, religious or secular, short or long, written or oral. What matters is that the narrative mode of presenting information is able to communicate a moral lesson that remains in our hearts and memories long after the specifics of the story are forgotten. Storytelling, as a way of teaching the young what behaviors and attitudes are acceptable and what ones are not, as well as revealing the consequences of behavior, is implemented in all cultures. It was the method Jesus used when He presented in parable form the deep truths of the kingdom of God.

Using Scripture to teach right and wrong is another traditional approach. The Bible is God's word to us, communicating the story of Creation and of redeeming love. It sets forth a standard of morality that exceeds anything we can attain by our own efforts. Because of our weakness, a holy and righteous God, unable to tolerate sin in any form, devised a plan that enables those who trust in Him to be declared righteous and holy. How this came about is the greatest story ever told.

The values of this world — wealth, power, and prestige — are not the values of the kingdom of God. Jesus blessed those who were willing to give up the values of the time and follow Him. Jesus turned everything on its head. As teachers, parents, and pastors we need to endeavor to counteract the message of today's world that material possessions, physical strength, or a prestigious position is what matters. A good place to start is with ourselves, by listening to what we say and watching what we do. Do we communicate by our lives that following Christ is more important than the values of those around us? Do we teach the Bible and its truths to our children?

Character education, the third traditional approach, is coming back into its own, having fallen out of favor during the fifties, sixties, and seventies. The social adjustment programs that took the place of character education were designed to make for democratic living, but they deteriorated in some circles to little more than getting in touch with your feelings and developing a good self-concept. Without a standard of right and wrong that surpasses what each person thinks, the result, according to many educators and pastors, is rebellion against authority or any universal moral code. Irresponsible behavior and hedonism became the norm. It is for this reason that leaders in moral education are once again asking for programs in character education (e.g., Bennett,

1991; Kilpatrick, 1992; Lickona, 1991; Ryan & McLean, 1987).

The new character education programs of the eighties and nineties combine a presentation of values accepted in all democratic cultures and by all religions with opportunities for student input as to how these values can be implemented in everyday life. In this way universal truths are taught while indoctrination is avoided. Differentiation is made between those values that must be adopted by everyone in order for the society to thrive and those values a person has the right to choose for himself or herself. The new character education programs are gaining in popularity and appear to be quite effective. As teachers, pastors, and parents, we can use them in both religious and secular contexts.

Psychological Methods of Teaching for Moral Growth

Each of the four major psychologies that comprise the main body of this book gives a different answer to the important question of how we can teach for moral growth. *Psychoanalytic* psychologists stress the conflicts brought about by the advent of the ego and the superego, see the child as born depraved, and maintain that identification with the parents during the child's early years is the natural way for conscience development to take place. Parents are the child's first and most important teachers.

Learning psychologists accent the behavioral component of morality, say the child is born neither good nor bad, and advocate a control of the environment in order to produce responses that are moral. As teachers, parents, and pastors we are responsible for the kinds of environment children find themselves to be in.

Cognitive psychologists emphasize the rational or thinking processes in moral development, say that the child is born with the ability to construct his or her own experiences and knowledge of self and the world, and make use of moral dilemma stories to encourage moral reasoning. Knowing Kohlberg's stages of moral reasoning will greatly enhance our opportunities for helping children to grow morally (cf. Lickona, 1985).

Humanistic psychologists underscore the emotional and motivational aspects of morality, say that the child is born a goodly individual with the capacity to become morally mature, and favor the encouragement of the child's natural propensity to be moral by the use of values clarification strategies. Humanistic methods are fun to use and can be implemented in the school, the home, and the church.

Each psychology, then, calls for a different strategy. From psychoanalysis we learn that a close, loving relationship of parent with child in which the parent shows joy when the child is "good" and disappointment when the child is "bad" is the natural way for superego development to take place. Talking with the child about the consequences of behavior and giving the child opportunity to engage in the correct behavior is far more effective than punishing the child when misbehavior occurs. For those children who may not have parents oriented to love-oriented techniques of discipline, teachers and pastors can show deep interest and concern for the child, thereby creating a relationship in which the young person does not want to disappoint the "surrogate" parent and consequently will develop internal controls so this does not occur.

From learning psychology we learn the significance of behavior and of the environment that brings about that behavior. Rather than expecting children to be good, we realize that none of us continues behaviors for which we are not rewarded in some way. Good behavior needs to be reinforced, thus insuring its continuance. We learn it is better to reinforce good behavior than to punish bad behavior although sometimes both reinforcement and punishment are necessary. We learn the use of behavior modification procedures so we can implement them in any context including the school, the home, and the church. Programmed learning also is helpful and is increasingly being used by parents and pastors as well as by teachers. And always we must keep in mind that children and young people imitate the people they are around. The *how* of teaching for moral growth begins first with our attitudes and behaviors and speech. We learn the importance of ourselves as role models for the children entrusted to our care.

From cognitive psychology we learn the advantages of thinking through possible solutions to moral problems. As children get older and are able to function at higher levels of cognitive organization, they can solve problems they could not handle at a younger age. The use of stories (including the child's own story) to present moral dilemmas, followed by discussion as to the best course of action the characters in the story should take, or the kind of punishment that would be fair to the culprit, or how different people in the story looked at the same situation, will help children develop in moral understanding. Children are naturally drawn to the next stage of moral judgment when they hear someone give reasons at the next higher stage. As teachers, parents, and pastors we can be "plus-one" models, providing possible solutions that are at a higher level. But this is not to be confused with indoctrination in which we tell children what the correct answers are. We must remember that children should come to an understanding on their own as to why one course of action is better than another.

From humanistic psychology we learn that being human means we have within us a potential not seen in any other species. Programmed within each person is the desire to grow up, to become mature. This includes moral growth as well as physical, emotional, and mental growth. The desire of each child is to become self-actualized, and this takes place naturally when one is in an environment that is supportive. As teachers, parents, and pastors we need to encourage children to be all they can be, to make their own choices freely and without restraint, to change their minds when they have made a mistake, to celebrate the choices they have made, and to act upon those choices in their daily lives.

"In Thy Light Shall We See Light" (Ps. 36:9, kjv)

We have seen that the Scriptures include all the emphases of the major psychological approaches: moral conflict as hypothesized by the psychoanalyst, moral behavior as observed by the learning psychologist, reasoning and judgmental processes of morality studied by the cognitive psychologist, and moral potential postulated by the humanist. Rather than centering on only one aspect of morality, as does each psychology, the Bible encompasses within its definition all four ways of looking at morality and consequently provides a more accurate picture. As a complete creation "fearfully and wonderfully made" (Ps. 139:14), the totality of what it means to be moral can be understood only in the context of Christian belief.

For those of us who are believers in Jesus and in the written Word, *teaching for moral growth* will include not one but all four aspects of morality. We will teach that victory over conflict is possible, that the behaviors we engage in are to be acceptable in the sight of God, that our thoughts and the words that express those thoughts are known by our Creator, and the potential we have by virtue of being human comes from our Redeemer rather than from ourselves. In Christ is the ultimate and complete expression of what it means to be moral. He is our model; He is our teacher.

NOTES

1. Bruce Narramore (1985) puts it succinctly when he writes that "the structural division of personality into the id, ego, and superego" has "no apparent biblical parallel. As hypothetical constructs, concepts such as ego, id, and superego can be seen as biblically neutral" (p. 900), "Psychoanalytic psychology," in D.G. Benner (Ed.), *Baker Encyclopedia of Psychology,* pp. 896–900. Grand Rapids: Baker.

2. John Elias (1989) in *Moral education: Secular and religious* (Malabar, FL: Krieger) speaks of the functioning of superego as being that of "repressor, accuser, censor, and tormentor" (p. 70). Freud saw one of the purposes of therapy as bringing into consciousness the repressive superego so that it could be dealt with by the ego and integrated into a rational system of values.

3. A number of other Christian authors have taken this same position. Examples include John Hammes (1973) who writes, "One cannot fault Skinner's experimental data, which stand on their own merit. It is his theoretical formulations, based on this data, that can seriously be questioned" (p. 8); Roger Bufford (1978) who states, "Metaphysical behaviorism is inherently in conflict with the biblical view; however, methodological behaviorism does not pose this problem. Practical application of behavior modification may make a significant contribution in helping us put biblical principles into practice" (p. 125); and Bolin and Goldberg (1979) who comment, "Behavioral psychology has been slow in being accepted as a viable source of theological integration because of the questions it raises concerning man's freedom, dignity, self-control, and responsibility. Although these are valid concerns of philosophical behaviorism, they are merely pseudo-issues regarding methodological behaviorism. Reflecting the natural laws of God's universe, methodological behaviorism integrates with Scripture on many points" (p. 167). Mark Cosgrove (1982) shared this view when he said, "The Christian has no quarrel with Skinner's data. Skinner has uncovered some of God's laws governing certain animal and human behaviors. The problem arises only when Skinner generalizes from his data and makes broad assumptions about the nature of reality that are unsupportable by data and in conflict with biblical revelation" (p. 108).

4. See chapter 9 for an explanation of the following Piagetian terms.

5. For a more detailed examination of Kohlberg's stages and Christian belief, Jack Pressau (1977) *I'm saved, you're saved — Maybe* is recommended.

6. Not all studies report a negative relationship between stage of moral judgment and adherence to Christianity. For a positive correlation between moral reasoning and literal scriptural belief, see M.B. Brown & L. Annis (1978), Moral development level and religious behavior, *Psychological Reports, 13,* 1230; and for moral judgment and religious background, see N.J. Bull (1969), *Moral judgement from childhood to adolescence,* Beverly Hills: Sage. Two unpublished doctoral dissertations show moral reasoning related to religious knowledge (see R.P. O'Gorman [1979], *An investigation of moral judgment and religious knowledge scores of Catholic high school boys from Catholic and public schools,* Boston College), and to religious education (see D.A. Stoop [1979], *The relation between religious education and the process of maturity through the developmental stages of moral judgments,* University of Southern California).

7. For a discussion of why law and love in Scripture comprise one morality rather than two, see B. Clouse (1990), Jesus' law of love and Kohlberg's stages of moral reasoning, *Journal of Psychology and Christianity, 9*(3), 5–15.

REFERENCES

Barclay, O. (1978). The nature of Christian morality. In B. Kaye & G. Wenham (Eds.), *Law, morality, and the Bible* (pp. 125–150). Downers Grove, IL: InterVarsity.

Beck, J.R. (1992). The role of theology in the training of Christian psychologists. *Journal of Psychology and Theology, 20,* 99–109.

Benner, D.G. (1989). Toward a psychology of spirituality: Implications for personality and psychotherapy. *Journal of Psychology and Christianity, 8*(1), 19–30.

Bennett, W.J. (1991). Moral literacy and the formation of character. In J.S. Benninga (Ed.), *Moral, character, and civic education in the elementary school* (pp. 131–138). New York: Teachers College Press.

Bolin, E.P., & Goldberg, G.M. (1979). Behavioral psychology and the Bible: General and specific considerations. *Journal of Psychology and Theology, 7,* 165–175.

Brown, D.W. (1970). *Brethren and pacifism.* Elgin, IL: Brethren Press.

Bufford, R.K. (1978). God and behavior mod II: Some reflections on Vos' response. *Journal of Psychology and Theology, 6,* 215–218.

A Christian humanist manifesto. (1982, January). *Eternity,* pp. 15–18.

Clouse, B. (1981). The teachings of Jesus and Piaget's concept of mature moral judgment. In J.R. Fleck & J.D. Carter (Eds.), *Psychology and Christianity: Integrative readings* (pp. 200–210). Nashville: Abingdon.

_____. (1985). Moral reasoning and Christian faith. *Journal of Psychology and Theology, 13*, 190–198.

_____. (1991). Religious experience, religious belief and moral development of students at a state university. *Journal of Psychology and Christianity, 10*, 337–349.

Collins, G.R. (1977). *The rebuilding of psychology: An integration of psychology and Christianity.* Wheaton, IL: Tyndale.

Cosgrove, M.P. (1982). *B.F. Skinner's behaviorism: An analysis.* Grand Rapids, MI: Zondervan.

Dirks, D.H. (1988). Moral development in Christian higher education. *Journal of Psychology and Theology, 16*, 324–331.

Ernsberger, D.J., & Manaster, G.J. (1981). Moral development, intrinsic/extrinsic religious orientation and denominational teachings. *Genetic Psychology Monographs, 104*, 23–41.

Fromm, E. (1980). *Greatness and limitations of Freud's thought.* New York: Harper & Row.

Getz, I. (1984). The relation of moral reasoning and religion: A review of the literature. *Counseling and Values, 28*, 94–116.

Gordon, E. (1980). *Me, myself and who? Humanism: Society's false premise.* Plainfield, NJ: Logos International.

Grimley, L.K. (1991). A theological perspective on Kohlberg's sixth stage of moral development. *Journal of Psychology and Christianity, 10*, 293–299.

Haan, N., Smith, M.B., & Block, J. (1968). Moral reasoning in young adults: Political-social behavior, family background, and personality correlates. *Journal of Personality and Social Psychology, 10*, 183–201.

Hammes, J.A. (1971). *Humanistic psychology: A Christian interpretation.* New York: Grune & Stratton.

_____. (1973). Beyond freedom and dignity: Behavioral fixated delusion? *Journal of Psychology and Theology, 1*(3), 8–14.

Holley, R.T. (1991). Assessing potential bias: The effects of adding religious content to the Defining Issues Test. *Journal of Psychology and Christianity, 10*, 323–336.

Humanist Manifesto II. (1980). *The Humanist, 40*(5), 5–10.

Joy, D.M. (1983). Kohlberg revisited: A supra-naturalist speaks his mind. In D.M. Joy (Ed.), *Moral development foundations* (pp. 37–62). Nashville, TN: Abingdon.

_____. (1986). Some critical adaptations for Judaeo-Christian communities. In S. Modgil & C. Modgil (Eds.), *Lawrence Kohlberg: Consensus and controversy* (pp. 401–413). Philadelphia: Falmer.

Teaching for Moral Growth

Kilpatrick, W.K. (1992). *Why Johnny can't tell right from wrong.* New York: Simon & Schuster.

LaHaye, T. (1980). *The battle for the mind.* Old Tappan, NJ: Fleming H. Revell.

Lamont, C. (1957). *The philosophy of humanism.* New York: Philosophical Library.

Lawrence, J.A. (1978). *The component procedures of moral judgment making.* Unpublished doctoral dissertation, University of Minnesota.

Lickona, T. (1985). *Raising good children.* New York: Bantam.

_____. (1991). *Educating for character: How our schools can teach respect and responsibility.* New York: Bantam.

Llewellyn, R.C. (1973). A second look at B.F. Skinner. *Journal of Psychology and Theology, 1*(3), 3–7.

MacKay, D.M. (1979). *Human science & human dignity.* Downers Grove, IL: InterVarsity.

May, W.E. (1975). *Becoming human: An invitation to Christian ethics.* Dayton, OH: Pflaum.

McKenna, D.L. (1977). *The Jesus model.* Waco, TX: Word.

McKeown, B. (1981). Myth and its denial in a secular age: The case of behaviorist psychology. *Journal of Psychology and Theology, 9,* 12–20.

Meehl, P.E. (1958). *What, then, is man? A symposium of theology, psychology, and psychiatry.* St. Louis: Concordia.

Moore, M.E. (1979). *The differential effect of a church-related college environment and a state college or university environment on the moral development of self-described students.* Unpublished doctoral dissertation, University of Virginia.

Motet, D. (1978). Kohlberg's theory of moral development and the Christian faith. *Journal of Psychology and Theology, 6,* 18–21.

Packer, J.I. (1978). *Knowing man.* Westchester, IL: Cornerstone.

Piaget, J. (1932). *The moral judgment of the child* (M. Gabain, Trans.). London: K. Paul, Trench, Trubner, & Co.

Pinnock, C.H. (1973). Conscience. In C.F.H. Henry (Ed.), *Baker's dictionary of Christian ethics* (pp. 126–127). Grand Rapids: Baker.

Pippert, R.M. (1989). *Hope has its reasons: From the search for self to the surprise of faith.* San Francisco: Harper & Row.

Ple, A. (1976). Christian morality and Freudian morality. In B.B. Wolman (Ed.), *Psychoanalysis and Catholicism* (pp. 97–109). New York: Gardner.

Pressau, J.R. (1977). *I'm saved, you're saved—Maybe.* Atlanta, GA: John Knox.

Rest, J.R. (1986). *Moral development: Advances in research and theory.* New York: Praeger.

Richards, P.S. (1991, June). The relationship between conservative religious ideology and principled moral reasoning: A review. *Review of Religious Research, 32,* 359–368.

Runestam, A. (1958). *Psychoanalysis and Christianity* (O. Winfield, Trans.). Rock Island, IL: Augustana.

Ryan, K., & McLean, G.F. (Eds.). (1987). *Character development in schools and beyond.* New York: Praeger.

Ryrie, C.C. (1986). *Basic theology.* Wheaton, IL: Victor Books.

Sanderson, S.K. (1973). *Religion, politics, and morality: An approach to religious and political belief systems and their relation through Kohlberg's cognitive-developmental theory of moral judgment.* Unpublished doctoral dissertation, University of Nebraska at Lincoln.

Sapp, G.L. (1986). Moral judgment and religious orientation. In G.L. Sapp (Ed.), *Handbook of moral development: Models, processes, techniques, and research* (pp. 271–286). Birmingham, AL: Religious Education.

Sapp, G.L., & Jones, L. (1986). Religious orientation and moral judgment. *Journal for the Scientific Study of Religion, 25,* 208–214.

Skinner, B.F. (1971). *Beyond freedom and dignity.* New York: Alfred A. Knopf.

Slavson, S.R. (1973). A group of problem girls. In H. Greenwald (Ed.), *Great cases in psychoanalysis* (pp. 227–251). New York: Jason Aronson.

Steckel, C.J. (1979). *Theology and ethics of behavior modification.* Washington, DC: University of America Press.

Stott, J.R.W. (1970). *Christ the controversialist.* London: Tyndale.

Vos, A. (1978). A response to "God and behavior mod." *Journal of Psychology and Theology, 6,* 210–214.

Wynn, J.C. (1977). *Christian education for liberation and other upsetting ideas.* Nashville, TN: Abingdon.

Zilboorg, G. (1962). *Psychoanalysis and religion.* New York: Farrar, Straus, and Cudahy.

INDEX